Lecture Notes in Computer Science 10131

Commenced Publication in 1973
Founding and Former Series Editors:
Gerhard Goos, Juris Hartmanis, and Jan van Leeuwen

More information about this series at http://www.springer.com/series/7410

Victor Chang · Muthu Ramachandran
Robert J. Walters · Gary Wills (Eds.)

Enterprise Security

Second International Workshop, ES 2015
Vancouver, BC, Canada, November 30 – December 3, 2015
Revised Selected Papers

 Springer

Editors
Victor Chang
International Business School Suzhou
Xi'an Jiaotong-Liverpool University
Suzhou
China

Muthu Ramachandran
School of Computing, Creative
Technologies, and Engineering
Leeds Beckett University
Leeds
UK

Robert J. Walters
Department of Electronics and Computer
Science
University of Southampton
Southampton
UK

Gary Wills
Department of Electronics and Computer
Science
University of Southampton
Southampton
UK

ISSN 0302-9743   ISSN 1611-3349   (electronic)
Lecture Notes in Computer Science
ISBN 978-3-319-54379-6   ISBN 978-3-319-54380-2   (eBook)
DOI 10.1007/978-3-319-54380-2

Library of Congress Control Number: 2017934328

LNCS Sublibrary: SL4 – Security and Cryptology

Printed on acid-free paper

This Springer imprint is published by Springer Nature
The registered company is Springer International Publishing AG
The registered company address is: Gewerbestrasse 11, 6330 Cham, Switzerland

Preface

Enterprise security is an important area since all types of organizations require secure and robust environments, platforms, and services to work with people, data, and computing applications. There are instances where security breaches and privacy concerns have been the main factors preventing organizations from putting their resources in public and community domains. Even in private domains, there is no escape from the threats to cyber security, privacy, trust, and risk. We live in an information age whereby there is a massive and rapid dissemination of information. Protecting our data, privacy, and rights has become increasingly important regardless of where we are based and in which organization we work. Challenges such as data ownership, trust, unauthorized access, and big data management should be resolved by using innovative methods, models, frameworks, case studies, and analysis to reduce risks imposed by data leakage, hacking, breach of privacy, and abuse of data. To adopt the best practices, papers that can fully address security, privacy, and risk concerns are welcome. We seek papers from both technical security (theory, prototype, experiments, simulations, proofs-of-concept, and product development) and information system security (review, frameworks, best practices, statistical analysis based on surveys and recommendations) that provide good recommendations and research contributions to enterprise security. The best papers from the ES 2015 workshop were selected for this book. This book presents comprehensive and intensive research into various areas of enterprise security including a chapter on "Challenges of Cloud Forensics" by Hamid Jahankhani and Amin Hosseinian-Far, who discuss how cloud computing has generated significant interest in both academia and industry, but it is still an evolving paradigm. Cloud computing services are also a popular target for malicious activities, resulting in the exponential increase of cyber attacks. Digital evidence is the evidence that is collected from the suspect's workstations or electronic media that could be used to assist computer forensics investigations. Cloud forensics involves digital evidence collection in the cloud environment. The current established forensic procedures and process models require major changes in order to be acceptable in a cloud environment. This chapter aims to assess the challenges that forensic examiners face in tracking down and using digital information stored in the cloud and discusses the importance of education and training for handling, managing, and investigating computer evidence.

Similarly, a chapter on the relationship between public budgeting and risk management – competition or driving? – by Yaotai Lu discusses how the world is rife with uncertainties. Risk management plays an increasingly important role in both the public sector and the private sector. Considering that government is the risk manager of last resort, government faces a vast variety of risks and disasters, either natural or man-made. Owing to scarce public resources and increasing public needs, government is not capable of financing all risk management programs. However, once a catastrophic event occurs, government must take immediate actions to control the event. Another interesting chapter on "Iris Biometrics Recognition in Security Management" by

Ahmad Ghaffari, Amin Hosseinian-Far, and Akbar Sheikh-Akbari discusses an application of iris recognition for human identification, which has significant potential for developing a robust identification system. This is due to the fact that the iris patterns of individuals are unique, differentiable from left to right eye, and are almost stable over the time. However, the performance of existing iris recognition systems depends on the signal processing algorithms they use for iris segmentation, feature extraction, and template matching. Like any other signal processing system, the performance of the iris recognition system depends on the existing level of noise in the image and can deteriorate as the level of noise increases.

The chapter on "Robust Enterprise Application Security with eTRON Architecture" by M. Fahim Ferdous Khan, Ken Sakamura, and Noboru Koshizuka presents the eTRON architecture, which aims at delineating a generic framework for developing secure e-services. At the core of the eTRON architecture lies the tamper-resistant eTRON chip that is equipped with functions for mutual authentication, encrypted communication, and strong access control. Besides the security features, the eTRON architecture also offers a wide range of functionalities through a coherent set of API commands so that programmers can develop value-added services in a transparent manner. This chapter discusses various features of the eTRON architecture, and presents three representative eTRON-based e-services in order to evaluate its effectiveness by comparison with other existing e-services.

We believe the approaches discussed in this chapter will significantly impact on industrial practice as well as research in the area of enterprise security. Enterprise security also includes new models of cloud-based enterprises. We hope you enjoy reading this book.

February 2017

Victor Chang
Muthu Ramachandran
Gary Wills
Robert J. Walters

Organization

Workshop Chairs

General Chair

Victor Chang   Xi'an Jiaotong-Liverpool University, China

Co-chairs

Muthu Ramachandran   Leeds Beckett University, UK
Gary Wills   University of Southampton, UK
Robert John Walters   University of Southampton, UK

Publicity Chairs

Mario Hoffmann   Fraunhofer Institute for Applied and Integrated
                             Security (AISEC), Germany
Neil N. Yen   University of Aizu, Japan
Laurence T. Yang   St. Francis Xavier University, Canada
Chung-Sheng Li   IBM, USA
Wendy Currie   Audencia Nantes, France

Keynote Speaker

Dr. Konstantin (Kosta) Beznosov

Program Committee

Mitra Arami   American University of Middle East, Kuwait
Reinhold Behringer   Leeds Beckett University, UK
Victor Chang   Xi'an Jiaotong-Liverpool University, China
Sidney Chapman   Freelance, Australia
Tzu-chun Chen   TU Darmstadt, Germany
Chung-Sheng Li   IBM, USA
Muthu Ramachandran   Leeds Beckett University, UK
Jose Simao   Instituto Superior de Engenharia de Lisboa, Portugal
Robert John Walters   University of Southampton, UK
Gary Wills   University of Southampton, UK
Fara Yahya   University of Southampton, UK

Contents

Challenges of Cloud Forensics

Hamid Jahankhani[1] and Amin Hosseinian-Far[2](✉)

[1] Department of Digital Technology and Computing,
GSM London, London, UK
Hamid.Jahankhani@gsmlondon.ac.uk
[2] School of Computing, Creative Technologies and Engineering,
Leeds Beckett University, Leeds, UK
A.Hosseinian-Far@leedsbeckett.ac.uk

Abstract. Legal requirement for cloud forensics is currently uncertain and presents a challenge for the legal system. These challenges arises from the fact that cloud environment consists of distributed shared storages so there is a level of necessary interactions forensic examiners and law enforcement officers require from the cloud provider in order to conduct their investigations. Cloud computing has generated significant interest in both academia and industry, but it is still an evolving paradigm. Cloud computing services are also, a popular target for malicious activities; resulting to the exponential increase of cyber-attacks. Digital evidence is the evidence that is collected from the suspect's workstations or electronic medium that could be used in order to assist computer forensics investigations. Cloud forensics involves digital evidence collection in the cloud environment. The current established forensic procedures and process models require major changes in order to be acceptable in cloud environment. This chapter aims to assess challenges that forensic examiners face in tracking down and using digital information stored in the cloud and discuss the importance of education and training to handle, manage and investigate computer evidence.

Keywords: Cloud computing · Cloud forensics · Digital evidence · Cyber security strategy · Computer misuse act · Anti-forensics · Challenges of cloud forensics

1 Introduction

In a fully connected truly globalised world of networks, most notably the internet, mobile technologies, distributed databases, electronic commerce and E-governance E-crime manifests itself as Money Laundering; Intellectual Property Theft; Identity Fraud/Theft; Unauthorised access to confidential information; Destruction of information; Exposure to Obscene Material; Spoofing and Phishing; Viruses and Worms and Cyber-Stalking, Economic Espionage to name a few.

According to the House of Commons, Home Affairs Committee, Fifth Report of Session 2013–14, on E-crime, "Norton has calculated its global cost to be $388bn dollars a year in terms of financial losses and time lost. This is significantly more than the combined annual value of $288bn of the global black market trade in heroin, cocaine and marijuana." (Home Affairs Committee 2013).

© Springer International Publishing AG 2017
V. Chang et al. (Eds.): Enterprise Security, LNCS 10131, pp. 1–18, 2017.
DOI: 10.1007/978-3-319-54380-2_1

Since the launch of the UK's first Cyber Security Strategy in June 2009 and the National Cyber Security Programme (NCSP) in November 2011, UK governments have had a centralised approach to cybercrime and wider cyber threats.

Until recently E-crimes had to be dealt with under legal provisions meant for old crimes such as conspiracy to commit fraud, theft, harassment and identity theft. Matters changed slightly in 1990 when the Computer Misuse Act was passed but even then it was far from sufficient and mainly covered crimes involving hacking.

Over the years, the exponential growth of computing era has brought to light many technological breakthroughs. The next radical wave of this growth appeared to be outside the traditional desktop's realm. An evolving terminology that can describe this paradigm is cloud computing. Smith (2011) and Martini and Choo (2012) argued that cloud computing has recently become a prevalent technology and currently is one of the main trends in the ICT sector. In cloud computing several tangible and intangible objects (such as home appliances) surrounding people can be integrated in a network or in a set of networks (Cook 2007).

Migration to cloud computing usually involves replacing much of the traditional IT hardware found in an organisation's data centre (such as servers and network switches) with remote and virtualised services configured for the particular requirements of the organisation. Hence, data comprising the organisation's application can be physically hosted across multiple locations, possibly with a broad geographic distribution (Grispos et al. 2012).

As a result, the use of cloud computing can bring possible advantages to organisations including increased efficiency and flexibility. For instance, virtualised and remote services can provide greater flexibility over a physical IT infrastructure as they can be rapidly Re-configured to meet new requirements without acquiring a new or potentially redundant hardware (Sammons 2015). Further, Khajeh-Hosseini et al. (2010) found that cloud computing can be a significantly cheaper alternative to purchasing and maintaining system infrastructure In-house.

Though, the other side of the coin supports that cloud computing services are a popular target for malicious activities; resulting to the exponential increase of cyber-crimes, Cyber-Attacks (Bluementhal 2010). Consequently, this phenomenon demonstrates the need to explore the various challenges and problems of cloud computing in the forensics community to potentially prevent future digital fraud, espionage, Intellectual Property (IP) theft as well as other types of concern.

2   Cloud Computing; Concept, Technology & Architecture

In 1980's the main centralized processing power for various computation tasks was through mainframes (Jadeja and Modi 2012), however this centralized public utility architecture is gaining momentum in today's industries and numerous applications therein. According to (Givehchi and Jasperneite 2013) *"the main goal of cloud computing is to provide on-demand computing services with high scalability and availability in a distributed environment with minimum complexity for the service consumers"*. According to Chang et al. (2016a) many businesses are now considering cloud computing as an option to reduce their costs and to enhance the efficiency in their business processes. Cloud computing offers a variety of advantages as opposed to non-distributed architectures. Users can access the application only using a browser, regardless of the geographical area they reside in, and the type of system are using. Knowing the centralised nature of the cloud, it is an ultimate solution in disastor recovery and and for crucial nature of business continuity (Jadeja and Modi 2012).

There are three known cloud categories; Romgovind et al. (2010) depicted these categories in a so called 'Cloud Computing Map':

They also outlined three main cloud delivery models i.e. 'Software as a Service', 'Platform as a Service', and 'Infrastructure as a Service', in the same figure (Fig. 1). In the SaaS delivery model, the focus is on how the user is accessing the software on a cloud. The software is accessible by the user through his/her browser and the user would not need to be concerns about the software deployment, installation and the system's resources, etc. (Kumar 2014). Instances include but not limited to Mobile Application, Thin Clients, etc. PaaS delivery model is where the cloud provider offers the required platform for the user in which software can be created and deployed. This is not a single technology/platform and entails a range of different resources and services (Devi and Ganesan 2015). Instances include but not limited to Database, Web Server and Tools required for Development, etc. Considering the cloud architecture as stack, Infrastructure as Service (IaaS) would be the base layer offering the full required computing infrastructure for the above mentioned delivery models. The infrastructure will be available and distributed through the Internet and Web; an instance include Amazon Web Services (Alhadidi et al. 2016).

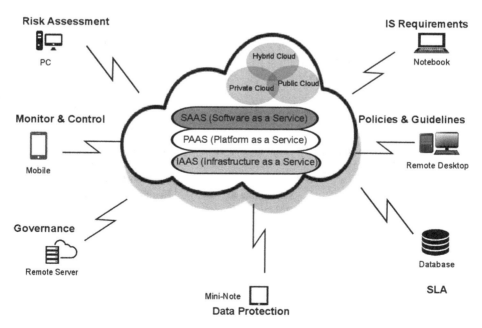

Fig. 1. Cloud computing map; adapted from (Romgovind et al. 2010)

With regards to generic cloud categorisation, there are numerous definitions and characteristics for the above-mentioned three categories. Batra and Gupta (2016) define the categories as:

Private Cloud: In private cloud computing, cloud services are offered to pre-defined and selected users. Overall security and users' authentication and access levels are imperative in this category.

Public Cloud: In this type of cloud computing, the cloud services are provided; Usually through a third party, and via the Internet.

Hybrid Cloud: This category is a mixed representation of the above two types of cloud computing. Many businesses are benefitting from both private and public cloud services.

Table 1. Advantages and disadvantages of different cloud types; by Hu et al. (2011)

	Public cloud	Private cloud	Hybrid cloud
Advantages	Simplest to implement and use	Allows for complete control of server software updates patches, etc.	Most cost-efficient through utilization flexibility of public and private clouds
	Minimal upfront costs	Minimal long-term costs	Less susceptible to prolonged service outages
	Utilization efficiency gains through server virtualization	Utilization efficiency gains through server virtualization	Utilization efficiency gains through server virtualization
	Widespread accessibility	–	Suited for handling large spikes in workload
	Requires no space dedicated for data center	–	–
	Suited for handling large spikes in workload	–	–
Disadvantages	Most expensive long-term	Large upfront costs	Difficult to implement due to complex management schemes and assorted cloud center
	Susceptible to prolonged services outages	Susceptible to prolonged services outages	Requires moderate amount of space dedicated for data center
	–	Limited accessibility	–
	–	Requires largest amount of space dedicated for data center	–
	–	Not suited for handling large spikes in workload	–

According to Batra and Gupta (2016), organisations offer the private cloud services in cases where the service has a high importance and the security of the operation is vital, whilst the public cloud services are offered for the lengthy tasks and will be offered when required.

Hu et al. (2011) summarizes the advantages and disadvantages of Private, Public and Hybrid cloud (Table 1):

3   Cloud Storage Models

The goal of cloud storage system is an effective organizational system node to store data. Following are the common four types of services:

3.1   Elastic Compute Clusters

A compute cluster includes a set of virtual instances that run a customer's application code. Each virtual instance can be a bare-metal VM (in an infrastructure-as-a-service provider, such as AWS and Cloud Servers) or a sandbox environment (in a platform-as-a-service provider, such as AppEngine). Clusters are elastic in that the number of instances can scale dynamically with the application's workload. For instance, in a cloud-based Web application, the number of front-end server instances can scale according to the incoming request rate, so that each server instance won't be overwhelmed by too many simultaneous requests.

3.2   Persistent Storage Services

These services store application data in a non-ephemeral state; all instances in the cluster can access them. They're different from the local storage (for example, the local hard drive) in each virtual instance, which is temporary and can't be directly accessed by other instances. They're also different from block storage services that some providers offer (for example, Amazon's Elastic Block Storage). The latter can't be accessed by multiple instances simultaneously and serves primarily as backup. There are several common types of storage services. Table storage (SimpleDB, Google's DataStore, and Azure's Table Storage) is similar to a traditional database. Blob storage (S3, Rackspace's Cloud Files, and Azure's Blob Storage) keeps binary objects such as user photos and videos. Queue storage (SQS and Azure's Queue Storage) is a special type of storage service.

Persistent storage services are usually implemented as RESTful Web services (REST stands for Representational State Transfer) and are highly available and scalable compared to their non-cloud siblings.

3.3   Intracloud Networks

These networks connect virtual instances with each other and with storage services. All clouds promise high-bandwidth and low-latency networks in a data centre. This is because network performance is critical to the performance of distributed applications such as multitier Web services and MapReduce jobs.

3.4   Wide-Area Networks

Unlike intra cloud networks, which connect an application's components, wide-area networks (WANs) connect the cloud data centres, where the application is hosted, with end hosts on the Internet. For consumer applications such as websites, WAN performance can affect a client's response time significantly. All cloud providers operate multiple data centres at different geographical regions so that a nearby data centre to reduce WAN latency can serve a user's request.

3.5   Putting It All Together

These four types of services are fundamental in building a generic online computation platform. Imagine a typical online cloud application, such as a social network website. Its servers can run in the compute cluster, leveraging the scaling feature to absorb flash-crowd events. Its user data can be stored in the various storage services and accessed through the intracloud network. Its Web content can be delivered to users with just a short delay, with a WAN's help. Other important cloud services, such as MapReduce (Hadoop) services and backup services, aren't as common, probably because they aren't essential to most cloud applications.

Considering the complexities of digital oil fields in the cloud, oil and gas industry still is geared to migrate to the cloud because of the various advantages in exploration and production information deliver, collaboration and decision-support. However, for an effective migration to cloud environment, it is paramount that a set of clear metrics based on business analytics objectives are defined. Of course, the choice of appropriate deployment model is based on the security, compliance, cost, integration and quality of service.

4   Cloud Storage Challenges

Cloud services are applications running in the Cloud Computing infrastructures through internal network or Internet. Cloud computing environments are multi domain environments in which each domain can use any security, privacy, and trust needs and potentially employ various mechanisms, interfaces, and semantics (Zhou et al. 2010). Such domains could signify individual enabled services or other infrastructural or application components. Service-oriented architectures are naturally relevant technology to facilitate such multi domain formation through service composition and orchestration.

4.1   Authentication and Identity Management

By using cloud services, users can easily access their personal information and make it available to various services across the Internet. An identity management (IDM) mechanism can help authenticate users and services based on credentials and characteristics. The key to the issue concerning IDM in clouds is interoperability drawbacks that could result from using different identity tokens and identity negotiation protocols. Existing password-based authentication has an inherited limitation and poses significant risks. An IDM system should be able to protect private and sensitive information related to users and processes. How multi-tenant cloud environments can affect the privacy of identity information isn't yet well understood. In addition, the multi-jurisdiction issue can complicate protection measures. While users interact with a front-end service, this service might need to ensure that their identity is protected from other services with which it interacts. In multi-tenant cloud environments, providers must segregate customer identity and authentication information. Authentication and IDM components should also be easily integrated with other security components.

4.2   Access Control and Accounting

Heterogeneity and diversity of services, as well as the domains' diverse access requirements in cloud computing environments, demand fine-grained access control policies particularly, access control services should be flexible enough to capture dynamic, context, or attribute- or credential-based access requirements and to enforce the principle of least privilege. Such access control services might need to integrate privacy-protection requirements expressed through complex rules.

It's important that the access control system employed in clouds is easily managed and its privilege distribution is administered efficiently. We must also ensure that cloud delivery models provide generic access control interfaces for proper interoperability, which demands a policy-neutral access control specification and enforcement framework that can be used to address cross-domain access issues. The access control models should also be able to capture relevant aspects of SLAs. The utility model of clouds demands proper accounting of user and service activities that generates privacy issues because customers might not want to let a provider maintain such detailed accounting records other than for billing purposes. The out-sourcing and multi-tenancy aspects of clouds could accelerate customers' fears about accounting logs.

4.3   Trust Management and Policy Integration

Even though the multiple service providers coexist in the cloud and collaborate to provide various services, they might have different security approaches and privacy mechanisms, so it is important that we must address them heterogeneity among their policies. Cloud service providers might need to compose multiple services to enable bigger application services. So mechanisms are placed to ensure that such a dynamic collaboration is handled securely and that security breaches are effectively monitored during the interoperation process. Now, even though individual domain policies are verified, security violations can easily occur during integration and providers should carefully manage access control policies to ensure that policy integration doesn't lead to any security breaches.

In cloud computing environments, the interactions between different service domains, which are driven by service requirements, can also be dynamic, transient, and intensive and a trust framework should be developed to allow for capturing a generic set of parameters required for establishing trust and to manage evolving trust and interaction/sharing requirements. The cloud's policy integration tasks should be able to address challenges such as semantic heterogeneity, secure interoperability, and policy-evolution management. Furthermore, customers' behaviors can evolve rapidly, thereby affecting established trust values. This suggests a need for an integrated, trust-based, secure interoperation framework that helps establish, negotiate, and maintain trust to adaptively support policy integration.

4.4   Privacy and Data Protection

Privacy is a core issue here, including the need to protect identity information, policy components during integration, and transaction histories. This helps to store their data and applications on systems that reside outside of their on-premise data centers. This might be the single greatest fear of cloud clients. By migrating workloads to a shared infrastructure, customers' private information faces increased risk of potential unauthorized access and exposure (Tianfield 2012). Cloud service providers must assure their customers and provide a high degree of transparency into their operations and privacy assurance. Privacy-protection mechanisms must be embedded in all security solutions. In a related issue, it's becoming important to know who created a piece of data, who modified it and how, and so on. Provenance information could be used for various purposes such as trace back, auditing, and history-based access control. Balancing between data provenance and privacy is a significant challenge in clouds where physical perimeters are abandoned (Carroll et al. 2014).

Chang et al. (2016a) strongly believe that privacy is one of the most important factors in cloud security. They also argue that many organisations are willing to invest in making the cloud private and ultimately secure. In a recent research work conducted by Chang et al. (2016b), privacy was considered as the most imperative factor with regards to the overall security of the system. That was followed by identity management, trust, etc.

4.5   Risk Management

Cloud computing provides several benefits to an organization including, cost, investment on physical or software infrastructure, users can access their data anywhere and finally, easier and faster data sharing.

The cloud computing concept arises from the notion of "software as a service" (SaaS). A set of services is provided on a set of platforms at various locations. The five key characteristics and benefits of cloud computing can pose downside risks that require identification, evaluation, assessment and mitigation. For example, unavailability of on-demand self-service, sensitivities to location-independent resource pooling such as security concerns, unresponsive elasticity/scalability are illustrative downside risks that a fully cloud dependent/migrated enterprise may need to be aware of and provide requisite solutions for.

The code of practice for the implementation of the ISO31000 standard on risk management highlights a number of principles that any risk management system shall ideally follow and embed (Jahankhani et al. 2015). The key principles relevant to cyber risk management are:

- Risk management should be systematic and structured, the approach to risk management should, where practicable, be consistently applied within the organisation
- Risk management should take into account organizational culture, human factors and behaviour
- Risk management should create and protect value, the organization should optimize risk management to contribute to the demonstrable achievement of objectives and maximize overall business and commercial benefits
- Risk management should be transparent and inclusive, Management and stakeholders should be actively involved in risk identification, assessment and response
- Risk management should be dynamic, iterative and responsive to change; the organization should ensure its risk management continually identifies and responds to changes affecting its operating environment.

A comprehensive risk register, identifying, characterizing, assessing and mitigating all risks need to be devised to ensure business continuity should any of the promised key benefits be interrupted due to local or global disruptions or threats. The Institute of Risk Management (IRM) has also issues guidelines on the risk management process framework of related to ISO31000 (Theirm.org 2010).

Chang (2014) discusses the concept of Business Intelligence as a Service (BIaaS) in which financial risk assessment is considered as one of the intelligent services that can be offered on cloud. Fan and Chen (2012) argue that many risks and cost exposures that arise as a result of cloud implementation are due to social factors, and have proposed a risk management strategy. It can be argued that education and training would minimise such social risks (Jahankhani and Hosseinian-Far 2014). This risk management strategy can be useful for executive decision making. Theoretically, Bedford et al. (2014) propose a probabilistic risk analysis using minimum information methods which can also be applied to the cloud risk assessment.

4.6   Disaster Recovery in Cloud Systems

Considering all the above mentioned challenges, there is always a risk of using key and vital business data at the time of disastrous incidents. Although many scholars focus on different security challenges in cloud computing, few outline the contingency planning and recovery procedures in the event of system failure as a result of an incident (Chang 2015). The disaster recovery plans and systems are usually context dependent and vary application by application. There are also automatics systems that can be accessible when it comes to disaster recovery. Clarkson (2016) has a patent on an automatics disaster recovery system in which restoration devices are used to get the copied data for post-disaster recovery. The significance and vitality of disaster recovery techniques become apparent when, the incident is viewed from the business perspective. Considering 'business continuity' or survival as one of the key business objectives, we would agree that despite the higher costs of contingency planning, disaster recovery techniques worth the investment. Disaster recovery and contingency planning depends on the context and the utilised system, however some scholars have generalised the procedure using a macro perspective. There are numerous examples of disaster recovery in cloud systems. Haji (2016) has defined the set of requirements, challenges and some procedures for contingency planning in the Airline business context. The concept of business continuity and sustainability is also perceived from a different perspective. The virtualisation in cloud has already helps the business to maintain a solid disaster recovery plan through using cloud services (Pulsant Business Limited 2015). There are numerous platforms for disaster recovery of cloud services. Khoshkholghi et al. (2014) have conducted a thorough survey on disaster recovery techniques and properties for cloud services; in which strengths and weaknesses of each system are methodically assessed.

5 Challenges Raised by Cloud Computing with Respect to Existing Digital Forensics Models

It has been observed that use of cloud computing currently presents several challenges to its users (i.e. individuals, organisations, regulatory and law enforcement authorities).

In 2006 two new laws were passed to tackle E-crime namely the Fraud Act 2006 which came into force in 2007 which "the new law aims to close a number of loopholes in proceeding Anti-fraud legislation, because, the Government said was unsuited to modern fraud", and the Police and Justice Act 2006 (part 5) which prohibits "unauthorised access to computer material; unauthorised acts with intent to impair operation of computer and the supply of tools that can be used for hacking" (The National Archives 2006).

Documented guidance, practices and procedures were outdated and wholly inadequate to help tackle electronic evidence in a forensic manner, until first E-crime publication by ACPO in July 2007 and subsequently revised in November 2009 and 2012. This is recognised as the best guidelines ever produced to assist law enforcement in handling digital evidence (ACPO 2012). On one hand these guidelines seem sustainable and functional; however on the other hand it is still yet practically unclear how digital evidence used in courts produced by a digital forensic investigation could be gathered by such guidelines in a cloud environment.

Digital evidence is the evidence that is collected from the suspect's workstations or electronic medium that could be used in order to assist computer forensics investigations.

There are basically two types of evidences that could support a digital forensic investigation, which are, physical evidence and digital evidence. Physical evidences are categorised as touchable and substantial items that could be brought to court and shown physically. Examples of physical evidence that could assist in the investigations are computers, external hard disk drives and data storage (memory sticks and memory cards) handheld devices including mobile phones/smart phones, networking devices, optical media, dongles and music players. Digital evidence would be the data that is extracted from the physical evidence, or the computer system.

In order to perceive a bit of information or data as evidence, it needs to satisfy the 5 rules that are:

(1) The evidence should be admissible and excepted in the court of law
(2) The evidence needs to be authentic and not contaminated
(3) The evidence needs to the whole piece, not just indicative parts
(4) The evidence has to be reliable, dependable
(5) The evidence needs to be believable

Digital evidence, as compared to hard evidence, are difficult to find, in terms of defining the nature of the data, and classifying it as a digital evidence that is worthy to be presented in court.

Proving evidence which is reliable has been proven to be a difficult task, not just because the nature of evidence, but also the wide scope and environment in which the evidence are extracted from.

In a corporate environment, the forensic investigator team will need to identify, contain and maintain the integrity of the evidence, and differentiate whether the piece of evidence is relevant or not to the current crime being investigated, and whether it would stand a chance in finding the culprit and charging them through legal proceedings.

Among the considerations that need to be evaluated by the investigators when dealing with collecting digital evidence are the expenses, cost and loss incurred and the availability of the service during and after the incident.

However, the question here is, can we investigate a crime in the cloud using the existing computer forensics models, frameworks and tools?

According to Grispos et al. (2012), the available digital forensic practices, frameworks and tools are mainly intended for Off-line investigation, therefore if an investigation is conducted in a cloud computing environment new challenges come to light since the potential evidence that arises is likely to be ephemeral and stored on media beyond the investigator's immediate control.

In addition, digital forensics investigation processes heavily rely on theoretical frameworks and enhanced Digital Investigation Process Models which are practically not very useful for the current available cloud technologies as they were developed prior to their advent; and mainly assume that the investigator has physical access and control over the storage media of the targeted network, system or device (Grispos et al. 2012).

As a result, it is apparent that the current cloud technologies face numerous significant challenges as the majority of available forensic process models do not respond adequately to the requirements of a digital forensic investigation and therefore they do not meet the needs of a complex cloud environment. All of the assumptions of the suggested forensic process models are likely to be invalidated when investigating forensic activities in a cloud environment as the majority of them strictly follow tactics of a physical investigation.

Roussev et al. (2009) argues that, although the digital forensics models comprehensively reviews the stages of a digital forensic process and analyses the cloud forensics' impact on this process; most of its assumptions are not yet valid in the context of cloud computing and the problem will only get worse with the explosive growth of data volumes. As a result they proposed the Distributed Digital Forensic (DDF). This of course is not new and several researchers have already proposed models for DDF services for cloud computing paradigm. However, Roussev et al. (2009) proposal is based on the MPI MapReduce (MMR) framework.

Grispos et al. (2012) have summarises the challenges of cloud forensics in Table 2.

Dykstra and Sherman (2013) introduced FROST which is three new tools for the OpenStack cloud platform. These tools are integrated into the management plane of cloud architecture; hence, forensic investigators can obtain trustworthy forensics data independent of the cloud providers. OpenStack (2016) is an Open-Source cloud computing platform and users includes many large organizations such as Intel, Argonne National Laboratory, AT&T, Rackspace and Deutsche Telekom.

Table 2. Summary of challenges to digital forensics in cloud environments (Grispos et al. 2012).

Phase	Action	Challenges
Identification	Identifying an illicit event	Lack of frameworks
Preservation	Software tools	Lack of specialist tools
	Sufficient storage capacity	Distributed, virtualized and volatile storage; use of cloud services to store evidence
	Chain of custody	Cross-jurisdictional standards, procedures; proprietary technology
	Media imaging	Imaging all physical media in a cloud is impractical; partial imaging may face legal challenges
	Time synchronization	Evidence from multiple time zones
	Legal authority	Data stored in multiple jurisdictions; limited access to physical media
	Approved methods, software and hardware	Lack of evaluation, certification generally, but particularly in cloud context
	Live vs. Dead acquisitions	Acquisition of physical media from providers is cumbersome, onerous and time consuming data is inherently volatile
	Data integrity	Lack of write-blocking or enforced persistence mechanisms for cloud services and data
Examination	Software tools	Lack of tested and certified tools
	Recovery of deleted data	Privacy regulations and mechanisms implemented by providers
	Traceability and event reconstruction	Events may occur on many different platforms
Presentation	Documentation of evidence	Integration of multiple evidence sources in record
	Testimony	Complexity of explaining cloud technology to jury

Legal requirement for cloud forensics is currently uncertain and presents a challenge for the legal system. These challenges arises from the fact that cloud environment consists of distributed shared storages so there is a level of necessary interactions forensic examiners and law enforcement officers require from the cloud provider in order to conduct their investigations. This means they are at the mercy of their public cloud providers to assist in an investigation. In cloud investigation this lack of physical access due to the decentralized nature of the data processing causes enormous technical and legal disruptive challenges Orton et al. (2013). There are two legal issues:

(1) Validity-Of-the-Warrant – Establishing a specific location for search warrant that evidence is believed will be found together with the specifics required in the warrant.

(2) Authenticity – Making sure that the data is of the suspect (defendant) alone when searching shared storages.

The National Institute of Standards and Technology released a draft report in 2014 (NIST 2014), highlighting the requirement for cloud forensics standards to aid law enforcement. In that report NIST identified 65 challenges in 9 major groups that forensics investigators face in gathering and analysing digital information stored in the cloud. The nine major groups are architecture, data collection, analysis, Anti-forensics, incident first responders, role management, legal, standards, and training. Figure 2 is the NIST mind map of forensic challenges.

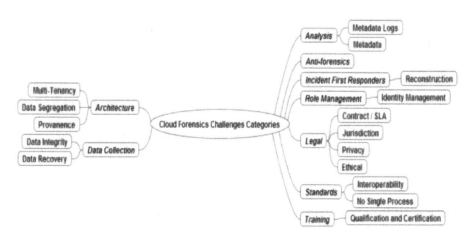

Fig. 2. NIST mind map of forensic challenges (NIST 2014).

Considering all the above-mentioned challenges with regards to cloud forensics, the complexity of the cloud architecture on its own would also make the overarching security processes very challenging. This complexity is outlined in a conceptual model in Fig. 3.

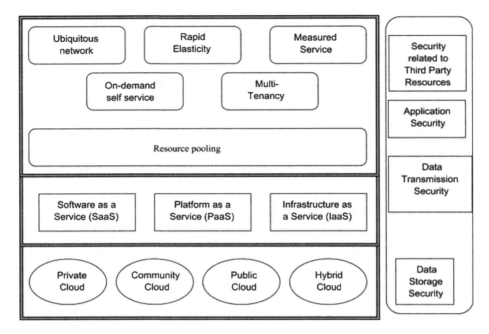

Fig. 3. Cloud computing complexity and challenges for cloud security (Subashini and Kavitha 2011)

6 Anti-forensics

Anti-forensics as a concept is as old as the traditional computer forensics. Someone that commit a punishable action use any possible way to get rid of any evidence connected with the prohibited action. The traditional forensics can have a range of Anti-forensics that start from a trivial level (e.g. wiping fingerprints from a gun) and to a level where our fantasy can meet the implementation of an Anti-forensic idea (e.g. alteration of DNA left behind in a crime). In digital Anti-forensics the same rules exists, with the difference that they are fairly new with little research and development (Jahankhani et al. 2007).

There are number of techniques that are used to apply Anti-forensics. These techniques such as obfuscation, data hiding, and malware are not necessarily designed with Anti-forensics dimension in mind.

While in theory the forensics investigator should monitor everything available around the suspect, in reality the post incident response could end up quite dramatically. This could be due to; ignorance regarding the network activity logs, legal barriers between the access point and the forensics acquisition, non–cooperative ISP's, etc.

Anti-forensics is a reality that comes with every serious crime and involves tactics for "safe hacking" and keeps the crime sophistication in a high level. Computer forensic investigators along with the forensic software developers should start paying more attention to Anti-forensics tools and approaches.

If we consider the Computer Forensics as the actions of collection, preservation, identification and presentation of evidence, Anti-forensics can affect the first three stages. Because these stages can be characterized as "finish to start" between them from a project management point of view, the failure of one of them could end up as a failure of the lot. Thus, there is a high impact of Anti-forensics to the forensics investigations.

Officially there is no such thing as Anti-forensic investigations because the Anti-forensic countermeasures are still part of the investigator's skills.

7 The Main Difficulties Faced by Law Enforcement Officers Fighting Cyber-Crime

It is evident that cybercrime is no longer in its infancy. It is 'big business' for the criminal entrepreneur with potentially lots of money to be made with minimal risks. Cloud computing has generated significant interest in both academia and industry, but it is still an evolving paradigm. Confusion exists in IT communities about how a cloud differs from existing models and how its characteristics affect its adoption. Some see cloud as a novel technical revolution; some consider it a natural evolution of technology, economy, and culture (Takabi et al. 2010). Nevertheless, cloud computing is an important concept, with the strong ability to considerably reduce costs through optimization and increased operating and economic efficiencies. Furthermore, cloud computing could significantly enhance collaboration, agility, and scale, thus enabling a truly global computing model over the Internet infrastructure. However, without appropriate security and privacy solutions designed for clouds, this potentially revolutionizing computing paradigm could become a huge failure. Several surveys of potential cloud adopters indicate that security and privacy is the primary concern hindering its adoption. At the same time cloud creates unique challenges for digital forensic investigators, and one of the areas which have been recognised as the contributory elements in the failing by law enforcement officers is lack of proper training.

From law enforcement point of view the task of fighting Cyber-Crime is a difficult one. Although crime is irrespective of how big or small, a decision has to be made on the merits of each case as to whether investigating and prosecuting is in the public's interest and therefore, it is becoming necessary to understand and manage the Computer Forensics process in the cloud.

Computer Forensics is no longer a profession where training on the job to get experience is sufficient, especially when dealing in cloud environment. Most other professions require one to have a degree before one can progress to train in their vocation i.e. teachers, lawyers, forensic scientist and doctors etc., the same should be with Computer Forensic as the work done is as important as those in other fields and be it positive or negative does affect people's lives.

Numerous universities in in UK and abroad are offering Computer Forensic and Information Security courses to graduate and Post-Graduate level which will help those taking on the courses to have a good grounding in computer science, a better understanding of computer forensic theories and most of all help them develop to be more innovative in coming up with new forensically sound ways of fighting E-crime and to "think outside the box".

It is time for the government to actively work in partnership with universities to encourage people to take on these courses especially those already working in the field in the public sector.

A degree is now a prerequisite in the private sector as well as experience, as it is becoming a lot more difficult for one to claim to be an expert in the field of computer forensics and an expert witness in a court of law. Gone are the days where Do-It-Yourself forensics will be accepted (Jahankhani and Hosseinian-Far 2014).

This leads us to another area a lot of experts in the field of computer forensics have been reserved about and that is the idea of accreditation. It is an area that is very difficult to make decisions on. Most agree and recognize that a board should be set up, but what cannot be agreed upon is who should lead it. Some have suggested that it should be led by universities, by government, by their peers or jointly by universities, government and businesses.

If it is government lead, without set of standards the situation will be no different from what we have at present. It will also involve those working in the profession to give it some direction and it is still doubtful as to whether those people are in a position to decide what form of accreditation to be embarked upon.

This brings us to the option of, a joint partnership with government, universities and businesses. This is the most feasible option but a lot of joint effort will be required to come up with a credible accreditation that will be accepted by all.

One thing is for sure having a form of accreditations will force government, academics, researches and those working in the field of computer forensics to set more appropriate standards and controls for those who handle, analyse and investigate computer evidence.

8 Conclusions

Cloud computing is still an evolving paradigm and has already created challenges for law enforcement around the globe to effectively carry out cloud forensics investigations. Although the digital forensics models comprehensively reviews the stages of a digital forensic process and analyses the cloud forensics' impact on this process; most of its assumptions are not yet valid in the context of cloud computing and the problem will only get worse with the explosive growth of data volumes.

Legal requirement for cloud forensics is currently uncertain and presents a challenge for the legal system. These challenges arises from the fact that cloud environment consists of distributed shared storages so there is a level of necessary interactions forensic examiners and law enforcement officers require from the cloud provider in order to conduct their investigations. One of the areas, which have been recognised as the contributory element in the failing by law enforcement officers, is lack of proper training. Education and training will help to provide good grounding in computer science, a better understanding of computer forensic theories and most of all help to develop to be more innovative in coming up with new forensically sound ways of fighting E-crime and to "think outside the box".

References

ACPO. ACPO Good Practice Guide for Digital Evidence (2012). http://www.digital-detective. net/digital-forensics-documents/ACPO_Good_Practice_Guide_for_Digital_Evidence_v5.pdf

Alhadidi, B., Arabeyat, Z., Alzyoud, F., Alkhwaldeh, A.: Cloud computing security enhancement by using mobile PIN code. J. Comput. **11**(3), 225–231 (2016)

Batra, M., Gupta, N.: Various security issues and their remedies in cloud computing. Int. J. Adv. Eng. Manag. Sci. (IJAEMS) **2**(2), 18–20 (2016)

Bedford, T., Wilson, K.J., Daneshkhah, A.: Assessing parameter uncertainty on coupled models using minimum information methods. Reliab. Eng. Syst. Saf. **125**, 3–12 (2014)

Bluementhal, M.S.: Hide and seek in the cloud. IEEE Secur. Priv. **8**(2), 57–58 (2010)

Carroll, N., Helfert, M., Lynn, T.: Towards the development of a cloud service capability assessment framework. In: Mahmood, Z. (ed.) Continued Rise of the Cloud: Advances and Trends in Cloud Computing, pp. 289–336. Springer, London (2014)

Chang, V.: The business intelligence as a service in the cloud. Future Gener. Comput. Syst. **37**, 512–534 (2014)

Chang, V.: Towards a big data system disaster recovery in a private cloud. Spec. Issue Big Data Inspired Data Sens. Process. Netw. Technol. **35**, 65–82 (2015)

Chang, V., Kuo, Y., Ramachandran, M.: Cloud computing adoption framework: a security framework for business clouds. Future Gener. Comput. Syst. **57**, 24–41 (2016a)

Chang, V., Ramachandran, M., Yao, Y., Li, C.: A resiliency framework for an enterprise cloud. Int. J. Inf. Manag. **36**(1), 155–166 (2016b)

Clarkson, D.B.: Automatics Cloud-Based Disaster Recovery System. United States Patent Application, Patent No. 20160036623 Kind Code: A1 (2016)

Cook, T.: The Cloud of Unknowing, 1st edn. Harcourt Inc., Orlando (2007)

Devi, T., Ganesan, R.: Platform as a Service (PaaS): model and security issues. Indones. J. Electr. Eng. **15**(1), 151–161 (2015)

Dykstra, J., Sherman, A.T.: Design and implementation of FROST: digital forensic tools for the OpenStack computing platform. Digit. Investig. **10**, 87–95 (2013)

Fan, C.K., Chen, R.-C.: The risk management strategy of applying cloud computing. Int. J. Adv. Comput. Sci. Appl. (IJACSA) **3**(9), 18–27 (2012)

Givehchi, O., Jasperneite, J.: Industrial Automation Services as part of the Cloud: First Experiences. Jahreskolloquium Kommunikation in der Automation, Magdeburg (2013)

Grispos, G., Storer, T., Glisson, W.B.: Calm before the storm: the challenges of cloud computing in digital forensics (2012)

Haji, J.: Airline business continuity and IT disaster recovery sites. J. Bus. Contin. Emerg. Plan. **9** (3), 228–238 (2016)

Home Affairs Committee: E-Crime, Fifth Report of Session 2013–14. House of Commons, London (2013)

Hu, F., et al.: A review on cloud computing: design challenges in architecture and security. J. Comput. Inf. Technol. - CIT **19**, 25–55 (2011)

Jadeja, Y., Modi, K.: Cloud computing - concepts, architecture and challenges. In: IEEE International Conference on Computing, Electronics and Electrical Technologies (2012)

Jahankhani, H., Altawell, N., Hessami, A.G.: Risk and privacy issues of digital oil fields in the cloud. In: Jahankhani, H., Carlile, A., Akhgar, B., Taal, A., Hessami, A., Hosseinian-Far, A. (eds.) Global Security, Safety and Sustainability: Tomorrow's Challenges of Cyber Security. ICGS3 2015. Communications in Computer and Information Science, vol. 534, pp. 275–284. Springer, Heidelberg (2015). doi:10.1007/978-3-319-23276-8_25

Jahankhani, H., Anastasios, B., Revett, K.: Digital Anti Forensics: Tools and Approaches. Defence College of Management and Technology, Shrivenham (2007)

Jahankhani, H., Hosseinian-Far, A.: Digital Forensics Education, Training & Awareness. In: Cyber Crime and Cyber Terrorism Investigator's Handbook. Elsevier, pp. 91–100 (2014)

Khajeh-Hosseini, A., Greenwood, D., Sommerville, I.: Cloud migration: A Case Study of Migrating an Enterprise IT System to IaaS. IEEE, Miami (2010)

Khoshkholghi, M.A., et al.: Disaster recovery in cloud computing: a survey. Comput. Inf. Sci. 7(4), 39–54 (2014)

Kumar, M.K.: Software as a service for efficient cloud computing. IJRET: Int. J. Res. Eng. Technol. 3(1), 178–184 (2014)

Martini, B., Choo, K.: An integrated conceptual digital forensic framework for cloud computing. Digit. Investig. 9, 71–80 (2012)

NIST: NIST Cloud Computing Forensic Science Challenges - NISTIR8006. NIST Cloud Computing Forensic Science Working Group - Information Technology Laboratory (2014)

OpenStack. OpenStack Open Source Cloud Computing Software (2016). http://www.openstack.org/

Orton, I., Alva, A., Endicott-Popovsky, B.: Legal process and requirements for cloud forensic investigations. In: CyberCrime and Cloud Forensics: Applications for Investigation Processes. IGI Global (2013)

Pulsant Business Limited: Rethinking Business Continuity with the Cloud. Pulsant, Reading (2015)

Romgovind, S., Eloff, M.M., Smith, E.: The Management of Security in Cloud Computing, pp. 1–7. IEEE, Johannesburg (2010)

Roussev, V., Wang, L., Richard, G., Marziale, L.: A cloud computing platform for large-scale forensic computing. Advances in Digital Forensics, pp. 201–214. Springer, Heidelberg (2009)

Sammons, J.: The Basics of Digital Forensics, 2nd edn. Elsevier, Waltham (2015)

Smith, D.M.: Hype cycle for cloud computing (white paper). Gartner Inc. (2011)

Subashini, S., Kavitha, V.: A survey on security issues in service delivery models of cloud computing. J. Netw. Comput. Appl. 34(1), 1–11 (2011)

Takabi, H., Joshi, J.B., Ahn, G.: Security and privacy challenges in cloud computing environments. IEEE Computer and Reliability Societies (2010)

The National Archives. Police and Justice Act 2006 (2006). http://www.legislation.gov.uk/ukpga/2006/48/contents

Theirm.org: A structured approach to Enterprise Risk Management (ERM) and the requirements of ISO 31000 (2010). https://www.theirm.org/media/886062/ISO3100_doc.pdf. Accessed 2016

Tianfield, H.: Security Issues in Cloud Computing. IEEE, Seoul (2012)

Zhou, M., et al.: Security and privacy in cloud computing: a survey, pp. 105–112 (2010)

Could the Outsourcing of Incident Response Management Provide a Blueprint for Managing Other Cloud Security Requirements?

Bob Duncan[1]([✉]), Mark Whittington[2], Martin Gilje Jaatun[3],
and Alfredo Ramiro Reyes Zúñiga[4]

[1] Computing Science, University of Aberdeen, Aberdeen, UK
bobduncan@abdn.ac.uk
[2] Business School, University of Aberdeen, Aberdeen, UK
[3] Department of Software Engineering, Safety and Security SINTEF ICT,
Trondheim, Norway
[4] Department of Telematics, NTNU, Trondheim, Norway

Abstract. In this chapter, we consider whether the outsourcing of incident management is a viable technological approach that may be transferable to other cloud security management requirements. We review a viable approach to outsourcing incident response management and consider whether this can be applied to other cloud security approaches, starting with the concept of using proper measurement for a cloud security assurance model. We demonstrate how this approach can be applied, not only to the approach under review, but how it may be applied to address other cloud security requirements.

Keywords: Cloud · Requirements · Measurement · Assurance · Outsourcing · Incident response · Security

1 Introduction

The cloud has been referred to as "outsourcing on steroids" (Jaatun et al. 2011), and in the following we review a proposed approach to outsourcing incident response management (Reyes and Jaatun 2015), and consider whether this approach might be transferable to other cloud security requirements, starting in this case with a particular approach to cloud security addressing the importance of proper measurement for a cloud security assurance model (Duncan and Whittington 2015e). Reyes and Jaatun (2015) indicate that outsourcing of incident management is a viable security approach for many organizations, but that transitioning between providers frequently is a challenge. Duncan and Whittington (2015e) suggest that defining proper measures for evaluating the effectiveness of an assurance model, which they have developed to ensure cloud security, is vital to ensure the successful implementation and continued running of the model. The authors recognise that responsibility must lie with the board. However, in this work, we consider the viability of outsourcing these requirements to deliver an independent assurance of delivered security.

V. Chang et al. (Eds.): Enterprise Security, LNCS 10131, pp. 19–39, 2017.
DOI: 10.1007/978-3-319-54380-2_2

The fundamental concepts of information security are confidentiality, integrity, and availability (CIA). Beautement and Pym (2010) provide an account of the misunderstandings prevalent in information security which arise through confusion between (declarative) objectives of (Parker and Crime 1998; Neumann 1995) information security operations with the (operational) mechanisms deployed in order to achieve these objectives. Achieving information security in the cloud is not a trivial process. There are a great many challenges to overcome and, with Pym, Duncan and Whittington addressed some of those in earlier work (Duncan et al. 2013), developing a conceptual model for cloud security assurance, where they addressed three key challenges, namely standards, proposed management method and complexity. Duncan and Whittington (2015e) extended these key challenges to address a total of six possible challenges, which we expand on in Sect. 3.

The rest of this chapter is organised as follows: Sect. 2 summarises the main points related to outsourcing of incident response. In Sect. 3, we outline the work of Duncan and Whittington which highlights the requirements to be addressed. In Sect. 4, we consider whether these requirements might reasonably be provided through outsourcing, and how we might approach this. In Sect. 5, we discuss the implications of our findings and in Sect. 6 we offer our conclusions.

2 Outsourcing of Incident Management

An organization may have several motivations for outsourcing incident management. Reyes and Jaatun (2015) list the following:

- Cost
- Difficulties in hiring, training and retaining staff
- Services you might not want to provide yourself
- Physically hardened facilities with latest infrastructure
- Enterprise-wide management of security strategy
- Access to threat and countermeasure information
- Global prosecution
- Service performance 24×7

Reyes interviewed representatives from organizations who are transnational organizations selected based on the managed security service provider's (MSSP) market presence (Reyes 2015; Reyes and Jaatun 2015). Six large MSSPs and an emerging one (dubbed "A" to "G") contributed to the interviews; for more details on each MSSP, see Reyes (2015).

The findings are organized based on three different stages: Pre-operation, Operation and Post-operation. *Pre-operation* refers to the stage where an organization has not created a contract with any provider to acquire incident management services. *Operation* describes the stage where there is an ongoing contract between the customer and the provider to outsource incident management services. Finally, the *Post-operation* stage deals with a normal contract completion or an early termination.

2.1 Pre-operation

Identifying the Services Needed. Many similar services have different names at different providers, which makes it difficult for customers to choose the right service. Organization A recommends making an in-depth search of the services and then get an independent view from a third party, to understand what their strengths and weaknesses are, and what might be suitable for the company. Organization C recommends that providers should be clear about where these services are located in the incident management process, where the starting point is, where the ending point is and what resources are required from the customer in order to implement the services. Organization D, F and G recommend providers to devote time helping potential clients to understand how what they are doing is different from what others do and what some of the differences in their proposal are. Organization F advises the customers to not choose services through technical specifications but according to the real challenges that they are trying to address.

Choosing the Right Provider. Companies are not aware of the broad diversity of providers that offer incident management services. Organization A advises the companies to have a subscription or a working relationship with an analyst company or a neutral third party in order to get an independent view of the providers, helping to understand the MSSP market segmentation, provider's capabilities, flexibility and customer satisfaction. Organization F recommends to find out about the provider's pro-activity, the skills and knowledge from their personnel and the methodology which their processes are aligned to.

Taking Staff Morale into Consideration. Staff morale might be affected by outsourcing services that were previously run in-house. Organization B recommends involving the staff, and making them understand why the decision was made. Organization F advises MSSPs to persuade their customers that what they are doing is to take away the repeatable processes, so that the customer's security personnel can do the interesting and new tasks. Instead of losing job positions, the in-house personnel would be benefited by improving its tasks.

Adapting to Foreign Language Communication When Using Global Outsourced Services. Outsourcing services to global companies might impact internal communication, since staff might not be used to talking to people in another language. Organization B recommends taking internal communication into account when choosing a service provider.

Predicting Resources and Justifying Them Inside the Business. Customers may have difficulties predicting how much resources or help they are going to need and justifying it within their business. Organization E advises to take advantage of cyber attacks reported in the news to make justifications easier.

Having Control over the Outsourced Service. MSSPs prefer to have control of the process because that allows them the ability to keep a particular price for a commodity. The customers on the other hand, are reluctant to provide the control. Organization F recommends MSSPs to negotiate this with the customers especially at contract time because constant changes are required in a rapid manner and should be aligned to good security practices.

2.2 Operation

Communication Between External and Internal Incident Management Teams. If clear roles and communication mechanisms have not been established in the internal incident management team, this can cause communication conflicts. Organization A describes that it is important that the customers have developed some forensic readiness and incident management documentation describing IRT roles and responsibilities.

Multiple Providers Interaction During an Incident. Customers may have multiple providers supporting the same incident which, even if they are assigned to do different tasks, can have some overlap. Organization C recommends that there should be some hierarchy involved when multiple providers are engaged in the same incident, to make sure that somebody is in charge and perhaps solve overlapping tasks. Organization E describes that the customer should be the one dictating how the investigation would be done and defining the separation of duties to be handled by the companies that are brought in. Organization G recommends to inform the customer about overlaps and to be proactive and address the rest of the providers in charge of a specific security component overlapping, providing them with specifications for modifications.

Collecting Logs from Systems and Infrastructure. The use of logs is something that does not necessarily require many resources, but it provides great help when having an incident. Organization D advises to collect sufficient logs and data in order to facilitate and improve the customer's incident response process. This will allow verifying the information of an incident and would significantly speed the provider's response enabling some response functions to be performed remotely.

Providing Emergency Response Services to New Customers. Emergency response services are available 24 h a day, every day. Organization A advises that experienced security professionals which have developed their skills through different cases are the most suitable to provide help quickly in an unknown infrastructure. Organization C describes that some customers prefer to engage multiple providers when emergency response services are required.

Having Appropriate Staff to Provide Response to Emergency Response Calls. MSSPs require having people available to respond when needed. Organization C advises that providers should be prepared to provide the appropriate people at the appropriate time, since their staff might be actively engaged in different tasks.

Reaching Global Support When System Breaches Involve Global Companies. Some companies might have complex systems either in their internal infrastructure or due to mergers with other companies. When there is a breach in companies with complex systems such as cloud services, international forensics might be an issue. Organization A recommends not looking at the whole company, but first finding the breach and then working your way through it and related systems. If there are complex systems involved in the breach, only then global resources might be required.

Combine the Strategic Information and Intelligence. Not all vendors have access to the same level of intelligence. Organization A describes that the quality of the input that you have access to as a vendor is a big differentiator, but its meaning can only be extracted by combining it with strategic information either from history or from experience. Organization E advises that intelligence can help with detection of anomalies and indicators of compromise to stop targeted attacks.

Implementing Massive Security Services that Will Work Without False Positives. Many customers want to get security services alerting only about the real issues and not being alerted by stuff that is not relevant. Organization A describes that it depends on the quality of the services but this would achieved once a broader integration of IT, network and security systems occurs.

Keeping the Customers. Customers might switch providers due to not getting the agreed service or because the service is or becomes too expensive. Organization A describes that in order to keep a customer it is important to build a trusted relationship between the provider and the customer.

Cultural Differences Might Impact the Working Behavior. Offshoring is the relocation of an outsourced service from one country to another that provides cheaper labor costs. The cultural differences in those outsourcing destinations might impact the communication and the working behavior in the provider's staff. Organization B explains that having workers with big cultural differences demand follow up activities and inter-cultural communication in order to understand the differences and get the job done.

Unavailable Personnel Working in Countries with Natural, Societal or Political Risk Factors. Different circumstances such as natural disasters, strikes or riots among others might restrict offshore workers to reach their working place. Organization B describes that having offshore offices spread over different locations is a good way to spread the risk.

Remote Response Enabled by Agents. IT departments might be reluctant to the use of agents because increased complexity on an endpoint may cause increased customer service calls, help desk calls, and time for evaluating new software releases. Organization D and E recommend working with customers to help convincing their ultimate decision maker as to why the benefit of running the agent at the endpoint is greater than the cost.

Lack of Skilled Personnel. Shortage of people with capabilities for incident response activities. It is difficult to hire as many people as is needed. Organization D advises to hire more junior talent to develop their skills providing them with formal training and in-depth hands-on experience. Organization E advises to create bonds with universities and research groups to find dedicated people and train them. Organization G recommends offering students a part time job while they write their thesis. Once the students graduate, organizations can select those that are skilled and want to keep inside by offering a full time job position.

Incident Response Roles Are Not Clearly Defined. Incident response roles are not clearly defined in the industry, when hiring incident response experts there is a wide variation of the capabilities, level of experience and expertise that is needed. Organization D recommends defining internally what these roles actually are for the company's needs. It is important to understand, when hiring new personnel, what they really have experience in and how that is related to what it is needed at any particular point.

2.3 Post-operation

Knowledge Transition of Customer Services from One Provider to Another When a Customer Changes Provider. Providers might be reluctant to pass knowledge that took many years to get. Organization B describes that providers might transition the problem knowledge that they are obliged to but not the rest. Having a proper documentation and a continuous revision of it during the meetings with the customer might help to keep everything documented so that there won't be any gaps when a provider transition will occur. Organization D highlights that the new provider should be aware that the previous provider may not have much incentive to participate in the process. Some cases it is needed to educate and train the new people that have been hired to perform the same services.

Understanding the Customer Needs and Expectations When Switching Providers. Not understanding the new customer's expectations and its infrastructure could make the transition challenging for the provider receiving the new costumer and deteriorate the relationship from the beginning. Organization A emphasizes the importance of getting familiar with the infrastructure both at the customer and previous provider's facilities. It is important to understand what the critical assets are, what does the customer want to protect, and where did the previous provider fail. The more the provider knows about the customer then the better it would be in shape to provide protection and build a trusted relationship between the parties. Organization C describes that the provider needs to understand the new customer's challenges in order to identify the services that can be offered in that category and propose something to address them based on their prior experience.

3   The Importance of Proper Measurement for a Cloud Security Assurance Model

In this section, we summarize the Duncan and Whittington (2015e) paper on the importance of proper measurement for a cloud security model.

3.1   The Challenges

The fundamental concepts of information security are confidentiality, integrity, and availability (CIA), a concept developed when it was common practice for corporate management to run a company under agency theory. We have all seen how agency theory has failed to curb the excesses of corporate greed. The same is true for cloud security, which would suggest a different approach is needed. We have identified six key points to address: definition of security goals, compliance with cloud security standards, audit issues, the impact of management approaches on security, and how complexity and the lack of responsibility and accountability affects cloud security.

In looking at the definition of security goals, we have recognised that the business environment is constantly changing, as are corporate governance rules and this would clearly imply changing measures would be required. More emphasis is now being placed on responsibility and accountability (Huse 2005), social conscience (Gill 2008), sustainability (Ioannidis et al. 2013; Kolk 2008), resilience (Chapin et al. 2009; Chang et al. 2016) and ethics (Arjoon 2012).

Responsibility and accountability are, in effect, mechanisms we can use to help achieve all the other security goals. Since social conscience and ethics are very closely related, we can expand the traditional CIA triad to include sustainability, resilience and ethics. This expansion of security requirements can help address some of the shortcomings of agency theory, but also provides a perfect fit to stewardship theory. Stewardship carries a broader acceptance of responsibility than the self-interest embedded in agency. This breadth extends to acting in the interests of company owners and potentially society and the environment as a whole.

On the matter of achieving compliance with standards in practice, we have identified the use of assurance to achieve security through compliance and audit. With compliance, there are a number of challenges to address. Since the evolution of cloud computing, a number of cloud security standards have evolved, but there is still no standard which offers complete security, which is a limitation. Even compliance with all standards will not guarantee complete security, which, presents another disadvantage (Duncan and Whittington 2014).

The pace of evolution of new technology far outstrips the capability of international standards organizations to keep up with the changes (Willingmyre 1997), adding to the problem and meaning it may not be resolved any time soon. We have argued that companies need to take account of these gaps in the standards when addressing issues of compliance. In (Duncan and Whittington 2014), we have addressed the question of whether compliance with standards, assurance and audit can provide security, and in (Duncan and Whittington 2015d), we have addressed one of the fundamental weaknesses of the standards compliance process.

Auditing in the accountancy world has enjoyed the benefit of over a century of practice and experience, yet there remain differences of opinion and a number of problems are yet to be resolved. Duncan and Whittington (2014) provide some background on this issue. Cloud audit can not be considered a mature field, and there will be some way to go before it can catch up with work done in the accounting profession. Clearly further research will be needed in this area.

Looking at management approach, we would argue that a shift from agency behaviour to a stewardship approach (Duncan and Whittington 2015a) can go a long way to reducing the major weaknesses inherent in an agency approach to security in cloud ecosystems. We have observed that cloud service providers (CSPs) have developed their cloud business models using agency theory. Pallas (2014) suggest that agency theory models the current relationship between CSPs and cloud users very well, further suggesting this expresses all the weaknesses of agency and highlights many of the issues still faced today.

Given the potential multiplicity of actors, and the complexities of their relationships with each other in cloud ecosystems, it is clear that simple traditional agency relationships (where each actor looks to their own short term ends) will no longer be able to handle fully the security implications for users of these ecosystems. There is a clear need for developing a stronger mechanism to ensure that users of such ecosystems can be assured of the security of their information. We have addressed (Duncan and Whittington 2015a) the cloud security issue with management method, and argued that the historic reliance on agency theory to run companies can present a barrier to effective security.

In considering complexity, we have observed that since cloud computing was developed, the majority of security based research has concentrated on providing technical solutions to solve the security problem. While many excellent solutions have been proposed, cloud security can never be achieved by technical means alone.

First, the core business architecture comprises a combination of people, process and technology (PWC 2012), thus a solution which addresses only one of these key elements will always be doomed to failure. Second, a cloud user can take as many steps to secure their business as they wish, but a key ingredient in the equation is the fact that all cloud processes run on someone else's hardware, and often software too — the CSP's. The cloud relationship needs to include the CSP as a key partner in the pursuit of achieving security. Unless and until CSPs are willing to share this goal, technical solutions will be doomed to failure. Third, the additional complexities which cloud brings into the security equation must be recognised, and dealt with appropriately. Increased complexity brings with it increased risk. If this risk is not recognised, and dealt with appropriately, this will inhibit the possibility of achieving good security.

Currently, cloud users effectively have to treat cloud services as a black box, since they have no control over what goes on inside, or behind the scenes. This puts cloud users at a singular disadvantage when it comes to issues of privacy and security. Regulators are taking a far more aggressive approach to breaches, and the cloud user is the one who ends up carrying the can and getting the punitive fines issued by the regulator.

This leads to the issue of lack of responsibility and accountability. Standard service level agreement (SLA) offerings from the major players currently ignore accountability, assurance, audit, confidentiality, compliance, integrity, privacy, responsibility and security, merely offering availability as the focus of their measure of performance. The onus for measuring and proving unacceptable performance is neatly passed to the customer, which, with the inclusion of some suitably deeply buried clauses in the small print, assures the buck invariably never stops with the CSP.

Companies who are cloud users are quite properly legally held responsible and accountable to a variety of regulators throughout industry under privacy and security regulations. Fines for non-compliance are reaching punitive levels, and many regulators have extreme levels of sanction at their disposal. Yet, CSPs are not held to account for their often not inconsiderable role in such failures! This issue with CSP SLAs is not a trivial issue to address. CSPs need to provide users with assurance, through compliance and audit, that they can provide a level of service capable of meeting user requirements in confidentiality, integrity, privacy and security. CSPs should be prepared to offer cloud users performance guarantees in all their required areas, not just on availability. CSPs need to become accountable to users for meeting these requirements, by which means they will be able to demonstrate a responsible and ethical approach to their customers, and at the same time, providing an extremely robust and dependable service to all cloud users.

We further argue that the CSPs should provide monitoring tools to collect sufficient information to demonstrate that they have achieved the required level of performance, rather than leaving it for customers to find out when something goes wrong. CSPs are much better placed to do this, since cloud customers will not necessarily have access to all the systems necessary for this to happen. We have further argued (Duncan and Whittington 2015b) that this will require a significant change in attitude from the CSPs, leading to the development of better security oriented SLAs, which will improve the approach to security for all actors within the cloud ecosystem.

This was the basis on which, with Pym, we developed a conceptual framework for cloud security assurance (Duncan et al. 2013), expanding on earlier works (Beautement and Pym 2010; Baldwin et al. 2011), which seeks to address the issues faced in trying to achieve security in the cloud, and provides a more effective means for business to achieve both cloud security assurance along with appropriate standards compliance, by providing continuous assurance through both compliance and audit. We draw on natural resource management research (Chapin et al. 2009; Kao 2007) which provides some very clear illustrations of the effectiveness of stewardship, presenting a clear systems view of the issues addressed. The framework we have proposed addresses these key challenges facing cloud users.

3.2   How Our Framework Operates

The framework functions by taking a 3 dimensional security approach to how the company is organised. On one dimension there is the business architecture, which covers people, process and technology; the second dimension covers the security properties, which extends the traditional CIA approach by adding sustainability, resilience and ethics; and the third dimension is the systems architecture of the business, which addresses the systems, services and applications used by the business, to which we must add the cloud models of infrastructure, platform and software as a service (IaaS), (PaaS) and (SaaS). The framework then identifies and addresses every point in the matrix where each of the three dimensions intersect (Fig. 1).

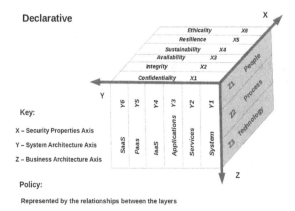

Fig. 1. A declarative cloud three-dimensional security matrix

There are 4 stages of process involved in running the model. There is the declarative stage, where management set the goals to be achieved. Next the operational stage collects data to measure how well the company is meeting these declarative goals. Then, internal audit will provide assurance through audit and compliance checks to confirm the integrity of the process. Finally, external audit will essentially double check that everything undertaken will have been compliant and thus compliance with standards can be achieved, together with the assurance that the declarative goals of management are being met.

Thus, management need to determine their declarative position on each of these intersecting points, and further, must determine how performance will be measured. Management are responsible for defining proper measurements and metrics to be used in the framework, and this is what we will now address.

3.3   How to Develop Useful Measurements

Duncan and Whittington (2015e) provide an extensive list of literature on the subject of measurement, which we will not reiterate here. We will simply focus on the development of useful measures for a company. Defining a generic set of measures is unlikely to be useful, since every business is different. This is a task for management. However, we think it will be useful to provide some general assistance by way of a few examples of how to go about it. We will start by looking at each dimension in turn.

Measuring people can be relatively straightforward. Each employee has a unique employee number, a unique computer access code and password, and access rights to whatever areas are appropriate for carrying out their job. Some companies will already have electronic or biometric systems installed and functioning, others might not, but identifying who is who ought to be relatively straightforward. Most companies will have their processes well documented with a unique reference number assigned to each process.

While these processes may well have been documented for a considerable period of time, it is important to recognise that they may have been defined before security formed part of the requirements. This should be recognised and appropriate steps taken to address this. Technology, too, should be simple enough, as each piece of technology, whether servers, desktop, or mobile device will have a unique asset number, and internet connectivity can be recorded via the unique media access control (MAC) address inside the hardware, as well as the internet protocol (IP) address used to connect to the network, whether from inside the company, or from outside the company via the internet.

Looking at systems next, each piece of technology will have an operating system, which will be identifiable. There will be one or more services running on the equipment, which will be identifiable, and there will be one or more applications running on the equipment, all of which will be identifiable. Where access to cloud systems is available, this will be either at a high level, such as SaaS or some service such as desktop as a service (DaaS), which can be identified. Equally, if the access is to a lower level of service such as PaaS or IaaS, this too can be identified. There may be multiple systems accessed, operated by multiple providers, which may also involve brokers or other service providers, all of which can be identified.

This brings us to a more difficult area, the security properties. Confidentiality can be achieved by ensuring only the correctly authorised people can be granted access to confidential information. This can be achieved by proper access control, and monitoring. Integrity is slightly more challenging, as it is technically more challenging to ensure that information, once saved into a system has not been tampered with, particularly in the case of databases. This can be addressed by logging every change made to every transaction within a system, logging who made the change, when, from what location and so on. Thus each change in the information state can be preserved, which would allow recreation of the original if the change was malicious.

However, our requirement to address the new security properties of sustainability, resilience and ethics presents the biggest challenge. We could address sustainability of security by using redundancy to ensure continuity of operations in the event of some business disaster or major security breach. This may involve an element of lost time due to set up and configuration time needed to restore systems.

Resilience could be addressed by having a permanently running system mirror which allows for an extremely rapid recovery from unexpected shock. The additional costs of addressing sustainability and resilience would need to be considered. For business critical systems, the additional costs of ensuring sustainability and resilience may end up providing cheap insurance.

Ethics, which generally would include company approach to corporate social responsibility, could be addressed by viewing how suppliers approach these issues, usually disclosed in annual reports, corporate social responsibility reports or on the company website.

Clearly CSPs who concentrate on availability in their SLAs without considering accountability, assurance, audit, confidentiality, compliance, integrity, privacy, responsibility and security, thus leaving the cloud user to carry the can, might well be considered as irresponsible and unethical in their behaviour. The same might be said for companies who provide poor service in other areas, such as outsourced activities which might have an impact on security and privacy.

3.4 Addressing Two Critical Remaining Obstacles to Cloud Security

We would like to think that there are no weaknesses in the conceptual framework we have developed for cloud security assurance. But to do so would be naïve, as the framework has been necessarily developed to address all aspects of cloud security under the control of the company operating the framework. Unfortunately, the very mechanism of cloud computing means that not all areas are completely under the control of the company operating the framework. At least one or more companies involved in the cloud ecosystem will not be under the control of the company operating the framework, and this presents a key weakness.

Our proposed framework addresses all three areas of people, process and technology, yet is still not foolproof, and here are some of the main reasons for this: CSP SLA limitations, and unwillingness to change; The threat environment; Standards issues; Management reluctance to take security seriously. One of the most important of these is the SLA between the company and the CSP. It is no accident that the standard SLA offerings from the major CSPs focus on availability. Their business model is geared to providing availability as the main service performance measure to which they purport to be accountable.

Accountability, assurance, audit, confidentiality, compliance, integrity, privacy, responsibility and security do not feature in the standard SLA (Duncan and Whittington 2015b). It is important that companies recognise that this represents the current status. Any additional requirements must be negotiated directly with the CSP, although it is encouraging to note that following an EU pilot study (EU 2012), the EU Commission proposed new guidelines for a standard EU SLA (EU 2014).

Another key area to be considered is the magnitude of the threat environment. Companies are bound by legislation, sometimes regulation, the need to comply with standards, industry best practice and are accountable for their actions. Attackers have no such constraints. They have different agendas, different skills levels, capabilities and resources at their disposal. Between them all, they can attack 24/7, 365 days a year. They don't work to rule, go home at 5:00 pm, take weekends off or go on holiday, at least not until they have the cash, in which case there are plenty more happy to take their place. In addition to this, Kaspersky (2013) suggest that over 200,000 new malware threats are being developed globally every day.

We are concerned about developing proper metrics for the six security goals of our proposed security assurance model. This will not be a trivial exercise and clearly we cannot do justice to all these areas within the space of this chapter. Accordingly, we will address each of these areas individually during the next year as part of our ongoing research.

4   Can We Outsource Measurement and How Would We Do It?

Management guru Harrington (1999) once said "Measurement is the first step that leads to control and eventually to improvement. If you can't measure something, you can't understand it. If you can't understand it, you can't control it. If you can't control it, you can't improve it."

In considering whether we can outsource measurement and thinking about how we can do it, we look at Duncan and Whittington (2016) where the authors first consider the cloud audit problem, and how this can impact on our plan. We also consider in Duncan and Whittington (2016) how correct use of the audit trail can help us ensure that a good solution to this problem can be achieved.

In previous work (Duncan and Whittington 2015b) on enhancing cloud security and privacy, the authors addressed issues arising due to the cloud service provider's (CSP)'s lack of accountability in the standard service level agreement (SLA). The authors discuss the importance of the role assurance plays, and the two main mechanisms used to achieve this, namely compliance and audit.

Before understanding how the use of cloud impacts on the audit process, and how it differs from conventional IT audit, we need to first understand what audit is, why we need to do it, who should be doing it and how it should be done. We must also understand what special difficulties the use of cloud brings to audit. We therefore revisit the authors' definition of audit.

The Oxford English Dictionary (OED) defines audit as (OED 1989): ("To make an official systematic examination of (accounts), so as to ascertain their accuracy") and requires outsiders who are deemed to be both objective and expert to form their own opinion of what is being audited and then to publicly state their confidence (or otherwise) in the reliability of what they have investigated. Auditing is not straightforward or easy. Just as with accounting auditors, objectivity is difficult when companies pay auditors directly and auditors would also like to be retained for the following year. Audit is also potentially very expensive if done well by the best experts in the field and there is a temptation to reduce the experts' role to one of advising, often writing checklists to be administered by qualified technicians.

We first consider the three main purposes of audit, who should be carrying it out, and how it should be done. First, the most widely understood of which is the statutory requirement for financial statements to be audited by an independent external auditor, which has been a cornerstone of confidence in global financial systems since auditing was introduced. It provides assurance that company managers have presented a "true and fair" view of a company's financial performance and position, underpinning the trust and obligation of stewardship between company management and the owners of the company, the shareholders.

A second purpose of audit is IT systems audit. Traditional audit approaches often involved treating IT systems as "black box" systems, meaning trust was placed in the IT systems, and looking at the functioning of the IT system was not considered part of the statutory audit. These audits are usually conducted by IT specialists, often in conjunction with accounting audit professionals to ensure the functioning of these systems are properly understood. However, these are not mandated under statute, and there is no requirement for an annual audit to be undertaken.

A third purpose of audit is compliance, either with regulations, or more often with standards. This is often undertaken to assure shareholders and other stakeholders that the company is using best practice in its operations. This is particularly the case in cloud computing, where systems are operated by third parties beyond the control of the cloud user. Currently, the difficulties associated with performing an adequate cloud audit present one of the key barriers to cloud adoption (Armbrust et al. 2010). Again, these audits are not mandated under statute, nor is there a requirement for an annual audit to be undertaken.

Clearly, in order to take an economic approach to providing a satisfactory level of service, utilising the first purpose of audit would not be appropriate, due to the high costs involved. However, the second purpose of audit would provide a high level of assurance to cloud users if it were carried out on the monitoring system at the beginning of the contract. Thereafter, using the third purpose of audit could provide assurance in the long run that the outsourcing company is providing an adequate level of performance.

Having said that, there are some shortcomings with the cloud audit trail process, as discussed by (Duncan and Whittington 2016), which we would do well to take into account. The six security issues addressed in Duncan and Whittington (2015c) have been expanded to ten, with the addition of the following four security issues: measurement and monitoring; management attitude to security; security culture in the company; and the threat environment.

Since the Duncan and Whittington (2015e) paper already covered the measurement issue, this leaves the last three to consider. There is no doubt that management approach to security will have a major impact on how well a company can stand up to attack, and indeed this approach will also determine how good the security culture within the company will be. Our approach to solving these issues is to minimise the impact any adverse management approach is likely to have on security. Obviously, we have no control over the threat environment, our only approach being to make life as difficult as possible for attackers to gain access.

A fundamental element of the audit process is the audit trail, and having two disciplines involved in providing cloud audit services means there are two different disciplines to contend with, namely accounting professionals and security professionals. An obvious concern is what is meant by the term "audit trail". It is easy to assume that everyone is talking about the same thing, but is that actually the case? To an accounting professional, the meaning of an audit trail is very clear.

The Oxford English Dictionary (OED) (OED 1989) has two useful definitions of an audit trail: "(a) Accounting: a means of verifying the detailed transactions underlying any item in an accounting record; (b) Computing: a record of the computing processes which have been applied to a particular set of source data, showing each stage of processing and allowing the original data to be reconstituted; a record of the transactions to which a database or a file has been subjected". This suggests common understanding, but often this is not evident in computing research.

What is abundantly clear, both from an accounting and a computing security perspective, is that users should only be able to read the audit trail (Anderson 2008). While it is simple enough to restrict users to read-only access, this does not apply to the system administrators. This presents an issue where an intruder gets into a system, escalates privileges until root access is obtained, and is then free to manipulate, or delete the audit trail entries in order to cover their tracks.

A simple solution to this key problem would be for the outsourcing contractor to run the audit trail on their own systems, thus removing all vulnerabilities from the user's system and ensuring continuity of monitoring and preservation of a full and proper audit trail.

Turning back to the questions of the chapter, we have now established the mechanics of how we might achieve this goal, meaning we have a viable methodology that can be used to achieve these goals. Thus we need to consider in which cases this methodology might be deployed. Whether or not they have the will, it is certainly the case that large corporates can afford the calibre of staff necessary to take care of these issues in-house.

However, in the case of small to medium sized enterprises (SME)s and micro enterprises (ME)s, these companies may well not have the resources to deploy an adequate calibre of staff to handle this challenging technical task. Equally, the management may not have sufficient knowledge to be able to define adequate and proper metrics to measure. This is likely to put such companies at a commercial disadvantage as compared to large corporates.

However, by providing them with an opportunity to have access to this service as an outsourced service, provided to a high standard, this will free them and their staff to concentrate on the areas of business which they are most skilled at. This should permit them to take comfort that a vital, and highly specialised, requirement needed to ensure the security of their business is being properly taken care of, while at the same time, removing some of the competitive disadvantage that they would otherwise suffer from.

5   Discussion

Pearson and Charlesworth (2009) argue that *accountability* may be a solution to the privacy problem in the cloud, but this may be true also in the general case if we can persuade providers that "doing the right thing" may be a business advantage (Jaatun et al. 2016). Incident response in the cloud is difficult for many reasons, not least because many cloud services are delivered as part of complex provider chains, and incidents that occur at one part of the chain may have implications at the other end (Jaatun and Tøndel 2015).

Some recent developments may provide additional incentives to an accountability-based approach. The European Data Protection Regulation (EDPR) (EU 2016), which will come into force by 2018, has specific provisions for data breach notification, which may encourage providers to use notification technology that is already available. However, it may be argued that being too open about incidents that have occurred in your system both could create bad publicity and allow your competitors (not to mention other attackers) too much insight into your weak spots (Frøystad et al. 2016).

Against this backdrop emerges a major selling point for outsourcing incident management services to a trusted third party. Cloud customers could ensure that their MSSP either covers the entire provider chain, or that the provider chain is covered by a set of MSSPs that collaborate. This avoids having to reveal "arbitrary" incident information to the next provider in the chain, instead sending it to the MSSP, who in this context would fill a similar role as an auditor. It is not a long stretch to imagine that such an MSSP also could do other forms of security-relevant measurements, either using agents or other mechanisms (Doelitzscher et al. 2013).

Organization A describes that good communication with internal incident management teams depends on the customer's forensic readiness, meaning that the customer is prepared and the stakeholders are involved in the case. If there is not a proper working model in the internal incident management team, there might be communication conflicts due to a lack of internal communication (Tøndel et al. 2014).

A customer that has security controls in place, trains its people, has implemented security awareness, and knows what the threats might be, gets more benefit from the outsourced incident management services. Organization E describes that when internal incident management teams are mature and self-sufficient, they look for assistance in services that are too complex. Organization A and C explain that outsourced incident management services could benefit an internal incident management team by providing it with more manpower, specialized services, managerial skills, a global perspective on threats and multiple sources of intelligence. However, in some cases it might affect internal teams that are trying to respond in the same manner if there are not clear lines of responsibility in terms of which team does what type of tasks. Moreover, some internal incident management teams might get affected by a reduction of staff.

Organization B comments that current incident management teams benefit from participating on discussions and inputs coming from the provider getting a different perspective in order to make decisions and reach agreements to deal with an incident. Organization D highlights that some internal incident management teams might perceive the MSSPs as the help needed to prevent being fired when an incident is out of control. Ahmad et al. (2015) highlight the importance of learning from incidents, and the difficulties some experience with information sharing even within the same organization. Using professional third party could be a way to bridge this gap.

Organizations A and D describe that they offer different types of SLAs in terms of different services. Organization A's responsibilities and penalties are dependent on what the customer is looking for and is willing to pay. The penalties differentiate on what services are outsourced, traditional managed security services or managed incident handling services, the level of the incident missed and the severity of the attack.

Organization B explains that the roles and responsibilities are dependent on what the client wants. Organization B offers different types of SLAs not only in terms of different services but also according to the environment (production, test, development, etc.). The SLAs related with the production environment have higher cost and penalties than the rest of the environments. The penalties at the SLAs might differ from account to account. However, Organization B has compensation agreements, meaning that if an SLA is missed and there is a penalty, the compensation agreement could be used in order to condone the penalty as long as the compensation agreement is achieved.

Organization C has very specific SLAs for incident reporting or detection. If there is an incident or suspected incident, there is an escalation process to notify the customer, which is done by phone or by other means, based on its severity. But Organization C uses a different set of SLAs when it comes to incident response. Responsibilities and penalties are dependent on what is being offered and what the consequences are for the customer.

Organization E considers that there is no way to promise some customer that the provider's resources will be on site within a very specific amount of time. Everything is done in a best effort manner, and there are no artificial time limits. There is no way that a provider can promise to get to the bottom of something in an investigation in a certain period of time, because each situation is different (Schneier 2014). It is hard to state SLAs because there is no level of predictability in these kinds of situations.

Proper measurement and monitoring can not only provide an effective means of ensuring proper standards of security and privacy can be maintained on a day to day basis, but in addition, can provide effective compliance assurance to ensure cloud users can demonstrate a highly ethical approach to the stewardship of customers' data. Where the measurement and monitoring solution is added to the incident response solution, this can provide a repository of additional long term forensic material in the event of a cloud breach, as well as freeing internal company resources to address other important company issues.

6   Conclusion

Outsourcing incident management security services is a viable option to get security competence for responding to today's threats. Outsourcing incident management services seems to be a good option for small and medium size organizations that don't require tailored services. These organizations can reap affordable comprehensive security without investing in new infrastructure or being burdened by deployment and management costs. Large organizations are benefiting from specialized services or by having the chance to focus on tasks that demand specialized skills instead of repeatable tasks. Tailored solutions are not easily achieved by outsourced services. It is a complex process that requires both internal and external staff to accomplish.

All organizations can evaluate and assess what MSSPs offer according to their needs. However, the service descriptions at the provider's websites are unclear, and often confusing. Mapping those services to either the incident management model, or, e.g., the Observe-Orient-Decide-Act (OODA) decision-making lifecycle phases (Boyd 1987) will enable better understanding of what the customers are lacking to increase the effectiveness of their organizational cyber-defense capabilities.

Knowledge transition of customer services from one provider to another requires proper documentation. This documentation is not effectively done, according to some of the interviewees, and in some cases there is knowledge that doesn't reach the new provider. Therefore exchange formats between providers to transfer the customer services knowledge could help to guarantee the customers that their data will be properly handled during and after the transition. A public file format for exchange of customer services knowledge should be developed to automate as much of the knowledge transition process as possible. It would make cross-organizational coordination more efficient and cost effective.

We have looked at some of the challenges facing companies who seek to obtain good cloud security assurance. We have seen how weaknesses in standard CSP SLAs can impact on cloud security. We have identified issues with cloud security standards, and how that might impact on cloud security. We have considered how the lack of accountability can impact on security. We have briefly outlined how our cloud security assurance framework operates, and have discussed how the above issues must additionally be addressed.

In looking at measurement literature, we see how some aspects are quite mature and well understood, but that more modern methods of management such as sustainability, resilience and ethics present new challenges due to the dearth of research in these areas. In looking at how our framework operates, we have discussed how the best security approach needs to consider not just a technical solution, but must address people, process and technology.

We have touched on how these difficult areas of security might be approached as part of a comprehensive security solution based on our proposed framework. Clearly, companies could benefit from further research in several of these areas, and in particular, measurement. However, we would caution that action is needed now, not several years down the line when research reaches a more complete level of success in these areas. The threat environment is too dangerous. Companies have to act now to try to close the door, otherwise it may be too late.

Where a company is prepared to use an outsourced service for incident response, it is clear that there will be synergies to be gained by also using the same outsourced service to measure and monitor the effectiveness of the ongoing security position of the company as a whole. Our proposal will address one of the fundamental weaknesses of security monitoring, namely the lack of security which conventional systems impose on the audit trail, which will clearly provide a considerable improvement on the status quo.

Acknowledgements. The research in this paper has partly been supported by the European Commission (A4Cloud project, grant no. 317550).

References

Ahmad, A., Maynard, S.B., Shanks, G.: A case analysis of information systems and security incident responses. Int. J. Inf. Manag. **35**(6), 717–723 (2015)

Anderson, R.J.: Security Engineering: A Guide to Building Dependable Distributed Systems, vol. 50. Wiley, Hoboken (2008)

Arjoon, S.: Corporate governance: an ethical perspective. J. Bus. Ethics **61**(4), 343–352 (2012)

Armbrust, M., Fox, A., Griffith, R., Joseph, A.D., Katz, R., Konwinski, A., Lee, G., Patterson, D., Rabkin, A., Stoica, I., Zaharia, M.: A view of cloud computing. Commun. ACM **53**(4), 50–58 (2010)

Baldwin, A., Beres, Y., Mont, M.C., Shiu, S., Duggan, G., Johnson, H., Middup, C.: An experiment in decision making WEIS 2011. In: WEIS, pp. 1–28 (2011)

Beautement, A., Pym, D.: Structured systems economics for security management. In: WEIS, pp. 1–20 (2010)

Boyd, J.R.: Organic design for command and control. A discourse on winning and losing (1987)

Chang, V., Ramachandran, M., Yao, Y., Kuo, Y.H., Li, C.S.: A resiliency framework for an enterprise cloud. Int. J. Inf. Manag. **36**(1), 155–166 (2016)

Chapin, F.S., Kofinas, G.P., Folke, C.: Principles of Ecosystem Stewardship: Resilience-Based Natural Resource Management in a Changing World. Springer, Heidelberg (2009)

Doelitzscher, F., Ruebsamen, T., Karbe, T., Reich, C., Clarke, N.: Sun behind clouds - on automatic cloud security audits and a cloud audit policy language. Int. J. Adv. Netw. Serv. **6**(1&2) (2013)

Duncan, B., Pym, D.J., Whittington, M.: Developing a conceptual framework for cloud security assurance. In: 2013 IEEE 5th International Conference on Cloud Computing Technology and Science (CloudCom), Bristol, vol. 2, pp. 120–125. IEEE (2013)

Duncan, B., Whittington, M.: Compliance with standards, assurance and audit: does this equal security? In: Proceedings of the 7th International Conference on Security of Information and Networks, Glasgow, pp. 77–84. ACM (2014)

Duncan, B., Whittington, M.: Company management approaches stewardship or agency: which promotes better security in cloud ecosystems? In: Cloud Computing, Nice, pp. 154–159. IEEE (2015a)

Duncan, B., Whittington, M.: Enhancing cloud security and privacy: broadening the service level agreement. In: The 14th IEEE International Conference on Trust, Security and Privacy in Computing and Communications (IEEE TrustCom 2015), Helsinki, Finland, pp. 1088–1093 (2015b)

Duncan, B., Whittington, M.: Information security in the cloud: should we be using a different approach? In: 2015 IEEE 7th International Conference on Cloud Computing Technology and Science (CloudCom), Vancouver, pp. 1–6 (2015c)

Duncan, B., Whittington, M.: Reflecting on whether checklists can tick the box for cloud security. In: Proceedings of the International Conference on Cloud Computing Technology and Science, CloudCom, Singapore, vol. 2015-February, pp. 805–810. IEEE (2015d)

Duncan, B., Whittington, M.: The importance of proper measurement for a cloud security assurance model. In: 2015 IEEE 7th International Conference on Cloud Computing Technology and Science (CloudCom), Vancouver, pp. 1–6 (2015e)

Duncan, B., Whittington, M.: Enhancing cloud security and privacy: the power and the weakness of the audit trail. In: Submitted to Cloud Computing, Rome, pp. 1–6. IEEE (2016)

EU: Unleashing the Potential of Cloud Computing in Europe (2012)

EU: Cloud service level agreement standardisation guidelines. Technical report, EU Commission, Brussels (2014)

EU: Reform of EU data protection rules (2016)

Frøystad, C., Gjære, E.A., Tøndel, I.A., Jaatun, M.G.: Security incident information exchange for cloud services. In: Proceedings of International Conference on Internet of Things and Big Data (2016)

Gill, A.: Corporate governance as social responsibility: a research agenda. Berkeley J. Int. Law **26**(2), 452–478 (2008)

Harrington, H.J.: Measurement. CIO, 19 September 1999

Huse, M.: Accountability and creating accountability: a framework for exploring behavioural perspectives of corporate governance. Br. J. Manag. **16**(S1), S65–S79 (2005)

Ioannidis, C., Pym, D., Williams, J.: Sustainability in information stewardship: time preferences: externalities and social co-ordination. In: WEIS 2013, pp. 1–24 (2013)

Jaatun, M.G., Nyre, Å.A., Alapnes, S., Zhao, G.: An approach to confidentiality control in the cloud. In: Proceedings of the 2nd International Conference on Wireless Communications, Vehicular Technology, Information Theory and Aerospace Electronic Systems Technology (Wireless Vitae Chennai 2011) (2011)

Jaatun, M.G., Pearson, S., Gittler, F., Leenes, R., Niezen, M.: Enhancing accountability in the cloud. Int. J. Inf. Manag. (2016, to appear)

Jaatun, M.G., Tøndel, I.A.: How much cloud can you handle? In: 2015 10th International Conference on Availability, Reliability and Security (ARES), pp. 467–473 (2015)

Kao, R.: Stewardship Based Economics. World Scientific, Singapore (2007)

Kaspersky: Global Corporate IT Security Risks. Technical report, May 2013

Kolk, A.: Sustainability, accountability and corporate governance: exploring multinationals' reporting practices. Bus. Strateg. Environ. **17**(1), 1–15 (2008)

Neumann, P.G.: Computer-Related Risks. Addison-Wesley, Reading (1995)

OED: Oxford English Dictionary (1989)

Pallas, F.: An agency perspective to cloud computing. In: Altmann, J., Vanmechelen, K., Rana, O.F. (eds.) GECON 2014. LNCS, vol. 8914, pp. 36–51. Springer, Heidelberg (2014). doi:10.1007/978-3-319-14609-6_3

Parker, D.B., Crime, F.C.: Fighting Computer Crime: A New Framework for Protecting Information. Wiley, Hoboken (1998)

Pearson, S., Charlesworth, A.: Accountability as a way forward for privacy protection in the cloud. In: Jaatun, M.G., Zhao, G., Rong, C. (eds.) CloudCom 2009. LNCS, vol. 5931, pp. 131–144. Springer, Heidelberg (2009). doi:10.1007/978-3-642-10665-1_12

PWC: UK Information Security Breaches Survey. Technical report, London, April 2012

Reyes, A.: Outsourced incident management services (2015)

Reyes, A., Jaatun, M.G.: Passing the buck: outsourcing incident response management. In: IEEE 7th International Conference on Cloud Computing Technology and Science (CloudCom), pp. 503–508 (2015)

Schneier, B.: The future of incident response. IEEE Secur. Priv. **12**(5), 96–96 (2014)

Tøndel, I.A., Line, M.B., Jaatun, M.G.: Information security incident management: current practice as reported in the literature. Comput. Secur. **45**, 42–57 (2014)

Willingmyre, G.T.: Standards at the crossroads. StandardView **5**(4), 190–194 (1997)

The Relationship Between Public Budgeting and Risk Management: Competition or Driving?

Yaotai Lu[(⊠)]

Qingdao University, Qingdao, China
yaotailu@163.com

Abstract. This world is rife with uncertainties. Risk management plays an increasingly important role in both the public sector and the private sector. Considering that government is the risk manager of last resort, government faces a vast variety of risks and disasters, either natural or manmade. Owing to scarce public resources and increasing public needs, government is not capable to finance all risk management programs. However, once a catastrophic event occurs, government must take immediate actions to control the event. This essay intends to explore the relationship between risk management and budgeting in the public sector. It attempts to demonstrate to what extent and in which areas risk management depends on budget and competes against other public expenditures, and if budget austerity blocks risk management. The analyses of risk management activities and budget cycles find that budgeting generally serves as a facilitator and catalyst to risk and disaster management; and risk and disaster management is mostly a competitor in budget process; and severe unexpected disasters and crises drive and overshadow budgets to deal with the serious consequences ever incurred. This essay suggests particular measures that may help establish a virtuous relationship between budgeting and risk management.

Keywords: Risk management · Budgeting · Management process · Budgeting cycle · Vulnerability management · Sustainability

1 Introduction

Since risks may bring about enormous loss of properties and human lives, risk management has been a popular topic in both the public and private sectors. In the private sector, businesses focus on management of risks that come from every source and endanger benefits of all stakeholders. The risk sources may include hazards (natural catastrophes, liability torts, and property damage), financial management (such as pricing, asset, currency and liquidity), business operation, and strategic development (such as competition, social trend, and capital availability). In the public sector, risk management is considered as a public good because government utilizes public resources for mitigation against risks, preparedness for risks, responding to risks, and recovering from risks. In this sense, risk management in the public sector has become a subtle area that attracts much more concern and attention than before from the public and

© Springer International Publishing AG 2017
V. Chang et al. (Eds.): Enterprise Security, LNCS 10131, pp. 40–72, 2017.
DOI: 10.1007/978-3-319-54380-2_3

private entities. Compared with risk management in the private sector, risk management in the public sector involves a wide scope of risks, crises, and emergencies. Traditionally, risk management focuses more on health and environmental issues and emphasizes natural disasters rather than man-made disasters and crises (Regens et al. 1983; Zimmerman 1985). This means that government used to invest largely in policies and management in terms of funds and assets against possible natural disasters to diminish losses and expedite recovery from disasters; and that government, especially national government, paid much attention to people's health and environmental protection. In the United States, federal agencies like Environment Protection Agency, Food and Drug Administration, and Federal Emergency Management Agency (including federal disaster relief agencies in pre-FEMA ages) made enormous efforts to deal with health and environmental issues and relieve natural and technological disasters.

With time going on and with higher sensitivity of the public to occurrence of risks and crises, risk management in the public sector covers broader ranges of risks and crises. Besides natural disasters and technical risks, people tend to worry about terrorism attacks, economic turndown, unemployment, riots, gun-shooting, armed strife, contagious diseases, environmental changes, and violent strikes. Hot spots all over the world have caused feeling threat and relevant crisis in the affected regions. The Islam State in Syria and Iraq has rampaged across cities and villages in Syria and Iraq, killing thousands of innocent, unarmed civilians, and causing large swarms of victims to flee from home. As a result, refugee migration crisis occurred in most European countries in 2015. Japanese military expansion has created threats and incurred panic in East Asian and Southeastern Asian countries. Conflicts in South China Sea between China, the Philippines, Vietnam, and the United States have resulted in lots of uncertainties. North Korea rocket launch and nuclear weapons tests have caused threats and risks of war in Northeastern Asia. These situations call for strategies and counter-measures to deal with crises that have occurred and manage risks before they proceed to cause disasters.

In addition, nowadays risk management has become more complicated than before. Risk management in the public sector involves so many triggering agents, functional areas, variables, actors, and disciplines that it is a system in which each factor acts upon other factors in different extent (McEntire et al. 2002; Somers and Svara 2009). The concept of risk management system in the public sector requires that governments at each level play a variety of roles throughout risk management cycles. In different cases and under different situations of risk management, government operates as a policy maker, a regulator, a coordinator, an administrator, a service provider, a provider of program funds, a project/program manager, a risk assessor, a loss compensator, a loan provider, and a program evaluator. This suggests that government must invest manpower and material resources in risk management to effectively and efficiently fulfill its responsibilities. According to Wildavsky (1961, p. 183), "the budget is the life-blood of the government, the financial reflection of what the government does or intends to do." Risk management cannot be implemented without budget. However, decision makers in the public sector are always confronted with scarce public resources to satisfy all demands they consider desirable or worthwhile (Lewis 1952). Therefore, a crucial aspect of budgeting with regard to risk management is to determine if risk management preferences prevail over other alternatives of expenditure in the light of limited resources in final budgetary decisions. Since budgets are "a viable compromise among competing interests" (Caiden 1993, p. 13), some risk management demands may be ignored in one year's budget if they are not considered more valuable than other budgetary alternatives.

This essay intends to explore the relationship between risk management and budgeting in the public sector. It will analyze the organization theories that support risk and disaster management, the roles that government plays in risk and disaster management, and the efforts that government needs to make throughout the risk management cycles. The analysis intends to demonstrate to what extent, in which areas, and at what rate risk management depends on budget and competes against other public expenditures to fulfill organizational goals and objectives. Likewise, this essay will analyze budget functions and cycles to find out how budget process interacts upon risk management. Based on these analyses, this essay delves into the working relationships between risk management and budgeting. The analyses find that budgeting generally serves as a facilitator and catalyst to risk and disaster management; and risk and disaster management is mostly a competitor in budget process; and severe unexpected disasters and crises drive and overshadow budgets to deal with the serious consequences caused by disasters and crises. In addition, this essay suggests that decision makers and risk managers need to take particular measures that benefit both risk management and budgeting, and that help establish a virtuous relationship between budgeting and risk management.

2   Risks and Risk Management

2.1   Risk Definition and Categorization

Risk can be defined in a number of ways according to standards of different professions. Merriam-Webster Dictionary defines risk as "possibility of loss or injury." In this definition, risk is unpleasant and unwelcome. In general business, a risk is defined as "a probability or threat of damage, injury, liability, loss, or any other negative occurrence that is caused by external or internal vulnerabilities, and that may be avoided through preemptive action" (BusinessDictionary.com). This definition suggests somewhat different particular consequences in distinct areas of business. International Organization for Standardization (2009) developed and published its international standard for risk management—ISO 31000: 2009 Risk Management—Principles and Guidelines, which can be used by any public, private or community enterprise, association, or group. This document defines risk as "effect of uncertainty on objective." So far, there is no universally accepted definition of risk. However, similar to ISO 31000 definition of risk, most definitions have a connotation of uncertainty and adverse effect, which is a substantial feature of any risk (see Beck et al. 2005; Dickson 1991; Hardy 2015; Holmes 2002; Pritchard 2015; Smith and Toft 1998).

Risks fall into a variety of categories based on triggering agents and sources in relations to an organization. In a holistic disaster management system they have developed, McEntire et al. (2002) specify four categories of disaster-triggering agents, including natural agents, technological agents, civil agents, and environmental agents. Natural agents may include earthquakes, flooding, volcanoes, hurricanes, or any other natural disasters caused by degraded physical environment and depletion of natural resources in certain regions. Technological agents consist of nuclear plant accidents, utility failure, industrial explosions, computer malfunctions, airplane accidents, hazardous material spills, and biotechnology-related disasters. Civil disasters may be caused by abnormal social, political, and economic relationships, riots, violence, terrorist attack, and incomplete security mechanism. Environmental or biological disasters may include global warning, foot-and-mouth diseases, small pox and other infectious diseases due to inability to protect environment and insufficient medical measures to control contagious diseases. Since a disaster is the actual hazard occurrence of a risk (ICDRM/GWU 2010), agents that trigger disasters also trigger risks at inception. One defect of this categorization is that it does not include some particular crisis a national government may face, such as regional or international conflicts that may cause wars and migrant crisis.

Table 1. Risk categories

Risk category	External unpredictable	External predictable	Internal non-technological	Technological	Legal
Natural risks	Earthquakes, flooding, volcanoes, hurricanes, tsunami, tornado, environmental catastrophe				
Technological risks				Technology shifts, design imprecision, improper implementation, operation or quality demand changes, reliability challenges, requirement changes	
Civil or international risks	Terrorism attack, violence, riots, social upheaval, political unrest, unpredictable financial collapse or economic turndown, unplanned regulatory change, sabotage, migrant crisis, regional conflicts	Financial market fluctuation, inflation, health regulation, competitive shifts, taxation, safety	Inappropriate operation procedures, unqualified team member, poor HR coordination, ambiguous policies, operation mistakes, senior official change, financial fault, neglected or delayed work		Contract failure, lawsuits with stuff, citizens, private organizations, or other governments, higher government actions
Environmental or biological risks	Global warning, foot-and-mouth diseases, small pox, BSE, END, and other contagious diseases				

Based on relations of risks to an organization and controllable or incontrollable factors, Pritchard (2015) puts risks into five categories, including external unpredictable, external predictable, internal non-technical, technical, and legal. External unpredictable risks usually refer to natural or unintentional hazard events, which occur without warning. Natural disasters, societal upheavals, and capricious government acts belong to this category. External predictable risks are events externally incurred; some factors that relate these risks, such as outcomes and time frames, can be foreseen through systematic analysis and research although impact scale of these risks may be difficult to perceive. Internal nontechnical risks are caused by organization structure, administrative procedures, and organization policies, among other managing factors. Technical risks include all risks that occur in the course of technical operation. Legal risks are mainly based on contractual issues with external actors, either contractors or customers. One important strength of this categorization is that it helps organizations understand what risks can be managed and controlled under their range of responsibilities and what risks can be avoided through making changes in organization, policy, contract terms, relations, and other premises that result in risks. Risks are internal to one organization but external to another organization. Since government takes responsibilities for all risks that endanger benefits of the public, there is no difference of internal and external risks. In this sense, priority matters. However, for each government agency, owing to differences in responsibilities and objectives from other agencies, the categorization of internal and external risks makes difference in achieving agency objectives and fulfilling risk management objectives. Table 1 demonstrates fundamental risks mainly based on risk categorization by McEntire et al. (2002) and Pritchard (2015).

2.2 Risk Management

In the research on risk management, scholars and practitioners define risk management from various perspectives. International Organization for Standardization (2009) defines risk management as coordinated activities an organization conducts to control its risks. The Chartered Institute of Management Accountants defines risk management as a process in which an entity understands and manages the risks it faces to attain its corporate objectives (CIMA 2008). The most effective definition combines the goal of risk management and the means for fulfilling the goal. In this respect, risk management is a process in which risks are managed to achieve organizational objectives by means of "maximizing potential opportunities and minimizing potential adverse effects" (Drennan et al. 2015, p. 2). Since risk management in the public sector relates public resources, government must take into account both the weight of a risk management program in achieving its objectives and the budget (or the public resources) that is to be expended in relation to the total budget of a government.

The definition of risk indicates that risk is the main cause of uncertainty in any organization because it may bring about damage, injury, loss of properties and lives, liability, and other negative consequences. Since risk sources include both internal and external factors, risk management is an essential part of the general operation of an organization. This means that an organizations, either public or private, need to establish an effective risk management system that is implemented organization-wide to control and coordinate all relevant internal factors that may directly cause risks, and monitor relevant external factors (either natural or manmade) that directly or indirectly endanger the organization's regular operation. In the United States, the federal government has promulgated a number of laws, such as Federal Manager's Financial Integrity Act (FMFIA), Federal Information Security Management Act, Federal Financial Management Information Act, and American Recovery and Reinvestment Act of 2009, to manage financial risks, administrative risks, operation risks, information technology risks, financial management information risks, and contract and grants management risks. The federal Government Accountability Office (GAO) has issued the GAO Standards (Green Book) for federal agencies to establish internal control frameworks. The federal Office of Management and Budget (OMB) has issued Circular A-123 Management's Responsibility for Internal Control as implementing guidance for FMFIA to ensure that federal agencies have well-controlled and effective framework to manage and mitigate risks to achieve operational and financial objectives. Currently, OMB requires all federal agencies to measure risk at the enterprise level. The 2014 Annual CFO survey demonstrated that twenty percent (20%) of federal agencies have a Chief Risk Officer role; and roughly fifty-one percent (51%) of federal agencies have a role similar to that of a Chief Risk Officer that is performed through a variety of roles such as Chief Operating Manager, Chief Financial Officer, Chief Safety Officer, and Performance Improvement Officer (Bureau of Fiscal Service 2015). Advertizing evidence shows that many more federal agencies, such as Department of Education, Department of Housing and Urban Development, Department of Interior, Federal Thrift Retirement Investment Board, Veterans Administration, Internal Revenue Services, to name a few, are hiring chief risk officers or risk management officers whose responsibility is to lead risk management from across their entire portfolio (Hardy 2015). This means that most federal government agencies have implemented mechanisms of enterprise risk management and strategic risk management plans within the enterprise. Although risk management at enterprise level started in the financial industry, it has spread into other industry sectors.

Since the issue of GAO Risk Management Framework[1] in 2005 and the publication of both COSO Enterprise Risk Management-Integrated Framework[2] in 2004 and ISO 31000 Risk Management-Principles and Guideline in 2009, risk management has been given more attention by state and local governments in the United States. The 2014 ERM Core Competency Survey for the Public Sector demonstrated that state and local governments have established their own risk management framework although not

---

[1] The GAO Risk Management Framework was development by Government Accountability Office, a nonpartisan federal government agency that provides auditing, evaluation, and investigative services for the US Congress. The framework incorporates requirements and standards the Government Performance and Results Act of 1993, the Government Auditing Standards (2003 revision), GAO Standards for Internal Control in the Federal Government, guidance from OMB, the work of the President's Commission of Risk Management, and the enterprise risk management approach of the COCO.

[2] COSO Enterprise Risk Management-Integrated Framework was created and published by the Committee of Sponsoring Organizations of the Treadway Committee in 2004. The framework consists of three dimensions of enterprise risk management, each of which includes components that may affect fulfillment of organizational objectives.

every state or local government agency manages internal and external risks at the enterprise level (Hardy 2015). About forty-five percent (45%) of respondents indicated that their organizations have taken risk management into account when making all decisions (Hardy 2015). In addition, approximately fifty-three percent (53%) of respondents reported that their agencies have implemented or considered ISO 21000 Risk Management guideline; forty percent (40%) indicated that their agencies have adopted a hybrid risk management system that incorporates the three approaches previously mentioned (Hardy 2015). With regard to key ERM components, eighty percent (80%) of respondents indicated that their agencies have risk management policies. About 69 percent (69%) of state and local respondents have more than ten years of experience in the areas of risk management, internal control, and financial management (Hardy 2015).

3   Organization Theories Supporting Risk Management

3.1   Chaos Theory and Risk Management

The concept of chaos means that a hazardous event happens; that there appears "a state of non-equilibrium, instability, turbulence, rapid or rupturing changes that scramble plans and cause unpredictability, with consequences of anxiety, fear of the unknown, and triggering and tripling effects of destruction and system breakdowns" (Farazmand 2002, p. 78). Chaos theory claims that society and nature do not evolve absolutely in a linear and regular form so that barriers, crisis, emergencies, and disasters can be reasonably predicted, avoided, or controlled (Farazmand 2002). This explains why the world is rife of risks; and why turbulent hazardous events, such as natural and man-made disasters and crises, happen almost every day and discontinue normal societal life and development.

Chaos theory (Laszlo 1972; Miller 1978; Prigogine and Stengers 1984; Maturana and Varela 1980) focuses on change and the way in which change takes place. Chaos is the consequence of either long-term macrocosmic forces or short-term microcosmic forces. The macrocosmic forces are mainly the great historic events of paramount importance and extreme forms of evolution that contribute to overriding systemic changes, long-wave crises throughout the entire globe, and pressure among people and concern about the future requiring present decision and action. The microcosmic forces are either wide-range or global crises, like financial crises, global waning, environmental crises, population problem, widening gap between poor and rich countries, or natural, political, social, and cultural crisis, such as terrorist attacks, tsunami, hurricane, flooding, and nuclear disasters. From the perspective of public administration, short-term crises and chaotic events are worth more attention and study (Capra 1982; Drucker 1969; Loye and Eisler 1983; Salk 1983).

Throughout a system, a small change may lead to disequilibrium and cause enormous unexpected consequence, resulting in breakdown of the entire system (Daft 1995). This means that a small internal factor in a system is likely to produce significant changes, either good or bad. Similarly, a small force out of a system may also cause outcomes far beyond expectation. Chaos theory claims that an organization as an open system may "make changes from order to chaos and make order out of chaos possible" (Farazmand 2002, p. 80). An organization has the characteristics of self-governance, self-control, and self-regulation (Prigogine and Stengers 1984; Maturana and Varela 1980). Once chaotic state comes up, an organization is able to self-correct its chaos through generating capacity and producing internal forces of changes that may generate a new form of system structures. This feature provides two suggestions for risk and crisis management. One is that an organization needs to systematically build up its capacity to manage risks, crises, and disasters in the light of its resources and organization objectives. Once a hazardous event occurs, the organization is able to start its self-controlling and self-regulating mechanism in no time to restore its smooth operation in a short period of time. The other suggestion is that risk management provides opportunities to improve or reform an organization's structure so that the organization may be well balanced to achieve its selected goals and objectives.

3.2 Rational Model and Risk Management

The concept of rationality is fundamental in public management. Comprehensive rational theorists claim that decision makers are capable of identifying a social problem and rank their organizational goals or objectives; they can obtain full information to predict consequence of each alternative to a goal; they are able to work out the best alternative to achieve the organizational goal they select (Edwards 1967; Forester 1984; Zey 1992). However, considering actual complexity of problems in real life, individuals' capacity is limited in finding appropriate solutions that require objectively rational behavior (Simon 1957). Individuals' rationality is bounded because of a variety of uncertainties and limitations (Simon 1947, 1997; Forester 1984; Morçöl 2007; Lindblom 1959). First, some problems in real life are ambiguous and complicated. They are neither easy to formulate nor easy to solve. Second, owing to incomplete, imperfect information and inconsistent criteria, it is almost impossible to rank alternatives and select the most rational one to solve problems. Third, decision makers are limited in time, skill, and resources for solving the problems they face.

Considering the fact that rationality is bounded, individuals may conduct limited search for alternatives and select the first satisfactory alternative to the problem they attempt to solve rather than seek the best alternative (Perrow 1986). In practice, although they do not seek the best objective by obtaining complete information and analyzing all possible objectives, decision makers must seek rational objectives and try to maximize utilities to whatever extent possible (Denhardt 2004). Generally, rationality means seeking "consistent and value maximizing" objectives and actions when confronted with constraints and bounds (Allison 1971, p. 30). Following the rational model, rational decision makers take four procedures in their decision-making process, including (1) prioritizing values and set appropriate objectives; (2) designing a list of alternatives to each objective, (3) examine each alternative and relevant consequence; and (4) selecting the alternative that might maximize utilities in achieving the predetermined objectives (Allison 1971; Lindblom 1959; Simon 1997).

In most cases, risk management is a complicated process in which risk managers make rational decisions regarding risk assessment, risk evaluation, risk communication, disaster mitigation, disaster preparedness, responding to disasters and crises, and recovery from disasters and crisis. While analyzing the information collected from risk analysts and finance managers, risk managers prioritize risk management programs in the light of their organizational goals and objectives. They develop rational alternatives and examine the impact of a risky occurrence. They select the alternative that may maximize the potential opportunity and utility of management resources and minimize potential adverse effects to help their organization achieve its objective (Drennan et al. 2015). They implement programs based on the selected alternative in each phase of disaster and crisis management.

3.3   Systems Theory and Risk Management

Based on systems theory (Buckley 1967; von Bertalanffy 1968; Katz and Kahn 1966; Scott 1961; Thompson 1967), a modern organization is an open system that receives inputs from outside environments, has internal factors interrelated and interacting upon each other to keep the organization working efficiently and maintaining equilibrium, transforms inputs to outputs, and exchanges outputs with environments. The internal factors of an organization consist of the organization structure, human and material resources, technological elements, operation procedures, organization policies, value, culture, and other relevant factors of the organization (Blau and Scott 2003; Mentzberg 1979; Beckhard 2006). The environments of an organization are cultural, social, economic, political, religious, demographic, international, and even natural facets with which an organization constantly interacts.

Risk management in the public sector is an open, complex system that involves organization, laws, policies, public resources, decision making process, technologies, and other necessary elements to prevent or diminish losses and help achieve expected organization objectives (McEntire et al. 2002; U.S. Environmental Protection Agency 2004). This means that a risk management entity, either a government agency, or a local, state/provincial, national government, needs to understand the internal components of its risk management system as well as the external factors in the outside environment. When it comes to assessing risks, risk assessors of a jurisdiction need to be clear about what information or factors to analyze, if a disaster will occur, and how adverse the impact will be (Somers and Svara 2009; U.S. EPA 2004; Regens et al. 1983). When making decisions regarding how to manage risks in different phases, risk managers need to understand what resources are needed, what ability the management entity has, and if government has laws, policies, and regulation that relate the risk or disaster being managed, among other issues (Wallace and De Balogh 1985; Clary 1985).

3.4   Organizational Sustainability Model

Sustainability is an essential factor for an organization to operate effectively and develop healthily. Organizational sustainability can be defined as the capacity of an organization to develop a strategic plan and maintain resources for its operation in secure environment over time (Francois 2014). Sustainability highlights such elements an organization has: a long-term value, performance, social equity, and ecological survival in environments (de Lange et al. 2012; Gladwin et al. 1995; Hundermark

2012). An organization faces change every day; and it needs change and adapts to environments to sustain its operation and long-term development. However, risks bring about change to a direction adverse to organization growth. Disasters and crises may cause loss or injury of life, harmful impact on health, damage to properties, loss of jobs, environmental damage, and social and economic disruption, among other consequences.

An organizational sustainability model (OSM) developed by Chang et al. (2016) suggests that an organization needs to build up its capacity of managing all risks associated with its projects and to improve actual performance in the course of controlling and ameliorating risks, thus increasing return from organization operation and inputs. Based on OSM (Chang et al. 2016), an organization need set up a reliable system that deals with all risks related to operation of the organization that can be controlled within a bearable, organizational bound. With that said, an organization must take reasonable measures to establish a risk management mechanism or system that consists of goals, objectives, procedures, communication modes, policies, structure, resources, managerial responsibilities, management standards, and other essential elements. Thus, organizational sustainability is built up and strengthened during operation of the organization. Risks, disasters, crises can be mitigated, prevented, controlled, or ameliorated so that loss and damage can be minimized and expected return maximized.

Actually, the risk management requires organizational sustainability planning or sustainable development, which is financially supportive, operationally secure, and ecologically viable (Gladwin et al. 1995). To develop a sustainability planning, an organization need create a vision of sustainability, establish standards and/or guidelines that help the organization translate the vision into actionable ideas, identify the impacts and priorities, develop sustainability metrics and reports, create implementation strategies and choose appropriate projects, develop effective management system, and set up a structure to manage efforts (Hitchcock and Willard 2008). Sustainability planning helps an organization avoid and control risks, and effectively and efficiently fulfill its goals and objectives.

3.5   The New Public Management and Risk Management

Considering scarce public resources and unlimited public needs, the new public management intends to seek approaches to an efficient government that works better and costs less. Based on principles of economic rationalism, the new public management attempts to solve the problem of low performance and poor quality of governmental work through fiscal austerity measures, new scheme to improve productivity, and alternative platform to deliver public service (Denhardt 2004; Lynn 1996). To attain these goals, government agencies need to reform their work structure, redefine their mission, streamline work process, establish work benchmark, and develop partnership relations with private businesses (Denhardt 2004; Osborne and Gaebler 1992; Kettl 2000).

According to Osborne and Gaebler (1992), government is good at making policies, but weak in managing business. Based on this theorem, government is encouraged to privatize certain public services, or rely more on charges and fees for public services and investments to fund future public projects, contract out/outsource some public services and/or production of some public goods. To reduce cost in managing government programs, government decision makers, employing principles of scale economy, create public procurement policies to make purchase of goods, services, projects, and technologies. Following these policies, government agencies select appropriate contractors, suppliers, and service providers through a fair, transparent tendering and bidding process. To improve efficiency and effectiveness in public management, government may implement market-oriented strategies, such as competition within government units, or among public, private, and nongovernmental service providers (Barzelay 2000; Hood 1995; Kaboolian 1998; Kamensky 1996; Osborne and Gaebler 1992; Pollitt and Bouckert 2000).

Moreover, the new public management highlights a number of innovative strategies and approaches to manage some government functions. Government agencies are more mission-driven and customer-driven, which means that agency programs and activities are implemented using alternative budget techniques and performance benchmarks to target at the overall mission and higher customer (citizen) satisfaction (Osborne and Gaebler 1992). In addition, traditional hierarchical system gives way to a decentralized decision-making mechanism. Government needs to become anticipatory and take proactive strategies to prevent problematic issues from happening.

The new public management provides valuable theoretical and practical backup for risk management in the public sector. To improve efficiency and effectiveness of risk management, government needs to readjust its roles because it cannot conduct everything to mitigate against, prepare for, respond to, and recover from disasters or crises. Government at different levels needs to understand its mission and responsibilities and remove all barriers that block efficient ways to risk management (Braig et al. 2011). The new public management calls for an innovative platform of risk management, where government, private businesses, and nonprofit organizations work together, and limited public resources are used for crucial needs in managing risks, emergencies, crises, and disasters.

4   Risk Management Process

4.1   The Role of Government in Risk Management

Traditionally, the primary role of government is to govern all societal activities in the domains of legal framework and policy. According to Stiglitz (2000), the vast array of government activities can be simply divided into four categories: production of goods and provision of services, regulating and subsidizing private businesses, purchase of goods and services, and redistribution of resources.

Considering risk phases, risk categories, and risk severity, government plays multiple roles in the domain of risk management. Before a disaster or crisis happens, government formulates and implements policies regarding private business in each industry, enforces laws to regulate private business through technological inspection, safety and health oversight, and code compliance checkup (Baker and Moss 2009; Godschalk and Brower 1985; Clary 1985; Zimmerman 1985). Government also provides information regarding industry status and even research findings for businesses to make decisions. In the arena of governmental operation, decision makers select risk management programs and other public service programs. Chief executives and agency managers establish operation procedures, take anticipatory measures to prevent risks in each area of every program, and create information system for risk analysis and management (Hardy 2015). They also make technological, material, personnel, organizational, and communication preparation for risks that may affect smooth operation of each field that government controls and manages (Wallace and De Balogh 1985; Beck et al. 2005). In the case of a disaster or crisis, government takes over risk management to protect public interest if a disaster striking private businesses is beyond control of private risk managers. Government acts directly as a risk manager when a disaster occurs within arenas of government operation, or when a disaster, such as an earthquake or a severe terrorist attack, produces enormous adverse effects on the public. Government works as both a coordinator and manager in the phase of recovery from a disaster, especially in the case of natural and man-made catastrophes (Rubin and Barbee 1985).

In actuality, government at different levels plays distinct functions in the course of risk management because constitution fundamentally assigns government at different levels distinct jurisdictions. For instance, in the United States, the Constitution requires that state governments take responsibility for public health and safety; and that the federal government be assigned a supporting role (Bullock et al. 2009). Traditionally, the federal government intervenes in crisis and disaster management when state and local governments are overwhelmed and officially request the federal government to provide aids. However, in recent years, the federal government has been playing an increasingly important role in managing risks, emergencies, crises, and disasters in such domains as public security, finance, economic growth, public health, globalization issues, environmental protection, and hurricane. In addition, more local governments have learned to put risk management at high priority. More than half of state and local governments take into account risk management in all decisions they have made (Hardy 2015).

4.2 Efforts of Government in Risk Management

As stated previously, risk management is an open, complex system that encompasses a large variety of factors, such as triggering agents, functional areas, actors, and relevant disciplines. Risk management is also a complicated process in which government deals with legislation regarding public health, safety, and security; identifies and analyzes public hazards; mitigates against and prepares for emergencies, crises, and disasters; and coordinates and expends resources in response to and recovery from hazardous events, either natural or man-made. Therefore, confronted with all sorts of possible risks, government needs to establish a reasonable, effective, and efficient risk management mechanism through which to prevent, control, and ameliorate destructive events. It is of supreme importance that government clearly defines its obligations for risk management within its jurisdiction and decides which risk management program to finance, although this is actually not an easy job (Bullock et al. 2009). Generally, government activities fall into four categories based on functional areas.

4.2.1   Mitigation Efforts

Risk mitigation usually refers to sustained actions that focus on three goals: modifying hazards, protecting people and property from hazards and their effects, limiting use of hazardous areas (Godschalk and Brower 1985). The first mitigation effort that government needs to exert is to identify potential risks and hazards by means of risk and vulnerability analysis and evaluation. Three major elements for analysis and evaluation are risk type in next ten years or twenty years, likelihood, and consequences (Kaplan 1997). This means that for each potential risk, analysts need to focus on likelihood and consequences. Table 2 presents a qualitative risk analysis. In some cases, analysis may take into account joint possibilities of two or more disasters occurring simultaneously, such as tsunami and earthquake. From business intelligence perspective, an organization can analyze risks in terms of asset price and notify all stakeholders the risk analysis results (Chang 2014).

Table 2. Qualitative risk analysis matrix

	Consequences				
Likelihood	Insignificant	Minor	Moderate	Major	Catastrophic
Almost certain	High	High	Extreme	Extreme	Extreme
Likely	Moderate	High	High	Extreme	Extreme
Possible	Low	Moderate	High	Extreme	Extreme
Unlikely	Low	Low	Moderate	High	Extreme
Rare	Low	Low	Moderate	High	High

Source: Emergence Management Australia, Emergency Risk Management: Application's Guide. Australian Emergency Manual Series, 2000

For public programs, it is high necessity that government compares risks against each other to prioritize all risk management programs and determine which one(s) to fund. Since government has limited resources and it is not possible to finance all risk management programs, prioritization helps government staff who are in charge of risk management ensure that limited resources are expended wisely (Bullock et al. 2009). Once decision makers identify risk management programs in the budgetary document, the programs are executed in accordance with government policies and legal requirements. Public facilities may be established, buildings constructed, land acquired, personnel trained, equipment purchased, technology created, information system established, communication means set up, building code complied, organization structure established, financial resources secured, and so on. With regard to government program operation, executives and managers must make sure that safety measures, operation procedures, and emergency measures are established and strictly followed.

In the private sector, each private business needs to have a risk management system established and appropriately manages any risk it faces (Bullock et al. 2009). Government must regulate activities and oversee risk measures of private businesses, especially large-scale, labor-intensive businesses, chemical companies, businesses manufacturing hazardous materials, businesses that are subject to natural and geological hazards, and businesses that provide public venues for large groups of customers or audience, such as airports, shopping centers, stadiums, and theatres. It is of supreme importance that government puts these large or special businesses under its mitigation plans to protect lives and property. Specifically, government needs to conduct inspections, security surveillance, threat investigations, public health and agricultural surveillance, immunizations, isolation and quarantine if appropriate, law enforcement aiming at deterring, preempting, interdicting, or disrupting illegal activities (Bullock et al. 2009).

4.2.2   Preparedness Efforts

Preparedness ensures a state of readiness and testing of all necessary actions and plans that a risk management entity will actually implement in response to an incident or a disaster or a crisis. It usually consists of activities, programs, and systems that aim to support response promptness, effectiveness, and efficiency. Typical examples of preparedness efforts by government may include

- preparation of sufficient inventories and convenient location of resources,
- determination of local jurisdiction to be involved,
- generation of scenarios for emergency response and specific measures under each scenario,
- training of emergency operations in all relevant organizations,
- provision of services for disaster rescue,
- evacuation drills in case of fire or other threats, and
- testing of warning system (Wallace and De Balogh 1985).

Government agencies may provide employees and local residents with first-response training and family disaster plans that cover top priority things to deal with in response to disasters and crises (Bullock et al. 2009).

Government needs to pay close attention to preparedness for special incidents, disasters, and crises, such as fire emergencies in an oil refinery, biological and chemical attacks and incidents, health and medical incidents, nuclear and radiological incidents, and terrorist attacks. Preparedness for these incidents and disasters involves quick decisions, particular technologies and equipment to control the incident or disaster, professional processing of hazardous material exposure, safe reallocation of hazardous material, treating of enormous medical needs, and reallocation of affected people.

4.2.3   Response Efforts

Traditionally, local government bears the responsibility for first response to disasters, crises, or any other emergency (Clary 1985; Bullock et al. 2009; Drabek 1985). Once an emergency, a disaster, or a crisis occurs, local officials must take immediate action to respond to the hazardous event. In the United States, National Response Framework provides a guide to how the nation conducts hazard response; and it defines the responsibilities of local, tribal, state, and federal governments. Considering specific issues and actual situations, major response measures may be as the follows:

- initiating alert procedures and mobilizing emergency or disaster operations,
- assessing the urgent situation and initial damage,

- estimating imminent danger conditions and getting prepared for them,
- assessing the amount of emergency or disaster resources, utilizing the available resources, and purchasing more resources if necessary,
- mobilizing all departments and related actors in the private and non-profit sectors if possible,
- taking evacuation measures if appropriate,
- taking whatever measures to control the disaster and exert rescue efforts to diminish loss,
- obtaining information for official briefing,
- initiating assistance request to state/provincial government if response requirements exceed local capabilities,
- state/provincial government providing personnel, equipment, and funding within its jurisdiction if appropriate,
- state/provincial government filing request for assistance to the central/federal government if the disaster exceeds its management ability, and
- if appropriate, the central/federal government declaring an emergency state in the disaster area and providing required support (Bullock et al. 2009; Wallace and De Balogh 1985).

Mostly, local government appropriately manages minor emergencies or disasters (Bullock et al. 2009; Drabek 1985). Firefighters, police officers, and emergency medical personnel respond to disasters to maintain order, conduct search and rescue, treat the injured, suppress hazardous conditions, and retrieve the dead. Within its jurisdiction, a local government may coordinate or mobilize efforts from private or nonprofit sectors in response to a disaster. However, major disasters or special disasters, such as hurricanes, earthquake, and nuclear meltdown, are out of control of local capacities, and require efforts from the higher-level government, private and nonprofit actors, volunteers from a variety of fields, and even other nations and international organizations (Drabek 1985; Farazmand 2007; Rubin and Barbee 1985).

4.2.4   Recovery Efforts

Recovery from disasters or crises is a difficult, complicated process that involves a variety of stakeholders in both public and private sectors. First of all, recovery plans must comply with relevant laws, policies, and regulations promulgated by national, state or provincial, and local governments because relevant statutes define not only responsibilities of government (including international relations) and private entities, but also request of funds, grants, loans and other financial resources to compensate losses and support reestablishment of buildings and facilities. Considering damages incurred and future recurrent disasters, a local government may change its zoning policy or update its requirements on construction projects, buildings, facilities, and structures. Secondly, in the case of damages to portions of government operation and running of private businesses, restoration involves a series of decision making regarding a number of issues, such as replacing property, resuming employment, restoring business, and repairing and rebuilding infrastructure. These issues require input of financial resources and manpower. Similarly, families may face harsh situations of building or purchasing homes, purchase of household utensils and appliances, and finding schools for their children. Thirdly, recovery requires short-term and long-term actions that include multifaceted programs and involve various actors. Government needs to coordinate different activities as well as entities in both the public and private sectors.

Although it faces complicated situations in recovery from a disaster or a crisis, government must clarify the major responsibilities it is supposed to take, considering its administrative roles. Specifically, government at different levels may take the following major responsibilities:

- assessing current, short-term, medium-term, and long-term damage and damage area,
- identification of tasks, priorities, budget, and schedule of the recovery program in the public sector,
- reexamination of local policies regarding zoning, public facilities, building, and construction and making amendments if appropriate,
- determination of jurisdictions to be involved in recovery,
- initiating recovery assessment procedures and operating the recovery reporting system,
- identification of public programs that are eligible for state/provincial assistance and central/federal government assistance,
- filing request to higher-levels governments for assistance to eligible public programs,
- formulating and implementing long-term evacuation project if appropriate,
- implementing and evaluating self-funded programs as scheduled,
- state/provincial governments briefing officials to inform them the public assistance available in the case of a major disaster and how to apply for it,
- recovery coordination being established at a government of a higher level to coordinate assistance programs to help individuals and businesses meet basic needs, to coordinate donations and other recovery activities, to coordinate with private businesses on restoration and recovery, to coordinate public assistance grant programs and hazard mitigation grant programs; and
- national government providing financial and technical support (Bullock et al. 2009; Wallace and De Balogh 1985).

In addition, after a major disaster or crisis occurs, the relevant national government usually implements particular policies, including loss compensation programs, public assistance projects, and/or economic stimulus plans, to help local government, state/provincial government, private businesses, individuals, or the whole country recover from a natural catastrophe, or a manmade disaster, or an economic/financial crisis. The policies may be issued in a form of recovery act, or a declaration of emergency state and grant.

4.3 Comprehensive Vulnerability Management

Generally, a risk exists in a program or a system because vulnerability exists. That is to say, a composing element, or a part of a system is a vulnerable component that may result in uncertainty and possible loss. Vulnerability management is to reduce risks and impacts of disasters through liability reduction and capacity building (McEntire et al. 2002). Comprehensive vulnerability management (CVM) intends to reduce emergencies and disasters through holistic and integrated activities of diminishing vulnerability and building resistance (McEntire et al. 2002). It deals with risk and disaster management through analysis of triggering agents, functional areas, actors, variables, and disaster-related disciplines. Triggering agents and functional areas in the public sector are analyzed in the previous sections of this essay. The other factors may provide public managers with suggestions on disaster or crisis management.

Public, private, and nonprofit actors are all indispensible players in disaster management. As discussed previously, government regulates social activities and distributes resources throughout all social segments. Private and nonprofit organizations manage risks and disasters under their jurisdiction. Government gets involved in risk management in the private or nonprofit sectors in the case of disasters that produce severe adverse impact on public. Therefore, government is inevitably "the risk manager of last resort" (Baker and Moss 2009, p. 107). Government plays leading and coordinating roles in response to major natural and manmade catastrophes. Private entities contribute to search-and-rescue activities and bear some other liabilities and capacities. Nonprofit organizations provide both help with vulnerable population and professional services in health care, education, and distribution of relief (McEntire et al. 2002).

Comprehensive vulnerability management emphasizes reduction of disasters in physical devices, education about disaster, improvement of emergency management agencies, provision of sufficient resources for risk management, up-to-date technological strategies for emergency communication and processing of hazardous materials, and rural and urban planning to reduce risks (McEntire et al. 2002). It also calls for public risk managers to pay attention to research on vulnerability reduction in a number of fields, such as environmental science, criminal justice, political science, law, and meteorology, among other disciplines (McEntire et al. 2002). Relevant research in these disciplines may provide effective measures and technology for prevention, control, and amelioration of disasters and crises.

5 Public Budgeting Process

5.1 Budget Functions

In the public sector, budget plays multiple functions. Budget means not only money and other sorts of financial resources, but also public needs and how public needs are financed, and how well public needs are satisfied. In this sense, budget is an administrative instrument by which projects are financed and performance audited (Niskanen 1992; Rubin 2010). Specifically, for government management, budget is first of all a tool of strategic planning that determines both the goals and objectives of a budget entity and resources to attain these goals and objectives (Schick 1966; Mikesell 2007). Actually, goals and objectives are attained through programs and projects identified by decision makers and financed by public resources. Budget is also an instrument of financial management to secure that a budget entity appropriately obtains public resources, and expends public resources efficiently and effectively to attain organizational objectives and goals (Schick 1966; Hyde 2002; Willoughby 2002; Axelrod 1988). In addition, budget is an operation guide that instructs government agencies to manage their specific tasks and programs in effective and efficient ways (Schick 1966; Axelrod 1988).

From a political perspective, budget is a political instrument by which policy makers, who represent certain interest groups and citizens in a jurisdiction, allocate limited public resources among a variety of needs (Wildavsky 1961; Rubin 1990). From the perspective of economists and top government officials, budget may serve as an economic instrument that helps direct a budget entity's economic growth, investment, and development through particular economic, financial, and taxation policies (Axelrod 1988; Hyde 2002).

5.2   Budget Cycles

In a democratic society where the executive branch and the legislative branch are separated, a budget is usually formulated and executed throughout a budget cycle that consists of four phases. In the first phase, executive preparation, the chief executive of a government instructs departments and agencies to prepare budget requests for the next fiscal period. The chief executive's instruction is based on preferences of the chief executive and financial information the chief executive has obtained through budget analysts. It specifies budget ceilings, program priority directions, and performance requirements. Each department creates its budget estimates based on services the department has provided or is going to provide in the next budget period and the forecast of conditions in the upcoming year (Mikesell 2007). When each department submits its budget requests, the budget office consolidates all budget requests and adjusts them based on the budget policies of the chief executive and budget analysis. If necessary, the budget administrator may call administrative hearings to reconcile departmental budget requests. Finally, the chief executive approves the administrative budget and has it submitted to the legislative branch for approval.

The second phase of budget cycle begins with legislators reviewing the budget document the chief executive transmits. The legislators may take into account interest of their constituents, or the preferences of interest groups that support them at election campaign, or the values of their political parties. If the legislative chambers have their own budget personnel or budget office, they prefer to collect information from sources different from those of the executive branch. Therefore, they can build up their own budget and review the executive budget based on their preferences and the information they collect. Considering the difference of information sources and the difference of budget preferences, there are usually considerable differences between the executive budget requests and the legislative edition of budget estimate. In the United States, this case exists in both federal government and state governments since legislatures have more than one fiscal office at each state government and the federal government (Short 2013). Conversely, when the legislative branch does not have capability of conducting financial and economic analysis and cannot make a justifiable estimate of budget, legislators may select to approve the executive budget without making a large portion of adjustments. When a government faces financial difficulties, political competition for limited budget to satisfy conflicting needs is much fierce.

In addition, modern technology of communication makes it easy for citizens to express their preference on resource allocation and taxation policies through public hearings, citizen advisory committees, citizen surveys, public meetings, citizen panels, open community meetings, focus groups, open forums, and balanced budget exercise (Callahan 2002; Ebdon 2002; Ebdon and Franklin 2006). With establishment of e-government, citizen participation has produced affirmative effects in budget decision-making (Xu 2012; Alateyh et al. 2014; Olphert and Damodaran 2007). It also helps improve budget efficiency, responsiveness and accountability, and guard against corruption (Becket and King 2002; Tanaka 2007).

The third phase of budget cycle focuses on budget execution. Departments and agencies request apportionments or allotments to their legislature branch. They spend the appropriations to implement budgeted programs after their request is approved. Pursuant to budget regulations, departments and agencies are not allowed to overspend their budget; if not permitted by the legislature, neither can they use budget for a purpose that is different from what is stated in the budget document. In addition, while implementing budgeted programs, departments and agencies must improve efficiency and effectiveness of spending appropriations. In addition, the finance department of the executive branch and the legislative offices in charge of fiscal activities at each level of government must take effective measures, such as preventive, feed-forward controls, feedback controls, and internal controls, to oversee budget execution process (Mikesell 2007; Thompson and Zumeta 1981).

In the fourth phase, budget is audited and evaluated by both internal personnel and external auditing firms based on the information generated in the first three phases. Budget audit falls into two categories: financial audit and performance audit (Mikesell 2007). The former focuses on financial statement audits and financial-related audits whereas the latter targets on economy and efficiency audits and program audits. Financial audits intend to assure that the budget entity has presented appropriate financial statements in accordance with generally accepted accounting principles, and that the budget entity has complied with relevant laws when implementing the adopted budget. Performance audits purport to secure that budget entity has acquired and used its resources economically and efficiently, and that the budgeted programs have achieved intended goals and objectives effectively and efficiently in compliance with laws and regulations.

6   Relationship Between Budgeting and Risk Management

As stated previously, budget is the life-blood of government management. Since risk and disaster management is a part of public management, budget is also the life-blood of risk and disaster management. However, risk management is a complicated process that encompasses a series of decision-making activities. In one dimension, risk management is a part of regular government operation. It is implemented in the course of program operation. In another dimension, risk management is a sort of special work that involves mitigation against, preparedness for, response to, and recovery from disasters and crises. In either dimension, budget is indispensible throughout each phase of risk and disaster management. However, the discussion of risk management process and budget process demonstrates that not every risk management element needs extra budget. On the other hand, risk management ensures sustainability of social and economic activities so that financial resources are continually supplied to provide sustainable budget inputs.

It is of high necessity to note that budgeting for risk and disaster management is different from other budgeting activities in that some budgeted resources are not put to use if a disaster or emergency does not occur while other programs need funds. In addition, once an emergency occurs and results in a disaster or crisis that exceeds expected magnitude, extra budget is needed immediately; and financial resources must be provided in any form without delay. In this case, emergencies and disasters are a driver to public budget.

6.1   Budget as Facilitator of Risk Management

When government prepares budget and makes budget decisions, each department or agency analyzes all potential risks that may have adverse effects on attainment of departmental or agency objectives. Priorities are given to internal risks that may adversely affect regular operation of the department or agency. This is because most of disasters are minor ones, and minor disasters are mostly related to a department's major responsibilities (Bullock et al. 2009). Effective holistic risk management over department operations may eliminate considerable amount of risks within departmental jurisdiction, and this does not necessarily lead to increase of budget. Research has found that a considerable number of disasters occurred because of inappropriate operation or other causes that relate regular maintenance and design defects (Lu 2012). Some examples in recent years in the United States include the collapse of the I-35W Mississippi River Bridge in Minneapolis, Minnesota, the collapse of the Mianus River Bridge in Greenwich, Connecticut, the steam pipe eruption in New York City, the coal dust explosion in Upper Big Branch Mine, Chatsworth train collision in Chatsworth, California, and the collapse of Cypress Street viaduct in Oakland, California. While investigating the failure of rescue work during and after Hurricane Katrina that struck five southern states in U.S., some experts questioned why the levees in New Orleans, whose elevation is under sea level, were not originally built for a severer category of hurricane and why an unexpected management system was not created for such an emergency (Farazmand 2007). Previous disasters have confirmed that failures in operation of budgeted programs are likely to lead to a disaster immediately or one day in the future.

Furthermore, while making budget estimates, departments and agencies must take into account every possible element or event that may cause a disaster, and make it a part in budge estimate. They need to take mitigation and preparedness measures through new programs or projects, reconstruction projects, facility updating, restructuring management system, replacing equipment, training of emergency operations, and preparation for inventory of resources, among other means. Each government department or agency must establish a holistic and integrated risk management system throughout budget cycles; and it must build up capacity to prevent risks, thus sustaining operations to fulfill organization goals and objectives.

Besides risks related to operations, departments and agencies must make appropriate plans for adverse effects from external risks, either predictable or unpredictable, when preparing departmental budgets. The risk management department, whatever names such a department is named, needs to consider possible external risks that may cause disasters within jurisdiction of the government. Considering intergovernmental relationships, some risk management programs may have funds and grants from state/provincial government and central/federal government (Bullock et al. 2009). In the United States, federal Department of Homeland Security provides a variety of grants for state and local governments to prevent, protect against, respond to, and recover from acts of terrorism and other disasters. In some cases, such as fire fighting and environmental protection, coordination can be established with adjacent communities, municipalities, states or provinces. In addition, risk management can be improved and strengthened through market actions with government as a guarantor (Baker and Moss 2009).

Overall, budgeting facilitates risk government in a variety of ways. For one thing, the budgeting process promotes risk management through combination of providing funds and enforcement of performance standards so that vulnerability can be enhanced. For another, mitigation and preparedness programs can be established with public resources to prevent and ameliorate disasters and crises.

6.2   Risk Management as Budget Competitor

Government has scarce public resources in comparison with public needs (Lewis 1952). This indicates that some government programs may not be funded. As discussed previously, budget process is a political process in which all actors, such as administrators, chief executives, legislators, and interest groups, compete for public resources. When government makes budget decisions, decision makers take into account budget preferences of all actors. Based on financial and economic analysis as well as other information, budgeters prioritize budget requests from government departments and agencies, committees of the legislative branch, and other sources. Risk management programs are among budget alternatives. Only those risk management programs that need attention immediately are to be funded because disasters and crises are on their way or because emergencies will ultimately happen if the programs are not taken care appropriately.

On the other hand, most people are near-sighted. They do not prefer to consider potential emergencies, disasters, and crises when they have mountains of other things they think they have to deal with (Smith and Toft 1998). Decision-makers are no exception. They may not choose to put large amounts of resources as inventory in stock or as cash in a bank account. From this perspective, risk management is considered a competitor in the budget process. However, considering possibilities that they may have emergency spending during a budget cycle, a large majority of state/provincial and local governments have established rainy day funds, also called budget stabilization funds, and emergency funds, also called contingency funds (Carroll 2016; Douglas and Gaddie 2002; Rodriguez-Tejedo 2012). The rainy funds cap is different from government to government. It usually accounts for 1–15% of general funds (Carroll 2016). To provide funds for emergency spending, local governments may also use risk sharing and adjusting services if legally allowed (Elder and Wagner 2013).

6.3   Emergency and Disaster as Budget Driver

As stated in the second section of this essay, some disasters and crises occur unexpectedly. Earthquakes, flooding, volcanoes, hurricanes, tsunami, tornado, terrorism attacks, financial collapses, and other catastrophes occur without prediction and expectation. Although they develop with a series of unfolding events, these disasters may either leave no time for response or call for immediate integrated, systematic response that involves successive quick and rational decisions and actions. When a disaster occurs, government at different levels takes immediate actions based on local, state/provincial, and/or national disaster plans. From a budget perspective, government needs emergency funds or rainy day funds immediately after a non-expectable disaster occurs. In addition, budget may be readjusted to meet emergency needs after the readjustment request is approved by the legislature. Pursuant to legal requirements, government may have access to other financial means, such as emergency grants or additional budget through a legislative process.

In the United States, the federal Department of Homeland Security provides grants for first responders of disasters. State government may file request for grants based on risks they face. The President may approve emergency grants after he declares emergency state in the disaster-affected areas. When an economic and financial crisis occurs, financial support may be provided through legislative action, such as American Recovery and Reinvestment Act of 2009 to stimulate economy throughout the country.

In Europe, the Migrant Crisis of 2015 caused by refugees and migrant from Syria, Afghanistan, Iraq, and Eritrea forced European Union countries to open borders and accept migrants and refugees. As a result, the countries that accepted migrants and refugees were put under great budget pressure. Some EU countries that accepted a large number of migrants were running a risk of derailing the budget (AFP 2015). Grace, Austria, and Sweden had to raise money to take care of the migrants. Moreover, compared to the huge number of migrants, EU budget was too small to handle the migrant crisis (Holehouse 2015) and EU Council had to approve additional financial assistance (Unterhuber 2015). The migrant crisis has caused a number of problems in those countries that accepted migrants and refugees. The Director of German Refugee Bureau resigned because of inability to deal with migrant and refugee issues.

In fact, non-expectable emergencies and crises that cause severe casualties and enormous loss of properties have become a driver to budgeting. Each time a catastrophic event happens and affects a large number of citizens, local budgets are put under considerable pressure; and local financial sustainability may be weakened and broken because local revenue bases may be severely affected. Simultaneously, local economy is stuck; and local unemployment is on rise. The list of adverse effects could be longer than this.

6.4   Budget as Catalyst for Disaster Recovery

Since local government has limited resources, it mainly provides fundamental services for local citizens such as water, electricity, sewer, and streets. State or provincial government is considerably stronger in economy to serve many more functions within its jurisdiction. Generally, local and state/provincial governments are able to deal with minor disasters that relate operations, or that are caused by natural agents. Considering its financial capacity and particular budget requirements, it may hardly handle some catastrophic events that have overwhelming adverse effects on people and properties, such as Hurricane Katrina and Bovine Spongiform Encephalopathy crisis. This is especially true in the recovery phase of disaster management. Once a disaster is beyond local and state/provincial control, national government may declare emergency state in the affected areas. However, national government may not approve all requests for disaster declaration. Statistics indicates that from April, 1974 to September, 1983, the President had approved only about 59% of all requests submitted by governors for a presidential disaster declaration (Settle 1985). In spite of this, the federal government still provided assistance to state and local governments pursuant to laws that relate disaster management. Generally, the federal government plays the most important role in providing financial and technical support to recovery from disasters in the United States (Bullock et al. 2009).

In the United States, federal grants flow to disaster recovery from a variety of federal departments and agencies. The major departments and agencies include Department of Homeland Security (mainly its Federal Emergency Management Agency), Department of Housing and Urban Development, Small Business Administration, Department of Commerce, Economic Development Administration, Department of Defense, Department Energy, Department of Interior, Department of Labor, Department of Transportation, and Department of Treasury. The federal grants serve recovery in disaster-affected areas mainly in three general categories: public assistance, individual assistance, and hazard mitigation assistance. With regard to public assistance, federal grants cover 75% or more of total expenses in such projects as debris removal, emergency protective measures, road system and bridges, water control facilities, public buildings and contents, public utilities, and parks, recreational and other facilities. Local governments are obligated to match 25% of project expenses from its own resources unless the state provides financial assistance (Settle 1985). Disaster relief projects supported by Corps of Engineers, Department of Education, and Federal Highway Administration are 100% funded with federal grants. Federal grants for individual assistance cover individual and households programs, such as temporary housing, repair, replacement, permanent housing construction, and other needs assistance. In addition, Small Business Administration provides homeowners and business owners with home disaster loans, business physical disaster loans, and economic injury disaster loans. Other federal programs provide financial aids regarding disaster unemployment and legal service. Special tax terms are accessible to taxpayers who have sustained a casualty loss from disasters declared by the federal government (Bullock et al. 2009). However, federal grants do not fund property projects that are covered by commercial insurances.

Besides federal grants, a local government may use its own financial resources to cover the costs of recovery from disasters, such as rainy day funds, emergency funds, and funds transferred from general funds to special funds if approved by the legislative body. In addition, local government may also use other strategies for financial resources to fund its recovery programs. These strategies may include mutual aid agreements if any, joint power agreements or joint power insurance agreements, tax anticipation notes, municipal bonds, insurance programs, and benefit assessment districts.

Overall, financial resources serve as a catalyst that makes recovery happen and ensures that recovery proceeds efficiently, effectively, and equitably as expected. Budgeting serves as a mechanism by which government obtains and appropriates financial resources to fund the needs in recovery from disasters, either natural or manmade. Governments at different levels must coordinate and work together to restore order and provide sustainable services while attaining organizational goals objectives.

7 Recommendations for Improving Risk Management and Budgeting to Attain Organization Goals and Objectives

Risk management involves a wide variety of factors that constitute the risk management system. The functioning of this system depends on appropriate institution, organization, leadership, management, technology, personnel, culture, and financial sources. The characteristics of risk management and public budgeting suggest that risk management and budgeting interact upon each other. An effective, sustainable budgeting framework provides funds (even though budgeting is sometimes driven by severe unexpected disasters and crises) and operation guides for risk management. Similarly, efficient and effective risk management benefits budgeting in that risk management helps find and improve ineffective and inefficient elements in budgeting process. From perspectives of both budgeting and risk management, the following suggestions are essential for these two facets to work together to attain governmental goals and objectives.

7.1 Establishing an Effective Enterprise Risk Management System

It is important that governments at different levels establish an effective risk management system that is implemented at the enterprise level of each government agency. This is required by principles of both risk management and fiscal administration. Enterprise risk management (ERM) is an integrated management mechanism throughout an enterprise (Hardy 2015). By ERM, the chief executive of a government, managers of departments and agencies, and other personnel, in a strategic setting and throughout the whole government, identify potential events that may incur adverse effects, manage risks in an integrated manner to provide assurance for the achievement of the government's objectives (COSO 2004; Ernst & Young LLP 2014; Pickett 2006).

Enterprise Risk management requires that a government agency should have risk management policies, set up systematic organization from top to bottom, clearly define responsibilities of all actors, clarify procedures, train personnel, create necessary technologies, and allocate financial resources. By doing so, a government agency intends to prevent, control, and ameliorate disasters and crises to attain organizational goals and objectives. A system of enterprise risk management helps government build up capacities of managing uncertainties to ensure smooth organizational operation of government. In addition, fiscal administration calls for rational allocation and efficient use of public money so that performance of budgeted programs meets expected standards (Mikesell 2007). Budget techniques, such as program budgeting, planning, programming, and budgeting system, performance budgeting, and new performance budgeting, target at different strategies and orientations (Lu and Thai 2012). These strategies and orientations are essential factors of risk management.

7.2 Building Enterprise Risk Management into Government Operation

Government and its agencies need to implement enterprise risk management and apply risk management throughout their operations (Stanton 2013). Since budget is an administrative instrument and an operation guide, performance can be improved through preventing and controlling risks and disasters. Specifically, risk identification, risk analysis, and risk mitigation is a part of budgeted tasks in budget process; response to and recovery from risks are measures to reduce losses and remedial actions to complete budgeted programs. When implementing enterprise risk management, a government establishes a risk management office and creates the position of a chief risk officer to lead and supervise government-wide risk management activities, and monitor emerging major disasters in each procedure of governmental operation. Agency managers and other personnel need to acquire necessary skills to complete regular activities and manage risks and disasters when they arise. In addition, government needs to train its employees and provide education for them to be capable of identifying, controlling, and ameliorating risks and disasters while complying with codes and policies, dealing with technical issues, and accomplishing activities related to organization operation.

7.3 Determined Support of Long-Term Strategic Risk Management Goals

Decision makers of each government can never compromise long-term goals in risk management with short-term political and financial benefits (Farazmand 2007). Political factors in making budgetary decisions indicate that legislators, chief executives, and department managers may have distinct interest and preferences in distributing public money. When a government is under budgetary constraints and takes austerity measures, competition for public funds is much fierce between budget actors (Drennan et al. 2015). Considering their term of office, decision makers may consider more of the interest they are seeking in short terms than interest for the general public in long terms. Comparatively, they would prefer to fund building of local parks rather than reinforce local levees to resist the severest hurricane that may occur once every fifty or one hundred years. For some long-term projects, smaller financial input for a higher grade of original construction may avoid future losses that are ten to twenty times of initial financial inputs.

7.4 Eradicating Barriers to Risk Management

Government must take strategic measures to eradicate the factors that contribute to decision makers' and department managers' disinterest in risk management (Somers and Svara 2009). There are political, social, managerial, and financial causes that lead to the disinterest. The major courses may include

- not being aware of their role in risk management,
- a low perception of risk,
- lack of understanding the way in which disasters and crises are created,

- a tendency to deem risk management programs as lower priorities,
- insufficient emphasis on risk management in public administration programs and training,
- lack of resources and staffing for risk management especially in mitigation and preparedness phases,
- low prestige of public risk managers, and
- low performance of some risk management programs (Drennan et al. 2015; Grant 1996; Labadie 1984; Tierney et al. 2001; Smith and Toft 1998).

Only when government eradicates the barriers to risk management, can it treat risk management appropriately by establishing an effective risk management system, implementing enterprise risk management mechanism, creating efficient risk management organization, and appropriately allocating financial resources. While it prevents and controls risks, disasters, and crises, government may find it possible to attain its goals and objectives in effective and efficient manners.

7.5   Establishing a Culture of Risk Management Learning

Organizational learning is an important tool by which a government keeps sustainable operation. It occurs when an organization's system and culture retain the knowledge its members acquire and incorporate the knowledge into the organization system (Yeung et al. 1999). Organizational learning is a process in which an organization processes, interprets, and responds to information both inside and outside the organization (Easterby-Smith and Araujo 1999; also see Argyris and Schon 1978; Gilley and Maycunich 2000; Lassey 1998; Senge 1990). Organizational learning helps government obtains knowledge, experience, practice, new ways of performing tasks, efficient organization, international relations, and technology for risk management. Generally, government and its departments and agencies learn risk and disaster management from education, virtual experience, other organizations, information system, and previous events (Drennan et al. 2015; Moynihan 2008). A culture of risk management learning promotes not only correction of inappropriate operation and procedure, but also pursuit of new alternatives to solving problems and strategic planning in risk management.

7.6   Establishing a Holistic Financing Framework for Risk Management

It is of supreme importance that government executives and risk managers understand the position of risk management in the light of budget austerity. To ensure that risk management programs are sufficiently financed, government may have to cut some programs and save money. However, government agencies must make sure what laws and regulations they must comply with regarding risk management. This relates not only to operation standards but also to governmental funding during recovery from disasters and crises (Settle 1985). In addition, risk managers must understand how much budget is available from their government's own finance, and how much from higher-level governments, and under what conditions they cannot obtain any grants from higher-level governments in different phases of disaster management. Government must make strategic plans for multiple financial means to fund risk management, such as mutual aid agreement with other governments, joint power insurance agreements, tax anticipation notes, municipal bonds or industrial development bonds, insurance programs, assessment district, and tax increases.

7.7   Improving Risk Management Efficiency to Back Up Budget Austerity

Risk management has been a challenge to public administration (Petak 1985). In the case of budget austerity, policy makers find it hard to determine what risk programs to fund, and what roles different levels of government may play. However, risk management may not be a minus in the budgeting process, nor does it relate only bad things government agencies must prevent or control. Risk analysis may help government agencies find ineffective and inefficient elements in budgeted programs. Eradicating or improving those elements may help save financial resources. In addition, risk management may provide creative ways of performing routine tasks or solutions to certain problems in budgeted programs.

Moreover, risk management can be combined with other activities in the budgeting process. Since risk and disaster management relates to prevention measures, which are crucial "in terms of identifying faults and preventing errors" (Drennan et al. 2015, p. 54), it provides important information for budget audit. Risk management can be a part of internal budget audit with regard to performance evaluation and compliance to laws and regulations. These measures suggest that improving risk management is a mechanism to back up budget austerity (Leitch 2003).

To sum up, considering the relationship between risk management and budgeting, a government needs first to examine if it has an effective enterprise risk management system as required by ISO 31000 risk management guideline, or GAO Risk Management Framework, or COSO ERM-Integrated Framework. The government needs to establish such a system if it does not have one. After establishing the ERM system, the government needs to incorporate risk management into governmental operation. In this process of incorporation, the government needs to establish a culture of learning to managing risks, eradicating barriers to effective risk management, supporting long-term

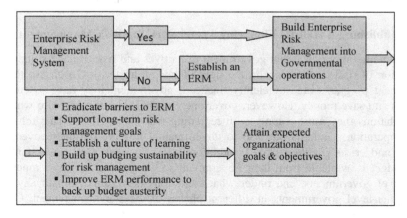

Fig. 1. Examination of relationship between risk management and budget

risk management goals, building up financial sustainability for risk management, and improving management efficiency to back up budget austerity. These recommendations are illustrated by Fig. 1.

8   Conclusion

Nowadays people have considered government as an accountability bearer in risk and disaster management. Although there is no clear definition with regard to in what degree government should provide safety, security, and health services, risk management is generally considered a key responsibility of government. Generally, people do not pay much attention of risks management because they do not think risk is potential in any fields of social life. However, when a disaster is pressing, it causes chaos among residents. Therefore, considering limited budget resources and possible huge losses a disaster may incur, government at each level must find a balance point for both risk management and budget resource allocation so that major risks can be managed effectively while budget resources are distributed equitably and efficiently.

Government needs to establish an effective risk and emergency management framework that defines responsibilities, organization, communication, and funding in the process of preventing against, preparing for, responding to, and recovering from disasters and crises. Risks that relate government operation may be managed through regular budgetary process in which public programs are financed and performance evaluated. Unexpected catastrophic events, either natural or manmade, drive an emergency budgetary process and overshadow a variety of aspects of social life. It is high necessity that government builds risk management into its operation, eradicates all barriers to effective risk management, and establishes a culture of risk learning.

Government needs to build up finance and budget sustainability to appropriately fund risk and disaster management. It must allocate resources to ensure public safety and disaster recovery services because they are public goods. This suggests that government needs to establish a financial risk management mechanism and make strategic planning to sustain spending and revenue polices so that public finance remains on its sustainable track and provides funds for risk and disaster management.

Acknowledgement. The author would like to thank Dr. Victor Chang sincerely for his suggestion and for the opportunity to work on this essay.

References

AFP: Migrant crisis 'may derail' EU budget: Dijsselbloem, 2 November 2015. http://www.msn.com/en-za/news/world/migrant-crisis-may-derail-eu-budgets-dijsselbloem/ar-BBmKs8t. Accessed 17 Feb 2016

Alateyh, S., Chang, V., Crowder, R., Wills, G.: Citizen intention to adopt e-government service in Saudi Arabia. In: Emerging Software as a Service and Analytics, ESaaSA 2014, Barcelona, ES, 03–05 April 2014 (2014)

Allison, G.T.: Essence of Decision: Explaining the Cuban Missile Crisis. Little Brown, Boston (1971)

Argyris, C., Schon, D.: Organizational Learning. Addison-Wesley, Readings (1978)

Axelrod, D.: Budgeting for Modern Government. St. Martin's Press, New York (1988)

Baker, T., Moss, D.: Government as risk manager. In: Moss, D. (ed.) New Perspectives on Regulation, pp. 87–109. The Tobin Project Inc., Cambridge (2009)

Barzelay, M.: The New Public Management. University of California Press, Berkeley (2000)

Beck, M., Asenova, D., Diskson, G.: Public administration, science, and risk assessment: a case study of the U.K. bovine spongiform encephalopathy crisis. Public Adm. Rev. **65**(4), 396–408 (2005)

Becket, J., King, C.: The challenge to improve citizen participation in public budgeting: a discussion. J. Public Budg. Acc. Financ. Manag. **14**(3), 463–485 (2002)

Beckhard, R.: What is organization development? In: French, W.L., Bell, C.H., Zawacki, R.A. (eds.) Organization Development and Transformation: Making Effective Change, 6th edn, pp. 12–15. The McGraw-Hill Companies, New Delhi (2006)

Blau, P.M., Scott, W.R.: Formal Organizations: A Comparative Approach. Stanford Business Books, Stanford (2003)

Braig, S., Gebre, B., Sellgren, A.: Strengthening risk management in the U.S. public sector. McKinsey working papers No. 28 (2011). https://www.mckinsey.com/ ~ /media/mckinsey/ dotcom/client_service/Risk/Working%20papers/28_WP_Risk_management_in_the_US_ public_sector.ashx. Accessed 15 Feb 2016

Buckley, W.: Sociology and Modern Systems Theory. Englewoods Cliffs, Prentice-Hall (1967)

Bullock, J.A., Haddow, G.D., Coppola, D.P., Yeletaysi, S.: Introduction to Homeland Security, 3rd edn. Butterworth-Heinemann, Burlington (2009)

Bureau of Fiscal Service, US Department of the Treasury. Enterprise risk management: developments and application in the U.S., 15 October 2015. https://fiscal.treasury.gov/ fstraining/events/Colloq_Enterprise_RM_US.pdf. Accessed 2 May 2015

Callahan, K.: The utilization and effectiveness of advisory committees in the budget process of local governments. J. Public Budg. Acc. Financ. Manag. **14**(2), 295–319 (2002)

Capra, F.: The Turning Point. Simon & Schuster, New York (1982)

Carroll, J.: Which states have rainy day funds? (2016). http://www.csg.org/knowledgecenter/ docs/sgn0104WhichStatesHave.pdf. Accessed 3 Mar 2016

Chang, V.: The business intelligence as a service in the cloud. Future Gener. Comput. Syst. **37**, 512–534 (2014)

Chang, V., Walters, R., Wills, G.: Organizational sustainability modeling—an emerging service and analytics model for evaluating cloud computing adoption with two case studies. Int. J. Inf. Manag. **36**(1), 167–179 (2016)

CIMA: Introduction to managing risk. Topic Gateway Series, No. 28 (2008). http://www. cimaglobal.com/Documents/ImportedDocuments/cid_tg_intro_to_managing_rist.apr07.pdf. Accessed 20 Feb 2016

Clary, B.B.: The evolution and structure of natural hazard policies. Public Adm. Rev. **45**(Issue Special-Jan85), 20–28 (1985)

Committee of Sponsoring Organizations of the Treadway Committee (COSO): Enterprise Risk Management Framework. American Institute of Certified Public Accountants, New York (2004)

Daft, R.: Organization Theory and Design, 5th edn. West, New York (1995)

de Lange, D.E., Busch, T., Delgado-Ceballos, J.: Sustaining sustainability in organizations. J. Bus. Ethics **110**(2), 151–156 (2012)

Denhardt, R.B.: Theories of Public Organization, 4th edn. Belmont Wadsworth/Thomson Learning, Belmont (2004)

Dickson, G.: Risk Management. Chartered Insurance Institute, Cambridge (1991)

Douglas, J., Gaddie, R.: State rainy day funds and fiscal crisis: rainy day funds and the 1990–1991 recession revisited. Public Budg. Financ. **22**(1), 19–30 (2002)

Drabek, T.E.: Managing the emergency response. Public Adm. Rev. **45**(Issue Special-Jan85), 85–92 (1985)

Drennan, L.T., McConnell, A., Stark, A.: Risk and Crisis Management in the Public Sector, 2nd edn. Routledge, New York (2015)

Drucker, P.: The Age of Discontinuity: Guidelines to our Changing Society. Harper & Row, New York (1969)

Easterby-Smith, M., Araujo, L.: Organizational learning: current debates and opportunities. In: Easterby-Smith, M., Burgoyne, J., Araujo, L. (eds.) Organizational Learning and the Learning Organization, pp. 1–21. SAGE Publications Ltd., London (1999)

Ebdon, C.: Beyond the public hearing: citizen participation in the local government budget process. J. Public Budg. Acc. Financ. Manag. **14**(2), 273–294 (2002)

Ebdon, C., Franklin, A.L.: Citizen participation in budgeting theory. Public Adm. Rev. **66**(3), 437–447 (2006)

Edwards, W.: The theory of decision-making. In: Edwards, W., Tversky, A. (eds.) Decision-Making: Selected Readings, pp. 13–64. Penguin Books, Middlesex (1967)

Elder, E., Wagner, G.: Revenue cycles and risk sharing in local governments: an analysis of state rainy day funds. Natl. Tax J. **66**(4), 939–959 (2013)

Ernst & Young LLP: Government and public sector enterprise risk management (2014). http://www.ey.com/Publication/vwLUAssets/EY_Government_and_Public_Sector_Enterprise_Risk_Management/$FILE/EY-Government-and-Public-Sector-Enterprise-Risk-Management.pdf. Accessed 23 Feb 2016

Farazmand, A.: Emergent theories of organization: an overview and analysis. In: Farazmand, A. (ed.) Modern Organizations: Theory and Practice, 2nd edn, pp. 63–96. Praeger, Westport (2002)

Farazmand, A.: Learning from the Katrina crisis: a global and international perspective with implications for future crisis management. Public Adm. Rev. **67**(Special Issue), 149–159 (2007)

Forester, J.: Bounded rationality and the politics of muddling through. Public Adm. Rev. **44**(1), 23–31 (1984)

Francois, E.J.: Financial Sustainability for Nonprofit Organizations. Springer Publishing Company, New York (2014)

Gaiden, N.: Processes, policies, and power: budget reform. Public Manager **28**(1), 13–17 (1993)

Gilley, J.W., Maycunich, A.: Beyond the Learning Organization. Perseus Books, Cambridge (2000)

Gladwin, T., Kennelly, J.J., Krause, T.: Shifting paradigms for sustainable development: implications for management theory and research. Acad. Manag. Rev. **20**(4), 874–907 (1995)

Godschalk, D.R., Brower, D.J.: Mitigation strategies and integrated emergency management. Public Adm. Rev. **45**(Issue Special-Jan85), 64–71 (1985)

Grant, N.K.: Emergency management training and education for public administrators. In: Selves, R.T., Waugh Jr., W.L. (eds.) Disaster Management in the U.S. and Canada: The Politics, Policymaking, Administration, and Analysis of Emergency Management, 2nd edn, pp. 313–326. Charles C. Thomas, Springfield (1996)

Hardy, K.: Enterprise Risk Management: A Guide for Government Professionals. Jossey-Bass, San Francisco (2015)

Hitchcock, D.E., Willard, M.L.: The Step-by-Step Guide to Sustainability Planning: How to Create and Implement Sustainability Plans in Any Business or Organization. Earthscan, Sterling (2008)

Holehouse, M.: Migrant crisis: EU running out of money, warns Jean-Claude Juncker, 27 October 2015. http://www.telegraph.co.uk/news/worldnews/europe/eu/11959111/Migration-crisis-EU-running-out-of-money-warns-Jean-Claude-Juncker.html. Accessed 17 Feb 2016

Holmes, A.: Risk Management. Wiley, Oxford (2002)

Hood, C.: The new public management in the 1980s. Acc. Organ. Soc. **20**(2–3), 93–109 (1995)

Hundermark, G.: Learning and the sustainability of small organizations: an examination of Senge's theory of a learning organization in a South African context. Int. J. Learn. **18**(12), 195–214 (2012)

Hyde, A.C.: The development of budgeting and budget theory: the threads of budget reform. In: Hyde, A.C. (ed.) Government Budgeting: Theory, Process, and Politics, 3rd edn. Thompson Learning, Toronto (2002)

ICDRM/GWU: Emergency Management Glossary of Terms. The Institute for Crisis, Disaster, and Risk Management (ICDRM) at the George Washington University (GWU), Washington, D.C. (2010). George Washington University website www.gwu.edu/~icdrm. Accessed 22 Feb 2016

International Organization for Standardization: Risk Management: Principles and Guidelines (2009). https://www.iso.org/obp/ui/#iso:std:iso:31000:ed-1:v1:en. Accessed 14 Feb 2016

Kaboolian, L.: The new public management. Public Adm. Rev. **58**(3), 189–193 (1998)

Kamensky, J.: Role of reinventing government movement in federal management reform. Public Adm. Rev. **56**(3), 247–256 (1996)

Kaplan, S.: The words of risk analysis. Risk Anal. **17**(4), 408–409 (1997)

Katz, D., Kahn, R.L.: The Social Psychology of Organizations. Wiley, New York (1966)

Kettl, D.F.: The Global Public Management Revolution. Brookings Institution, Washington, DC (2000)

Labadie, J.R.: Problems in local emergency management. Environ. Manag. **8**(6), 489–494 (1984)

Laszlo, E.: Introduction to Systems Philosophy: Toward a New Paradigm of Contemporary Thought. Gordon and Breach, New York (1972)

Lassey, P.: Developing a Learning Organization. Kogan Page, London (1998)

Lewis, V.B.: Toward a theory of budgeting. Public Adm. Rev. **12**(1), 43–54 (1952)

Leitch, M.: Risk management and beyond budgeting, 6 March 2003. http://www.internalcontrolsdesign.co.uk/RMandBB/. Accessed 13 Feb 2016

Lindblom, C.: The science of muddling through. Public Adm. Rev. **19**(1), 79–88 (1959)

Loye, D., Eisler, R.: The failure of liberalism: a reassessment of ideology from a new feminine-masculine perspective. Polit. Psychol. **4**(2), 375–391 (1983)

Lu, Y.: Public Asset Management: Empirical Evidence from the State Governments in the United States. Lambert Academic Publishing, Berlin (2012)

Lu, Y., Thai, K.V.: Information management for public budget decision making: insights from organization and budget theories. In: Vaidya, K. (ed.) Inter-Organizational Information Systems and Business Management: Theories for Researchers, pp. 206–228. IGI Global, Hershey (2012)

Lynn Jr., L.E.: Public Management as Art, Science, and Profession. Chatham House, Chatham (1996)

Maturana, H., Varela, F.: Autopoiesis and Cognition: The Realization of the Living. Reidel, Boston (1980)

McEntire, D.A., Fuller, C., Johnson, C.W., Weber, R.: A comparison of disaster paradigms: the search for a holistic policy guide. Public Adm. Rev. **62**(3), 267–281 (2002)

Mentzberg, H.: The Structure of Organizations. Prentice-Hall, Inc., Upper Saddle River (1979)

Mikesell, J.L.: Fiscal Administration: Analysis and Applications for the Public Sector, 7th edn. Thomas Wadsworth, Belmont (2007)

Miller, G.: Living Systems. McGraw-Hill, New York (1978)

Morçöl, G.: Decision-making: an overview of theories, contexts, and methods. In: Morçöl, G. (ed.) Handbook of Decision-Making, pp. 3–18. Taylor & Francis Group, Boca Raton (2007)

Moynihan, D.P.: Learning under uncertainty: networks in crisis management. Public Adm. Rev. **68**(2), 350–365 (2008)

Niskanen, W.A.: A reflection on bureaucracy and representative government. In: Blais, A., Dion, S. (eds.) The Budget-Maximizing Bureaucrat: Appraisals and Evidence, pp. 13–31. University of Pittsburgh Press, Pittsburgh (1992)

Olphert, W., Damodaran, L.: Citizen participation and engagement in the design of e-government service: the missing link in effective ICT design and delivery. J. Assoc. Inf. Syst. **8**(9), 491–507 (2007)

Osborne, D., Gaebler, T.: Reinventing Government. Addison-Wesley, Reading (1992)

Perrow, C.: Complex Organizations: A Critical Essay, 3rd edn. McGraw-Hill Inc., New York (1986)

Petak, W.J.: Emergency management: a challenge for public administration. Public Adm. Rev. **45**(Issue Special-Jan85), 3–7 (1985)

Pickett, S.K.H.: Enterprise Risk Management: A Manager's Journey. Wiley, Hoboken (2006)

Pollitt, C., Bouckert, G.: Public Management Reform. Oxford University Press, Oxford (2000)

Prigogine, I., Stengers, I.: Order Out of Chaos. Bantam, New York (1984)

Pritchard, C.L.: Risk Management: Concepts and Guidance, 5th edn. Taylor & Francis Group, LLC, Boca Raton (2015)

Regens, J.L., Dietz, T.M., Rycroft, R.W.: Risk assessment in the policy-making process: environmental health and safety protection. Public Adm. Rev. **43**(2), 137–145 (1983)

Rodriguez-Tejedo, I.: The determinants of structure of rainy day funds. Public Adm. Rev. **72**(3), 376–386 (2012)

Rubin, I.S.: The Politics of Public Budgeting: Getting and Spending, Borrowing and Balancing. Chatham House of Publishers Inc., Chatham (1990)

Rubin, I.S.: The Politics of Public Budgeting, 6th edn. CQ Press, Washington, D.C. (2010)

Rubin, C.B., Barbee, D.G.: Disaster recovery and hazard mitigation: Bridging the intergovernmental gap. Public Adm. Rev. **45**(Issue Special-Jan85), 57–63 (1985)

Salk, J.: The Anatomy of Reality. Columbia University Press, New York (1983)

Schick, A.: The road to PPB: the stages of budget reform. Public Adm. Rev. **26**, 243–258 (1966)

Scott, W.G.: Organization theory: an overview and an appraisal. Acad. Manag. J. **4**(1), 7–26 (1961)

Senge, P.M.: The Fifth Discipline: The Art & Practice of the Learning Organization. Currency & Doubleday, New York (1990)

Settle, A.K.: Financing disaster mitigation, preparedness, response, and recovery. Public Adm. Rev. **45**(Issue Special-Jan85), 101–106 (1985)

Short, A.D.: An examination of the effects of institutional and individual characteristics on the importance of information sources to analysts in state legislative fiscal offices. ProQuest Dissertations Publishing. North Carolina State University (2013)

Simon, H.A.: Administrative Behavior: A Study of Decision-Making Process in Administrative Organization. McMillan Co., New York (1947)

Simon, H.A.: Administrative Behavior: A Study of Decision-Making Processes in Administrative Organizations, 2nd edn. Free Press, New York (1957)

Simon, H.A.: Models of Bounded Rationality, vol. 3. The MIT Press, Cambridge, MA (1997)

Smith, D., Toft, B.: Risk and crisis management in the public sector: Editorial: Issues in public sector risk management. Public Money Manag. **18**(4), 7–10 (1998)

Somers, S., Svara, J.H.: Assessing and management environmental risk: connecting local government management with emergency management. Public Adm. Rev. **69**(2), 191–193 (2009)

Stiglitz, J.E.: Economics of the Public Sector, 3rd edn. W.W. Norton & Company, New York (2000)

Stanton, T.H.: Risk management is essential at a time of downsizing. Public Adm. Rev. **73**(2), 219–220 (2013)

Tanaka, S.: Engaging the public in national budgeting: a non-government perspective. OECD J. Budg. **7**(2), 139–177 (2007)

Thompson, J.D.: Organizations in Action. McGraw-Hill, New York (1967)

Thompson, F., Zumeta, W.: Control and controls: a reexamination of control patterns in budget execution. Policy Sci. **13**(1), 25–50 (1981)

Tierney, K.J., Lindell, M.K., Perry, R.W.: Facing the Unexpected: Disaster Preparedness and Response in the United States. Joseph Henry Press, Washington, DC (2001)

von Bertalanffy, L.: General Systems Theory. George Braziller, New York (1968)

Unterhuber, J.: Council approves more money to tackle the refugee crisis, 8 October 2015. http://www.consilium.europa.eu/en/press/press-releases/2015/10/8-council-approves-money-refugee/. Accessed 18 Feb 2016

U.S. Environmental Protection Agency: An Examination of EPA Risk Assessment Principles and Practices. U.S. EPA Office of the Science Advisor, Washington, DC (2004)

Wallace, W.A., De Balogh, F.: Decision support systems for disaster management. Public Adm. Rev. **45**(Issue Special-Jan85), 134–146 (1985)

Wildavsky, A.: Political implications of budgetary reform. Public Adm. Rev. **21**(3), 183–190 (1961)

Willoughby, W.F.: The movement for budgetary reform in the states. In: Hyde, A.C. (ed.) Government Budgeting: Theory, Process, and Politics, pp. 20–23. Thomson Learning, Toronto (2002)

Xu, H.: Information technology, public administration, and citizen participation: the impacts of e-government on political and administrative processes. Public Adm. Rev. **72**(6), 915–920 (2012)

Yeung, A.K., Ulrich, D.O., Nason, S.W., Glinow, M.A.V.: Organizational Learning Capability. Oxford University Press, Oxford (1999)

Zey, M. (ed.): Decision-Making: Alternatives to Rational Choice Models. Sage, Newbury Park (1992)

Zimmerman, R.: The relationship of emergency management to government policies on man-made technological disasters. Public Adm. Rev. **45**(85), 29–39 (1985)

Iris Biometrics Recognition in Security Management

Ahmad Ghaffari[✉], Amin Hosseinian-Far, and Akbar Sheikh-Akbari

School of Computing, Creative Technologies and Engineering,
Leeds Beckett University, Leeds, UK
A.Ghaffari6582@student.leedsbeckett.ac.uk,
{A.Hosseinian-Far,A.Sheikh-Akbari}@leedsbeckett.ac.uk

Abstract. Application of iris recognition for human identification has significant potential for developing a robust identification system. This is due to the fact that iris pattern of individuals are unique, differentiable from left to right eye and is almost stable over the time. However, performance of the existing iris recognition systems depends on the signal processing algorithms they use for iris segmentation, feature extraction and template matching. Like any other signal processing system, the performance of the iris recognition system is depend on the existing level of noise in the image and can be deteriorated as the level of noise increases. The building block of the iris recognition systems, techniques to mitigate the effect of the noise in each stages, criteria to assess the performance of different iris recognition techniques and publicly available iris datasets are discussed in this chapter.

Keywords: Iris recognition systems · Iris segmentation · Iris feature extraction · Iris template matching · Iris datasets · Iris image pre-processing

1 Introduction

1.1 Background

In this changing world, authentication of people is necessary in order to admit themselves in to different places, such as: international travel, ATMs and gaining entry to the buildings. Different methods for authentication of individuals have been developed over the years, e.g. password, smartcard (with identity information stored in the chip or printed on the surface of a card e.g. a bank card) and biometric identification. Biometric identification methods seem to be taking over other verification methods. Biometric passports, electronic fingerprints and palm-prints (Minaee and Abdolrashidi 2015) are existing examples of current biometric identification methods. Fingerprints, the most well-known and highly robust biometric identification method in some cases may fail to identify the person due to injuries and basic wear and tear on ridges part of the finger pattern. Iris recognition methods use iris patterns of a person's eyes to identify the person (Alrifaee and Hsuuien 2014), are much more reliable. Every single iris's pattern is unique and it is different from the left to the right eye of a person. In addition,

© Springer International Publishing AG 2017
V. Chang et al. (Eds.): Enterprise Security, LNCS 10131, pp. 73–96, 2017.
DOI: 10.1007/978-3-319-54380-2_4

it remains unchanged throughout a person's lifetime. Iris recognition systems analyse the random patterns of the iris, to identify the person (Bowyer et al. 2008). Since the iris of a person is unique, stable and complex, it can easily be used as a lifetime passport for the person. The accuracy of the iris based identification methods is very high because of the extraordinary dimensionality of the iris. Hence the chances of error in identification are extremely low. Furthermore, iris recognition systems can provide ease of use, as people do not have to remember any passwords to verify their identity.

1.2   Iris Anatomy

The iris is a part of an eye which controls the amount of light that reaches the retina by monitoring and adjusting the size and diameter of the pupil. It has a colourful circular shape with a rich texture (Bowyer et al. 2008), as shown in Fig. 1.

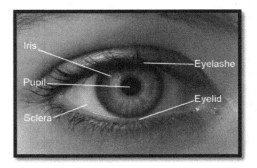

Fig. 1. Eye anatomy (Dovey 2015)

In the optical world, the iris acts as a diaphragm adjusts the size of the pupil as an aperture to control the amount of the light to pass through. Iris makes the colour of the eye. Every iris contains extensive patterns of pigment spots, furrows and ridges. The internal dark circle of the eye is called pupil. The white region of the eye, which contains blood vessels and connective tissue surrounding the iris, is the sclera. The pupil and iris are covered by cornea which is a clear covering. Every iris has two regions separated by the collarets. These two regions are outer ciliary zone of iris and central pupillary zone, as illustrated in Fig. 2.

The pattern of the iris is developed during the eye development at the time of the birth. The iris pattern is believed to vary from a person to others and also from the right to the left eye (Noh et al. 2002). Throughout the lifetime of a person the pattern of the iris does not change but the colour can change with the increase in the level of pigmentation.

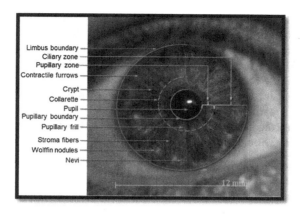

Fig. 2. Iris regions (Drewes 2014)

1.3   Iris Datasets

Biometric recognition system has gained great popularity in the last thirty years. Extensive research has been done to develop accurate iris recognition systems over the past years. Current iris recognition systems analyse features of the iris to identify the person. To assess and compare the performance of these systems, a comprehensive test on an iris dataset comprising of a variety of iris images is needed. Hence a number of iris datasets have been created to facilitate these tasks. Some of the existing iris databases, which are publicly available, are:

- *CASIA dataset:* Produced by the Chinese Academy of Science. It has four versions of datasets (V1 to V4) (Tan 2010).
- *BATH dataset:* It was created by Smart Sensor Limited in Bath University (Bath 2007).
- *MMU dataset:* It was generated by the Multimedia University and has two versions (MMU 2010).
- *ICE dataset:* It was created by the National Institute of Standards and Technology (NIST 2011).
- *WVU dataset:* It was formed at West Virginia University (Li 2007).
- *UBIRIS dataset:* It contains noisy iris images (SOCIA Lab 2010).

2   Iris Recognition

A general iris recognition system consists of four stages; image acquisition, iris segmentation, feature extraction and template matching. There are some challenging points within the iris images such as: noise, light reflection, low image quality and object movement, which could significantly affect the performance of the iris recognition systems. Over the years, many researches (Daugman 1993; Clover 2014; Alrifaee and Hsuuien 2014; Noh et al. 2002; Tajbakhsh et al. 2009) have done to improve the speed and accuracy of the iris recognition systems in the presence of these parameters. Some researchers have claimed that the limits specified for iris recognition systems can be eased by using techniques to deal with the movement of the subject over an extensive space from the camera (Bashir et al. 2008); dealing with low resolution iris images (Jeong et al. 2005); and interacting with iris images, which are unclear due to noise (Proenqa 2009). False Acceptance Rate (FAR) and False Rejection Rate (FRR) are two measurement factors for comparing the performance of different iris recognition systems when using a particular dataset (Daugman 1993). For verification of the iris recognition systems, the samples of the claim on the earlier taken samples are tested. This process produces four distinct results:

- *True Acceptance (TA):* if the biometric picture is saved in the dataset and the recognition system matches the person correctly.
- *False Acceptance (FA):* if the picture is not stored in the dataset and the recognition system incorrectly find a match for it in the dataset.
- *True Rejection (TR):* if one's biometric iris information has not been saved in the dataset and the recognition system does not match it with any images in the dataset.
- *False Rejection (FR):* if one's iris image is stored in dataset but his/her biometric is discarded.

The iris recognition test results are concluded in a Receiver Operating Characteristics (ROC) parabola in which FRR is represented as a function of FAR. The point where the FRR and FAR are intersected is termed as Equal Error Rate (EER).

- FAR are the chances that someone else gets recognized by the system as a registered person and this happens when iris images of different classes from different humans are matched (inter-class comparison).
- FRR: it is the chance of the system to not being able to identify a registered person in the dataset. This happens when an iris recognition system does not match current iris image of a person with another image of the same iris stored in the dataset (intra-class comparison).
- ROC: it is the plot of FRR against FAR and is used to determine the best matching threshold for the iris recognition system. ROC is used to determine the threshold values for FRR and FAR of the system.
- Equal Error Rate (EER): EER is used to determine the accuracy of the system. It is the point that FAR and FRR are equal, the lower the EER value the greater the accuracy of the system.

In image acquisition, the first step of iris recognition, an eye image from a predefined distance is captured, when the eye is illuminated by either a visible or an infra-red illuminant. The captured image is then segmented to extract the iris boundaries. The segmented iris is then normalised, where the doughnut shaped iris image is converted from the Cartesian coordinate into a rectangular polar coordinate. A new step known as the pre-process step has recently been added to the image processing stage. In the pre-processing, the noisy input image is enhanced to mitigate the effect of noise on the iris recognition process. The discriminating features of the iris are obtained from the normalized form of the iris in the feature extraction stage and stored in its feature vector. The resulting features vector is stored and used for iris recognition. Various steps of the iris recognition will be explained in the following sub-sections.

2.1   Image Acquisition

Various methods have been developed to capture eye images from short or long distances (More et al. 2015). Kennell and Matey (Labati et al. 2009) and while Wheeler et al. (Tajbakhash et al. 2009) reported iris images capturing for the range of 1 and 1.5 m, respectively. Near Infra-Red (NIR) illumination, 700 to 900 nm wavelength, is usually used in commercially available iris recognition systems (Daugman 2004a, 2004b), an example of such a system is shown in Fig. 3. In these kinds of systems, audio feedback is used to guide the person to accurately position his/her head (Clover 2014).

Fig. 3. Iris recognition machine used in airport (Canada) (Addleton 2012)

High resolution cameras like LG, OKI, SARNOFF and PANASONIC are used in some iris recognition systems to capture eye images from distance as far as 3 m (Matey et al. 2006). Multiple cameras are used in IOM (Iris On Move) system for capturing multiple images of an iris from different angles. The quality of the captured images can be improved by engineering the image acquisition system (Matey et al. 2006). Researchers have suggested using image processing algorithm to categorize and improve the quality of the captured image further (Alexandra and Proenqa 2007).

2.2   Image Processing

The resolution of the captured iris image is a function of the illumination source, camera parameters (distance of the camera from the human eye, orientation of the camera with respect to the eye and camera zooming). Furthermore, unwanted data like eyelashes, pupil, eyelids, sclera and extra parts of the human skin will also be captured along with the iris. Therefore, eye images must be segmented to extract the iris area.

2.2.1   Segmentation

In segmentation stage, the unwanted data is eliminated and the outer and inner boundary of the iris is identified (Tay and Mok 2008). These boundaries are used to extract the iris region, as shown in Fig. 4 (Daugman 1993).

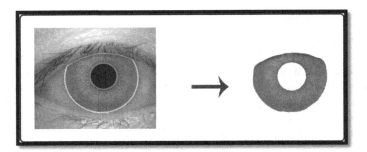

Fig. 4. Iris segmentation

Performance of the iris recognition systems depends on the accuracy of the iris segmentation algorithm. Hence, precise iris segmentation is vital for achieving robust iris recognition. The segmentation is the process of dividing the image into its components wherein the iris needs to be isolated form the rest of the eye image (the two circles shown in Fig. 4). These differentiate the different parts of the eye in terms of the sclera, iris and pupil, as shown in Fig. 4, while two curves encompass the structure within the upper and lower eyelids. The accuracy of the segmentation process depends on the quality of the eye images. Hence, most of the iris recognition machines use high quality eye images, which captured eye image under NIR light sources (cancelling out light reflections by using the NIR light sources). The images are generally taken from a short distances. This needs the individual to be photographed stand still and look into the camera when capturing the image. This has been considered in the images of the CASIA dataset wherein such images could be accurately segmented. The majority of the iris recognition systems use NIR eye images. Although there are some studies comparing the application of the NIR image and visible wavelengths image for the iris recognition. The primary difference between these two images is that a clear pigmentation is obtained using the NIR images while a fainter texture of the iris achieved from visible images. In addition, the NIR lights are considered not to reflect the noise within the picture, while it is reflected in images captured under visible wavelengths sources (Figs. 5 and 6).

The centre of the pupil is considered to be the reference point for the iris recognition systems, prior to localizing the iris. The segmentation algorithm in NIR images is starts from inner circle, as there is significant intensity transition from the pupil to iris

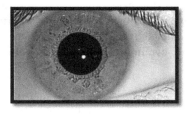

Fig. 5. An eye image captured under NIR illuminant.

Fig. 6. An eye image captured under visible wavelength illuminant.

regions, as shown in Fig. 5, while this is true for iris outer layers in images captured under visible light source, as shown in Fig. 6. With reference to this fact (Grabowski et al. 2008), Grabowski concluded to use a strong whitened visible wavelength light source, an average colour temperature of 5780 °K, for capturing images under visible wavelength light. They reported a greater clarity within the iris image in comparison to the use of NIR images, as shown in Fig. 7.

Fig. 7. Visible wavelength vs NIR (Grabowski et al. 2008)

While a bright light source is used, the conclusions derived through the experiments, which reflected how the iris is more efficiently recognised in consideration of NIR light sources, in comparison to visible wavelengths including those within FRR and FAR. This could be attributed to the light source wherein the texture of the iris being impacted through reflection. The image would also be reflective of associated aspects including muscle fibre or caverns influencing the overall segmentation process. The low level of accuracy within (Grabowski et al. 2008) can be explained in how the Daugman method was used in relation to integro-differential operators towards segmenting the image, and Gabor filter was used towards extracting the features of the iris images using eye images captured under visible wavelengths lights. The algorithm was ensured to successfully conclude the features excluding the noise within NIR iris images. Towards concluding more efficient results, a revised extraction algorithm can be used.

Advances in iris recognition technologies have contributed to enhancing the accuracy of the segmentation process, enabling the handling of pictures with heterogeneous aspects including those in the UBIRISv.1 and UBIRISv.2 databases.

Iris Segmentation Methods

Existing iris recognition systems mainly using one of the following three iris segmentation methods:

- Iris template (De Martin-Roche et al. 2001)
- Iris outer and inner boundaries (Wildes 1997).
- Hybrid (Proenqa 2010) based on iris colour template and iris boundaries.

In the following sections sate of the art iris segmentation techniques are discussed:

I. Daugman's Method

This method perhaps constitutes the most common methodology, which was implemented by Daugman for the first time in 1993 (Daugman 1993) and later owned by Iridian Technologies. The new Daugman's method is used in most of the existing iris recognition systems. Daugman assumes that the iris and the pupil are both circular. Therefore, he considers the integro-differential operator as follows:

$$max_{r,x_0,y_0}\left|G_\sigma(r) * \frac{\delta}{\delta_r}\oint_{r,x_0,y_0}\frac{I(x \cdot y)}{2\pi r}d_s\right| \tag{1}$$

where $I(x,y)$ is the intensity of the eye grey image at location of (x,y); r is the variable radius; G is the Gaussian smoothing factor while ds represents the circular path. The operator concludes the circular path relative to the circumference towards maximizing the variations within the pixel intensity values relative to $N3$ spatial domains. To start off, pixels constituting localized minima intensity are concluded towards constituting the central points of the circumference, reflected in Fig. 8.

Fig. 8. Minimum intensity pixels

Both the iris and the pupil are considered to constitute the minimum values, in consideration of the areas being amongst the darkest within the eye. Prior to the implementation of the integro-differential operator, the grey level image should be pre-processed in consideration of the operator failure. This is particularly valid in relation to less intensity separation between the coloured regions of the ring and the white colour of the sclera. In resolving this issue, a histogram based contrast enhancement technique is used to increase the level of contrast within the sclera, iris and the pupil as illustrated in Fig. 9.

Alrifaee and Hsuuien (2014) have reported that the Daugman integro-differential operator have been successful in segmenting high quality eye images using CASIA, Bath and UPOL datasets. However, this method is less effective in segmenting noisy images such as images of the UBIRIS.v1 and UBIRIS.v2 datasets.

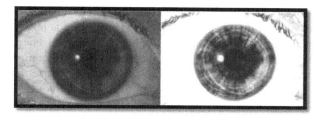

Fig. 9. Original and resulting contrast enhanced image.

II. Avilla and Snchez's Method

Dependent upon template-based strategies, the methodology (De Martin-Roche et al. 2001) is close to the Daugman's process in drawing upon a grey-scale image and applying the histogram stretch, emphasizing towards the intensity of the separation. Once the histogram is stretched, the image is gridded in concluding pixels with the lowest intensities to be considered the centre point for further searches. To conclude, the maximum of the differences relative to the five circumferences is calculated in regard to the next radius. The methodology is considered twice in relation to the image domain towards concluding the outer and the inner ring of the iris in terms of:

$$\sum_m \left(\sum_{k=1}^{5} \left(I_{n,m} - I_{n-k,m} \right) \right) \tag{2}$$

and

$$I_{i,j} = I(x_0 + i\Delta_r \cos(j\Delta_\theta), y_0 + i\Delta_r \sin(j\Delta_\theta)) \tag{3}$$

wherein (x_0, y_0) is the centre point for the gridding, Δ_θ and Δ_r constitute the changes of the angles and the radius, while $I_{i,j}$ is the grey scale image at location of i and j. The prior methodologies are expressed in terms of N^3 spaces relative to the tri-circular parameters under consideration, the x and y axis are related to the radius r. This has a direct link with the time for the iris to be segmented in relation to the size of the image (the larger the size of the image, the slower the segmentation process).

III. Camus and Wildes Method

Camus and Wildes (2002) proposed an iris segmentation for the subjects' iris from up close like that adopted within the Daugman process by maximizing the summation of directional derivation. The algorithm searches within the N^3 spaces relative to the circumferential parameters of the centre (x, y) and the radius, r, can reflect in maximizing the functions in terms of:

$$max_{r,x_0,y_0} = \sum_{\theta=1}^{n} \left((n-1)g_{\theta,r} - \sum_{\emptyset=\theta+1}^{n} \left(\|g_{\theta,r} - g_{\emptyset,r}\| \right) - \frac{g_{\theta,r}}{n} \right) \tag{4}$$

Herein, n is the discrete values relative to the polar variable of θ and $g_{\theta,r}$ constitutes the directional derivative with regard to the radius. The process is initially divided into three stages, named: specularity filling, seed point selection and boundary representation. In terms of specularity filling; this contributes towards minimizing specular reflections in consideration of high intensity pixels valuing greater than 250. In the subsequent seed point selection stage, the centre point and radius of the pupil is considered relative to the location of the local minima intensity pixels within the application of the formulae in the iris. At the concluding stage, the boundary of the process is drawn relative to the centre and the radius. The process is relatively effective for images considered to be derived where the pupil and the intensity of the iris is clearly observable in relation to the sclera, and where the images have minimal noise reflections. Alternatively, the overall accuracy of the algorithm is degraded.

IV. Wildes Method

The Wildes method (Wildes 1997) performs iris segmentation using circular contours fitting in two stages. In first stage, it applies Canny edge detector to the input image creating an edge map for the image. In the second stage, the circular Hough transform is applied on the resulting binary edge map in which or a specific contour for every edge point is chosen to instantiate radius and centre coordinate values that satisfy the following equation.

$$x = a + R\cos\theta \qquad (5)$$

$$y = b + R\sin\theta \qquad (6)$$

Where (a, b) represent the centre of coordinates, R is the radius and θ shapes a circle.

The method of edge map detection involves the construction of a map using the gradient-based canny edge detector to consolidate directional selection. Varieties of orientations are created through the grey scale image intensity. As shown in Fig. 10, the edge points are extracted in horizontal, vertical and diagonal directions.

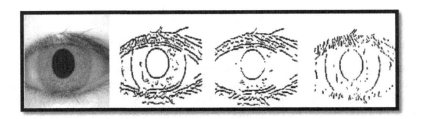

Fig. 10. Edge map

More development for the detection of upper and lower eyelids arcs is proposed by the horizontal points, whereas in the vertical edge map the edge points are suitable for the detection of sclera, iris and pupil circles.

For circular parameters (centre, radius), each point from the vertical edge map chooses the Hough space for iris-sclera and iris-pupil detection, where the edge point works as a focal point for a circle with increasing radius. As demonstrated in Fig. 11, the point that have highest number of circumferences intersection will signify the circle centre and the radius will be signified as the distance between the detected centre and the extracted edge points that forms the circumferences. The parabolic Hough transform is used onto the horizontal edge map with arcs parameter rather than circular parameters for the detection of the upper and lower eyelids, as seen bellow:

$$(-(x - hj)sin\,\theta j + (y - kj)cos\,\theta j)2 = aj((x - hj)cos\,\theta j + (y - kj)sin\,\theta j) \qquad (7)$$

Where the curvature controlled by aj, and θj is the rotation angle and (hj, kj) is the peak of parabola.

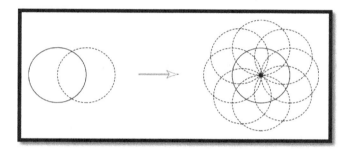

Fig. 11. Edge detection

V. Proenca Method UBIRIS.v1

Proenca and Alexandre in (2006) were proposed an iris segmentation method using moments function, clustering, Canny edge detection and circular Hough transform, as shown in Fig. 12. The proposed technique was the first effective method that could segment noisy iris images such as images of UBIRIS dataset, which have some level of noise.

The feature extraction step is the first stage of the Proenca and Alexandre's method. In this stage a moment texture segmentation algorithm proposed by Tuceryan (1992) is applied on the input image and the image moments over the image intensity domain are calculated in small size windows as a texture features. For every pixel from the input image, the compound moment offers three distinct features, where (x, y) signifies the pixel position and $I(x, y)$ signifies pixel intensity. The moment computed over the image intensity domain is characterized as:

$$M_{pq} = \left(\sum_{-\frac{w}{2}}^{\frac{w}{2}} \left(\sum_{-\frac{w}{2}}^{\frac{w}{2}} (I(m, n) x_m^p y_n^q) \right) \right) \qquad (8)$$

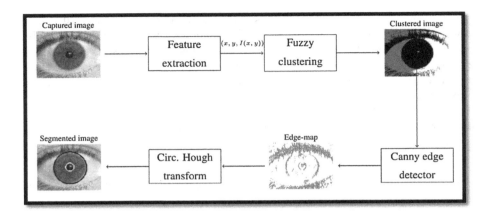

Fig. 12. A block diagram of the Proenca and Alexandre iris segmentation method (Proenca 2006)

Where, $I(m, n)$ is the pixel intensity, (x, y) are the moment windows' width and coordinate and Mpq is the geometric moments of p and q. The author calculates the average of the hyperbolic tangent for all moment functions to focus the discriminating limit between these regular order geometric moments as it follows:

$$F_{pq}(i,j) = \frac{1}{L^2} \sum_{(a,b)\in w_{ij}} \left(tanh\left(\sigma\left(M_{pq}(a,b) - \overline{M}\right)\right)\right) \tag{9}$$

Where, σ is the controller parameter for the logistic function shape, w_{ij} variable is the average window at (i, j) centre location and F_{pq} is the feature image for all moments with M mean.

To create a moderate image that has variety of intensities, which are smaller than the input image variety of intensities, Proenca and Alexandre were used the Fuzzy K-Means as clustering algorithm for discrimination between the pixels that are a part of iris region and the pixels that are a part of the rest of the eye regions. The Fuzzy K-Means can be characterized as:

$$J_{fuz} = \sum_{i=1}^{c} \left(\sum_{j=1}^{n} \left(\hat{P}\left(w_i|x_j, \hat{\theta}\right)^P \|x_j - \mu_i\|^2 \right)\right) \tag{10}$$

Where value P adjusts the blending of the clusters, μ_i represent the value of cluster. As in Fig. 13, the resulting image from the second stages is a moderate image with negligible range of intensity.

After the clustering step, to create edge map image from the resulting clustered image the canny edge detector will be applied on the clustered image that is less penetrating to light reflection noise and obstruction of eyelashes and eyelids. Finally, the circular Hough transform is used to determine the inner and outer iris rings.

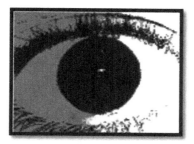

Fig. 13. Clustered image

2.2.2   Iris Image Normalization

In Normalization stage, the circular shape Cartesian coordinate iris image is converted into polar coordinate of the predefined rectangular size so that a more accurate matching can be done, as shown in Fig. 14. The distance at which the image is captured and type of the light sources cause a discrepancy in the dimension of the iris and the pupil to dilate. Several methods for performing the normalization process have been presented in the literature. Amongst the proposed methods, Wildes image registration (Wildes 1997) and Daugman rubber sheet model (Daugman 1993) are the most commonly used methods for iris image normalization.

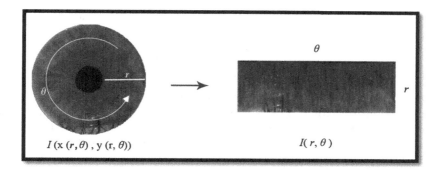

Fig. 14. Rubber sheet

Daugman Rubber-Sheet

The segmented circular shape portion of the iris can be converted into dimensionless pseudo-polar coordinates using Homogenous Rubber Sheet Model (Daugman 1993). In this method instead of drawing the pixels forming concentric circles in the iris image which moves from the outer circle and reaches the pupil ring after moving along the iris, the pixels are to be kept in a linear pattern as in a rectangle after obtaining the pixels from the oval-shaped iris; this process has been illustrated in Fig. 14. This is achieved by obtaining the pixels from the first upper ring at 360° and plotting them in a straight line and then carrying out the same process by decreasing the diameter by one after each linear plotting (Daugman 2004a, 2004b). Therefore, the rectangle shape will have a width (θ) of 360 and height of difference radius size of the iris and the pupil (r), as formulated in the following:

$$x(r, \theta) = (1 - r)x_p(\theta) + rx_i(\theta) \qquad (11)$$

$$y(r, \theta) = (1 - r)y_p(\theta) + ry_i(\theta) \qquad (12)$$

where $I(x, y)$ is the iris image region, (x, y) is the Cartesian coordinates of the pixels, (r, θ) is polar coordinates, (xp, yp) and (xi, yi) are the coordinates of the outer and inner rings.

The next step of process is image registration. The main duty of the image registration is the calibration since the located iris cannot carry on the code for immediate iris image localization. This process adjusts each image to the same corresponding position and size by normalization (Wildes 1997). It warps the acquired image $(Ia(x, y))$ into alignment with a selected image $(Id(x, y))$ from the dataset the mapping function $(u(x, y), v(x, y))$ to transform the original coordinates. The image intensity values at $(x, y) - (u(x, y), v(x, y))$ in Ia are made to be close to those to (x, y) in Id then mapping function (u, v) chosen to minimize the error function:

$$err = \iint_{xy} (I_d(x, y) - I_a(x - u, y - u))^2 dx dy \qquad (13)$$

It captures a similarity transformation of image coordinates (x, y) to (x', y') that is

$$\begin{pmatrix} x' \\ y' \end{pmatrix} = \begin{pmatrix} x \\ y \end{pmatrix} - sR_{(\emptyset)} \begin{pmatrix} x \\ y \end{pmatrix} \qquad (14)$$

Where $R_{(\emptyset)}$ is a matrix representing the rotation, where $\emptyset$ and s are the scaling factor. The normalized iris images will still have some noise like low contrast and non-uniform illumination because of the position and light source intensity. In order to remove noise from the iris image, an image enhancement process is used. Junzhou et al. (2004) were proposed a method to remove reflection noise from the image by detecting high intensity valued region near 255 and eliminates the region by setting a threshold. For minimizing the noise due to non-uniform illumination Li et al. (2002) were suggested to use a local histogram on the normalized iris template.

Other methods for reducing the effect of noise on iris segmentation include the use of histogram equalization through edge detection, which was proposed by Wildes (1997), and using Gaussian low-pass filter for image enhancement that was proposed in Li et al. (2004). All above mentioned iris segmentation method use NIR eye images, which is less noisy in comparison to images captured under visible light sources. However, the strength of the iris recognition system can be improved by pre-processing the input image when visible wavelength light source is present. The determinations of different noises have been carried out recently using a new technique given by Proenca and Alexandre (2006); the noises are then classified into five different groups namely as it is illustrated in Fig. 15: eyelashes, specular reflection, eyelids and pupil light reflection.

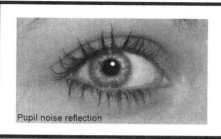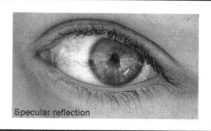

Pupil noise reflection   Specular reflection

Fig. 15. Light reflection (Photo MA 2009) (Anon 2010)

2.2.3 Feature Extraction

In the procedure of feature extraction, texture analysis methods are used to create a well-matched biometric template by extracting special features, like smooth, bumpy, silky or rough regions from normal iris image. In this process, several methods are used to normalize image in order to get appropriate features that can be used in the matching phase.

(a) **Gabor Filter**

Gabor filter is a linear function, which is appropriate for texture discrimination and representation. It is the result of the application of a mother wavelet for edge detection. 2D Gabor filter is characterized by multiplying the harmonic function with the Gaussian function: every pixel in the normalized image is regulated into two pits of binary code in the resulting iris template, which will be used in the template matching phase (Lim and Oppenheim 1981).

(b) **Wavelet Transform**

Wavelet transform splits the normalized iris area into space and frequency components with different resolutions. Iris image features are localized using wavelet transform, which is a set of low pass and high pass filters. Daubechies, Haar, Biorthogonal, Mexican Hat wavelet (Kocer and Allahverdi 2008) are the wavelets that have been used in various iris segmentation systems (Poursaberi and Araabi 2007).

(c) **Laplacian of Gaussian Filter**

The Laplacian of Gaussian filter disintegrate the iris image into a scrutinize form of image known as Laplacian pyramid. A series of Gaussian filters are then implemented on the resulting image to encode the iris features.

(d) **Key Local Variations**

Key local variation method is used to obtain the features and constitute the normalized iris image into a 1D intensity signals. Afterwards, to tally the prominent differences of the signal intensity, Dyadic wavelet transform is used. The resulting least points are encoded into a feature vector, which are then transformed into a binary template (Li et al. 2004).

(e) **Hilbert Transform**

The data from the iris texture is excerpted in Hilbert transform (Christel et al. 2002). This method relies upon the frequencies obtained from the iris image. The securitized frequency is modelled from instantaneous phase, called 'Emergent Frequency' and feature vectors are obtained from initiating the emergent frequency.

(f) **Discrete Cosine Transform (DCT)**

The encoding of the iris image in DCT is obtained by computing the variations in discrete cosine values (Monro et al. 2007). The normalized picture is partitioned into 8×12 patches and general width of the patch is windowed to shadow the image's features. The employing zero crossing method and the variation in discrete cosine coefficient are calculated to make a binary template.

(g) **Structure Preserving Projection – Maximum Margin Criterion**

This method was proposed in Li (2015). It integrates a Structure Preserving Projection (SPP) with the Maximum Margin Criterion (MMC) to extract iris features. This method creates a low-dimensional subspace of the iris data by limiting the dimension of sub-modes while the main iris information remains unchanged.

2.2.4   Template Matching

By using various matching algorithms, the template obtained from the iris feature extraction ought to be contrasted with the system dataset to find correspondence between two templates i.e. inter-class and intra-class.

Hamming Distance

Hamming distance measures the distance between two binary codes from the binary image template. A value close to 0.5 signifies two autonomous irises and a value close to 0 signifies an impeccable match. The quick matching procedure is the primary point of preference of Hamming distance. This is because it operates over a binary template with X-OR comparison.

Weighted Euclidean Distance

In the integer image template, this measures the distance between the two integer values.

Normalized Correlation

In a normalized iris region, the normalized correlation measures the distance between two points i.e. a pixel or a dot.

Nearest Feature Line

Two feature points of the same class are chosen and for the matching stage, nearest feature line of the chosen feature points will be employed.

Summary of Iris Recognition Systems

Uniqueness of the rich texture of an eye makes the iris recognition systems high-rank topic in both research and practical applications. As described, the researchers are trying to improve reliability and accuracy of the systems by different methods. Not only noises and system failure are challenging part of the iris recognition systems but also they are not completely spoof-proof. A fake iris can easily distract and spoof an iris recognition system. Therefore, the fake iris detection is the first step needs to be concerned.

3 Iris Recognition

The biometric recognition systems are, however, considered vulnerable to the fake copies which may be formed (Daugman 2004a, 2004b). For instance, the finger tips could be made of clay and gelatine which are available in the market. The same case lies with the iris system where a potential threat is existent. These potential threats may be the following (Daugman 1999, 2003a, 2003b)

1. Natural eye (user): Forced use
2. Capture/replay attacks: Eye image, Iris Code
3. Natural eye (impostor): Eye removed from body, Printed contact lens
4. Artificial eye: Glass/plastic etc.
5. Eye image: Screen image, Photograph, Paper print, Video signal

Some researchers have studied the feasibility of some of the attacks that have taken place (Lee et al. 2005). They believe that it is possible to make use of printed iris, photo iris (Fig. 16) and well-made colour iris lens to deceive the iris recognition systems. It is essential to be able to distinguish the fake iris from the real one. Various fake iris detection techniques have been proposed by researchers:

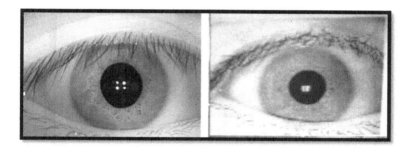

Fig. 16. Captured image (L), Printed image (R)

Daugman Method

The Fast Fourier Transform was introduced by Daugman in his previous research to test the printed iris pattern (Daugman 2004a, 2004b) (Daugman 2003a, 2003b). Within the frequency domain, the high frequency spectral magnitude is detected through his method. It is displayed in a period and distinct based on the periodic dot printing characteristics from the printed iris pattern. The counterfeit iris would be considered the live one if the input counterfeit iris is blurred and defocused on purpose. The counterfeit iris detection method was proposed by an iris camera manufacturer as well where he suggested that the illuminator must be turned off or on and upon the cornea, the specular reflection must be checked. This kind of method may however be spoofed at any time since a printed iris image could be developed, the printed pupil region could be cut off and seen using the eye of the attacker. All this activity would lead to the development of a corneal specular reflection.

Wavelet Packet Transform and SVM

Another fake iris detection method was proposed by authoress (He et al. 2009) who makes use of the wavelet packet transform and the SVM. This method is able to effectively detect the iris that is paper printed. The features can be extracted using the wavelet packet transform and the fake iris can be distinguished from the real using the SVM. In feature extraction step, for the hierarchical decomposing functions, the mathematical tool used is the wavelet transform. The wavelet transform has been generalized by forming the Wavelet Packets Transform (WPT). Through this generalization, a rich signal analysis is attained that allows zooming into the required frequency channels to carry out decomposition further (Laine and Fan 1993). For the WPT decomposition part, four output sub-images are formed. These sub-images consist of approximation (A), diagonal detail (D), vertical detail (V) and horizontal detail (H) coefficients respectively. For example, within a 2-level WPT, a single image consists of a quad tree with 20 output sub-images. The output sub-images have their own different frequency channels which can be observed in Fig. 17. Hence, the wavelet packet analysis is able to use the source image information much more as compared to the wavelet analysis. For feature extraction, the sub-images which do not have approximation are the suitable candidates.

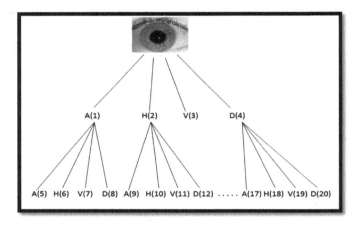

Fig. 17. The structure of WPT (He et al. 2009)

A fake iris feature extraction method has been stated by making use of the WPT. Using the WPT, the n-level coefficients of decomposition parts of iris image a used for feature extraction as part of the proposed scheme. The middle and high frequency channels consist of difference in the live and fake irises. However, for the discrimination, only the horizontal (H), diagonal (D) and vertical detail (V) coefficients are chosen. The WPT is used to decompose the iris image into n levels that formed 4^n components from the structure of the wavelet packet tree. High frequency decomposition is present within the iris feature vector and not the low frequency. For example, 18 sub-images are present for n which equal to 2 and this does not include

A(5) and A(1). The m-dimensional iris feature vector is formed through the standard deviation of the sub-images.

$$V = [std_1, std_2, std_3, \ldots, std_m]^T \tag{15}$$

where $std_i(i = 1, 2, \ldots, m)$ represents deviation of i sub iris image.

There are some issues in the iris pattern recognition which can be solved through the newly proposed technique SVM (Burges 1998). This technique was developed to cater to two class issues. The pattern recognition between two classes is carried out through the extraction of a decision surface which is stated by the specific training set points referred to as the Support Vectors (SV). The decision surface is also contain the maximum difference present between two classes. Hence, the fake iris classification is carried out through SVM.

The iris image is presented as the feature vector using m as the length after the feature extraction takes place. The classification carried out by SVM makes use of the features that have been extracted. In the method, the SVM function Radial Basis Functions (RBF) kernel function is used as the following.

$$K = (x, x_i) = exp\left\{ -\frac{|x - x_i|^2}{\sigma^2} \right\} \tag{16}$$

where:

- xi is the input features.
- σ is the standard deviation of the RBF kernel

The SVM texture classifier input is attained through feature vector of length m. The iris class is presented by the SVM output sign. The live iris class was assigned +1 for training purposes and the fake iris class was provided with −1. Hence, a live iris is present if the SVM output is positive for an input pattern.

Purkinje Image

Lee et al. in (Lee et al. 2005) proposed a method by using collimated IR-LED based on the Purkinje image. In this process, Daugman method is used to calculate the input image focus value (Daugman 2004a, 2004b). The predefined threshold is maintained at 50 and if the calculated focus value exceeds this amount, the iris recognition is carried out and the input image is focused as one. On the other hand, if the focus value is lesser, the iris image will be captured again by the system until the time recognition takes place of the focused image. When the completion of the user identification is done, the two 'collimated IR-LEDs' are turned on by the system in an alternative manner. A smaller illumination angle is present for a collimated IR-LED as compared to the conventional IR-LED in the case of iris recognition. Between the eye and camera, the Z- distance can be measured using the one of the collimated IR-LEDs. The other would then be used for the formation of the Purkinje image. Two images can be obtained if the two 'collimated IR-LEDs' are turned on in an alternative manner and become synchronized with the image frame. Using the 760 nm and 880 nm IR-LED a bright iris image is then captured which also helps detect the pupil ranges and the iris present within the image. Furthermore, the Z-distance is measured between the eye and the camera lens. This helps calculate a theoretical distance present amongst the Purkinje images. Using the Purkinje image model and Z-distance, the three Purkinje image searching boxes can be stated in Fig. 18.

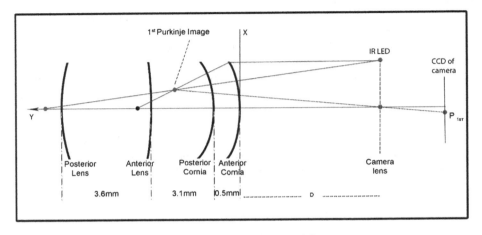

Fig. 18. The Parkinje model

The Gullstrand eye scheme helps attain the Purkinje image model (Gullstrand 1924). Processing time can be reduced by extracting the Purkinje images from the searching boxes. The 1st, 2nd and 4th Purkinje images are then detected from the searching boxes. Now it must be checked if the 1st and 2nd Purkinje images are present within the iris area searching box. This is because the system is configured with the collimated IR-LED and the iris region would contain the 1st and 2nd Purkinje images. Hence, it must also be assessed if the searching box of the pupil area contains the 4th Purkinje image. This 4th Purkinje image would be present in the pupil region as the system is configured with the collimated IR-LED. The input image is determined as the live iris and the user accepts it. However, if it is not, the input image would be determined as the fake iris. To practice the new method, the author (Lee et al. 2005) has used the conventional USB camera with CCD sensor with removed IR-cut. Two collimated IR-LEDs (760 and 880 nm) with 2.9° has been used. Four optical surfaces are present within the conventional human eye and each of these is expected to reflect bright light. It would be front and back surface of the lens and the cornea. The Purkinje images states the 4 reflected images present of the incident light upon each optical surface. The light sources geometry indicates the four Purkinje reaction images (Kording et al. 2001). The Gullstrand eye model is used to design the Purkinje image shaping model presented in Fig. 19 (Gullstrand 1924).

The Daugman method consists of several vulnerabilities when the Purkinje images are used. To resolve these issues, the Purkinje image shaping model must be considered. It is possible to attain the Purkinje images theoretical distances since the Gullstrand eye model has been used to design the model. The human eye model determines such distances and this model includes the lens, cornea diameter, refraction rate etc. The fake and live iris rates have different distances. The fake iris cannot be made using the Purkinje images which have the same distance to the live eye since the live iris and fake iris have different material characteristics. These characteristics are once again the diameter of lens and cornea, refraction rate etc. The method which helps calculate the Purkinje image theoretical distances is shown in Fig. 19.

Also, in Fig. 18, for each optical surface, the focal length and radius is shown (anterior cornea, posterior cornea, anterior lens, posterior lens).

The convex mirror reflection helps shape the 1st, 2nd and 3rd Purkinje image. At this point of time, these images are erect and virtual. The concave mirror is used to reflect the shape of the 4th Purkinje image. For the 4th image, it can be said that it is real and inverted. Hence, it is known that a symmetric position is present for the 1st and 2nd Purkinje images and within the centre of the iris is 4th Purkinje image. The anterior lens can be used to make the 3rd Purkinje image. The image does not show the 3rd Purkinje image since this image occurs behind the iris position when observed from a camera. The environmental light is used to change the size of pupil. The pupil size becomes smaller as the light becomes stronger. In the present case, the size of the pupil is smallest (2 mm) as a collimated IR-LED is used and it enters the pupil area. There is enlargement of the iris area and the iris area that is captured by the eye image hides the 3rd Purkinje image. It now cannot be observed.

Furthermore, the distance between the 1st, 2nd and 4th Purkinje images can be calculated through the proposed method in a theoretical manner. Convex mirror models can be supposed for the surfaces of anterior and posterior corneas as observed in Fig. 18. The concave mirror model can be used for the surfaces of posterior lens. Hence, the camera lens model can be used (Conzalez n.d.).

4 Conclusions

Biometric recognition systems have been used for identifying individuals in past years. Amongst biometric recognition system, iris recognition systems seem to be the most reliable one to be used. However, there are many challenges need to be solved to improve the robustness of these systems. Iris recognition systems like any other vision based systems are very sensitive to noise. Massive research and developments have been done to make iris recognition system robust to noise such as using NIR images, pre-processing algorithms and developing techniques to suppress the effect of noise in iris segmentation, iris feature extraction and iris template matching. However, due to the nature of the iris much more research needs to be done to speed up the iris recognition process and also to make it robust to noise.

References

Camus, T.A., Wildes, R.: Reliable and fast eye finding in close-up images. Pattern Recogn. **1**, 389–394 (2002)
Addleton, D.G.: Securityinfowatch (2012). http://www.securityinfowatch.com/article/10796789/fact-fiction-or-future-reality. Accessed 13 Mar 2016

Alexandra, L.A., Proenqa, H.: Toward non cooperative iris recognition: a classification approach using multiple signatures. Trans. Pattern Anal. Mach. Intell. **29**, 607–612 (2007)

Proenca, H., Alexandre, L.A.: A method for the identification of noisy regions in normalized iris images. In: Pattern Recognition, ICPR 2006, pp. 405–408 (2006)

Allahverdi, N., Kocer, E.: An efficient iris recognition system based on modular neural network. ETRI, **23** (2008)

Alrifaee, A., Hsuuien, M.M.: Unconstrained Iris Recognition. De Montfort University, Leicester (2014)

Anon: Print24 (2010). http://print24.com/blog/2010/11/tutorial-beaming-eyes-with-photoshop/. Accessed 15 Mar 2016

Anon: Medical dictionary (2011). http://medicine.academic.ru/17247/collarette. Accessed 2015

Bashir, F., Casaverde, P., Usher, D., Friedman, M.: Eagle-eyes: a system for iris recognition at a distance, pp. 426–431 (2008)

Bath: Irisbase (2007). http://www.smartsensors.co.uk/irisweb/. Accessed 2014

Boles, W., Boashash, B.: A human identification technique using images of the iris and wavelet transform. Trans. Signal Process. **46**, 1185–1188 (1998)

Bowyer, K.W., Hollingsworth, K., Flynn, P.J.: Image understanding for iris biometrics: a survey. Comput. Vis. Image Underst. **110**, 281–307 (2008)

Boyce, C., et al.: Multispectral iris analysis: a preliminary study, Morgantown (2006)

Burges, C.: A tutorial on support vector machines for pattern recognition. Data Min. Knowl. Disc. **2**, 955–974 (1998)

Christel, et al.: Person identification technique using human iris recognition. In: Vision Interface, pp. 294–299 (2002)

Clover, J.: MacRumors (2014). http://www.macrumors.com/2014/01/21/apple-iris-scanning/. Accessed 20 Sept 2015

Conzalez, R.C.: Digital Image Processing, 2nd edn. Prentice Hall, n.d

Cui, J., et al.: A fast and robust iris localization method based on texture segmentation. In: SPIE Defense and Security Symposium, vol. 5405, pp. 401–408 (2004)

Daugman, J.: Recognizing persons by their iris patterns: countermeasures against subterfuge. In: Personal Identification in a Networked Society, pp. 103–121 (1999)

Daugman, J.: Demodulation by complex-valued wavelets for stochastic pattern recognition. Wavelets Multiresolut. Inf. Process., 1–17 (2003a)

Daugman, J.: The importance of being random: statistical principles of iris recognition. Pattern Recogn., 279–291 (2003b)

Daugman, J.: How iris recognition works. Circ. Syst. Video Technol., 21–30 (2004a)

Daugman, J.: Iris recognition and anti-spoofing countermeasures, London (2004b)

Daugman, J.: New methods in iris recognition. Trans. Syst. Man Cybern. Part B **37**, 1167–1175 (2007)

Daugman, J.G.: High confidence visual recognition of persons by a test of statistical independence. Trans. Pattern Anal. Mach. Intell. **15**, 1148–1161 (1993)

De Martin-Roche, D., Sanchez-Avila, C., Sanchez-Reillo, R.: Iris recognition for biometric identification using dyadic wavelet transform zero-crossing. In: Security Technology. IEEE (2001)

Dovey, D.: Medicaldaily (2015). http://www.medicaldaily.com/blue-eyed-individuals-are-more-likely-be-alcoholics-coincidence-or-evidence-alcoholic-340780. Accessed 13 Mar 2016

Drewes, D.J.: Indreanilsinbaroy (2014). http://indranilsinharoy.com/2014/12/05/dissertation_series/. Accessed 13 Mar 2016

Feng, X., Ding, X., Wu, Y., Wang, P.: Classifier combination and its application in iris recognition. Int. J. Pattern Recogn. Artif. Intell. **22**, 617–638 (2008)

Grabowski, K., Sankowski, M., Napieralska, M.: Illumination influence on iris identification algorithms. In: 15th International Conference on Mixed Design of Integrated Circuits and Systems (2008)

Grabowski, K., Sankowski, W., Zubert, M., Napieralska, M.: Reliable iris localization method with application to iris recognition in near infrared light. In: International Conference on Mixed Design of Integrated Circuits and System (2006)

Gullstrand, A.: Helmholz's Physiological Optics, pp. 350–358. Optical Society of America, Rochester (1924)

Junzhou, H., Wang, Y., Tan, T., Cui, J.: A new iris segmentation method for recognition. In: 7th International Conference on Pattern Recognition (2004)

Hanho, S., Jaekyung, L., Jihyun, P., Yillbyung, L.: Iris recognition using collarette boundary localization, vol. 4, pp. 857–860 (2004)

Hosseini, M.S., Araabi, B.N., SoltanianZadeh, H.: Iris recognition for partially occluded images: methodology and sensitivity analysis, 71 (2007)

Shen, W., Khanna, R.: Prolog to iris recognition: an emerging biometric technology, vol. 85, p. 1347 (1997)

Kong, W., Zhang, D.: Accurate iris segmentation based on novel reflection and eyelash detection model. In: International Symposium on Intelligent Multimedia (2001)

Kording, K.P., Kayser, C., Betsch, B.Y., Koing, P.: Non-contact eye-tracking on cats (2001)

Labati, R., Piuri, V., Scotti, F.: Agent-based image iris segmentation and multiple views boundary refining. In: Theory, Applications, and Systems, pp. 1–7 (2009)

Laine, A., Fan, J.: Texture classification by wavelet packet signatures, pp. 1186–1191 (1993)

Lee, E.C., Park, K.R., Kim, J.: Fake iris detection by using Purkinje image. In: Zhang, D., Jain, A.K. (eds.) ICB 2006. LNCS, vol. 3832, pp. 397–403. Springer, Heidelberg (2005). doi:10.1007/11608288_53

Lim, J.S., Oppenheim, A.V.: The importance of phase in signals. **69**, 529–541 (1981)

Lim, S., Lee, K., Byeon, O., Kim, T.: Efficient iris recognition through improvement of feature vector and classifier. ETRI **23**, 61–70 (2001)

Li, M., Tieniu, T., Yunhong, W., Dexin, Z.: Efficient iris recognition by characterizing key local variations. Trans. Image Process. **13**, 739–750 (2004)

Li, M., Yunhong, W., Tieniu, T.: Iris recognition using circular symmetric filters. Pattern Recogn. **2**, 414–417 (2002)

Li, X.: WVU iris database (2007). http://www.csee.wvu.edu/~xinl/demo/nonideal_iris.html. Accessed 2015

Li, Y.: Iris recognition algorithm based on MMC-SPP. Image Process. Pattern Recogn. **8**(2), 1–10 (2015)

Masek, L.: Iris Recognition, Western Australia (2003)

Matey, J.R., et al.: Iris on the move: acquisition of images for iris recognition in less constrained environments, vol. 94, pp. 1936–1937 (2006)

Minaee, S., Abdolrashidi, A.: Highly accurate multispectral palmprint recognition using statistical and wavelet features (2015)

MMU: Pesona (2010). http://pesona.mmu.edu.my/~ccteo/. Accessed 2014

Monro, D.M., Rakshid, S., Dexin, Z.: DCT-Based iris recognition. Pattern Anal. Mach. Intell. **29**, 586–595 (2007)

More, M., Nagrale, V., Tonge, V.: A survey on iris recognition techniques. **2**(1), 89–94 (2015)

NIST: ICE - Iris Challenge Evaluation (2011). http://www.nist.gov/itl/iad/is/ice.cfm. Accessed 2015

Noh, S., Pae, K., Lee, C., Kim, J.: Multiresolution independent component analysis for iris identification, Phuket, Thailand (2002) jw Photo MA: Flicker (2009). https://www.flickr.com/photos/jwphotoma/3958111613. Accessed 15 Mar 2016

Poursaberi, A., Araabi, N.: Iris recognition for partially occluded images: methodology and sensitivity analysis (2007)

Prabhakar, S., et al.: Introduction to the special issue on biometrics: progress and directions. pp. 513–516 (2007)

Proenca, H.P.M.C.: Non-Cooperative Biometric Iris Recognition. University of Beria Interior, Covilha (2006)

Proenqa, H.: On the feasibility of the visible wavelength, at-a-distance and on-the-move iris recognition. In: IEEE Workshop on Computational Intelligence in Biometrics: Theory, Algorithms, and Applications, Issue CIB, pp. 9–15 (2009)

Proenqa, H.: Iris recognition: on the segmentation of degraded images acquired in the visible wavelength. Trans. Pattern Anal. Mach. Intell. **32**, 1502–1516 (2010)

Ritter, N., Owens, R., Cooper, J., Van Saarloos, P.: Location of the pupil-iris border in slit-lamp images of the cornea. In: Image Analysis and Processing, pp. 740–745 (1999)

SOCIA Lab: UBIRIS (2010). http://iris.di.ubi.pt/. Accessed 2015

Tajbakhsh, N., Misaghian, K., Bandari, N.M.: A region-based iris feature extraction method based on 2D-wavelet transform. In: Fierrez, J., Ortega-Garcia, J., Esposito, A., Drygajlo, A., Faundez-Zanuy, M. (eds.) BioID_MultiComm 2009. LNCS, vol. 5707, pp. 301–307. Springer, Heidelberg (2009). doi:10.1007/978-3-642-04391-8_39

Tan, T.T.: BIT. CASIA Iris Image Database (2010). http://biometrics.idealtest.org/. Last Accessed July 2014, Accessed 2015

Tay, Y., Mok, K.: A review of iris recognition algorithms. In: International Symposium on Information Technology, pp. 1–7 (2008)

Tiwari, U., Kelkar, D., Tiwari, A.: Iris recognition: study of different IRIS recognition methods, **2** (1) (2012)

Tuceryan, M.: Moment based texture segmentation. In: Image, Speech and Signal Analysis, pp. 45–48 (1992)

Vatsa, M., Singh, R., Noore, A.: Improving iris recognition performance using segmentation, quality enhancement, match score fusion, and indexing. Trans. Syst. Man Cybern. Part B **38**, 1021–1035 (2008)

Wei, Z., Tan, T., Sun, Z.: Nonlinear iris deformation correction based on Gaussian model. In: International Conference on Biometrics, pp. 780–789 (2007)

Wildes, R.P.: Iris recognition: an emerging biometric technology, vol. 85, pp. 1348–1363 (1997)

He, X., Lu, Y., Shi, P.: A new fake iris detection method. In: Tistarelli, M., Nixon, M.S. (eds.) ICB 2009. LNCS, vol. 5558, pp. 1132–1139. Springer, Heidelberg (2009). doi:10.1007/978-3-642-01793-3_114

Jeong, D.S., Park, H.-A., Park, K.R., Kim, J.: Iris recognition in mobile phone based on adaptive Gabor filter. In: Zhang, D., Jain, A.K. (eds.) ICB 2006. LNCS, vol. 3832, pp. 457–463. Springer, Heidelberg (2005). doi:10.1007/11608288_61

Zhi, Z., Yingzi, D., Belcher, C.: Transforming traditional iris recognition systems to work in nonideal situations. Trans. Ind. Electron. **56**, 3202–3213 (2009)

Automatic Clustering of Malicious IP Flow Records Using Unsupervised Learning

Muhammad Fahad Umer$^{(\boxtimes)}$ and Muhammad Sher

Department of Computer Science and Software Engineering,
Faculty of Basic and Applied Sciences, International Islamic University,
Islamabad, Pakistan
{fahad.phdcs62,m.sher}@iiu.edu.pk

Abstract. Anomaly based intrusion detection systems classify network traffic into normal and malicious categories. The intrusion detection system raises an alert when maliciousness is detected in the traffic. A security administrator inspects these alerts and takes corrective action to protect the network from intrusions and unauthorized access. Manual inspection of the alerts is also necessary because anomaly based intrusion detection systems have a high false positive rate. The alerts can be in very large number and their manual inspection is a challenging task. We propose an extension for anomaly based intrusion detection system which automatically groups malicious IP flows into different attack clusters. Our technique creates attack clusters from a training set of unlabeled IP flows using unsupervised learning. Every attack cluster consists of malicious IP flows which are similar to each other. We analyze IP flows in every cluster and assign an attack label to them. After the clusters are created, an incoming malicious IP flow is compared with all clusters and the label of the closest cluster is assigned to the IP flow. The intrusion detection system uses labeled flows to raise consolidated anomaly alert for a set of similar IP flows. This approach significantly reduces the overall number of alerts and also generates a high-level map of attack population. We use unsupervised learning techniques for automatic clustering of IP flows. Unsupervised learning is advantageous over supervised learning because the availability of a labeled training set for supervised learning is not always guaranteed. Three unsupervised learning techniques, k-means, self-organizing maps (SOM) and DBSCAN are considered for clustering of malicious IP flows. We evaluated our technique on a flow-based data-set containing different types of malicious flows. Experimental results show that our scheme gives good performance and places majority of the IP flows in correct attack clusters.

1 Introduction

Over the past decade, cyber attacks on computer networks have increased significantly. Intrusion detection systems are the core tool used for protection against cyber threats. Intrusion detection systems (IDS) analyze the log trails associated with the protected systems and decide whether these log trails contain traces of

© Springer International Publishing AG 2017
V. Chang et al. (Eds.): Enterprise Security, LNCS 10131, pp. 97–119, 2017.
DOI: 10.1007/978-3-319-54380-2_5

an attack or not. If the intrusion detection system detects an attack, it raises an alert. A human administrator or an automatic alert response system takes a corrective action based on the intrusion alert. Existing approaches for intrusion detection are broadly classified into two categories: misuse detection and anomaly detection (Liao et al. 2013). Misuse detection techniques use a signature database for detection of known attacks and malware. These techniques are very accurate and distinctly detect an attack with a very low false positive rate. Misuse detection systems already have detail information about all known attacks and no manual effort is required to determine the type and scale of attack. Most of the commercial intrusion detection products use misuse detection model (Wu and Banzhaf 2010).

Although commercially successful, misuse detection approaches have some drawbacks. These techniques are unable to detect zero-day attacks for which no signatures are yet available. Also when a new attack is discovered, all installations of the misuse based intrusion detection system need immediate signature update. Many sophisticated malware today use polymorphism which creates multiple variants of same malware. These variants easily bypass the signature comparison check in the misuse based intrusion detection system. To overcome these issues, intrusion detection systems use anomaly detection techniques to detect novel and unseen attacks. Anomaly based intrusion detection system learn normal network traffic behavior and use this knowledge to detect an abnormality (Garcia-Teodoro et al. 2009). The learning of traffic behavior can be supervised or unsupervised. Supervised learning uses a labeled training set, containing both normal and malicious examples, to train the algorithm until desired level of accuracy is achieved. After training, the algorithm process an incoming example to predict its class label. If the class label is malicious, the input example is classified as anomaly. Unsupervised learning does not use a labeled training set, instead it identifies statistical patterns in the data to create clusters. The algorithm calculates similarity of an incoming example with all clusters. If the similarity of input example and malicious traffic cluster is highest, then the algorithm declares the input example as anomaly. The anomaly based intrusion detection converts all anomalies into intrusion alerts and forward them to security administrator for corrective action. Anomaly based intrusion detection system have high detection rate than misuse based technique but they tend to produce many false positives.

Anomaly based intrusion detection systems are further classified into payload and flow based techniques (Alaidaros et al. 2011). In payload based techniques, the intrusion detection system analyzes the complete packet payload. This inspection is a type of strong packet filtration and has fine grain control over network traffic. These techniques can detect almost all types of network attacks because detail traffic information is available. However, payload inspection techniques have disadvantages which make them unsuitable for modern high-speed networks and cloud infrastructures (Golling et al. 2014). Inspection of complete packet payload is very difficult, if not possible, on high speed links where data is moving in gigabytes. In this case, intrusion detection system becomes a performance bottleneck (Husak et al. 2015). Also, payload inspection cannot be used if end-to-end encryption is implemented. Network level intrusion detection systems are unable to read anything from encrypted packet payload. Payload inspection also has legal implications due to privacy issues. The limitations of payload based intrusion detection techniques have shifted the focus of current research towards flow-based intrusion detection systems (Sperotto and Pras 2011).

Flow-based intrusion detection systems use IP flow records as input and decide if the flow of traffic is normal or malicious (Sperotto and Pras 2011). A flow is defined as a set of packets passing through an observation point in the network during a certain time interval. All packets belonging to an IP flow have similar attributes (Claise et al. 2013). An IP flow record, for instance, consists of attributes such as source and destination IP addresses, source and destination ports and the IP protocol number. The flow data is used for many purposes e.g. billing, traffic analysis, and congestion detection (Li et al. 2013). A flow export and collection protocol gathers flow data from the network using flow enabled devices and exports it in a flow record format. Almost all major vendors are now offering built-in flow collection and export support in their network hardware. Different flow collection and export protocols exist but Cisco Netflow has been the most popular. Other vendors also supported Netflow protocol but under different names like Netstream for HP and JFlow for Juniper. Internet Engineering Task Force (IETF) adopted Netflow and standardized it in the form of IP Flow Information Export (IPFIX) Protocol (Claise et al. 2013).

Flow-based intrusion detection systems only analyze IP flow records and no time-consuming packet payload inspection is performed. IP flow records contain aggregate packet information, and the size of flow packets are one the average equal to 0.1% of the network traffic. Whereas the network load measured in bytes, the overhead due to Netflow is on average 0.2% (Sperotto and Pras 2011). Therefore, flow-based intrusion detection is efficient than payload based detection. Flow-based techniques are not affected by the use of encryption for packet payload and have better intrusion detection rate (Amoli and Hamalainen 2013). At best, flow-based intrusion detection has near real-time response, low deployment cost and the ability to work in high-speed network environment (Golling et al. 2014). Flow-based inspection is well suited for intrusion detection layer in modern next generation networks (Koch 2011) and cloud infrastructures (Chang et al. 2016). Anomaly based intrusion detection systems, using either payload or flow level inspection, only classify network traffic as normal or malicious (Bolzoni et al. 2009). The intrusion detection system raises an alert when an anomaly is detected. However, the intrusion detection system does not provide additional information about the type of attack class. All these alerts are manually inspected to establish the validity of alert and to determine the attack type. On the basis of this information, the security administrator takes steps for any corrective action. Computer networks are a target of a wide range of attacks and every such attack requires different mitigation strategy (Hoque et al. 2014). Intrusion detection system raises a large number of alerts (Benferhat et al. 2013). In the absence of an automatic attack clustering system, it is difficult for a security administrator to manually inspect every alert and employ countermeasures.

This affects the overall usability of anomaly based intrusion detection system (Bolzoni et al. 2009). Therefore, structural organization of malicious traffic is required to reduce the number of alerts. A straight forward solution is to group similar malicious traffic together. A single alert can be generated for every set of malicious traffic. As a result, the overall number of alerts requiring manual inspection are reduced.

Bolzoni et al. (2009) has already proposed an automatic attack classification schemes for anomaly based intrusion detection systems. However, Bolzoni et al. (2009)'s technique uses payload inspection and supervised learning algorithms. In this paper, we propose an automatic attack clustering scheme for flow-based intrusion detection systems using unsupervised learning. Automatic clustering of malicious IP flows using unsupervised learning is a novel idea. Our scheme receives malicious IP flows from a flow-based intrusion detection system. We group similar malicious IP flows into different attack clusters. The flow-based intrusion detection system raises consolidated alert for every set of clustered IP flows instead of raising an alert for every malicious IP flow. We have used unsupervised learning for clustering therefore no labeled training set is required. Three unsupervised learning techniques k-means, self-organizing maps (SOM) and DBSCAN are considered. We have evaluated our technique on a realistic flow-based data-set. Experimental results show that our technique identifies all attack types in malicious IP and classify the majority of IP flows in correct attack clusters.

The remainder of this paper is organized as follows: Sect. 2 summarizes existing work related to the classification of malicious traffic and alert management. Section 3 gives an introduction to unsupervised learning techniques. We describe our proposed approach in Sect. 4. Experimental results are given in Sect. 5. Finally, the conclusion and future research direction are presented in Sect. 6.

2   Related Work

Numerous studies related to attack classification and alert management are presented in the literature. Bolzoni et al. (2009) proposed an automatic attack clustering technique, named Panacea, for packet-based intrusion detection systems. Panacea consists of two modules; Alert Information Extractor (AIE) and Attack clustering Engine (ACE). The AIE receives alerts from the intrusion detection system and extracts byte sequences from the alert packet payload. This information is sent to Attack clustering Engine (ACE) for clustering of attack packet. The clustering process has two main stages. First, the ACE is trained with several types of alert byte sequences to build a clustering model. The attack class information for training byte sequences is provided in several ways, either manually by an operator or automatically by extracting additional information from the original alert. When the training is complete, the ACE is ready to classify new incoming alerts automatically. The clustering engine uses Support Vector Machine (SVM) and RIPPER rule learner to group similar attack alerts together. Panacea is evaluated on alerts generated by Snort and promising results are obtained.

Rieck et al. (2011) have applied machine learning techniques for automatic clustering of malware. The proposed framework uses prototype based clustering and clustering algorithms to identify novel classes of malware and assigns unknown malware to the discovered classes. In the first step, the framework monitors malware behavior in a sandbox environment and generates a report of malware behavior. The malware reports are converted into vector space model. Machine learning clustering and clustering techniques are applied to the vector data for identification of novel and known malware classes. Using both, clustering and clustering, the behavior of malware can be analyzed incrementally. Two data sets of malware behavior have been used to evaluate the proposed framework. The first data-set consist of 24 known malware classes with 3133 reports of malware behavior. The second data-set contains 33,698 behavior reports with a unknown number of malware classes. Results show that clustering methods have F1-measure of 0.950 and classification methods have F1-measure of 0.981 and 0.997 for known and unknown malware classes respectively.

An alert correlation technique using Fuzzy Logic and Artificial Immune System (AIS) is proposed by Bateni et al. (2013). The system calculates the degree of correlation between two alerts and uses this knowledge to extract the attack scenarios. For each pair of input alerts, the system creates a feature vector which is matched with a set of Fuzzy rules. If it finds a matching rule with the value higher than the matching threshold, it uses the probability in that rule as the correlation probability of two alerts. If there is no matching rule with the required matching threshold, it uses the AIRS algorithm. AIRS algorithm is a supervised learning algorithm that uses a set of fuzzy rules as training set and discovers the relationships between the values of the features in the rules. The system can be converted to complete supervised learning system by setting the value of rule matching threshold to 1 and vice versa by setting it to 0. The system is evaluated on two data-sets, DARPA 2000 and netForensics honeynet data. Results show that average completeness and false alert rate for LLDoS1.0 attacks are 0.957 and 0.053 respectively. Average completeness and false alert rate for LLDoS2.0 attacks are 0.745 and 0.245 respectively.

Benferhat et al. (2013) proposed the use of expert knowledge in probabilistic Bayesian network classifiers for intrusion detection and alerts correlation. In this technique, a model for intrusion detection and alert correlation is learned using a training set. This model is used to determine malicious activities and validity of attack alerts. The authors argued that using expert knowledge has benefits when training data is insufficient or generates a large number of false negatives. Expert knowledge can be provided by a domain expert or is extracted from the probability distributions of the instances over attack class. A revised algorithm is proposed to modify the output of a probabilistic classifier with the use of available expert knowledge. The proposed technique is evaluation using two real network traffic data-sets and DARPA data-set. Results showed that performance of intrusion detection and alert correlation is improved with the use of expert knowledge.

Boukhtouta et al. (2015) presents a comprehensive evaluation of DPI and flow-based techniques for clustering of malware in network traffic. In flow-based detection, several supervised machine learning techniques including J48, Boosted J48, Naïve Bayesian, Boosted Naïve Bayesian, and SVM are used to identify malicious flows. Comparison between different algorithm results shows that J48 and boosted J48 perform better than other algorithms. Authors obtained a detection rate of 99% and a false positive rate of less than 1% for J48 and boosted J48 algorithms. In addition to detection of maliciousness of traffic, authors have used flows records for attribution of different malware families. The attribution process uses uni-directional IP flows through an iterative process to build Hidden Markov Models for every malware family. In deep packet inspection (DPI) based approach, machine learning techniques are applied on complete packet captures to fingerprint maliciousness. The DPI techniques performed well for less noisy malicious traffic.

A DDoS detection method based on the online processing of traffic time series using higher order F-transform is proposed in Hurtik et al. (2015). This approach extracts the relationship between traffic data to identify traffic patterns and detection of anomalies. The technique also determines the intensity of DDoS attack. A simulated data-set was used for evaluation which contained nine-classes with three classes for normal, slow and rapid attack categories. The proposed technique achieves a success rate of 100% and is also 166 times faster than naive approaches.

Yadav et al. (2015) propose a web attack clustering technique using the vector space model approach (VSMA). The vector space model converts a text document into real valued vectors based on the term frequencies (Umer and Khiyal 2007). Authors have converted HTTP requests into vector space data. The VSMA classifier has been evaluated on a data-set containing 250 malicious attacks including Redirecting URLs, script Injection, and XSS attacks. The VSMA classifier obtained 98% accuracy as compared to Naive bayes and Decision tree. Other approaches where authors have tried to determine the attack types are Haddadi et al. (2010) and Dharamkar and Singh (2014).

Review of literature shows that existing techniques suffer from a number of weaknesses such as use of payload inspection and requirement of labeled training set. Also the evaluation is carried out using non-representative old data-sets (e.g. DARPA) which are not relevant today. Our proposed technique differs from the existing work in a number of aspects. Instead of using an alert correlation or management system, we propose an additional internal component for intrusion detection system that automatically creates attack clusters of malicious traffic. Our technique is based on flow-based intrusion detection model therefore no payload inspection is performed. Also we use unsupervised learning algorithms for attack clustering therefore no labeled training data-set is required. We have evaluated our technique on a realistic flow-based data-set combined with IP flows of two well-known malware.

3   Unsupervised Learning Techniques

Unsupervised learning is an important feature of machine learning. Unsupervised learning techniques differ from supervised learning in the way that unsupervised learning does not require a labeled training set (Song et al. 2013). Unsupervised learning techniques derive their results using the statistical properties of data. Unsupervised learning techniques group a set of data examples in same dimension if they have similar statistical properties. Unsupervised learning has numerous application in machine learning because it is not always possible to obtain a labeled data-set for the training of algorithm (Hastie et al. 2009). In the case of intrusion detection, availability of labeled training set is also difficult. Use of unsupervised learning in intrusion detection has several advantages over supervised learning (Laskov et al. 2005).

Unsupervised learning techniques are divided into two categories; dimensionality reduction and clustering (Ghahramani 2004). Dimensionality reduction techniques map a set of examples from a high dimension feature space to low dimension feature space. The new features in low dimension space are not necessarily the same as those of original features in high dimension space. This process obtains a compact representation of data which is easy to process and analyze. Clustering techniques partition the data into different clusters such that distance between different clusters is maximized and the distance between a cluster boundary and its center is minimized. Clustering techniques discover new patterns in data which are not previously known.

Formally, clustering of input data X is defined as a set of k clusters $C = \{c_1, \ldots, c_k\}$ such that $X = \cup_{i=1}^{k}$. Every example in the data-set belongs to only one cluster where $C_i \cap C_j = \emptyset$ for $i \neq j$ (Rokach and Maimon 2005). Clustering techniques use a distance function (Euclidean distance, Manhattan distance) to calculate the similarity between different examples.

Main types of clustering algorithms include partitional, model and density based techniques (Xu and Tian 2015). Partitional clustering divides the data into different partitions where each partition represent a cluster (Jin and Han 2010). Partitional clustering algorithms include k-means and k-medoids. Model base clustering technique use a particular model for every cluster. An example becomes a part of the cluster if it fits the model. Model clustering algorithms include self-organizing map (SOM) and adaptive resonance theory (ART). Density based clustering techniques mark the areas with higher densities as clusters while lower densities areas are considered noise. Density based clustering techniques include density-based spatial clustering of applications with noise (DBSCAN), ordering points to identify the clustering structure (OPTICS) and Mean-Shift (Xu and Tian 2015). We have considered three unsupervised learning algorithms: k-means, SOM and DBSCAN, for clustering of malicious IP flows.

3.1   K-Means

K-means is a simple unsupervised learning algorithms based on partitional clustering technique. The k-means randomly choose centroid vectors for k clusters in the data. In next step, the algorithm calculates squared distance between all data examples and k centroids vectors and assigns all examples to their nearest cluster. The algorithm repeats the process and calculates k centroid vectors on the basis of new cluster membership. Again the membership of all example is calculated for new k centroid vectors. The process is repeated until no example moves the centroid vectors (Nazeer and Sebastian 2009). The k-mean algorithm minimize the following objective function:

$$\sum_{i=1}^{k}\sum_{j=1}^{n}||x_j - i|| \tag{1}$$

where k defines the total number of output clusters, i is the ith cluster center in k, n is the total number of examples, and j is the jth example in the n.

3.2   Self-organizing Map

The self-organizing map (SOM) is an artificial neural network based on unsupervised learning (Van Hulle 2012). The SOM network consists of a number of neuron units connected in multiple layers. SOM uses a particular type of unsupervised system called competitive learning. In competitive learning, the output neurons compete with each other and one neuron is active at a time. This approach is also called winner-take-all where the winning neuron supersedes all competing neurons. The competitive learning approach has three steps, competition, cooperation and adaptation.

Mathematically, Let $X = (x_1, x_2, \ldots, x_l)$ is a set of n-dimensional input vectors which we want to classify in k different clusters. The SOM network for this clustering consists of k output neurons, and every neuron has n inputs. In competition, k neurons compete with each other to win an n-dimension input vector. Each competing neuron has a weight vector associated with it. The value of the weight vector is initialized to random small values. When an input vector $x \ni X$, is presented to the SOM network, it is compared with weight vectors of all competing neurons using following equation:

$$v = argmin_k||w_k - x|| \tag{2}$$

A neuron v is declared "winner" if its weight vector is closest to the input example x. Winning neuron is also called BMU (best matching unit). In cooperation, the neurons closer to the BMU get excited more than distant neurons. This topological ordering is controlled using a neighborhood function. The effect of neighborhood function is maximum at the origin and decrease with distance and time. The range of the neighborhood is defined by a Gaussian function:

$$\sigma(t) = \sigma_0 e^{(-2\sigma_0 \frac{t}{t_m})} \tag{3}$$

where
$\sigma_0 =$ Initial value of neighborhood range
t and $t_m=$ The current and maximum iteration respectively
$\sigma(t) =$ The range of neighborhood at t stage.

Fig. 1. Self-organizing map learning process

The last step of adaptation defines a learning process and adjusts weights of neighboring neuron vectors to form a topographic self-organizing map:-

$$w_i(t+1) = w_i(t) + \eta(t)\sigma(t)(v - w_i(t)) \tag{4}$$

t and $\eta(t)$ represent the current iteration and learning rate. The effect of each learning iteration is to move the weight vectors w_i of the winning neuron and its neighboring neurons closer towards the input vector x_i. The continuous process of competition, cooperating and adaptation marks the cluster on the output layer as shown in Fig. 1.

3.3   DBSCAN

Density-based spatial clustering of applications with noise (DBSCAN) is a widely used clustering algorithm (Shrivastava and Gupta 2012). DBSCAN clusters the points together which are located in high density areas. The points situated in the less dense areas are considered outliers or noise.

The DBSCAN clustering algorithm is based on two important input parameters: Epsilon(eps) neighborhood and Minimum number of points (minPoints). Epsilon-neighborhood of a point p contains all points such that distance between p and all point q is less than the Epsilon. If the number of points within the eps-neighborhood of p is greater than or equal to minPoints, then p is called a core point. All points within p's eps-neighborhood are said to be directly density reachable from p if p is a core point. A point p is density reachable from the point q if there is a chain of objects $p_1, \ldots, p_n, p_1 = q$ and $p_n = p$ such that p_{i+1} is directly density-reachable from p_i(Birant and Kut 2007). A point p is a border point if it is not a core point but it is density-reachable from another core point. The DBSCAN algorithm starts with the first point p in data and creates a cluster of all points which are directly density reachable or density reachable from point p. The same process is repeated for all points in the data. A point is marked outlier if it is not part of any cluster. A DBSCAN clustering with 6 minPoints is shown in Fig. 2.

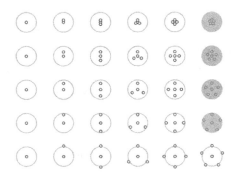

Fig. 2. DBSCAN clustering with minPoints = 6

4   Proposed Approach

Anomaly based intrusion detection systems classify network traffic into normal and malicious categories. In case of flow-based inspection, the IP flow records are classified as normal or malicious. These IP flows are in very large number and it is very difficult to inspect every individual flow manually. Our aim is to group malicious IP flows together into different attack clusters. IP flow records consist of a number of attributes which show the general behavior of the traffic. The flows generated by a network application generally follow a unique pattern. The key idea is that IP flows of an attack will also have similar values for flow attributes e.g. IP addresses, port numbers, protocol flags and packet sizes. Unsupervised learning algorithm uses the similarity in flow attributes for clustering of IP flows into different attack clusters.

The architecture of proposed approach is shown in Fig. 3. The malicious flow clustering component is placed between the intrusion detection system and alert triggering component. An unlabeled training set of n malicious IP flows is extracted from the flow-based intrusion detection. These malicious IP flow records are passed through feature selection and normalization steps. The clustering algorithm creates different attack clusters using the unlabeled malicious flows in training set. We assign an attack label to every cluster. After the clustering and labeling process is complete, the attack clustering component compares every incoming IP flow with all clusters and assigns them the label of the closest cluster. The intrusion detection system raises a consolidated alert for a set of malicious flows having same attack label.

4.1   IP Flow Collection

The attack classification component receives malicious flows from a flow-based intrusion detection system. The flow-based intrusion detection system separates malicious and normal IP flows. Normal flows are discarded while malicious IP flows are retained for further analysis. These malicious IP flows are forwarded to the attack clustering component. Initially, the IP flows are used to create

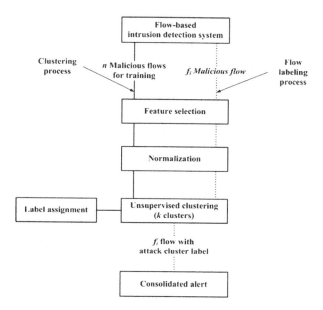

Fig. 3. Automatic clustering of malicious IP flows

attack clusters. After the clusters are created, all incoming IP flows are placed in different attack clusters. The flow-based intrusion detection system can use additional features computed using base flow attributes. However, these features may not be required for by the attack clustering component. The feature section step can add or remove additional features. In this paper, we have used standard Netflow v5 features[1].

We also normalize the IP flow records to control the variation in the flow data. Normalization process scale the values of flow attributes using a fixed range of values such that the larger value attribute cannot dominate smaller valued attributes. The normalization process only scales numeric attributes whereas nominal attributes are used as it. We have normalized flow data in the range of $[-1, 1]$ using the maximum and minimum value of a given attribute. If $x[i]$ is a given attribute value in an input vector x, its normalized value $x'[i]$ is calculated using the following equation:

$$x'[i] = \frac{x[i] - min(x[i])}{max(x[i]) - min(x[i])} \tag{5}$$

4.2   IP Flow Clustering

In this step, we use a training set of unlabeled IP flows to create different attack clusters. The clustering algorithm process all flow records in the training set, until the clusters are converged.

---

[1] https://www.plixer.com/support/netflow_v5.html.

We have used K-mean, SOM and DBSCAN algorithms for creation of clusters. Algorithm 1 outlines the process of k-mean clustering. The input to the algorithm is a set of unlabeled flows F and number of output clusters k. The algorithm normalizes the flow records and randomly select a flow for every cluster. This flow act as an initial cluster center for every cluster. In next step, membership of all examples is calculated and every example is assigned to the nearest cluster. In each iteration, the cluster centers are recalculated until the algorithm converges and cluster centers no longer change. The algorithm outputs a set of cluster centers C for k clusters.

Algorithm 2 shows the SOM clustering process. The input to the algorithm is a set of unlabeled flows F, number of output neurons(clusters) k, initial learning rate η and maximum number of iterations. The algorithm randomly initializes weight vectors for all neurons. In each iteration, a wining neuron is selected for every IP flows and weight of its neighboring neurons are adjusted using a time decay function $\sigma(t)$. The algorithm outputs a set of cluster centers C for k clusters.

Algorithm 1. Clustering of IP Flows using k-means

1: **procedure** CLUSTERFLOWKMEAN
        Input $F = \{f_1, f_2, f_3, \ldots, f_n\}$ set of malicious IP flows, k = number of output clusters
        Output $C = \{c_1, c_2, c_3, \ldots, c_k\}$ set of clusters
2:    $F' = Normalize(F)$
3:    **for** $c_i \in C$ **do**
4:        $c_i = Random(F')$
5:    **end for**
6:    **repeat**
7:        **for** $f' \ni F'$ **do**
8:            $l_i = argmin_k ||c_k - f'||$
9:            **for** k iterations **do**
10:               $s_k = \{x_i | l[i] = k\}$
11:               $c_k = \frac{\sum_{x_i \in s_k}}{|s_k|}$
12:            **end for**
13:        **end for**
14:    **until** clusters are converged
15: **end procedure**

The DBSCAN clustering does not require the number of clusters to be set initially. However, two parameters eps and minPoints have to be set. Slight changes in these value affect the placement and number of clusters. Algorithm 3 describes the process of clustering using DBSCAN. The input to the algorithm is a set of unlabeled flows F, minPoints and eps value. DBSCAN processes all flows in F and creates a cluster for flow f enclosing all flows which are directly density reachable or density reachable from f. The algorithm outputs a set of cluster C.

Algorithm 2. Clustering of IP Flows using Self-organizing maps

```
1: procedure ClusterFlowSOM
        Input F = {f₁, f₂, f₃, . . . , fₙ} set of malicious IP flows, k = number of output neurons
        (clusters), η = initial learning rate, max = maximum number of iterations
        Output C = {c₁, c₂, c₃, . . . , cₖ} set of clusters
2:      F' = Normalize(F)
3:      Random initialize weight vector W = {w₁, w₂, w₃, . . . , wₖ} for k neurons
4:      for max iterations do
5:          for f' ∋ F' do
6:              Select wining neuron c = argminₖ||wₖ − f'||
7:              for i neurons in neighborhood do
8:                  σ(t) = σ₀e^(−2η₀ t/tₙ) /*Determine neighborhood range
9:                  η(t − 1) > η(t) > 0
10:                 wᵢ(t + 1) = wᵢ(t) + η(t)σ(t)(−wᵢ(t)) /*Update weights
11:             end for
12:         end for
13:     end for
14: end procedure
```

Algorithm 3. Clustering of IP Flows using DBSCAN

```
1: procedure ClusterFlowDBSCAN
        Input F = {f₁, f₂, f₃, . . . , fₙ} set of malicious IP flows, eps = Epsilon value,
        minFlows = minPoints value
        Output C = {c₁, c₂, c₃, . . . , cₖ} set of clusters
2:      Initialize i = 0
3:      F' = Normalize(F)
4:      for f' ∋ F' do
5:          if f' is not visited then
6:              Mark e' visited
7:              if epsNeigborhoodPoints(f') ≥ minFlows then
8:                  i = i + 1
9:                  Assign f' to cluster cᵢ /* f' is a core point(flow)
10:                 for e' ∋ epsNeigborhoodPoints(f') do
11:                     if e' is not visited then
12:                         Mark e' visited
13:                         if epsNeigborhoodPoints(e') >= minFlows then
14:                             Assign e' to cluster cᵢ if e' ∉ C
15:                         end if
16:                     end if
17:                 end for
18:             end if
19:         end if
20:     end for
21: end procedure
22: procedure epsNeigborhoodPoints(p)
        output Return the number of points in eps neighborhood of point p
23: end procedure
```

4.3   Cluster and Flow Labeling

We label every cluster with the type of attack using domain knowledge of malicious traffic. The type of attack for every attack cluster is determined by analyzing IP flows at the center of every cluster. If the inspection of IP flows in an attack cluster does not reflect an attack type, the cluster number can be used as an attack label.

After the clusters are created, and labeling process is complete, the attack clustering component processes all incoming IP flows. An incoming malicious IP flow f_i is compared with all clusters centroids. The f_i is assigned the attack label of cluster c, if the it is closest to f_i.

$$c = argmin_k ||c_k - f_i|| \qquad (6)$$

These labeled IP flows are forwarded to the alert triggering component of the intrusion detection system. The alert triggering component raise consolidated alerts for every set IP flows with same attack label. The intrusion detections system can be configured with the minimum and maximum number of flows required for a consolidated alert.

5 Experimental Results

In this section, we describe experimental results for clustering of malicious IP flows using k-means, self-organizing map (SOM) and DBSCAN algorithms on a flow-based data-set.

5.1 Data-Set Description

Sperotto et al. (2009) developed a realistic flow-based intrusion detection data-set. The data-set contains IP flow records collected from a "honeypot" deployed at the University of Twente network. Three common services SSH, HTTP and FTP have been installed on the honeypot host with enhanced logging. The data-set mostly contains malicious SSH and HTTP flows. The SSH flows are result of automated brute-force dictionary attacks, where repeated tries are made for guessing user name and password from a list of dictionary words. The HTTP flows in the data-set were generated due to automated attacks carried out using tools like Nikto[2] and Whisker[3]. The data-set is available in Netflow v5 format. Detail of features in the flow records are given in Table 1. The original data-set has four time attribute to determine duration of flow; flow start time in seconds, flow end time in seconds, milliseconds part of flow start time and millisecond part of flow end time. We have converted all four attributes all to single variable of duration in milliseconds.

The data-set is very large and contains nearly 14M flow records. We have extracted a random subset of the data-set for evaluation. To make the data-set more comprehensive, we have mixed IP flows generated by two well known malware; Sality[4] and Asprox[5]. Sality infects executable and DLL files. It also generates P2P botnet traffic and receives URLs of other malware and security risks for downloading. This virus then executes these malware on the infected

---

[2] https://cirt.net/Nikto2.
[3] http://www.iss.net/security_center/reference/vulntemp/HTTP_WhiskerScan.htm.
[4] http://www.trendmicro.com/vinfo/us/threat-encyclopedia/malware/SALITY.
[5] https://en.wikipedia.org/wiki/Asprox_botnet.

Table 1. Features for IP Flow records

Feature	Description
Source IP Address	The IP Address of the source
Destination IP Address	The destination IP address
Packets	Number of packets in flow
Octets	Number of bytes in flow
Duration	The duration of flow in milliseconds
Source Port	Source port number
Destination Port	Destination port number
TCP Flags	Cumulative OR of TCP flags
Protocol	The transport layer protocol

computer system. Asprox malware uses SQL injections to spread itself and infect websites with malware containing redirects. Both malware have infected millions of computers worldwide.

We have obtained packet capture files for the malware from Contagio Malware Dump[6]. We converted packet capture files to uni-directional IP flows using nProbe[7]. Sality malware has both incoming and outgoing flows while Asprox malware dump has only outgoing flows. The resultant data-set contains malicious IP flows generated due to SSH brute force attack, HTTP server scanning and Sality malware. Distribution of malicious flows in data-set is given in Table 2.

The IP flows are uni-directional which means separate IP flow records are generated for incoming and outgoing traffic. Use of uni-directional IP flows is useful in identifying attacks classes because malicious incoming and outgoing traffic differs with each other (Boukhtouta et al. 2015). Table 3 shows a sample of malicious IP flows.

Table 2. Distribution of malicious flows

Type	No. of IP Flows
HTTP Incoming traffic	2127
HTTP Outgoing traffic	2113
SSH Incoming traffic	4140
SSH Outgoing traffic	3360
Sality Incoming traffic	3952
Sality Outgoing traffic	2603
Asprox Outgoing traffic	5705
Total	24000

---

[6] http://contagiodump.blogspot.com/.
[7] http://www.ntop.org/products/netflow/nprobe/.

Table 3. Malicious IP flow records

Packets	Bytes	Duration (msec)	Source port	Destination port	TCP flags	Protocol
5	736	33	80	1413	43	6
5	739	33	80	4416	43	6
12	2244	2052	22	1555	27	6
12	1152	3972	1084	22	27	6
5	721	20	80	3339	43	6
14	1969	2112	22	4165	27	6
5	722	20	80	4626	43	6
16	1739	4297	22	2042	27	6
5	729	32	80	1296	43	6
12	1152	2184	3316	22	27	6

5.2   Performance Measures

We have used precision, recall and F1-measure to evaluate the performance of clustering algorithms (Chang and Ramachandran 2016). Precision is defined as the ratio of correctly clustered IP flows to the number of clustered IP flows:

$$Precision = \frac{\text{number of true positives}}{\text{number of true positives} + \text{number of false positives}} \quad (7)$$

Recall is the ratio of correctly clustered IP flows to the number of actual number of IP flows:

$$Recall = \frac{\text{number of true positives}}{\text{number of true positive} + \text{number of false negatives}} \quad (8)$$

True positive refers to correctly clustered IP flows. False positives refers to the IP flows clustered but do not belong to the cluster. False negative refers to the number of IP flows incorrectly assigned to other clusters.

F1-measure is described as the harmonic means of precision and recall values:

$$F1\text{-}measure = \frac{2 \times \text{precision} \times \text{recall}}{\text{precision} + \text{recall}} \quad (9)$$

5.3   Results

We have performed the experiments on Weka[8] using Weka's class to cluster evaluation mode. In this mode, Weka uses a labeled data-set to validate the clustering algorithm. In training phase, Weka ignores the class attribute and generates clusters from unlabeled data-set. In testing phase, every example in the data-set is compared with all clusters and assigned to the closest cluster. The class label attribute is used to check that if an example is assigned to correct cluster or otherwise. The class to cluster evaluation also gives values for additional performance measures.

---

[8] http://www.cs.waikato.ac.nz/ml/weka/.

Experiment I: K-means. In first experiment, we have used k-mean algorithm for clustering of malicious IP flows. The number of output clusters has been set to 8 because the data-set has 7 attack types. The 8th cluster is included to hold IP flows which cannot be clustered in any of the 7 clusters. Table 4 gives the results of k-mean clustering. K-mean's performance is best in clustering of HTTP outgoing flows with F1-measure of 0.99. It has average performance in clustering of HTTP incoming, SSH incoming, and SSH outgoing traffic with F1-measure of 0.70, 0.87, 0.88 and 0.75 respectively. The Sality incoming and Asprox outgoing clustering has F1-measure of 0.75 and 0.87 respectively. However, k-mean do not perform well in clustering of Sality outgoing traffic and gives F1-measure of 0.39.

Table 4. K-mean clustering results

Attack cluster	Actual IP flows	Correctly clustered IP flows	Recall	Precision	F1-measures
HTTP Incoming	2127	1180	0.98	0.55	0.70
HTTP Outgoing	2113	2091	0.98	1.00	0.99
SSH Incoming	4140	3370	0.81	0.93	0.87
SSH Outgoing	3360	3360	1.00	0.78	0.88
Sality Incoming	3952	3400	0.86	0.66	0.75
Sality Outgoing	2603	960	0.36	0.41	0.39
Asprox Outgoing	5705	4503	0.78	0.99	0.87

Experiment II: Self-organizing map. We have used self-organizing map (SOM) in second experiment. The number of output clusters is set to 8. Table 5 gives the results for SOM clustering. The incoming and outgoing HTTP attack traffic is correctly clustered with F1-measure of 0.98 and 0.99 respectively. The incoming and outgoing SSH traffic has F1-measure of 0.70 and 0.98. SOM does not perform

Table 5. SOM clustering results

Attack cluster	Actual IP flows	Correctly clustered IP flows	Recall	Precision	F1-measures
HTTP Incoming	2127	2102	0.98	0.99	0.98
HTTP Outgoing	2113	2088	0.98	1.00	0.99
SSH Incoming	4140	3370	0.81	0.77	0.70
SSH Outgoing	3360	3360	1.00	0.96	0.98
Sality Incoming	3952	1879	0.86	0.76	0.80
Sality Outgoing	2603	961	0.63	0.55	0.58
Asprox Outgoing	5705	3036	0.53	0.99	0.69

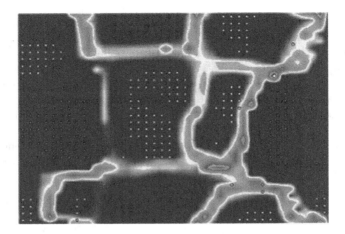

Fig. 4. Self-organizing clustering map

well in clustering of Sality and Asprox outgoing malware flows and gives F1-measure of 0.58 and 0.69 respectively. An additional benefit of SOM is generation of visual clustering map as shown in Fig. 4.

Experiment III: DBSCAN. In third experiment, we have used DBSCAN algorithm for unsupervised clustering of malicious IP flows. DBSCAN requires two parameters to be set manually; epsilon and minPoint. The value of epsilon and minPoint is chosen empirically and set to 0.4 and 6 respectively. DBSCAN has an advantage over k-mean and SOM that it automatically determine the number of output clusters from the data. Table 6 gives the results of DBSCAN clustering. The incoming and outgoing HTTP attack traffic is correctly clustered with F1-measure of 0.98. All IP flows for incoming and outgoing SSH attack traffic are also correctly clustered with F1-measure of 0.98 and 1.00 respectively. The Sality incoming and Asprox outgoing traffic has an F1-measure of 0.82 and 0.98 respectively. However, clustering of outgoing Sality attack traffic has low performance and gives an F1-measure of 0.59.

Table 6. DBSCAN clustering results

Attack cluster	Actual IP flows	Correctly clustered IP flows	Recall	Precision	F1-measures
HTTP Incoming	2127	2098	0.98	0.98	0.98
HTTP Outgoing	2113	2064	0.97	1.00	0.98
SSH Incoming	4140	3369	0.81	0.99	0.89
SSH Outgoing	3360	3360	1.00	1.00	1.00
Sality Incoming	3952	3407	0.86	0.78	0.82
Sality Outgoing	2603	1642	0.63	0.55	0.59
Asprox Outgoing	5705	5591	0.98	0.99	0.98

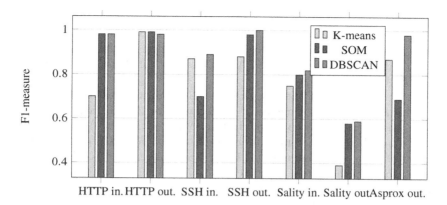

Fig. 5. Clustering results comparison

5.4   Discussion

The experimental results show that unsupervised clustering algorithms success-fully classify the majority of malicious IP flow records in different attack clus-ters. We have used three unsupervised learning algorithms, k-mean, SOM and DBSCAN for attack clustering. Figure 5 gives a visual comaprison of cluster-ing results. Table 7 lists the overall accuracy (OA) of all algorithms. The overall accuracy is calculated as the total number of correctly clustered IP flows divided by the total number of IP flows. The overall accuracy shows that DBSCAN gives the best performance as compared with k-means and SOM.

K-means clustering achieves an overall accuracy of 78%. K-means is a simple and efficient method of clustering and gives good performance when the IP flows are distinct. The k-mean clustering experiment shows that k-mean has very low accuracy in clustering of Sality malware traffic. The Sality malware's incoming and outgoing flows are similar to each other, therefore, k-mean is not able to cluster Sality IP flows accurately. Self-organizing map (SOM) gives better performance than k-mean and has an overall accuracy of 80%. SOM has good performance for all clusters but shows lower accuracy in clustering of Asprox IP flows. The Asprox malware traffic consists of variety of IP flows with different behavior and SOM is able to place them in a single attack cluster. SOM has an excellent capability of generating visual cluster map of malicious IP flows.

DBSCAN algorithm has the highest overall accuracy of 89% and places all types of IP flows in correct cluster. DBSCAN automatically determines the num-ber of output clusters using the *espsilon* and *minPoints* values. However, these

Table 7. Overall accuracy

Unsupervised learning algorithm	K-means	Self-organizing map	DBSCAN
Overall accuracy	78%	80%	89%

values have to be carefully set for best clustering performance. A slight change in these parameters affect the overall accuracy and also change the number of output clusters. DBSCAN has placed almost all types of flows in correct attack clusters. The performance of DBSCAN is also low for Asprox malware traffic due to variety in IP flows.

Both k-means and SOM algorithms require the number of clusters as an input parameter. The performance of clustering algorithms is largely dependent on correct estimation of number of clusters (Wang et al. 2009). Generally it is assumed that this parameters is user supplied (Pakhira 2012). Our proposed scheme also requires that number of clusters for k-means and SOM are carefully set using domain knowledge of malicious traffic. There also techniques which automatically determine the number of optimal clusters in the data (Pakhira 2012). If it is difficult to determine the number of clusters, algorithm such as DBSCAN can be used.

An important concern is the labeling of flow clusters. We have manually labeled clusters using the type of attack. The type of attack is determined by inspecting a sample of IP flows in every cluster. However, the correct labeling is also dependent on the number of output clusters. If the number of clusters is low, a cluster will contain flows of different attack types and a single attack label may not be enough to describe all malicious flows. Similarly, if the number of clusters is too high, IP flows of a single attack type will be distributed in multiple clusters.

In unsupervised clustering, clusters are created from unlabeled IP flows and no ground truth is available. Clustering is not accurate as compared with The clustering methods are not it is difficult to determine that an IP flow is placed in the correct cluster or not. This problem can be solved by allowing only those flows in a cluster which lie within a certain distance from the cluster centroid. We can define a threshold value on the probability or distance value of cluster membership. Our proposed technique uses IP flows to cluster different attacks. Flow-based intrusion detection system does not detect attacks which are hidden in the packet payload. These attacks do not affect the normal flow behavior. Web-based attacks such as SQL Injection, Cross-side scripting do not cause any variation in the flow attributes and flow-based detection can not detect them (Alaidaros et al. 2011). However, if an attacker makes repeated attempts for SQL injection, it will be reflected in IP flows and can be detected. Our technique is not able to cluster malicious flows of web-based attacks due to the limitation of flow-based detection.

6   Conclusion and Future Work

In this paper, we present a novel technique for automatic clustering of malicious IP flows. Our technique uses unsupervised learning techniques and creates attack clusters from the unlabeled training set of malicious IP flows. Once the clusters are created, incoming IP flows are compared with all clusters and placed in the closet attack cluster. The intrusion detection system raises a consolidated alert for every set of IP flows which belong to same attack cluster. We have used three unsupervised learning techniques, k-mean, SOM and DBSCAN and evaluated them on a flow-based data-set. Results show that our technique successfully identifies various attacks in malicious IP flows and places the majority of the IP flows in correct attack clusters. Overall, our work has following important contributions; First, the automatic clustering of malicious flows is helpful in reducing the total number of alerts generated by the intrusion detection system. Second, we use IP flow records for clustering of malicious traffic and no payload inspection is performed. IP flow records are capable of differentiating almost all type of attacks except those which are hidden in the packet payload. Third, we employ unsupervised learning techniques and no labeled training data-set is required.

There are several directions in which our work can be improved. We have used IP flow record based on standard Netflow v5 flow export protocol. Netflow v5 has a limited number of flow features. More accurate and valid results can be obtained by using additional flow attributes defined in Netflow v9/IPFIX. Our scheme does not have a way to determine the number of clusters in the malicious flows data. An automatic cluster finding technique can be integrated in our system for this purpose. We have only evaluated three unsupervised learning algorithm in our study. Additional unsupervised learning algorithms can be explored for automatic classification of malicious flow records.

References

Alaidaros, H., Mahmuddin, M., Al Mazari, A.: An overview of flow-based and packet-based intrusion detection performance in high speed networks. In: Proceedings of the International Arab Conference on Information Technology (2011)

Amoli, P.V., Hamalainen, T.: A real time unsupervised NIDS for detecting unknown and encrypted network attacks in high speed network. In: 2013 IEEE International Workshop on Measurements and Networking Proceedings (M&N), pp. 149–154. IEEE (2013)

Bateni, M., Baraani, A., Ghorbani, A.: Using artificial immune system and fuzzy logic for alert correlation. IJ Netw. Secur. **15**(3), 190–204 (2013)

Benferhat, S., Boudjelida, A., Tabia, K., Drias, H.: An intrusion detection and alert correlation approach based on revising probabilistic classifiers using expert knowledge. Appl. Intell. **38**(4), 520–540 (2013)

Birant, D., Kut, A.: St-DBSCAN: an algorithm for clustering spatial-temporal data. Data Knowl. Eng. **60**(1), 208–221 (2007)

Bolzoni, D., Etalle, S., Hartel, P.H.: Panacea: automating attack classification for anomaly-based network intrusion detection systems. In: Kirda, E., Jha, S., Balzarotti, D. (eds.) RAID 2009. LNCS, vol. 5758, pp. 1–20. Springer, Heidelberg (2009). doi:10.1007/978-3-642-04342-0_1

Boukhtouta, A., Mokhov, S.A., Lakhdari, N.-E., Debbabi, M., Paquet, J.: Network malware classification comparison using DPI and flow packet headers. J. Comput. Virol. Hacking Tech. **12**, 69–100 (2015)

Chang, V., Kuo, Y.-H., Ramachandran, M.: Cloud computing adoption framework: a security framework for business clouds. Future Gener. Comput. Syst. **57**, 24–41 (2016)

Chang, V., Ramachandran, M.: Towards achieving data security with the cloud computing adoption framework. IEEE Trans. Serv. Comput. **9**(1), 138–151 (2016)

Claise, B., Trammell, B., Aitken, P. (eds.): Specification of the IP flow information export (IPFIX) protocol for the exchange of flow information. Technical report, STD 77, RFC 7011, September 2013

Dharamkar, B., Singh, R.R.: Cyber-attack classification using improved ensemble technique based on support vector machine and neural network. Int. J. Comput. Appl. **103**(11), 1–7 (2014)

Garcia-Teodoro, P., Diaz-Verdejo, J., Maciá-Fernández, G., Vázquez, E.: Anomaly-based network intrusion detection: techniques, systems and challenges. Comput. Secur. **28**(1), 18–28 (2009)

Ghahramani, Z.: Unsupervised learning. In: Bousquet, O., von Luxburg, U., Rätsch, G. (eds.) Advanced Lectures on Machine Learning, vol. 3176, pp. 72–112. Springer, Heidelberg (2004). doi:10.1007/978-3-540-28650-9_5

Golling, M., Hofstede, R., Koch, R.: Towards multi-layered intrusion detection in high-speed networks. In: 2014 6th International Conference on Cyber Conflict (CyCon 2014), pp. 191–206. IEEE (2014)

Haddadi, F., Khanchi, S., Shetabi, M., Derhami, V.: Intrusion detection and attack classification using feed-forward neural network. In: 2010 Second International Conference on Computer and Network Technology (ICCNT), pp. 262–266. IEEE (2010)

Hastie, T., Tibshirani, R., Friedman, J.: Unsupervised learning. In: The Elements of Statistical Learning, pp. 1–101 (2009)

Hoque, N., Bhuyan, M.H., Baishya, R.C., Bhattacharyya, D., Kalita, J.K.: Network attacks: taxonomy, tools and systems. J. Netw. Comput. Appl. **40**, 307–324 (2014)

Hurtik, P., Hodakova, P., Perfilieva, I., Liberts, M., Asmuss, J.: Network attack detection and classification by the F-transform. In: 2015 IEEE International Conference on Fuzzy Systems (FUZZ-IEEE), pp. 1–6. IEEE (2015)

Husak, M., Velan, P., Vykopal, J.: Security monitoring of http traffic using extended flows. In: 2015 10th International Conference on Availability, Reliability and Security (ARES), pp. 258–265. IEEE (2015)

Jin, X., Han, J.: Partitional clustering. In: Sammut, C., Webb, G.I. (eds.) Encyclopedia of Machine Learning, p. 766. Springer, Boston (2010)

Koch, R.: Towards next-generation intrusion detection. In: 2011 3rd International Conference on Cyber Conflict (ICCC), pp. 1–18. IEEE (2011)

Laskov, P., Düssel, P., Schäfer, C., Rieck, K.: Learning intrusion detection: supervised or unsupervised? In: Roli, F., Vitulano, S. (eds.) ICIAP 2005. LNCS, vol. 3617, pp. 50–57. Springer, Heidelberg (2005). doi:10.1007/11553595_6

Li, B., Springer, J., Bebis, G., Gunes, M.H.: A survey of network flow applications. J. Netw. Comput. Appl. **36**(2), 567–581 (2013)

Liao, H.-J., Lin, C.-H.R., Lin, Y.-C., Tung, K.-Y.: Intrusion detection system: a comprehensive review. J. Netw. Comput. Appl. **36**(1), 16–24 (2013)

Nazeer, K.A., Sebastian, M.: Improving the accuracy and efficiency of the k-means clustering algorithm. In: Proceedings of the World Congress on Engineering, vol. 1, pp. 1–3 (2009)

Pakhira, M.K.: Finding number of clusters before finding clusters. Procedia Technol. **4**, 27–37 (2012)

Rieck, K., Trinius, P., Willems, C., Holz, T.: Automatic analysis of malware behavior using machine learning. J. Comput. Secur. **19**(4), 639–668 (2011)

Rokach, L., Maimon, O.: Clustering methods. In: Maimon, O., Rokach, L. (eds.) Data Mining and Knowledge Discovery Handbook, pp. 321–352. Springer, Heidelberg (2005). doi:10.1007/0-387-25465-X_15

Shrivastava, P., Gupta, H.: A review of density-based clustering in spatial data. Int. J. Adv. Comput. Res. (IJACR) **2**, 200–202 (2012)

Song, J., Takakura, H., Okabe, Y., Nakao, K.: Toward a more practical unsupervised anomaly detection system. Inf. Sci. **231**, 4–14 (2013)

Sperotto, A., Pras, A.: Flow-based intrusion detection. In: 2011 IFIP/IEEE International Symposium on Integrated Network Management (IM), pp. 958–963. IEEE (2011)

Sperotto, A., Sadre, R., Vliet, F., Pras, A.: A labeled data set for flow-based intrusion detection. In: Nunzi, G., Scoglio, C., Li, X. (eds.) IPOM 2009. LNCS, vol. 5843, pp. 39–50. Springer, Heidelberg (2009). doi:10.1007/978-3-642-04968-2_4

Umer, M.F., Khiyal, M.S.H.: Classification of textual documents using learning vector quantization. Inf. Technol. J. **6**(1), 154–159 (2007)

Van Hulle, M.M.: Self-organizing maps. In: Rozenberg, G., Bäck, T., Kok, J.N. (eds.) Handbook of Natural Computing, pp. 585–622. Springer, Heidelberg (2012). doi:10.1007/978-3-540-92910-9_19

Wang, L., Leckie, C., Ramamohanarao, K., Bezdek, J.: Automatically determining the number of clusters in unlabeled data sets. IEEE Trans. Knowl. Data Eng. **21**(3), 335–350 (2009)

Wu, S.X., Banzhaf, W.: The use of computational intelligence in intrusion detection systems: a review. Appl. Soft Comput. **10**(1), 1–35 (2010)

Xu, D., Tian, Y.: A comprehensive survey of clustering algorithms. Ann. Data Sci. **2**(2), 165–193 (2015)

Ram Naresh Yadav, B.V., Satyanarayana, B., Vasumathi, D.: A vector space model approach for web attack classification using machine learning technique. In: Satapathy, S.C., Raju, K.S., Mandal, J.K., Bhateja, V. (eds.) Proceedings of the Second International Conference on Computer and Communication Technologies. AISC, vol. 381, pp. 363–373. Springer, Heidelberg (2016). doi:10.1007/978-81-322-2526-3_38

A Hybrid Model of Attribute Aggregation in Federated Identity Management

Md. Sadek Ferdous[1]([✉]), Farida Chowdhury[2], and Ron Poet[3]

[1] Electronic and Computer Science, University of Southampton, Southampton, UK
S.Ferdous@soton.ac.uk
[2] Computing Science and Mathematics, University of Stirling, Stirling, UK
fch@cs.stir.ac.uk
[3] School of Computing Science, University of Glasgow, Glasgow, UK
Ron.Poet@glasgow.ac.uk

Abstract. The existing model of Federated Identity Management (FIM) allows a user to provide attributes only from a single Identity Provider (IdP) per service session. However, this does not cater to the fact that the user attributes are scattered and stored across multiple IdPs. An attribute aggregation mechanism would allow a user to aggregate attributes from multiple providers and pass them to a Service Provider (SP) in a single service session which would enable the SP to offer innovative service scenarios. Unfortunately, there exist only a handful of mechanisms for aggregating attributes and most of them either require complex user interactions or are based on unrealistic assumptions. In this paper, we present a novel approach called the *Hybrid Model* for aggregating attributes from multiple IdPs using one of the most popular FIM technologies: Security Assertion Markup Language (SAML). We present a thorough analysis of different requirements imposed by our proposed approach and discuss how we have developed a proof of concept using our model and what design choices we have made to meet the majority of these requirements. We also illustrate two use-cases to elaborate the applicability of our approach and analyse the advantages it offers and the limitations it currently has.

1 Introduction

In the last fifteen years or so, we have seen a tremendous expansion of the Internet and web-enabled online services. To allow users to access different online services in a seamless manner while maintaining security and privacy, the concept of Identity Management (IdM, in short) has been introduced which resulted in various different Identity Management Systems (IMS, in short). Shibboleth (Shibboleth 2016), OpenID (OpenID Authentication 2.0 - Final 2007), Microsoft's CardSpace (Chappell 2006), etc. are all examples of different IMS. Among different IMS, Federated Identity Management (FIM, in short) has gained much popularity. The FIM model is based on the concept of Identity Federation (also known as Federated Identities or Federation of Identities). Security Assertion Markup

© Springer International Publishing AG 2017
V. Chang et al. (Eds.): Enterprise Security, LNCS 10131, pp. 120–154, 2017.
DOI: 10.1007/978-3-319-54380-2_6

Language (SAML) (Standard 2005) and OpenID (OpenID Authentication 2.0 - Final 2007) are two of the most popular technologies used in identity federation.

Even though the federated services have improved the usability and experience of online services, there exists a serious limitation: a user can use only one IdP in one session (Chadwick and Inman 2009). This is an unrealistic restriction that assumes that one IdP would be able to provide any number of user attributes to the SPs where in reality users have different attributes stored in different providers. To illustrate the restriction, let us consider a real-life scenario in the setting of FIM. Imagine a user, named Alice, wants to buy an age restricted product from her favourite online shop. She might need to use her Governmental IdP (e.g. Passport or Driving authorities who issue her passport or driving licence) to prove her age, her bank details to pay for the product and her loyalty card information to collect loyalty points during this purchase. All this information are stored at different IdPs. Even if we assume that the online seller has a federated agreement with all these IdPs, the current setting of federated services does not allow Alice to provide all this information in a single session (e.g. during her purchase). Allowing users to aggregate attributes from different providers will enable them to release these attributes to an SP in a single service session which could be used to provide innovative services.

The concept of attribute aggregation has been introduced to tackle this very problem. A number of novel approaches exist for aggregating attributes targeted for federated services. Even though each model has their own strengths, most of them suffer from serious limitations: many of them are based on either complex user interactions, unrealistic assumptions or have not been implemented in practice. In this paper, we present a hybrid approach for federated services which is based on two existing models and has been designed to specifically address these limitations.

The contributions of the paper are:

- We present our hybrid model based on SAML that does not require complex user interactions.
- We present a threat model for identifying different threats for our proposed system.
- We formulate a list of functional, security, privacy and trust requirements for our model. The security and privacy requirements have been devised as mitigation strategies against the identified threats.
- We provide an in-depth analysis of the design choices that we have made to ensure that most of these requirements are met.
- The current SAML specification does not have any mechanism to allow an SP to pass any information regarding the requested attributes from the IdPs during the authentication process. We have proposed a mechanism to rectify this problem.
- We discuss the developed proof of concept based on our proposals to illustrate the applicability of our model using two use-cases.
- Finally, we discuss the advantages that our model offers and the limitations it has.

The rest of the paper is structured as follows. In Sect. 2, we present a brief background of Identity, Federated Identity Management, Attribute Aggregation and SAML along with a few relevant mathematical notations and definitions that will be used throughout the paper. We provide a comparative analysis of existing attribute aggregation models in Sect. 3. We present our Hybrid Model along with a threat model for the proposed approach, highlight different requirements imposed by our model and discuss the design choices we have made to develop a proof of concept in Sect. 4. A few use-cases using our model are illustrated in Sect. 5. Section 6 analyses how our proof of concept meets the stated requirements, discusses the advantages that our model offers, the limitation it has and the scope of future work. Finally, we conclude in Sect. 7.

2   Background

In this section, we provide a brief background of Identity, Identity Management and Federated Identity Management. Then, we Mathematically define the term *Attribute Aggregation*. Finally, we briefly describe Security Assertion Markup Language (SAML).

2.1   Entity, Identity, Identity Management and Federated Identity Management

An entity is a physical or logical object which has a separate distinctive existence either in a physical or logical sense (Ferdous et al. 2009.) Every entity has its own identity which is used to uniquely identify it in a certain context. In this paper, we are mostly interested about entities which digitally present users in an application system of an enterprise (organisation).

To define the identity of a user we utilise the Digital Identity Model (DIM) introduced in (Ferdous et al. 2014). According to this model, the (whole) identity of a user is actually distributed in different partial identities which are valid within a security domain (context) of an enterprise (organisation). Since the partial identity of a user is only valid within a domain, it is essential to specify the domain whenever a partial identity is mentioned. Each such partial identity consists of a number of attributes and their corresponding values, valid within the domain of a particular organisation.

Let us assume that D denotes the set of domains and d defines the domain of a single organisation whereas U_d denotes the set of users, A_d denotes the set of attributes and AV_d denotes the set of values for those attributes within d. Then, we can relate users and their attributes in a domain by the following partial function:

Definition 1. Let $atEntToVal_d : A_d \times U_d \to AV_d$ be the (partial) function that for an entity and attribute returns the corresponding value of the attribute in domain d.

The function is partial as not all entities have a value for each attribute. This also makes sense in practical systems as in many such systems, users are required to provide values for a number of attributes (e.g. email, telephone number, etc.). However, there remain some optional attributes (e.g. age, postal addresses, etc.) for which users may not provide any values.

Then, we can define the partial identity of a user (u) using the following definition.

Definition 2. For a domain d, the *partial identity* of a user $u \in U_d$ within d, denoted $parIdent_d^u$, is given by the set:

$$\{(a, v) \mid a \in A_d,\ atEntToVal_d(a, u) \text{ is defined and equals } v\}.$$

If we consider that there are n valid attribute-value pairs for a user u, the partial identity of u in d can also be defined as:

$$parIdent_d^u = \{(a_1, v_1), (a_2, v_2), (a_3, v_3) \ldots (a_n, v_n)\}.$$

The (total/whole) identity of an entity can be defined as the union of all her partial identities in all domains.

Definition 3. For an entity $u \in U$, the *identity* of u is given by the set:

$$ident^u = \bigcup \{(d, parIdent_d^u) \mid d \in DOMAIN \text{ such that } u \in U_d\}.$$

The concept of Identity Management (IdM) has been proposed to facilitate the management of digital identities (Ferdous et al. 2009). Formally, IdM consists of technologies and policies for representing and recognising entities with their digital identities (Jøsang et al. 2007). A system that is used for identity management is called an Identity Management System (IMS). Each IMS involves the following parties:

Client/User. A client/user receives services from a service provider (see below). Any entity can be a client, however we assume that each client is a user.

Service Provider. A Service Provider (SP, in short) is an organisation that provides services to the clients or to other SPs. It is also known as the Relying Party. We will use the notation SP to denote the set of service providers.

Identity Provider. An Identity Provider (IdP, in short) is an organisation that provides digital identities to allow clients to receive services from a SP. We will use the notation IDP for the set of identity providers.

There are different models of identity management. One of the most widely used IdM models is the Federated Identity Management (FIM) which is based on the concept of Identity Federation. A federation with respect to Identity Management is a business model in which a group of two or more trusted organisations legally bind themselves with a business and technical contract (Chadwick 2009; Ferdous et al. 2012). It allows a user to access restricted resources seamlessly and securely from other partners residing in different (identity/security)

domains. The IdPs and SPs who bind themselves in such a way form the
so-called Circle of Trust (CoT) which makes them a part of the same federation. One major advantage of the FIM is its Single Sign On (SSO) capability
that allows users to log in to one IdP and then access services from autonomous
and federated service providers without further logins, thus alleviating the need
to log in every time a user needs to access those related systems. A good example
is the Google Single Sign On service which allows users to log in to a Google
service, e.g., Gmail, and then allows them to access other Google services such
as Calendar, Documents, YouTube, Blogs and so on.

One of the functionalities of an IMS is to enable users to share their partial identities between different organisations (e.g. an IdP and SP). During this
process, for the sake of privacy, users usually do not share their full partial
identities between two organisations. Instead, a privacy-friendly approach is to
share a limited view of a user's data across organisational boundaries whenever needed. Such a limited view is defined as the profile of a user. Mathematically, a profile is a subset of the partial identity of a user within a domain:
$PROFILE_d^u \subseteq parIdent_d^u$. Hence, we can define the profile of a user $u \in U_d$ in
domain d in the following way, where $j \leq n$:

$$PROFILE_d^u = \{(a_1, v_1), (a_2, v_2), (a_3, v_3) \ldots (a_j, v_j)\}.$$

One of these attributes generally is an identifier which is used to identify a
user in an IdP and as well as in an SP. To protect the privacy of a user, an
IdP generally utilises two different types of identifiers. The first type is called
a persistent identifier which is used for authenticating a user using a special
attribute called a credential. In different systems, a persistent identifier takes
different forms such as a username, email and phone number. On the other
hand, passwords are the most widely used credentials nowadays. The second
type of identifier is called a transient or pseudonymous identifier which an IdP
generates for a user to be used in a specific SP. Such a pseudonymous identifier
is embedded within the profile of the user so that the SP can maintain a session
for the user. The main benefit of this approach is that one unique pseudonymous
identifier for a user is valid to be used within a single SP, hence, two malicious
SPs cannot collude together to track their users over two security domains. We
will use the notation id_u to denote a persistent identifier of a user and id_u' to
denote a pseudonymous identifier of the user. In addition, the notation $pass_{id_u}$
will be used to denote the credential for id_u.

2.2 Attribute Aggregation

Attribute Aggregation is the mechanism of aggregating or combining attributes of
a user retrieved from multiple identity providers in a single session. As mentioned
earlier, the profile of a user in an IdP contains the subset of attributes of that
user retrieved from that IdP. Therefore, this means that attribute aggregation,
in reality, is actually an aggregation of profiles of a user from different IdPs and
the terms "profile" and "attribute" will be used interchangeably. Formally, the
set of aggregated attributes can be defined in the following way:

For a user u, the set of aggregated attributes of u, denoted by $Att-Agg^u$ is given by:

$$Att-Agg^u = \bigcup \{PROFILE_d^u \mid d \in DOMAIN\}.$$

2.3   Security Assertion Markup Language (SAML)

SAML is one of the most widely deployed FIM technologies (Standard 2005). It is an XML (EXtensible Markup Language)-based standard for exchanging authentication and authorisation information between different autonomous domains. It relies on a request/response protocol in which one party (an SP) requests particular identity information about a user and the other party (an IdP) responds with the information using an assertion. An assertion may contain three different types of statements: (i) Authentication statements - which are used to state that a user has been authenticated by an asserted IdP at a specified time, (ii) Attribute statements - which are used to specify the attributes of a user and (iii) Authorisation statements - which are used to assert that a user is permitted a certain action on specified resources under certain conditions.

A SAML protocol flow between a user, an IdP and an SP is as follows. When a user tries to access a resource/service provided by the SP, if the user is already not authenticated and authorised, the SP forwards the user to a service called the *Discovery Service*, also known as the Where Are You From (WAYF) Service, where a pre-configured list of trusted IdPs is shown to the user. The user chooses her preferred IdP and then the user is forwarded to the IdP with a SAML authentication request. The authentication request consists of an identifier and the entity ID of the SP. We denote a SAML authentication request with *AuthnReq* and model it as presented in Table 1, where id_{req} denotes the identifier in each SAML request and id_{sp} denotes the identifier of the SP which is represented as the *entityID* in a SAML metadata (see below).

The IdP authenticates the user and a SAML response containing a SAML assertion is sent back to the SP. The assertion consists of the profile (user attributes) of the user as released by the IdP. We denote the assertion with *SAMLAssrtn* and model it as presented in Table 1. SAML also supports the notion of encrypted assertion where the assertion is encrypted with the public key of the SP. We denote an encrypted assertion with *EncSAMLAssrtn* and we model it as presented in Table 1, where K_{sp} represents the public key of the SP. The (encrypted or unencrypted) SAML assertion is at first digitally signed and then embedded inside a SAML response which also consists of the request identifier, the entity ID of the IdP and the entity ID of the SP. We denote a

Table 1. SAML notations

SAML Authentication Request:	$AuthnReq = (id_{req}, id_{sp})$
SAML Assertion:	$SAMLAssrtn = (PROFILE_{idp}^u)$
Encrypted SAML Assertion:	$EncSAMLAssrtn = (\{SAMLAssrtn\}_{K_{sp}})$
SAML Response:	$SAMLResp = (id_{req}, id_{sp}, id_{idp}, (\{SAMLAssrtn\}_{K_{idp}^{-1}} \mid \{EncSAMLAssrtn\}_{K_{idp}^{-1}}))$

SAML response with *SAMLResp* and model it as presented in Table 1, where id_{req} denotes the SAML request identifier whereas id_{idp} and id_{sp} denote the entity ID of IdP and the SP respectively. Furthermore, $\{SAMLAssrtn\}_{K_{idp}^{-1}}$ represents the a digitally signed assertion with the private key of IdP (K_{idp}^{-1}). On the other hand, $\{EncSAMLAssrtn\}_{K_{idp}^{-1}}$ represents a digitally signed encrypted assertion encrypted with the public key of the SP (K_{sp}) and signed with the private key of the IdP (K_{idp}^{-1}).

When the SP receives the response, it extracts the (encrypted/unencrypted) SAML assertion. If it contains an encrypted assertion, the assertion is decrypted with the private key of the SP (K_{sp}^{-1}) and then its signature is validated with the public key of the IdP (K_{idp}). If the response contains an unencrypted assertion, its signature is validated using the public key of the IdP. If the signature is valid, the SP retrieves the embedded user attributes (the profile, $PROFILE_{idp}^{u}$) from the assertion and takes an authorisation decision.

To enable the protocol flow discussed above, a notion of trust needs to be established between an IdP and an SP inside a federation. This notion of trust between the IdP and SP in SAML is established by exchanging the respective metadata of the IdP and SP and then storing such metadata at the appropriate repositories. This enables each party to build up the so-called Trust Anchor List (TAL). This exchange takes place in an offline fashion after a technical contract between the IdP and SP is signed. Moreover, this has to be done before any interaction takes place between the said IdP and SP. Once the exchange of metadata is complete, the IdP and SP are said to be part of the same federation (the CoT). A metadata is an XML file in a specified format that contains:

– an entity descriptor, known as *entityID* which represents an identifier for each party,
– service endpoints (the locations of the appropriate endpoints for an IdP and an SP where the request will be sent to and where the response will be consumed respectively),
– a certificate, containing the public key of the party,
– an expiration time, and
– contact information.

Metadata serves three purposes as explained below.

– Firstly, it allows each entity to discover the required service endpoint of another entity for sending SAML requests/responses.
– Secondly, the embedded certificate can be used by an SP to verify the authenticity of any SAML Assertion.
– Thirdly, metadata behaves like an anchor of trust for each party. During the discovery service at an SP, the list of IdPs returned to the user only contains those IdPs whose metadata can be found in its repositories (in other words in the TAL) and only those IdPs are considered trusted. An SP will allow a user to select only those IdPs which are trusted. Similarly, an IdP will respond only to those requests that are initiated from an SP whose metadata can be found in its TAL.

Table 2. Comparison of protocols and implementations

Protocol	Implementation	Attribute request	Attribute release	Attribute aggregation
SAML	Shibboleth	✓	✗	✗
	SSPHP	✓	✓	✗

SAML is a widely-used FIM technology in higher education and Governmental online services. It has many implementations such as Shibboleth (Shibboleth 2016), SimpleSAMLphp (SSPHP, in short) (SimpleSAMLphp 2016) and ZXID (ZXID 2016), however, only Shibboleth and SimpleSAMLphp are widely used. At first, we are interested to see if any particular implementation of SAML allows a specific set of attributes to be requested (denoted as *Attribute Request*), if the implementation allows the user to select and release specific attributes (denoted as *Attribute Release*), known as the Selective Disclosure in the Identity Management terminologies, and if the implementation allows any mechanism of attribute aggregation (denoted as *Attribute Aggregation*).

How and what attributes are requested and released in SAML depend on a specific implementation. Also, how attributes are selected is not standardised in SAML and depends entirely on the specific implementation. For example, a Shibboleth SP requests attributes from an IdP using the SAML *Attribute-Query* request and the attributes are released based on an attribute release policy (ARP) (Cantor 7 January 2008). On the other hand, SimpleSAMLphp also supports the *AttributeQuery* feature, however, this request cannot be used during the authentication process. Nonetheless, SimpleSAMLphp has a built-in module called *Consent* which allows selective disclosure of attributes.

Even though there are available frameworks that allow integrating different social networks with SAML federations (Chadwick et al. 2011) to offer federated services, the SAML specification has no mechanism to aggregate attributes nor does any SAML implementation provide this facility. However, the implementations of existing models of attribute aggregation are mainly based on SAML. The comparison between Shibboleth and SimpleSAMLphp for Attribute Request, Attribute Release and Attribute Aggregation is presented in Table 2. In the table, the symbol ✓ has been used to indicate that the particular implementation supports that particular function and the symbol ✗ indicates the absence of support.

3   Existing Attribute Aggregation Models

There are several existing attribute aggregation models. In the following sections, we provide a brief description of each model.

Application Database (AD) Model. This is the simplest form of attribute aggregation model (Klingenstein 2007; Hulsebosch et al. 2011). In this model, an SP might store additional user attributes such as a local identifier, user-preferences for that particular service, group membership, etc., in addition to the attributes supplied by an IdP. The SP creates a mapping of the SP-created identifier to the IdP-supplied identifier to store these additional attributes, into a local repository. Such local attributes can be retrieved later using this mapping to determine if the user is authorised to access a particular service.

SP-Mediated (SPM) Model. In this model, an SP allows a user to aggregate attributes from multiple IdPs in a single session (Klingenstein 2007; Hulsebosch et al. 2011). The user is forwarded to different IdPs one after another where she is authenticated separately. Then she is returned back to the SP with the IdP-supplied attributes. The SP combines the sets of attributes at its end to determine if the user can access a particular service.

Linking Service (LS) Model. Linking Service model is a combination of the linking and identity relay model (see below). It consists of a special type of SP called the Linking Service (LS) (Chadwick and Inman 2009; Hulsebosch et al. 2011) which is used by a user using a LS-supplied identifier. This identifier is used to link different IdPs using the IdP-supplied LS-specific persistent identifiers in a table called the Linking Table. To access any service of an SP, the user visits the SP and is forwarded to the first IdP. The user authenticates at the first IdP and then an assertion containing user-attributes, the persistent identifier for the LS and a reference to the LS is returned to the SP. The SP forwards the persistent identifier to the LS to aggregate attributes. At this point, two options are available: either the LS can retrieve the list of linked IdPs for this persistent identifier using the Linking Table and retrieve attributes from each of them which are then combined at the LS and is returned to the SP. Alternatively, the LS can send back the list of linked IdPs to the SP. The SP, then, retrieves attributes from each IdP. Based on the aggregated attributes, the SP determines if the user can access the service.

Identity Federation/Linking (IFL) Model. This model, introduced by the Liberty Alliance framework, is one of the first models to address the problem of attribute aggregation (Klingenstein 2007; Hulsebosch et al. 2011). In this model, IdPs allow a user to create a pair-wise link between two IdPs. To create the link, the user has to visit and authenticate to the first IdP. The first IdP will ask the user if she wants to federate this IdP with another IdP. If chosen, the user will be asked to federate the second IdP with the first one. At this point, both IdPs will interact with each other to create a random alias. During accessing services from an SP, one IdP will provide that random alias to the SP along with the assertion containing attributes. The SP can use that alias to retrieve another assertion containing attributes from the other IdP. Combining attributes from both IdPs, the SP can determine if the user can access a service.

Identity Proxying (IP) Model. In this model, an SP allows a user to aggregate attributes from multiple IdPs using a trusted IdP known as the *Proxy IdP* (Klingenstein 2007; Hulsebosch et al. 2011). The user is forwarded to the Proxy IdP at first and then the trusted IdP forwards the user to other multiple IdPs. After the user is authenticated separately at each IdP, the user returns back to the trusted IdP with an assertion including attributes. At this point, the trusted IdP validates each assertion, retrieves attributes from them and combines all these attributes. The trusted IdP might supplement the combined set with its own user-attributes and then reasserts all attributes to the SP as its own attributes. The SP, not being aware of other IdPs, assumes that all attributes have been released by the trusted IdP. Based on the combined attributes, the SP determines if the user can access the service.

Identity Relay (IR) Model. The Identity Relay model is a generalised case of the Proxying model (Klingenstein 2007; Hulsebosch et al. 2011). Since the Proxying model requires an SP to have a strong trust in the trusted IdP, it cannot function properly in situations when the Proxy IdP cannot be fully trusted. The Identity Relay model fits in such scenarios where an intermediary IdP, known as the *Relay IdP*, is used instead of a Proxy IdP. A user is forwarded to the Relay IdP at first and then the Relay IdP forwards the user to other multiple IdPs. The user is authenticated separately at each IdP and is returned back to the Relay IdP with encrypted assertions containing user-attributes. The encrypted assertions are encrypted with the public of the SP so that only the SP can decrypt them. The Relay IdP combines all encrypted assertions into a single assertion and forwards it to the SP. The SP extracts embedded encrypted assertions from this assertion, decrypts and validates each assertion one by one to retrieve attributes from other IdPs. Based on the combined attributes, the SP determines if the user can access the service.

Client-Mediated (CM) Model. This model is similar to the Relay Model. Here, the functionality of the Relay IdP has been replaced by an intelligent user-agent or application that has the capability to aggregate attributes from different IdPs (Klingenstein 2007; Hulsebosch et al. 2011) and hence the protocol flow of this model is similar to the Relay model. An SP informs the client about the IdPs that it trusts. The client forwards the user to each of these IdPs. After respective authentication at each IdP, the client receives assertions from all IdPs and present the combined set of assertions to the SP. The SP validates each assertion, retrieves all attributes and then determines if the user can access the service.

3.1   Analysis

Each of these models has their own strengths and weaknesses which is hard to comprehend at the first instance from the textual description as outlined above. Therefore, we present our analysis in tabular formats in Table 3 which outlines a side-by-side comparison of these models (Ferdous and Poet 2013a). The more requirements one model has to fulfil the more complex it will be to establish, maintain and scale. Therefore, an optimal aggregation model should have a relatively small number of requirements with a good number of advantages. It is clear from Table 3 that no model is unquestionably superior to other models. Next, we choose a suitable candidate for further research.

At the beginning, our main goal has been to investigate if there is any way we can leverage the advantages of different models by combining them together

Table 3. Aggregation models: strengths and weaknesses

Models	Advantages	Disadvantages
AD	Easy to implement and maintain. Small number of requirements	Aggregation from only one IdP in a session. Changing identifiers causes the system to fail
SPM	Aggregation from a number of IdPs in a session	Hard to maintain. Multiple logins at the IdPs in a single SP session. No implementation exists
LS	Secure and Privacy-preserving. Proof of concept implementation available. Attribute aggregation from multiple IdPs in a single session. SSO capability during service access	Unrealistic trust assumption. Hard to deploy and difficult to maintain. The LS represents a single point of failure
IFL	Secure and Privacy-preserving. Proof of concept implementation available. SSO capability during service access	Unrealistic trust assumption. Difficult to maintain and scale. Attribute aggregation from only two IdPs in a single session
IP	Attribute aggregation from multiple IdPs in a single session. The SP is easy to maintain. Relatively small number of requirements	The Proxy IdP requiring huge trust might not be suitable. The Proxy IdP is the single point of failure. No implementation exists
IR	Attribute aggregation from multiple IdPs in a single session. The SP is easy to maintain. Relatively small number of requirements. Less trust on the Relay IdP	The Relay IdP is the single point of failure. Hard to maintain. No implementation exists
CM	No need to rely on external IdPs. Attribute aggregation from multiple IdPs in a single session. Relatively small number of requirements	No implementation exists currently. Extensive changes are required to ensure that the IdPs, the SPs and the client can interact

to come up with a hybrid model that offers less complex user interactions, has a significantly smaller number of requirements as well as relatively fewer disadvantages and preferably has already been implemented. There is no direct available implementation of the AD, however, the model can be implemented with a little bit of additional code that will create, store and map the IdP-supplied identifier with the local identifier using any existing SAML implementation. Unfortunately, its main limitation is that it can aggregate attributes only from one IdP and therefore it has been ruled out of our consideration. Similarly, the CM model does not have any implementation and it will require a considerable number of changes in the existing standards to ensure that different IdPs, SPs and users can interact using this model. The next two models that have existing implementations are the LS and the IFL models. Even though, both these models, especially the LS model, have a good number of advantages, their weaknesses (in Table 3) limit their usefulness and hence we have also ruled them out of our consideration. The SPM model allows an SP to aggregate attributes from multiple IdPs, however, to deploy this model, a significant number of changes (e.g. saving and restoring sessions while the SP makes the SAML authentication request and receives the response, how the WAYF page displays the list of IdPs, etc.) are required at the SP side. We do not want an SP needing to make a vast number of changes to ensure that the existing SAML SPs are as less affected as possible. With all these goals in mind, the IP and the IR models seem to be the suitable candidates for our hybrid model. They both offer a good number of advantages and require a small number of trust assumptions. Moreover, one significant disadvantage of the IP model, the huge reliance on the Proxy IdP, can be tackled by allowing the Proxy IdP to act as the Relay IdP when it is required which will reduce the amount of trust needed on that IdP. This essentially brings us to this question: can we combine these two models to leverage the advantages in such a way that the advantages of one model can be used to reduce the disadvantages of the other model and then offer something more that none of the other existing models offer individually? In this work, we will seek answer to this very question.

4   The Hybrid Model

With the IP and the IR models chosen as the suitable candidates for our research, the next thing we would like to do is to design a model by combining the IP and IR model which will be denoted as the **Hybrid Model** and the trusted IdP of our model will be denoted as the **Hybrid IdP**. At first, we devise a threat model for identifying threats in our proposed model and for formulating different security and privacy requirements to minimise these threats.

4.1   Threat Modelling

Threat modelling is an integrated process of designing and developing a secure system. A well-defined threat model helps to identify threats on different assets of a secure system. In order to tackle such threats, different mitigation strategies need to be outlined by formulating security and privacy requirements (Myagmar et al. 2005). In essence, a threat modelling consists of the following steps (Desmet et al. 2005; De Cock et al. 2006):

1. llisting assets of the system,
2. identifying possible threats on those assets and
3. outlining mitigation strategies.

Each secure system since has different assets, the threat modelling process of one system will be considerably different than that of another system. Here, we would like to restrict our focus on modelling threats in the setting of a FIM System. There exist only a very few papers in this context; notably in (Khattak et al. 2010; Dominicini et al. 2010). Additionally, there are a few papers focusing on the issue of threat modelling in the setting of web services (Desmet et al. 2005; De Cock et al. 2006). Based on these works, each single step of our threat modelling process is described in the following sections.

4.1.1   Listing Assets

An asset is the abstract or physical resource in a FIM system that needs to be protected from an adversary (attacker) (Myagmar et al. 2005). It is the resource for which a threat exists and represents the target of the adversary in the system. Examples of physical assets include different hardware such as the server machine where a specific system is hosted, the network components such as routers by which data is transmitted from one system to another and machines such as computers, smartphones and tablets from which users access different online services. Examples of abstract resources include different software such as operating systems running the physical servers, web servers, web services and data. Since our focus in this paper is on federated web services, we are mostly interested about software resources. The motivation behind this step is to highlight those assets in the system which can be the target of an adversary so that associated threats for these assets can be identified. Based on the threat modelling of an Identity Management System in (Dominicini et al. 2010), we list the following assets:

- **Partial Identity of a user.** In a FIM system, the partial identity ($parIdent_d^u$) of a user u in a domain/system d can be regarded as the core asset since the main purpose of such a system is to help a user to manage her partial identity and leverage it for accessing online services.
- **Activities associated with a partial identity.** Not only the partial identity, but also how the partial identity of a user is leveraged for accessing different online services using a FIM system represents a valuable asset. This is because such associated activities offer a lucrative way for an adversary to track users across different application domains.
- **Web services.** In a FIM system, web services must be protected from unauthorised accesses and should be accessible to only those who can prove their rights to access them using their partial identities.

4.1.2   Identifying Threats

A threat represents the activity or capability of an adversary onto an asset of a system with an intention to invade the security of the system or invade the privacy of a user in the system (Myagmar et al. 2005). The main motivation behind this step is to identity possible threats on different assets of the system so that proper mitigation techniques can be carefully planned. Based on the treat modelling process presented in (Desmet et al. 2005; Dominicini et al. 2010; Khattak et al. 2010), we identify the following threats:

1. **Spoofing.** Information regarding the partial identity of a user is disclosed to another unauthenticated and unauthorised user allowing the second user to impersonate the first user.
2. **Tampering.** An attacker can intercept data while being transmitted and change it with malicious intent.
3. **Repudiation.** An attacker can deny performing a certain action and another party cannot prove it.

4. **Information disclosure.** User attributes are disclosed to service providers without the respective user's knowledge and consent.
5. **Escalation of privilege.** Aggregated attributes are released to an SP in such a way that it will enable an attacker to gain unprivileged accesses.
6. **Malicious providers.** Malicious service providers getting hold of unnecessary attributes can abuse them for their own benefit. Two or more malicious service providers can collude to track the activities of a user in order to build a profile of the user without her knowledge. A Hybrid IdP can abuse the aggregated attributes by storing them at its end.
7. **Lack of control.** Once attributes of a user is released to an SP, users have no control over them and the SP can abuse the attributes without any knowledge of the user.

4.1.3   Mitigation Strategies

Once the threats have been identified, mitigation strategies must be carefully planned and transformed into actions to minimise the threats as much as possible. One way to achieve this is to transform them into requirements which the system must fulfil as proposed in (Myagmar et al. 2005). We have adopted this approach. In the next subsection, we formulate several security and privacy requirements which act as the mitigation strategies and fulfilling them will ensure that threats are minimised.

4.2   A Study of Requirements

Next, we formulate a set of Functional, Security, Privacy and Trust requirements that we want our model to fulfil. The requirements are based on the requirements for the IP and IR models presented in (Ferdous and Poet 2013a) and have been rephrased with the reference of the Hybrid IdP. Among them, the security and privacy requirements formulated here act as mitigation strategies to minimise threats identified above as mentioned earlier. The requirements are presented below.

Functional Requirements (FR): The functional requirements ensure that a system behaves as desired. The requirements are:

F1. The Hybrid IdP and the SPs are part of the same federation. The other SAML IdPs and the Hybrid IdP are part of the same federation. The other SAML IdPs are part of the same federation with an SP, needed only for the IR model.

F2. A session is maintained at the Hybrid IdP so that the Hybrid IdP can correlate the attributes from the current IdP with attributes retrieved previously from other IdPs.

F3. The Hybrid IdP has dual capabilities of an IdP as well of an SP. The Hybrid IdP has to act as an IdP to the SP and as an SP to other IdPs.

F4. For the IP model, the assertion returned by other IdPs should be targeted for the trusted (Hybrid) IdP so that it can validate each assertion, extracts attributes from them and then aggregates all of them, possibly also with its own attributes.

F5. For the IR model, the assertions returned by other SAML IdPs should be targeted for an SP. The Hybrid IdP will just aggregate all assertions and embed them inside another assertion and send it back to the SP. The SP will validate the outer assertion and retrieve all embedded assertions. Then it must validate each assertion in turn to extract attributes from them.

Security Requirement (SR): The security requirements ensure the security during an interaction between entities. These requirements have been formulated to undermine the threats outlined above. The requirements are:

S1. The IdP should have a secure mechanism for user registration and authentication. A user must be authenticated before she can access her attributes and release those attributes to an SP. This requirement undermines threat 1.

S2. The transmitted data between two parties is not disclosed to any unauthorised entity.

S3. The transmitted data is not altered during transmission. Combinedly, S2 and S3 undermine threat 2.

S4. A user, once committed for a transaction, cannot deny her commitment in the transaction. It undermines threat 3.

Privacy Requirements (PR): The following privacy requirements ensure that the privacy of a user is preserved during attribute aggregation via any FIM system.

P1. The Hybrid IdP should allow a user to access services anonymously or using pseudonymous identifiers. This will ensure that two malicious SPs cannot collude to build a profile of a user.

P2. The Hybrid IdP should implement the selective disclosure of attributes to allow a user to select specific attributes before they are released to an SP. By this way, the user can choose specific attributes for a specific SP.

P3. The Hybrid IdP should allow a user to provide explicit consent before any data is released to an SP. Combinedly, P2 and P3 undermine threat 4.

P4. To ensure data minimisation, an SP must inform a user about the minimum number of attributes that the user must release to access any particular service of that SP.

P5. One way to enforce the control over the data, released to an SP, is to allow users to administer their data remotely, preferably using remote policies. If an IdP and an SP inside a federation offer this facility, there should be a user-interface at the IdP for the user to administer such policies and there should be a mechanism to exchange such policies between the IdP and the SP. This undermines threat 7.

Trust Requirements (TR): This set enlists those requirements that outline the scopes in which each entity trusts another entity during an attribute aggregation scenario using a FIM system.

T1. A user and an SP trust that an IdP has implemented satisfactory user registration procedures and authentication mechanisms. The SP trusts that the IdP will authenticate the user appropriately as per the requirement and will release user attributes securely.

T2. A user trusts that an IdP protects the user's privacy to an SP by using anonymous or pseudonymous identifiers and the IdP will release only those attributes to the SP that the user has consented to.

T3. A user trusts that an SP will ask only for the minimum number of user attributes that are required to access any of its services and will not abuse the released user attributes.

T4. The IdP and the user trust that the SP adheres to the agreed privacy policies regarding non-disclosure of user data.

T5. For the IR model, the user trusts that the other SAML IdPs release assertions in such a way that they are only accessible by the corresponding SP.

In essence, these functional, security and privacy requirements signify the technical conditions that must be considered while designing and developing an attribute aggregation mechanism using a FIM system and can be used to satisfy the trust requirements. Now, to design a model to aggregate attributes from other SAML IdPs, it will require formulating novel requirements. We have identified the gaps in the IP and IR models and formulated them as requirements which are enlisted below:

Functional Requirements (FR)

F6. There should be a mechanism to filter out an IdP once a user has aggregated attributes from that IdP to ensure that the user does not chose the same IdP over and over again.

F7. The existing proxy model assumes that the aggregated attributes, from the SAML IdPs, are combined to build a single assertion to pass over to an SP. The effect of this assumption is that the original sources of the attributes are lost, leaving the SP with the notion that the attributes have originated from the trusted Proxy IdP. This is a risky assumption to make which might escalate privileges since some (or even all) attributes might originate from the SAML IdPs which the SP might not trust at all. To prevent the SP from making such risky assumptions, the Proxy IdP must indicate the source of all attributes. Moreover, the Proxy IdP should use the NIST LoA (Level of Assurance or Level of Authentication (NISTWP 2006)) of level 1 to 4, where the level 1 signifies the lowest and the lever 4 signifies the highest level of assurance, to assert the assurance level of the attributes from each IdP. The best way to embed these values is to group attributes from a single IdP and then insert the source and the perceived LoA value for each group.

F8. An SP should have the capabilities to interpret such groupings to ensure that the SP can easily identify the source of each attributes as well as the LoA value associated with them.

F9. It is the user who should have the ability to choose between the IP and IR models. If the user chooses the IR model, it means that she wants the other IdP to release an encrypted assertion, instead of the regular unencrypted assertion, to an SP via the Hybrid IdP. In such cases, the Hybrid IdP should forward the information regarding the SP to the other IdP to enable it to generate the encrypted assertion properly.

Security Requirements (SR)

S5. To ensure the security of attributes, the Hybrid IdP must not store the aggregated attributes (assertions for the IR model) once the session with the Hybrid IdP is terminated. Combinedly, P1, P4 and S5 undermine threat 6.

S6. The LoA of other IdPs are properly determined by the Proxy IdP. This helps an SP to take correct authorisation decision and hence undermines threat 5.

Privacy Requirements (PR): There are no additional privacy requirements other than *P1 - P5*. However, it should be noted that all privacy requirements are applicable for external IdPs (including the Hybrid IdP).

Trust Requirements (TR): All mentioned trust requirements for the IP and IR models are applicable for our model. Note that $T4$ is applicable for the Hybrid IdP as well. In addition, we have the additional following requirements:

T6. A user trusts that the Hybrid IdP does not store any released attributes or assertions from the other IdPs.

T7. An SP trusts that the Hybrid IdP groups the attributes correctly according to their sources and the source for each group as well as the associated LoAs for each group are released to the SP.

4.2.1 Analysis

The trust requirement $T1$ can be satisfied by fulfilling requirements $S1$, $S2$ and $S3$ since these security requirements ensure that the IdP has implemented the required methods for adequate user registration and subsequent authentication. The requirement $T2$ can be satisfied by fulfilling $P1$ and $P3$ as these privacy requirements will enable a user to access services anonymously/pseudonymously and to provide explicit consent before releasing attributes to an SP. The requirement $T3$ is fulfilled by $P4$ as $P4$ ensures data minimisation. Since fulfilling $P5$ will enable a user and an IdP to determine how data are treated at an SP and if the SP adheres to the agreed policy, this will ensure $T4$ being satisfied.

Furthermore, if *F5* is satisfied, this will ensure that *T5* is fulfilled. Since meeting *S5* will ensure that aggregated attributes or assertions are not stored in the Hybrid IdP, this will fulfil *T6*. Finally, satisfying *F8* and *S6* will ensure that attributes are grouped according to their sources and the Hybrid IdP adds the correct LoA value for each source, this will fulfil the final trust requirement *T7*.

Table 4 illustrates a side-by-side comparison of requirements met by the IP, IR and Hybrid models. As mentioned earlier, the novel requirements of the Hybrid model are formulated to address the gaps in functionalities in the IP and IR models.

Table 4. Comparison of requirements

Models	TR	FR	SR	PR
IP	T1–T4	F1–F3, F4	S1–S4	P1–P5
IR	T1–T5	F1–F3, F5	S1–S4	P1–P5
Hybrid	T1–T7	F1–F9	S1–S6	P1–P5

4.3 Architecture

The architecture of our Hybrid Model is illustrated in Fig. 1. The dotted area in the figure represents the Circle of Trust (i.e. the federation) between two entities. The Hybrid IdP, which acts as the trusted third party (TTP), takes the central stage in our model. Any number of SAML IdPs can be added with the Hybrid IdP. These IdPs will act as the third party IdPs and a user can aggregate attributes from these IdPs using the Hybrid IdP. Any such third-party SAML IdPs (*SAML IdP1* and *SAML IdP2* in Fig. 1) must be federated with the Hybrid IdP. Furthermore, an SP has to be federated with the Hybrid IdP (as illustrated in Fig. 1). Thus, the Hybrid IdP takes the role of a Proxy IdP and the protocol flow for any use-case will be similar to that of the IP model.

One major limitation of this approach is that attributes are exposed to the Hybrid IdP during the aggregation process and hence, the Hybrid IdP needs to

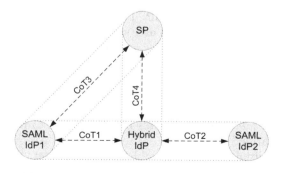

Fig. 1. Architecture of Hybrid model.

be trusted. Unfortunately, even if it is trusted, there is no guarantee that it will not abuse those attributes. One way to tackle this limitation is to enable the IR mode of the Hybrid IdP so that it acts as a Relay IdP. This will enable other SAML IdPs to release encrypted assertions to SPs via the Hybrid IdP. Since, all assertions will be exposed to the Hybrid IdP in encrypted formats, attribute will not be exposed. To enable this protocol flow, the SP must be federated with any other third-party SAML IdPs so that they can release encrypted assertions for the SP. The absence of any federation between an SP and any third-party SAML IdPs will prohibit the user to release any encrypted assertions from those IdPs to the SP via the Hybrid IdP. For example, in Fig. 1, the SAML IdP1 can release encrypted assertions to the SP whereas the SAML IdP2 cannot.

The whole architecture has been designed in such a way that it satisfies the majority of the requirements enlisted above. We will explain how our design choices achieve this in the subsequent section. Then, we will illustrate two use-cases for two different scenarios using our implementation.

4.4   Implementation

We have based our work using SimpleSAMLphp. This is for two reasons. Firstly, SimpleSAMLphp has built-in support for the Selective Disclosure of attributes based on its *Consent* module. Secondly, SimpleSAMLphp also has another built-in module called the *Multiauth* module that allows a SAML IdP to delegate the authentication task to an external SAML IdP and then release the attributes to an SP via a SAML assertion once the user has authenticated at the external IdP and returned back to the SAML IdP with attributes. This particular behaviour essentially allows the IdP to act as the Proxy IdP. However, it does not allow choosing more than one IdP for a particular session, hence attribute aggregation from multiple IdPs are not possible and cannot return an encrypted assertion to an SP, hence, it cannot perform as a Relay IdP. Even with these limitations, these two modules would give us a solid platform to base our work with the main focus to confine most of our changes to the Consent and the Multiauth modules and to modify the core code-base of SimpleSAMLphp only when there is an absolute necessity.

In SimpleSAMLphp, the consent module is loaded to show a consent form once a user is authenticated at an IdP. The consent form displays the list of attributes (the partial identity) of the user stored at the IdP and allows the user to choose the attributes that she wishes to release to an SP. We have modified the Consent module by adding two new inputs - a check box and a button - so that the consent form acts as the entry point for allowing users to aggregate attributes. The modified consent form is illustrated in Fig. 2. The check box with the text *Return Encrypted Assertion* is used to toggle between the IP and IR mode and the *Aggregate More Attributes* button is used to initiate the process of attribute aggregation.

The original Multiauth module enables an IdP to act as a Proxy IdP to delegate the authentication to other IdPs. A list of such IdPs is shown to the user at the IdP. Once the user selects the IdP, she is forwarded to the chosen

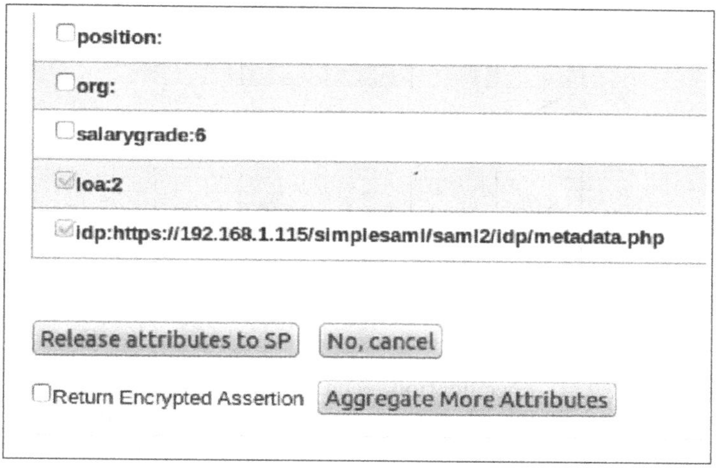

Fig. 2. The modified consent form.

IdP where the user authentication takes place. Then the user is redirected back to the Proxy IdP where a session is created. Once the session is created, the user cannot choose another IdP without logging out from the Proxy IdP. We need to change this behaviour of the Multiauth module and the SimpleSAMLphp IdP code-base to allow users to choose other IdPs even if there is a session at the IdP. For this, we have made two amendments: (i) the Multiauth module has been modified so that it shows the list of external IdPs, excluding those IdP(s) a user has already authenticated at, when the user clicks the *Aggregate More Attributes* button at the consent page and (ii) the SimpleSAMLphp IdP code-base has been modified to allow the user to initiate an authentication process even if the user has a session at an IdP and to retain that session when the user is redirected back from the chosen external IdP. This allows the IdP to collate attributes from the recently authenticated IdP with the attributes aggregated previously.

When attributes are aggregated from multiple sources at the Hybrid IdP and passed to an SP inside a single assertion, it will be impossible for the SP to identify the source of each single attribute. Without identifying the source of each attribute, it might be difficult for the SP to take access control decisions. None of the previous implementations considered this crucial issue. The best way to retian the source of the attributes is to group them according to their sources while aggregating them at the Hybrid IdP. In addition, the Hybrid IdP can also determine the LoA value for each IdP and add this information to each group. We need a data structure to hold all this information and one of the options for such a data structure is a list of lists where each entry of the list will signify a list holding the attributes from a particular IdP along with its LoA value. The structure is illustrated in Fig. 3.

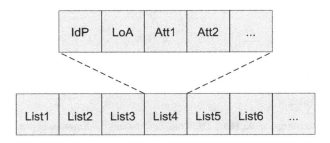

Fig. 3. The data structure for Attribute list.

In the current SAML specification, each attribute, with its value, is inserted inside an AttributeStatement element (Standard 2005). The schema for the AttributeStatement is given in Listing 1. If the grouped attributes following our data structure are inserted in the AttributeStatement element in this manner, there are chances that each group might get mixed up with each other. To mitigate this problem, we propose the inclusion of a new SAML element called *AttributeStatements*. The schema of the proposed element is given in Listing 2. The *AttributeStatements* element will essentially accommodate one or more AttributeStatement element(s) and will signify our proposed data structure. In this way, the Proxy IdP can include the IdP and LoA information for group of attribute inside each AttributeStatement element. We have modified the IdP and the SP code-bases of SimpleSAMLphp to reflect this mechanism.

The next amendment made is to handle the IR mode. The relay mode will enable the external IdP to release an encrypted assertion to the Hybrid IdP. To do so, we need two things: (i) a mechanism to signal to an external IdP that the Hybrid IdP (actually the user) is requesting an encrypted assertion and (ii) the Entity ID of an SP so that the external IdP can encrypt the assertion that is only decryptable by the SP. Since the SP is only communicating with the Hybrid IdP, not with the external IdP, the Hybrid IdP has the responsibility of passing on these two pieces of information. As stated earlier, a check box in the consent form is used to toggle between the IP and IR mode to indicate if a user wants to receive an encrypted assertion. Once the checkbox is ticked and the user clicks the *Aggregate More Attributes* button, an attribute called **EmbedAssertion** is added to the SAML authentication request which contains the Entity ID of the SP.

When the external IdP receives a SAML authentication request, it checks for an attribute called **EmbedAssertion**. If this attribute is not found, the IdP behaves as usual. However, if the attribute is found, the external IdP knows that it has to release an encrypted assertion. Then, the Entity ID of the SP is retrieved from that attribute which is used to create an encrypted assertion. The encrypted assertion is then Base64 encoded and added as the value of a special type of attribute called **encryptedAssertion** into an AttributeStatement element which is then embedded inside a regular unencrypted SAML assertion. This regular assertion is then passed to the Proxy IdP. After receiving an assertion from the external IdP, the Hybrid IdP validates it and if it finds that there is an attribute called ***encryptedAssertion***, it is treated specially (see below). Otherwise, the attributes retrieved from the external IdP are aggregated with the previously aggregated attributes and are presented in the consent form. We have added necessary amendments to SimpleSAMLphp code-bases to reflect this behaviour.

Listing 1. Schema for AttributeStatement Element

```
<element  name="AttributeStatement"
type="saml:AttributeStatementType"/>
<complexType  name="AttributeStatementType">
  <complexContent>
  <extension  base="saml:StatementAbstractType">
    <choice  maxOccurs="unbounded">
      <element  ref="saml:Attribute"/>
      <element  ref="saml:EncryptedAttribute"/>
    </choice>
  </extension>
  </complexContent>
</complexType>
```

Listing 2. Proposed Schema for AttributeStatements Element

```
<element  name="AttributeStatements"
type="saml:AttributeStatementsType"/>
<complexType  name="AttributeStatementsType">
  <complexContent>
  <extension  base="saml:StatementAbstractType">
    <choice  minOccurs="1"  maxOccurs="unbounded">
      <element  ref="saml:AttributeStatement"/>
    </choice>
  </extension>
  </complexContent>
</complexType>
```

To achieve data minimisation, the selective disclosure of attributes and to provide an optimal way of aggregating attributes, the user must know beforehand the attributes required by an SP to access its services. As mentioned earlier, one way to achieve this is to show the list of attributes for each specific service at the SP home page as adopted in (Chadwick and Inman 2013). However, it is not realistic to assume that a user will remember such a list for each service. A draft to extend the SAML AuthnRequest element has been proposed in (Sampo Kellomäki 2008) to include a SAML AttributeQuery statement within the authentication request. We have adopted this approach in this implementation. SimpleSAMLphp IdP and SP code-bases have been modified to include the AttributeQuery statement, containing the list of required attributes, with the SAML AuthnRequest statement at the SP side as well as to parse the list of attributes from the AttributeQuery statement of the authentication request at the IdP side and then to show them at the top of the consent form (Fig. 4). The modified SAML authentication request containing i number of requested attributes can be modelled in this way:

$$AuthnReq' = (id_{req}, id_{sp}, (a_1, a_2, \ldots a_i)).$$

We believe that the consent form is the best place to show the required attributes as it will allow a user to choose an IdP from where she can aggregate attributes as well as to decide the minimum number of attributes she needs to release to an SP. In addition, when a user chooses another external SAML IdP for attribute aggregation, these requested attributes will also be included within the AttributeQuery element of the SAML AuthnRequest that will be sent to the external IdP. This will enable any external SAML IdP to parse and show the requested attributes at any appropriate place. Moreover, the capability has been added to the SP code-base that will allow the admin to set the required attributes for each SP in the configuration file (called *config.php* in SimpleSAMLphp) which will be used to configure the AttributeQuery element which ultimately is embedded inside the AuthnRequest statement as described before. In this manner, the admin can set different attribute requirements for different SPs.

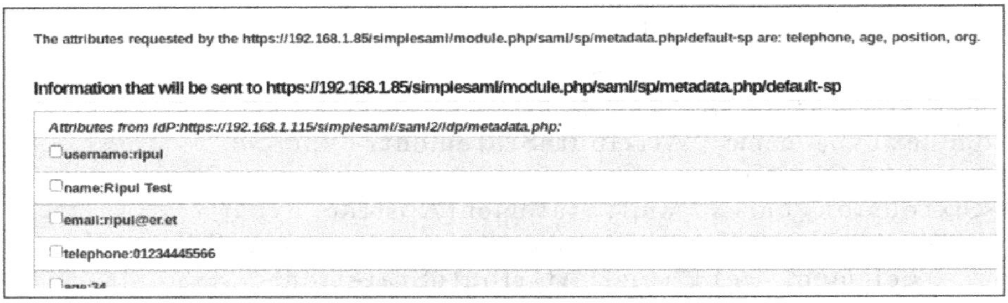

The attributes requested by the https://192.168.1.85/simplesaml/module.php/saml/sp/metadata.php/default-sp are: telephone, age, position, org.

Information that will be sent to https://192.168.1.85/simplesaml/module.php/saml/sp/metadata.php/default-sp

Attributes from IdP:https://192.168.1.115/simplesaml/saml2/idp/metadata.php:

□username:ripul

□name:Ripul Test

□email:ripul@er.et

□telephone:01234445566

□age:34

Fig. 4. The requested attributes at the consent form.

The current implementation equipped with all these features can aggregate attributes from different SAML IdPs. The implementation supports two types of SAML IdPs: trusted and semi-trusted. A trusted SAML IdP is the one which has been federated in the traditional way by exchanging metadata at the admin level whereas a semi-trusted SAML IdP is the one that has been federated using the concept of dynamic federation (Ferdous and Poet 2013b). In addition, the Hybrid IdP determines the LoA for each IdP in this way: attributes from the Hybrid IdP or from any trusted SAML IdP will have a LoA value of 2 whereas attributes from all other IdPs will have a LoA value of 1. The LoA level signifies the confidence the Hybrid IdP has on those IdPs.

At this point, we would like to compare our proposed approach with an already implemented attribute aggregation method. In (Chadwick and Inman 2013), authors have presented an approach for attribute aggregation from SAML IdPs. The approach is loosely based on the Identity Proxying model where the role of a Proxy IdP has been replaced with a web service called Trusted Attribute Aggregation Service or TAAS. To access any service from an SP, a user is forwarded to the TAAS which aggregates attributes from different IdPs and sends the aggregated set of attributes to the SP. As such, this is similar to the Identity Proxying capability of the Hybrid IdP. However, there are several distinct differences between our model and the TAAS. Firstly, TAAS does not have the Identity Relay capability meaning that all attributes released by other IdPs are exposed to TAAS. Secondly, TAAS requires every user to install a browser plugin to initate the protocol flow whereas our model does not rely on any such external component.

5   Use-cases

In this section we present two use-cases to show the applicability of our model. Each use-case illustrates the interaction between different entities utilising the implemented Hybrid model to aggregate attributes from multiple SAML IdPs. To present each interaction we use the following notation:

$$e_1 \xrightarrow{HTTPS} e_2 : \text{msg/resource}$$

The notation represents that a message (request/response) or a resource is transferred from entity e_1 to entity e_2 using a secure HTTPS channel. Moreover, we denote a user with u, an SP with sp, the Hybrid IdP as $hy - idp$ and other IdPs with idp_i where $i = 1 \ldots n$.

Each use-case is presented below.

5.1   Use-case 1

The first use-case illustrates the simplest form of attribute aggregation using the Hybrid model. The initial setup is: a user wants to access a service from an SP. The SP requires a set of user attributes from the IdP(s). The SP is deployed using our modified SimpleSAMLphp and is federated with the Hybrid IdP. The other SAML IdP is also implemented using SimpleSAMLphp. Moreover, the admin of the SP has configured the required attributes for each service in the configuration file as mentioned above. With this setup, the protocol flow for the use-case is illustrated in Fig. 5 and is described below:

1. The user visits the SP to access one of its services. The user submits an access request for the service.
2. The user is forwarded to the WAYF Page of the SP to choose the IdP.
3. The user chooses the Hybrid IdP.
4. The required attribute(s) for the requested service are read from the configuration file and are used to create a SAML authentication request. The user is redirected to the Hybrid IdP with the SAML authentication request ($AuthnReq'$).
5. The user is authenticated at the Hybrid IdP after providing his identifier (user-id) and credential (password).

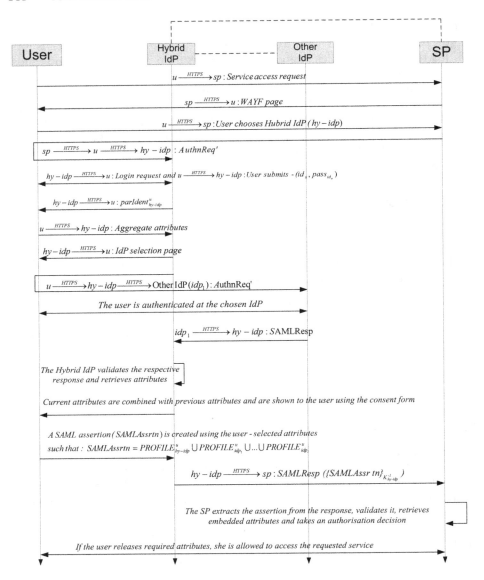

Fig. 5. Protocol flow for Use-case 1.

6. Once the user is authenticated, the consent form is shown which consists of the user attributes and their respective values (the partial identity, $parIdent_{hy-idp}^{u}$) stored in the Hybrid IdP.

7. The consent form displays the requested attributes from the SP (Fig. 4). In addition, the consent form allows the user to aggregate more attributes from other IdPs as well (Fig. 2). The user compares the requested attributes and the attributes shown in the consent form to decide if she needs to aggregate attributes.

8. Assuming the user decides to aggregate attributes, she clicks the *Aggregate More Attributes* button.
9. A session is created to keep track of the previous attributes and then the user is forwarded to the IdP selection page of the Hybrid IdP. The page contains the list of only those IdPs that have not been used already.
10. The user chooses one IdP (idp_1) and based on the user's selection, the respective protocol is initiated. For example, a SAML authentication request is created and the user is forwarded to the respective IdP.
11. The user authenticates at the respective IdP and releases the attributes to the Hybrid IdP using their respective protocol and implementations. For example, if the user chooses a SAML IdP that supports selective disclosure (e.g. SimpleSAMLphp), the user is shown a basic consent form where she chooses the attributes. Based on her selection, a SAML response will be returned to the Hybrid IdP.
12. Once the user returns to the Hybrid IdP, it validates the SAML assertion using its corresponding mechanism. Then, the attributes are retrieved from the assertion. Next, the previously aggregated attributes are retrieved using the saved session and these two sets of attributes are then merged together using the data structure mentioned previously and are shown to the user using the consent form (Fig. 6). From the figure, the attributes are grouped based on the IdP. The Hybrid IdP determines the LoA for each IdP. Note that, the IdP attribute and the LoA attribute for each attribute group are disabled so that the user cannot unselect them. If the user chooses to release at least one attribute from an attribute group, the respective IdP and the LoA value will be attached along with the chosen attribute(s).

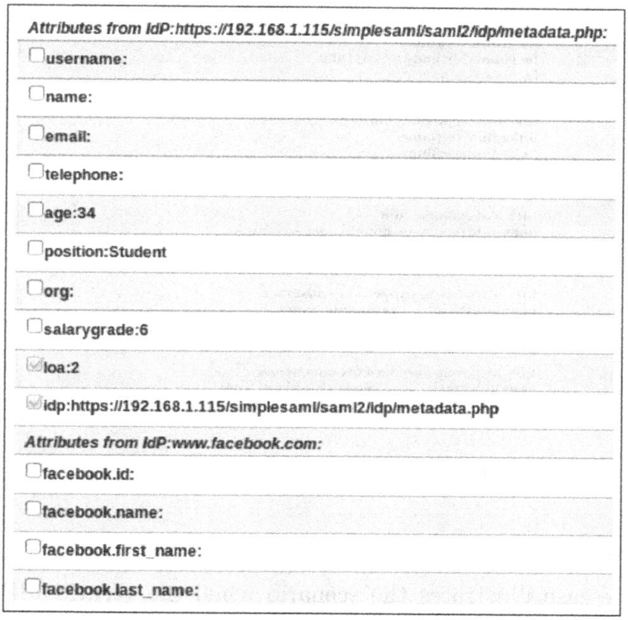

Fig. 6. Aggregated attributes from two IdPs at the consent form.

13. The requested attributes from the SP are listed at the consent form. The user can always consult that list to determine if she needs to aggregate more attributes. If so, the steps 4–7 are repeated.
14. Once the user has aggregated the required attributes, she selects those attributes and based on the user selection, attributes from each group are wrapped inside a SAML AttributeStatement element and then different such elements are wrapped inside a SAML AttributeStatements element. Then a SAML Response is created with the AttributeStatements element which is wrapped inside a SAML assertion and is sent back to the SP.
15. Upon receiving the assertion, the SP validates the assertion and retrieves the SAML AttributeStatements element. From there each attribute group is retrieved and from each group, all attributes are extracted. A sample of such attributes is illustrated in Fig. 7. Then, the SP can take authorisation decisions based on those attributes which is not explored any further.

Fig. 7. Released attributes from multiple IdPs in a single SP session.

5.2   Use-case 2

The second use-case illustrates the scenario when the Hybrid IdP acts as the Relay IdP using the IR model to ensure that another SAML IdP can release encrypted assertions to an SP as discussed previously. The setup is very similar to the first use-case except that the other SAML IdP needs to be federated with the SP to allow the other IdP to create an encrypted assertion targeted for the SP. We are also assuming that the user has already gone through the steps from 1–7 from the previous flow. With this setup, the protocol flow for the use-case is illustrated in Fig. 8 and is described below:

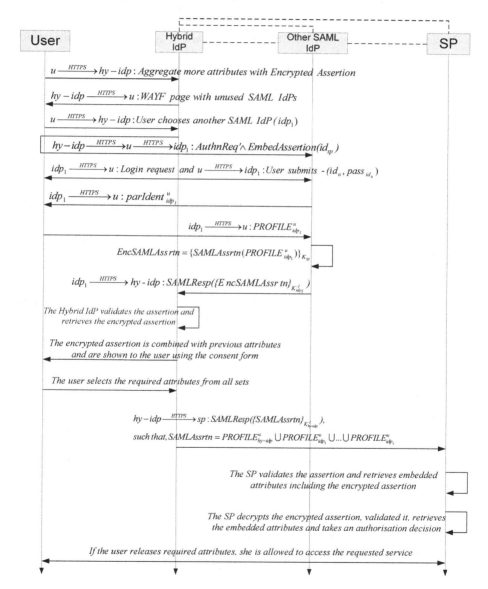

Fig. 8. Protocol flow for Use-case 2.

1. The user needs to aggregate attributes from a SAML IdP and she does not want to reveal the attributes to the Hybrid IdP. Therefore, she selects the *Return Encrypted Assertion* checkbox and clicks the *Aggregate More Attributes* button.
2. A session is created to keep track of the previous attributes and then the user is forwarded to the IdP selection page of the Hybrid IdP just like before. However, this time the page enlists only those SAML IdPs from which attributes have not been aggregated yet.
3. When the user chooses one SAML IdP (idp_1), a SAML authentication request is created. An attribute called *EmbedAssertion* in inserted within the request containing the Entity ID of the SP. Then the user is forwarded to the SAML IdP with the request.
4. The IdP notes the *EmbedAssertion* attribute in the request and the entity ID of the SP is stored in a session variable.
5. The user is authenticated at the IdP and then the consent form containing attributes (the partial identity of the user) stored at this IdP (idp_1) is shown.
6. The user chooses the attributes and clicks the *Release attributes to SP* button.
7. The IdP uses the entity ID from the session variable to create an encrypted assertion ($\{EncSAMLAssrtn\}_{K^{-1}_{idp_1}}$) targeted for the SP using the chosen attributes.
8. The encrypted assertion is then Base64 encoded and added as the value of the *encryptedAssertion* attribute and is used to create a regular unencrypted SAML assertion. The regular assertion is then sent back to the Hybrid IdP.
9. Upon receiving this assertion, the Hybrid IdP validates the assertion and retrieves the *encryptedAssertion* attribute. Since this encrypted assertion is not decryptable by the Hybrid IdP, the IdP treats it as it is.
10. Then, the Hybrid IdP merges the encrypted assertion with the previously aggregated attributes using the approach described before and displays all of them in different attribute groups in the consent page. Since, the Base64-encoded encrypted assertion can be quite a large value, it is not shown in the consent page. Instead, the text *Encrypted Assertion from the Other IdP* is shown (Fig. 9). Note that the Hybrid IdP assigns a LoA value of 2 for the encrypted assertion as the other SAML is assumed to be trusted in this instance.
11. When the user chooses the encrypted assertion (along with other attributes from other IdPs) and clicks the *Release attributes to SP* button, an assertion containing these attributes is created as described previously and is sent back to the SP.
12. The SP validates the assertion and retrieves attributes as discussed previously. However, when the SP finds the *encryptedAssertion* attribute, it is treated in a special way. The attribute is, at first, Base64-decoded. Then the SP decrypts the assertion, validates it and retrieves the attributes. Then the SP can take an authorisation decision as described above.

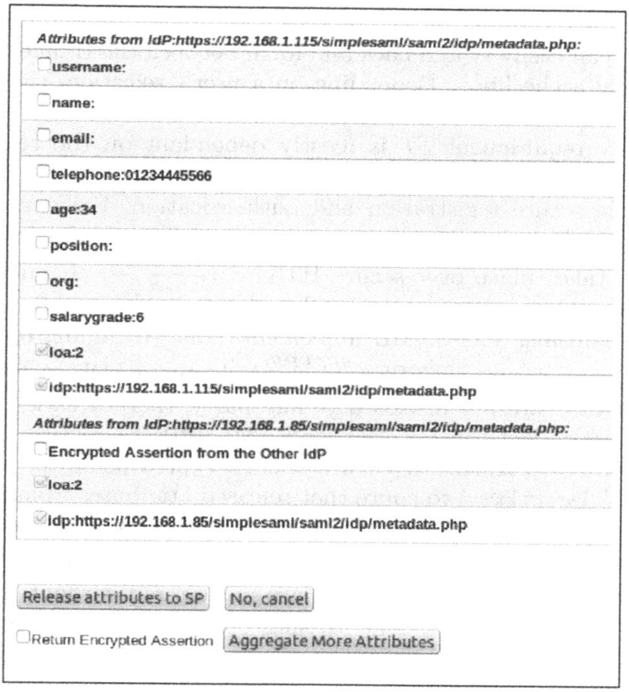

Fig. 9. Encrypted assertion as the attribute in the consent page.

6   Discussion

In this section, we will analyse if our proposed model can satisfy all the required functional, security and privacy requirements. We will also describe the advantages and the limitation of our model. In addition, possible future work will be discussed.

6.1   Analysis

The two use-cases illustrated previously require that the Hybrid IdP and the SP are part of the same federation as well as other SAML IdPs and the PPIdP are federated with the SP thereby satisfying *F1*. The Hybrid IdP also retains the sessions while the user is forwarded to aggregate attributes and performs a dual role as an IdP to the SP and as an SP to other IdPs thereby satisfying *F2* and *F3*. When other SAML IdPs return assertions to the Hybrid IdP, it validates the assertions as required by the SAML protocol and extracts the attributes and thus satisfies *F4*. Moreover, the approach of returning encrypted assertions to the Hybrid IdP satisfies *F5*. As evident from the use-cases, the Hybrid IdP filters out an IdP once it has been used for attribute aggregation and hence satisfies *F6*. The Hybrid IdP groups attributes according to their sources using the data structure described in Listing 2 with the proper LoA value and the SP has been equipped with the capability to interpret such groupings, therefore satisfying $F7$ and $F8$. A user can easily switch back and forth between the IP and the IR mode by just selecting a checkbox. Depending on a user's selection, the Hybrid IdP returns aggregated attributes or assertions. This satisfies $F9$.

The security requirement $S1$ is mostly dependant on the respective IdP. To prove its trustworthiness to its users, an IdP should deploy mechanisms that will enable secure registration and authentication. For our implementation, users can only access their attributes after being authenticated and the authentication takes place over secure HTTPS ($\xrightarrow{HTTPS}$) channel. Hence, $S1$ is fulfilled. Security requirements $S2$, $S3$ and $S4$ can be satisfied using cryptographic mechanisms. The SAML implementations (including ours) transmit user attributes over secure HTTPS ($\xrightarrow{HTTPS}$) channel which ensures that data during transmission are not disclosed to any party, thereby satisfying $S2$. Furthermore, the IR model can be used for SAML IdPs to release an encrypted SAML assertion ($EncSAMLAssrtn$) which is encrypted using the public key of the SP ($\{SAMLAssrtn\}_{K_{sp}}$) to enure that released attributes from a SAML IdP is not even disclosed to the Hybrid IdP. Similarly, these three standards use digital signature (e.g. $\{SAMLAssrtn\}_{K_{idp}^{-1}}$, the digitally signed SAML assertion) to ensure that data during transmission are not altered without being noticed and to enable non-repudiation. This satisfies $S3$ and $S4$. Moreover, the Hybrid IdP itself does not store any released attributes and it determines and assigns the LoA in a correct manner and thus satisfies $S5$ and $S6$.

The Hybrid IdP releases SP-specific pseudonymous identifiers to different SPs. This undermines the possibility of malicious SPs colluding together to track a user across multiple SPs and build a profile. Thus, it fulfils $P1$. The Hybrid IdP has support for the selective disclosure of attributes which enables users to select the attributes that they want to release to an SP. For other IdPs, how this property is fulfilled will depend on the respective IdP. As discussed before, Shibboleth SAML implementation does not have any support for the selective disclosure of attributes. In such scenarios, the Hybrid IdP provides another layer using the consent module to select attributes before they are released to an SP and hence it satisfies $P2$. Moreover, no attributes from the PPIdP are automatically released to an SP and the selective disclosure of attributes using the consent module ensures that users provide their explicit consent before they are released. This fulfils $P3$. Our implementation also enables an SP to inform a user which attributes are required to access a service and this ensures data minimisation as the user does not need to release all attributes to an SP. This satisfies $P4$. The SAML protocol does not have any mechanism for remote administration of policies that could be used to enforce $P5$ and also there is not a single SAML implementation that allows this features. We plan to work on this in future.

6.2 Advantages

The hybrid model offers a number of advantages which we describe below:

– By combining the features of the IP and IR models, we have been able to leverage the advantages of both models which allow a user to aggregate attributes almost seamlessly. The previously implemented models such as the LS and the IFL model require a user to engage in additional steps (e.g. the linking procedure) whereas the proposed approach does not require any such additional steps.

- Our model allows a user to switch between the IP and IR mode in the most convenient way - just by selecting a checkbox. Then all mechanisms are handled internally without burdening the user.
- Another added advantage that comes from the SSO feature of the SAML is that once the Hybrid IdP releases attributes to an SP, the user does not need to log in and choose attributes for the same SP until the session is lost. However, when the user accesses services from another SP and chooses the Hybrid IdP, the SSO feature directly takes the user to the consent form containing the already aggregated attributes from the first instance with the first SP. At this point, the user can aggregate more attributes if she wishes or chooses a separate set of attributes. In this way, the user can release completely different sets of attributes to different SPs using either the same or extended sets of aggregated attributes.
- None of the current SAML implementations allows an SP to pass on information regarding requested attributes along with the authentication request. The approach we have adopted to pass such request via the SAML authentication request is the first of its kind and could be widely adopted not only for the attribute aggregation mechanism but also for any general SAML implementation.

6.3   Limitations

There are a few limitations with our current implementation. These limitations are discussed below:

The LoAs of different IdPs are currently hard-coded. The way we have assigned LoAs might not suit every scenario. The best approach would be to allow the admin to assign the LoA at the configuration file and then read them during run-time.

There is another limitation when a PPIdP is used for aggregating attributes: the PPIdP allows a user to access the PPIdP only from a browser in the mobile phone where it is installed. This is not a realistic assumption for wide-scale adaptation of the approach.

Even though our approach allows any user to aggregate attributes from multiple SAML IdPs in single a session considering different security and privacy issues, the associated burden during the process from the perspective of a user needs to be considered. A user needs to go through several rounds of selection process - selecting the Hybrid IdP and then selecting a number of required IdPs and choosing required attributes from each of them - which might be a daunting experience for many users. For a successful deployment of the proposed approach, it must be justifiable to a user and the associated burden must be outweighed by its advantages. This will largely depend on the use-case scenarios for which the Hybrid model is deployed. This calls for a usability study for different scenarios. Depending of the result of that study, appropriate modifications may be suggested.

Furthermore, our approach assumes an SP to be honest in asking the number of attributes required for accessing its services. A malicious SP may request more than required attributes and once these attributes are received, they may be abused. This assumption finds it bases on the current setting of federated services in which an SP is never questioned on why it requires specified attributes for any specific services. One way to tackle this issue is to enforce privacy requirement *P5*. This will empower a user to understand how her attributes are utilised in an SP and help her to decide if the SP has been honest in requesting attributes. Furthermore, a dishonest SP can launch a phishing attack by redirecting users to a fake Hybrid IdP. From there, users can be redirected to fake IdPs which may have the same look and feel of the original IdPs. This would trick any user to expose their identifier and credential to the adversary. The authenticity of the Hybrid IdP can be verified using digital certificates with web PKI (Public Key Infrastructure) which can undermine this attack. Unfortunately, many general users still do not understand the technical details of this technology and hence are not proficient in verifying the authenticity of a website using digital certificates. This leaves them prone to such attacks.

6.4   Future Work

There are several directions to take from here:

- One major problem that still exists almost in every SAML system is the lack of control over the attributes once they are released to the SP. One way to achieve any control in this regard could be the use of remote administration of policies between two entities. None of the SAML implementation currently supports this mechanism. It will be interesting to investigate how such mechanisms can be integrated within the SAML.
- We are also working on how to allow the admin to configure LoAs for different IdPs at the configuration file.
- With the proliferation of online services and social networks, more and more user attributes will be stored online across multiple IdPs, most of which are non-SAML IdPs. Therefore, a mechanism to aggregate and manage those attributes from a central place will be useful for the users. We are investigating how the Hybrid model can be extended to aggregate attributes from non-SAML IdPs.

7   Conclusion

With the proliferation of online services, more and more user attributes will be stored online across multiple IdPs. Innovative service scenarios in the near future would definitely need a mechanism to allow users to aggregate attributes from multiple sources in the simplest of ways. The existing models are complex and require preliminary steps which are not intuitive. In this paper we present a hybrid way of aggregating attributes from differnt SAML IdPs in a single service session. The approach, based on the Identity Proxying and Relay model, is simple and does not require any preliminary step or complex user interactions like previous existing methods. Depending on the requirement, the user can switch back and forth between the proxy and relay model by selecting or un-selecting a single checkbox. Unlike any previous model, it allows the proxy and/or Relay IdP to retain the source of the aggregated attributes which would be beneficial for an SP to take any authorisation decision. We have proposed a few additional modifications of the SAML protocol and a novel way of letting an IdP know the attribute requirements of an SP which is missing in the current SAML specification. We strongly believe that our approach has true potential to advance federated service scenarios to the next step and to begin a new era of next generation federated services.

References

Hulsebosch, B., Wegdam, M., Zoetekouw, B., van Dijk, N., van Wijnen, R.P.: Virtual collaboration attribute management (2011). http://www.surfnet.nl/nl/Innovatiep rogramma's/gigaport3/Documents/EDS%2011-06%20AttributeManagement%20v1. 0.pdf. Accessed 1 May 2013

Cantor, S.: Shibboleth Attribute Release Policies, 7 January 2008. https://wiki.shibbo leth.net/confluence/display/SHIB/IdPARPConfig

Chadwick, D., Inman, G.: Attribute aggregation in federated identity management. Computer **42**(5), 33–40 (2009)

Chadwick, D., Inman, G.: The trusted attribute aggregation service (TAAS) - providing an attribute aggregation layer for federated identity management. In: Eighth International Conference on Availability, Reliability, Security (ARES), 2013, pp. 285–290, September 2013. doi:10.1109/ARES.2013.38

Chadwick, D.W.: Federated identity management. In: Aldini, A., Barthe, G., Gorrieri, R. (eds.) FOSAD 2007–2009. LNCS, vol. 5705, pp. 96–120. Springer, Heidelberg (2009). doi:10.1007/978-3-642-03829-7_3. http://www.cs.kent.ac.uk/pubs/2009/3030

Chadwick, D.W., Inman, G.L., Siu, K.W., Ferdous, M.S.: Leveraging social networks to gain access to organisational resources. In: Proceedings of the 7th ACM Workshop on Digital Identity Management, pp. 43–52. ACM, New York (2011). doi:10.1145/2046642.2046653

Chappell, D.: Introducing Windows CardSpace, April 2006. http://msdn.microsoft. com/en-us/library/aa480189.aspx

De Cock, D., Wouters, K., Schellekens, D., Singelee, D., Preneel, B.: Threat modelling for security tokens in web applications. In: Chadwick, D., Preneel, B. (eds.) CMS 2004. ITIFIP, vol. 175, pp. 183–193. Springer, Heidelberg (2005). doi:10.1007/0-387-24486-7_14

Desmet, L., Jacobs, B., Piessens, F., Joosen, W.: Threat modelling for web services based web applications. In: Chadwick, D., Preneel, B. (eds.) CMS 2004. ITIFIP, vol. 175, pp. 131–144. Springer, Heidelberg (2005). doi:10.1007/0-387-24486-7_10

Dominicini, C.K., Simplício Jr., M.A., Sakuragui, R.R., Carvalho, T.C., Näslund, M., Pourzandi, M.: Threat modeling an identity management system for mobile internet, Rio de Janeiro, Brasil (2010). http://www.teses.usp.br/teses/disponiveis/3/3141/tde-23032012-101827/publico/Tese_RonySakuragui.pdf

Ferdous, M.S., Chowdhury, M.J.M., Moniruzzaman, M., Chowdhury, F.: Identity federations: a new perspective for Bangladesh. In: 2012 International Conference on Informatics, Electronics Vision (ICIEV), pp. 219–224, May 2012

Ferdous, M.S., Jøsang, A., Singh, K., Borgaonkar, R.: Security usability of petname systems. In: Jøsang, A., Maseng, T., Knapskog, S.J. (eds.) NordSec 2009. LNCS, vol. 5838, pp. 44–59. Springer, Heidelberg (2009). doi:10.1007/978-3-642-04766-4_4

Ferdous, M.S., Norman, G., Poet, R.: Mathematical modelling of identity, identity management and other related topics. In: Proceedings of the 7th International Conference on Security of Information and Networks, p. 9 (2014)

Ferdous, M.S., Poet, R.: Analysing attribute aggregation models in federated identity management. In: Proceedings of the 6th International Conference on Security of Information and Networks, pp. 181–188. ACM (2013a)

Ferdous, M.S., Poet, R.: Dynamic identity federation using security assertion markup language (SAML). In: Fischer-Hübner, S., Leeuw, E., Mitchell, C. (eds.) IDMAN 2013. IAICT, vol. 396, pp. 131–146. Springer, Heidelberg (2013b). doi:10.1007/978-3-642-37282-7_13

Jøsang, A., Zomai, M.A., Suriadi, S.: Usability, privacy in identity management architectures. In: ACSW 2007: Proceedings of the Fifth Australasian Symposium on ACSW Frontiers', pp. 143–152 (2007)

Khattak, Z.A., Sulaiman, S., Manan, J.: A study on threat model for federated identities in federated identity management system. In: 2010 International Symposium in Information Technology (ITSim), vol. 2, pp. 618–623 (2010)

Klingenstein, N.: Attribute aggregation and federated identity. In: International Symposium on Applications and the Internet Workshops, SAINT Workshops 2007, p. 26 (2007)

Myagmar, S., Lee, A.J., Yurcik, W.: Threat modeling as a basis for security requirements. In: Symposium on Requirements Engineering for Information Security (SREIS), vol. 2005, pp. 1–8 (2005)

NISTWP: Electronic Authentication Guideline: Information Security, April 2006. http://csrc.nist.gov/publications/nistpubs/800-63/SP800-63V1_0_2.pdf

OpenID Authentication 2.0 - Final (2007). http://openid.net/specs/openid-authentication-2_0.html. Accessed 5 Dec

Kellomäki, S.: Query Extension for SAML AuthnRequest (Draft) (2008). http://zxid.org/tas3/anrq-index.html. Accessed 22 Apr

Shibboleth (2016). http://www.internet2.edu/products-services/trust-identity/shibboleth/

SimpleSAMLphp (2016) http://simplesamlphp.org/

Standard OASIS: Assertions and Protocols for the OASIS Security Assertion Markup Language (SAML) V2.0. (2005). http://docs.oasis-open.org/security/saml/v2.0/saml-core-2.0-os.pdf. Accessed 15 Mar

ZXID (2016). http://www.zxid.org/

Robust Enterprise Application Security with eTRON Architecture

M. Fahim Ferdous Khan[1($\boxtimes$)], Ken Sakamura[1,2],
and Noboru Koshizuka[1,2]

[1] Interfaculty Initiative in Information Studies,
The University of Tokyo, Tokyo, Japan
{khan, ken, koshizuka}@sakamura-lab.org
[2] YRP Ubiquitous Networking Laboratory, Tokyo, Japan

Abstract. With information and communication technologies progressing at a rapid pace and becoming increasingly affordable, the use of various e-services is gaining prevalence at all sectors and levels of enterprises, including government, commerce, education and health. As modern-day enterprise services become progressively virtual in terms of content, storage and delivery, the need for robust of security and privacy pertaining to such services increases proportionally. Despite the plethora of enterprise-scale e-services in use today, there seems to be no general framework for developing those, especially with regard to ensuring security of such services. In this chapter, we present the eTRON architecture which aims at delineating a generic framework for developing secure e-services. At the core of the eTRON architecture lies the tamper-resistant eTRON chip which is equipped with functions for mutual authentication, encrypted communication and strong access control. Besides the security features, the eTRON architecture also offers a wide range of functionalities through a coherent set of API commands so that programmers can develop value-added services in a transparent manner. This chapter discusses various features of the eTRON architecture, and presents three representative eTRON-based e-services in order to evaluate its effectiveness by comparison with other existing e-services.

Keywords: Enterprise application security · e-Services · e-Commerce · Secure filesystem · Smartcards · Location-based services · Authentication · Access control

1 Introduction

The twenty-first-century enterprises have embraced IT as an integral part to their very existence as business and commerce have been undergoing a significant paradigm shift in an era where Internet connection is omnipresent and use of mobile devices and smartphones is commonplace. With a modest start in the 1990s – despite being afflicted by the dot-com boom in the early 2000s – e-commerce has continued to proliferate and joined the lexicon of many languages. Use of information and communication technology has not only been limited to business, it has also successfully penetrated into other enterprises like education, health, government and so on, to offer a wider

© Springer International Publishing AG 2017
V. Chang et al. (Eds.): Enterprise Security, LNCS 10131, pp. 155–178, 2017.
DOI: 10.1007/978-3-319-54380-2_7

spectrum of e-services: e-government, e-health, e-learning, e-cash, e-voting, and e-tourism are a few to name. Many of these services are considered part and parcel in advanced societies, and – at the other end of the digital divide – e-services are playing an important role in making life easier for citizens, e.g., e-agriculture initiatives in Rwanda, and e-government initiatives in Colombia, Uruguay and Panama (Bilabo-Osorio and Lanvin 2013). As much as these e-services improve accessibility and efficiency to information and services, they bring along crucial security concerns as cyber security and privacy are under increasing threat in our expanding virtual world. Moreover, there are areas where the existing e-services can be made more efficient from both users' and application developers' perspectives. On this premise, this chapter explores the eTRON architecture as a generic architecture for developing various e-services that aim at striking a proper balance between security and efficiency.

Entity TRON or eTRON is a pervasive security concept (Fig. 1) that has grown out of the TRON project (Krikke 2005). The idea is to protect "electronic entities" that represent some kind of value (it could be encryption keys or concert tickets or commuter passes, etc.) by storing them inside a tamper resistant piece of hardware. This tamper-resistant hardware is the eTRON chip. The eTRON chips come in a number of generations, and are certified by the Japanese Ubiquitous ID Center (Koshizuka and Sakamura 2010) which is a subproject of TRON Forum (TRON FORUM 2016). The eTRON chips are not simply security co-processors as commonly used, but actually complete systems containing both processing power and memory for code and data. Though eTRON was initially intended as security support for TRON-based systems, it has eventually evolved – with research spanning over a decade – as a comprehensive architecture for building secure and efficient e-services.

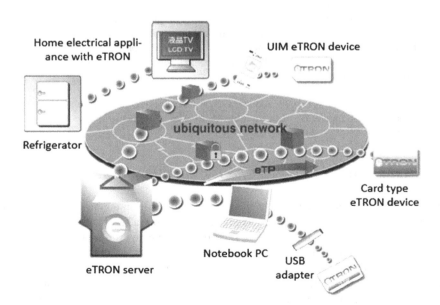

Fig. 1. High-level view of the eTRON architecture.

The rest of this chapter is organized as follows. Section 2 introduces basic eTRON security mechanisms and it software architecture including eTRON libraries. The next three sections briefly describes three applications developed using the eTRON architecture in e-commerce, location-based services and filesystem domains respectively. In light of the functionalities and security features of the three e-services, Sect. 6 discusses eTRON's viability as a generic architecture for e-service development, and chalks out a few avenues for future work. Finally, Sect. 7 concludes the paper.

2   The eTRON Architecture

eTRON is a basic architecture for "electronic entity" management. The term "electronic entity" or simply "entity", in eTRON parlance, represents special digital information that resembles real life objects like certificates or banknotes or keys. Certificates or banknotes are difficult to duplicate or alter as they use special papers, special ink, water marks or holograms. Keys are difficult to produce or reproduce as they have precisely cut edges made form hard materials. The "electronic entity", as envisioned in the eTRON architecture, should have such properties that make them difficult to produce, duplicate and alter. Creating an electronic entity is impossible with software alone, and hardware support is indispensable. The eTRON tamper-resistant hardware device can provide such support. Figure 2, shows the basic hardware module of eTRON, and Fig. 3, shows two different types of eTRON devices. An electronic entity produced by eTRON tamper-resistant hardware is composed of an indivisible unit of data. Such an electronic entity is difficult to counterfeit, produce a pirated copy, and illegally modify.

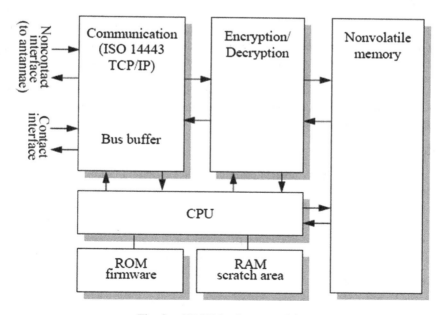

Fig. 2. eTRON hardware module.

Fig. 3. eTRON chips: SIM-type (left) and USB-type (right)

Manipulation of electronic entities inside eTRON hardware is strictly governed by the entity transfer protocol (eTP) which features only a limited set of operations that can be exerted only after stringent mutual authentication and access control requirements have been satisfied (Sakamura and Koshizuka 2001).

2.1 Mutual Authentication

The eTRON mutual authentication is performed by a challenge-response protocol using public key cryptography. After successful authentication, a session is created to share a secure key by Diffie-Hellman algorithm. By this session establishment an ephemeral key, valid only for the duration of the session, is shared between the interlocutors (in our case, the user and the authentication system at the healthcare institute) by Diffie-Hellman key sharing algorithm. In the eTRON architecture, this session is established in two phases; first a shared key is generated, and then the key is verified. For explaining the session establishment process, we assume that a session is established between A and B. For Diffie-Hellman key sharing, A and B have their respective secret and public keys, and certificates, which are denoted by x, y and $cert$ respectively, differentiated by A or B in the subscript. There are also two Diffie-Hellman protocol system parameters which are publicly known: p and g, where p is a prime number and g is an integer less than p, with the following property: for every number n between 1 and $p - 1$ inclusive, there is a power k of g such that $n = g^k \bmod p$. x and y are related as $y = g^x \bmod p$. The protocol is specified below.

Key Generation

- A generates a random number, R_A and calculates a commit value, $r_A = g^{R_A} \bmod p$ and sends $(r_A, cert_A)$ to B.
- B receives $(r_A, cert_A)$ from A. B verifies the validity of $cert_A$. B generates a random number R_B, and calculates a commit value, $r_B = g^{R_B} \bmod p$. B sends $(r_B, cert_B)$ to A. B calculates $K' = (r_A^{x_B}) \times (y_A^{R_B}) \bmod p$.
- A verifies B's certificate, $cert_B$ and then calculates $K = (r_B^{x_A}) \times (y_B^{R_A}) \bmod p$.

Key Confirmation

- A extracts the first 128 bits of K (which is represented in little-endian) as $w_0 = f_{128}(K)$. A then calculates $V_A = h(w_0|cert_B|r_B)$, known as authorization child, where $h(.)$ represents SHA-1 hash function. Then A calculates $c_A = E_{w_0}(V_A)$, where $E_{w_0}(.)$ represents symmetric key encryption with key $w_0.c_A$ is sent to B.

- B receives c_A. It extracts the first 128 bits of K' (which is represented in little-endian) as $w'_0 = f_{128}(K')$. B then calculates $V'_A = h(w'_0|cert_B|r_B)$ as authorization child, and $\tilde{V}'_A = D_{w'_0}(c_A)$, where $D_{w'_0}(.)$ is the decryption of the operand with key w'_0. If V'_A and $\tilde{V}'_A$ are same, then K' is registered as the session key. Next, B calculates its authorization child, $V_B = h(w'_0|cert_A|r_A)$ and $c_B = E_{w'_0}(V_B)$, where $E_{w'_0}(.)$ represents symmetric key encryption with key $w'_0.c_B$ is sent to A.

- A receives c_B. A calculates authorization child, $V'_B = h(w_0|cert_A|r_A)$ and $\tilde{V}'_B = D_{w_0}(c_B)$, where $D_{w_0}(.)$ is the decryption of the operand with key w_0. If V'_B and $\tilde{V}'_B$ are same, then K is registered as the session key. This way, a shared key $K(=K')$ is agreed between A and B.

The authentication protocol for session establishment is illustrated in Fig. 4.

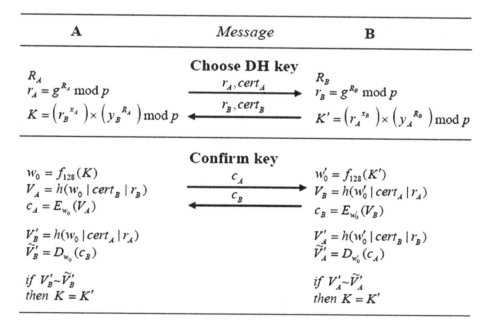

Fig. 4. eTRON authentication protocol.

2.2 File Access Control

In the eTRON architecture, mutual authentication has two modes: owner mode and issuer mode. By "owner" we mean owner of the chip or electronic entity and by "issuer" we mean issuer or creator of the entity (e.g., eTRON files or records). When an eTRON file is created, the eTRON ID of the issuer is attached to the file's file control block.

Issuer mode authentication is granted only when request to access an entity (file) comes from a party having the same eTRON ID as is written in the file control block of the entity. If the eTRON IDs match, the requesting party is given "issuer authority". Otherwise, "other authority" is given. On the other hand, in *owner mode* authentication, the requesting party proves himself as the owner of the chip by password or PIN, and upon successful authentication "owner authority" is granted.

eTRON's access control mechanism is based on access control lists. As shown in Table 1, the file access control list in eTRON is defined by setting or resetting different bits of a 16-bit value. "Issuer" of entity (file) has all rights by default, and rights for "owner" and "others" can be set for eight access privileges, namely updating record, reading record, changing mode of a file, acquiring status of a file, deleting file, transferring file, encrypting file, and decrypting file. The file access control list is defined by the issuer of the file during the file creation process. In comparison to the commonly followed state-based or rule-based access control techniques in smartcards (Mayes 2008; Rankl 2007), eTRON's access control mechanism offers several advantages.

- Firstly, it is straight-forward and explicit, and suitable for many applications.
- It has eight well defined access privileges and three different levels of access authorities. In contrast, state-based access control can be at times prohibitively complex with increasing number of states.
- Access definition of each file is part of the file control block, which is unlike the rule-based access control where compromise of the special reference file may lead to the compromise of all other files.
- The eTRON access control mechanism can work in flat file structure also, whereas state-based and rule-based access controls often rely on directory hierarchy to define states and rules respectively.

Table 1. File access control list in eTRON.

	Owner	Issuer	Others
Update record	ACL0	Always authorized	ACL1
Read record	ACL2		ACL3
Change file mode	ACL4		ACL5
Reference file	ACL6		ACL7
Delete file	ACL8		ACL9
Transfer file	ACLa		ACLb
Encrypt file	ACLc		ACLd
Decrypt file	ACLe		ACLf

Moreover, eTRON's access control mechanism allows programming multiple applications in a single chip very easily, just by defining different access rights to different files pertaining to different applications.

2.3   Secure Peer-to-Peer Communication

Each eTRON chip is assigned a unique identifier (eTRON ID), to create a persistent and reliable identification of each eTRON chip, regardless of communications channels and other variable factors. This is a key part of the end-to-end architecture, as it is used to ascertain the identity of the counterpart in a transaction. eTRON uses Public key infrastructure (PKI) where a certificate authority issues certificates to chips having valid eTRON IDs.

The eTRON architecture calls for eTRON chips to connect directly to each other over any available communications infrastructure, forming virtual, encrypted, and private end-to-end connections for the transfer of entities over the eTNet architecture (Yashiro et al. 2011).

2.4   eTRON Libraries

The eTRON access library, which mainly consists of eTRON client library and eTRON utility library, provides API commands for accessing eTRON chips and manipulating entities inside those. These libraries are compatible with C and C++, and can be used for application development in T-Kernel, Unix OS, MacOSX, and Windows.

eTRON Client Library. The eTRON client library provides functions for communicating with eTRON chips via the utility library. The client library can be divided into the following seven major modules (Fig. 5).

- *Entity module.* Applications and middleware basically use the entity module which provides API for issuing commands to eTRON entities for different applications. It also includes functions for connecting with the packet module, adapter module, authentication module, crypto module, and MAC/HASH module.
- *Packet module.* This provides protocol processing functions according to eTRON specifications such as eTRON/16 and eTRON/32. eTRON/16 chip has a 16-bit micro-controller, and eTRON/32 chip has a 32-bit microcontroller.
- *Device module.* A variety of interfacing devices and reader/writers can be used to interface eTRON chips to computers. Examples include PC/SC (personal computer/smartcard) compliant reader/writer, DENSO reader/writer, T-Engine SIM adapter, etc. Device module provides functions to treat streams defined by these interfacing devices, reader/writers, and also by the utility library.
- *Authentication module.* This module provides necessary parameter creation functions for the two-pass authentication according to eTRON specifications.
- *Crypto module.* This module provides encryption communication functions that are used between eTRON chips and computers. This can also be used as a stand-alone crypto library.
- *MAC/HASH module.* This module provides functions to compute MAC/HASH values to be appended to eTRON packets for packet transfer error- and alteration-detection, and message authentication.
- *Utility module.* This module provides auxiliary functions for using eTRON client library, such as error handling, time processing, and key management.

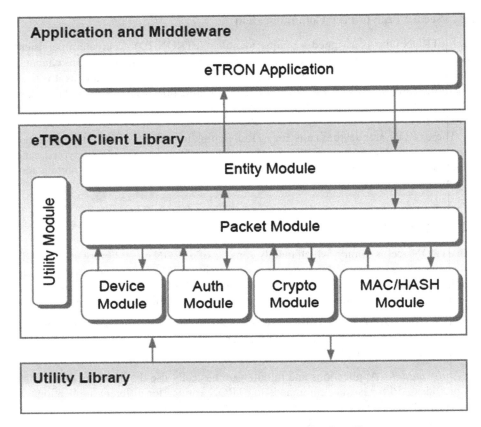

Fig. 5. Configuration of modules in eTRON client library.

eTRON Utility Library. The utility library mainly provides multi-platform support functions including string and task/thread handling, socket and time control, inter-process communication, etc.; and other basic functions like message list and buffer handling, debugging support and error handling, etc. These client library and utility library provide various API commands for interacting with and manipulating entities. As an example, API specification for creating a file in eTRON chip and reading it is shown in the Appendix at the end of this paper.

3   Electronic Ticket System

We developed an electronic-ticket system, eTRON/eTS (Khan et al. 2009), using the eTRON tamper-resistant chip, which was shown to have several security and performance advantages compared to traditional account-based systems and other smartcard-based systems. Most e-ticket systems involve only two main transactions. These are issue and verification (consumption) of e-tickets. However, for improved service quality a third type of transaction is also necessary which enables a user to seamlessly transfer e-tickets to his friends or other users.

3.1   E-Ticket Transactions

Once the session is established between the respective parties, e-ticket issuing, transfer and verification can proceed. In the following, eTRON chip is referred to as eTRON card, as we will see in Sect. 3.2 that the system is implemented using eTRON card that contains the chip.

Issue. An issuer machine creates an e-ticket in the user eTRON card. The following are the steps required for issuing an e-ticket. First, a session has to be established between the issuer machine and user eTRON card. Then the issuer defines the access control rights on the e-ticket (Sect. 2.1). Next, the issuer creates the e-ticket (eTRON file) in the user eTRON card. Finally, the issuer updates the e-ticket with ticket specific

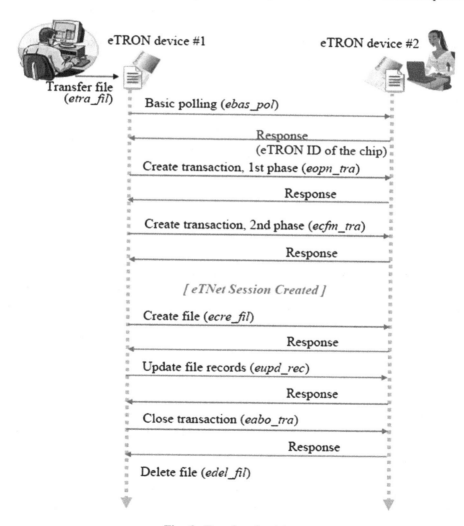

Fig. 6. Transfer of e-ticket.

information. For ticket specific information, we have included ticket ID, event ID, and validity interval of the e-ticket (start and end date).

Transfer. A user can transfer an e-ticket from his eTRON card to another user's eTRON card. First, a 'transaction' has to be established between the sending and receiving user eTRON cards attached to computers. A 'transaction' is a session with roll-back function provided by the eTRON chip in order to always keep the system in a consistent state in case of failures during the transfer process. An e-ticket (eTRON file) is created in the receiving eTRON card with the same file ID and issuer ID as they were in the sending eTRON card's e-ticket. Then the newly created e-ticket is updated with ticket specific information. After successful transfer of the e-ticket the transaction is closed, and e-ticket in the sending card is deleted. The operations involved in the transfer of an e-ticket are atomic. In case of any communication or peripheral failure, the system always rolls back to the previous consistent state so that only one copy of an e-ticket exists in the system. The message flow in transferring e-ticket is shown in Fig. 6.

Verification. A verifier machine verifies an e-ticket in the user eTRON card. Upon successful verification, the user is given access to the service. The following are the steps required for verifying an e-ticket. First, a session is created between the verifier machine and user eTRON card as described earlier. The verifier checks the existence of the desired e-ticket corresponding to the event in consideration, in the user eTRON card. If the e-ticket is found, the issuer ID, event ID and validity interval of the e-ticket are checked subsequently. If the verification is successful, the e-ticket (eTRON file) is deleted and session is closed.

3.2   Implementation

Based on the design outlined above, we implemented eTRON/eTS with both eTRON/16 and eTRON/32 cards on Microsoft Windows platform (with a relatively modest configuration of Intel Pentium M processor, 1.6 GHz) with Microsoft Windows SDK v6.1. The programming environment was Microsoft Visual C++. Both eTRON/16 and eTRON/32 are equipped with dual interfaces, i.e., they are compliant with ISO/IEC 7816, and ISO/IEC 14443 standards for contact and contactless communications respectively.

System Components

Access to eTRON Cards. The hardware interfacing with an eTRON card is a general-purpose PC/SC reader/writer, the GemPC Twin USB developed by GemPlus (see Fig. 7). The system communicates with an eTRON card (which is inserted into the card reader) via the Microsoft PC/SC Smartcard support provided by WIN32 system services. We chose to use PC/SC reader/writer over other choices of DENSO reader/writer and T-Engine SIM adapter for the following reasons. PC/SC, at least in principle, is platform-independent, since it works on all Windows-based PCs which make up the majority of personal computers. It allows smartcards to be integrated into any desired application in a manner that is largely independent of programming

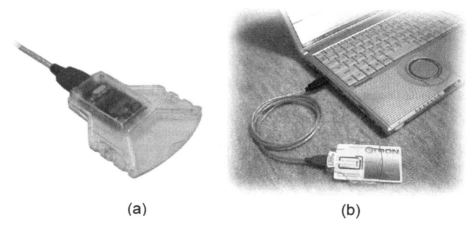

(a)   **(b)**

Fig. 7. (a) GemPC Twin USB, (b) eTRON card interfaced to PC.

languages, since it supports widely used languages such as C, C++, Java and Basic. The only prerequisites are that a suitable driver must be available for the terminal to be used, and the smartcard must be PC/SC-compatible. However, this compatibility requirement is reasonably non-critical, since the scope has been kept relatively broad. Moreover, it is very simple to use and install as the user requires no technical knowledge. The average cost is also relatively cheap.

Network Access. The system requires network access for communication with a remote eTRON card during e-ticket transfer. This network communication uses the TCP/IP network protocol provided by the Windows Operating System.

Runtime Environment. As a typical Windows application, the software requires the support of Windows runtime environments, the OS services provided by the Windows system DLLs. The Windows runtime environment should be available on any properly installed Windows computer. Additionally, eTRON client library and utility library should also be installed in the computer.

Authentication Mode and File Access Control. In our implementation of eTRON/eTS, we assume that the issuer and verifier are the same organization, which is often the case in real world. The two-phase session establishment requires specifying three parameters. These are the authentication mode, authentication algorithm and the crypto algorithm. The authentication mode is "issuer" for the issue and verification transactions and "owner" for the transfer transaction. For all transactions, we used Diffie-Hellman key sharing scheme as authentication algorithm; and Rijndael block cipher as the crypto algorithm. The rights on the e-ticket were defined according the following observations. The user (owner) should be able to view information of his e-ticket. He should be able to transfer an e-ticket to another user, and also acquire the status of any e-ticket in his eTRON card. The issuer (and verifier) has all the rights by default (Table 1). The following statement shows how to specify the file access control list (FACL) of the e-ticket using macros defined in eTRON library.

```
facl = UNL_etron_FACL_Owner_erea_rec
        | UNL_etron_FACL_Owner_eref_fil
          | UNL_etron_FACL_Owner_ etra_fil;
```

3.3 Evaluation

In this section, we present a comparative analysis of eTRON/eTS with respect to other e-ticket systems with a view to judging eTRON architecture for developing other e-commerce applications. Two main types of e-ticket systems are reported in the literature (Matsuyama and Fujimura 1999). These are account-based systems and smartcard-based systems. In account-based systems, e-tickets are managed in online accounts, and any processing of the e-tickets is handled by sending requests to an account manager through a network. As account has to be managed for every user, management cost can become very high. Moreover, central management of accounts may lead to single point of failure. Furthermore, accounts are safeguarded against malicious user but not against malicious service managers who can maliciously alter or delete user e-tickets. In smartcard-based systems, on the other hand, e-tickets are stored in and circulated among smartcards. The tamper-resistant storage offered by smartcards protects e-tickets from unauthorized exposure. Smartcard-based systems can be further divided into two categories based on the cryptographic scheme incorporated. Smartcards with shared key cryptography attains high speed authentication which comes at the cost of expensive key management. Smartcards with public key cryptography is more secure with low key management cost but lacks authentication speed. Among the smartcards that use shared key cryptography, the most popular ones are FeliCa-based cards (Sony Global Product Website 2016) which are used in many different countries. FlexTicket (Matsuyama and Fujimura 1999) is an example of e-ticket system that utilizes cards with public key cryptography although it is actually a hybrid of the account-based approach and smartcard-based approach.

eTRON/eTS, along with other smartcard-based systems, has clear advantages over account-based systems in that it incorporates hardware security, and prevents e-tickets from both malicious users and service managers through tamper- resistance. FeliCa- and other smartcard-based systems relying on shared key cryptography compromise security for the sake of high speed verification. Also, these systems have no provision for transfer of e-tickets, and hence lack the flexibility and service quality provided by FlexTicket and eTRON/eTS. However, FlexTicket assumes online presence of a central ticket-token manager for all three transactions, and hence, cannot support offline verification of e-tickets. Moreover, it requires user involvement in critical processes like selecting and storing keys. eTRON/eTS, in contrast, does not rely on any third party or user involvement in critical processes, and can support offline verification.

The verification time of eTRON/eTS, however, can be a problem in cases where high speed verification is imperative. In the present implementation, eTRON/16 and eTRON/32 require 5.3 s and 2.3 s respectively to verify e-tickets. This is relatively longer compared to systems with shared key cryptography. As eTRON/eTS uses public key cryptography to attain highest level of security, bulk of the verification time is spent for mutual authentication: 4.7 s for eTRON/16, and 2.04 s for eTRON/32.

However, as suggested by the data above, we have achieved a 57% speed-up from eTRON/16 to eTRON/32 implementation. With future versions of eTRON chips and in congruence to Moore's law, we expect further speed-up in verification time of e-tickets.

4   Security in Attestation Services

A secure user-centric attestation service (SUCAS) framework has been developed using the eTRON architecture, which enables user of location-based services to create, share, and verify spatio-temporal evidence relevant to user's action information using eTRON devices (Yap et al. 2012).

The generated evidences are used for protecting the owner's rights. A train-delay certificate application was developed using the SUCAS framework based on subway system in Tokyo. A delay certificate is a documented proof issued by a railway company stating that its scheduled train arrived at a station later than what is stipulated in the company's timetable. The delay certificate plays an important role in Japanese society as it can be used as evidence by the employee to prove that the reason for being late to work is due to the transportation system rather than personal negligence. However, the implementation of SUCAS is generic to other application domains that produce action-spatial-temporal evidence such as the digital receipt system, event participation certificate generation system and medical certificate generation system.

4.1   Architecture of SUCAS

The SUCAS architecture includes four main players. These are user, service provider, attestation and verifying center, and recipient.

User. Individual who uses the eTRON device to initiate evidence generation through secure communication channel. The generated evidences are managed by the user. User also involves in initiating the generation of attestation certificate which attests to the generated evidences. Besides that, user also initiates the evidence sharing process.

Service Provider. Provider who generates the action-spatial-temporal evidence through eTRON architecture. Service provider needs to register the ucode information which represents the evidence generation parameters and the service application code with the attestation and verifying center through offline channel prior to service deployment. (ucode is a standardized coding scheme under the uID architecture, details discussion of which out of the scope of this paper.) Service provider should install the action-spatial-temporal evidence generation infrastructure on unmovable objects such as turnstiles of subway system to prevent the movement of evidence providing infrastructure.

Attestation and Verifying Center. Trusted organization that issues and maintains the ucode information through eTRON architecture. Service provider's evidence generation parameters and application code are verified here prior to service deployment. Attestation certificate is also being generated here based on the generated evidence submitted by the user. Verification of the attestation certificate is also executed here.

Recipient. Individual who receives attestation certificate from the user through secure peer-to-peer communication channel. In the SUCAS implementation, recipient of the evidence must also possess the eTRON device. Recipient of the evidence interacts with the attestation and verifying center via secure communication channel to verify the integrity and authenticity of the received attestation certificate.

4.2 SUCAS Protocol

SUCAS works in four phases. These are: the generation phase, attestation phase, sharing phase and verification phase as shown in Fig. 8. All the phases are executed via secure communication channel. The detailed explanation of each phase is as follows:

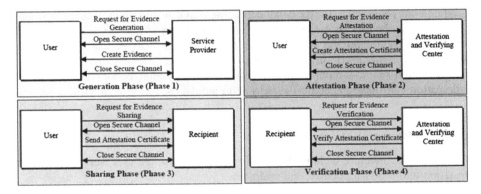

Fig. 8. Flow diagram of four phases of SUCAS protocol.

Generation Phase (Phase 1). In this phase, evidence generation is initiated by the user through secure communication channel. Evidence is generated by the service provider in eTRON environment. Information on location, action and event, user identity, service provider identity, time stamps, and time to complete the evidence generation are captured in the evidence. During this phase, FACL of the evidence file is set by the service provider. The user has only read and delete access rights to the evidence file, while others have only read access right. This feature ensures that no illegal modification can be made to the generated evidence for selfish interest. The FACL configuration also prohibits the user from transferring the evidence rights to others.

The generated evidence is stored at the user's eTRON device. Service provider is completely isolated from the management of user's evidence once evidence is generated. By examining the generated evidence, we can later infer that a particular individual has been engaged in certain activity at a particular location at a particular time. This information ascertains the action of the user.

Attestation Phase (Phase 2). The generated evidence is attested by the attestation and verifying center through secure eTP protocol defined in eTRON architecture. The validity and relationship of location, action, and event information, user identity, service provider identity and time-stamp information are checked. Also, the time to complete the evidence generation process is examined before passing the attestation test. Once attested, attestation certificates are issued. The number of attestation certificate to be issued is solely dependent on the user's request. Each attestation certificate is uniquely identified by an ucode. The FACL of the attestation certificate is being set such that only the owner of the certificate has read, delete and transfer access rights while others have only read and delete access rights.

Sharing Phase (Phase 3). This phase is launched when the owner of the evidence wants to share the evidence with others. The attestation certificates generated in the attestation phase (phase 2) are transferred to the recipient through secure peer-to-peer communication channel. No third party is involved in this process. For each recipient, a new attestation certificate is sent. Once the attestation certificate has been successfully sent to the recipient, the original copy at the user's eTRON device will be deleted. If the sharing phase ends abruptly, roll-back function of eTRON architecture is called to ensure the unsent copy remains at the user's eTRON device. Additional attestation certificates can be regenerated by the user at anytime by executing the attestation phase (phase 2). The redistribution of the attestation certificate by the recipient is prohibited through eTRON FACL. This is because the recipient of the certificate will not be granted certificate transfer right; only read and delete access rights are granted.

Verification Phase (Phase 4). In this phase, recipient of the attestation certificate verifies the authenticity of the received attestation certificate with the attestation and verifying center through secure communication channel dictated by the eTP. The attestation and verifying center checks the identity of the certificate issuer and the validity of the certificate's ucode information before verifying the integrity and trust of the attestation certificate. The SUCAS protocol ends with the verification phase.

4.3   Security Analysis of SUCAS

Let us analyze SUCAS in terms of integrity, confidentiality and privacy.

Integrity of Evidence. The analysis of evidence integrity is carried out to study the resistance of SUCAS towards evidence replay, evidence right transfer, relay attacks, illegal alteration of evidence generation parameters and unauthorized deletion of evidences.

Evidence replay occurs when malicious user tries to reproduce the action-spatial-temporal evidence obtained from a particular location sometime later in another location. SUCAS is not susceptible to this kind of attack because time-stamp information provided by the service provider is captured when the evidence is being generated. The accuracy of the service provider's time-stamp information is governed by the network time protocol.

Evidence right transfer is another prominent attack to evidence providing service. SUCAS prevents the owner of the evidence from transferring the evidence right to others through eTRON FACL configuration. Also, the generated evidence is linked to the ucode of the eTRON device. Even if the evidence is transferred from the owner's eTRON device to other eTRON device through illegal means, the owner's eTRON ucode still remains in the action-spatial-temporal evidence.

Relay attack happens when malicious user acts as a proxy by forwarding the evidence generation request for a user who is not present at the context environment. This attack is prevented in SUCAS by recording the evidence generation time during the evidence generation process by the service provider. If the time for generating the evidence does not fall within the acceptable range, i.e., +10 ms of the mean generation time, the generated action-spatial-temporal evidence is considered invalid. This range is derived from experimental results (Yap et al. 2012). Under normal condition, the maximum ISO/IEC 7816 communication channel variances are within the range of 3–4 ms. Additional 6–7 ms is added for accommodating other potential delay factors. However, 10 ms is too short for completing the relay via IP network because the shortest round-trip-time of typical Internet Control Message Protocol flood (ICMP) ping command normally exceeds 10 ms.

Tampering with evidence generation parameters attack takes place when malicious user tries to manipulate with the evidence generation parameters such as the location information. Since SUCAS dictates that all evidence generation must take place at the service provider's side under secure environment, the modification of evidence generation parameters by malicious user can be thwarted.

Unauthorized deletion of evidence takes places when an attacker tries to delete the generated action-spatial-temporal evidence without the user's knowledge. This kind of attack is easy when user's information is stored at centralize server. SUCAS prevents this attack by offloading the evidence storage at the user's side. Moreover, access to user's eTRON device's file system is strictly protected by a four-digit password, making this kind of attack relatively challenging.

User Privacy and Confidentiality of Evidence. User privacy is breached when user's personal information is disclosed to others without user's consents. The confidentiality of evidences is maintained when the evidence is only disclosed to desired parties. In this section, we analyze how SUCAS achieves these security goals.

Attestation certificates are generated based on the action-spatial-temporal evidence generated during the evidence generation phase. The attestation certificate is created in such a way that only the owner of the certificate has the transfer right. Governed by the eTRON FACL, the recipient of the attestation certificate could not retransfer the received attestation certificate to others.

The generated evidences are being stored at the user's eTRON device; it minimizes the risk of information leakage to unwanted parties. Furthermore, all the files stored in the eTRON device are protected with a four-digit user password. In order to gain access to the stored evidences, authentication is imperative.

5   T-Kernel/SS Secure Filesystem

Using the eTRON chip, the T-Kernel/SS secure filesystem (Yashiro et al. 2010) provides passive access control, which ensures policy enforcement even when the operating system is replaced or when disks are peeked or tampered physically.

5.1   Motivation

Most of the existing secure filesystems aim at providing passive protection of data by using cryptography or tamper-resistant hardware. As such data on disks are protected data confidentiality is strongly kept even when disks are illegally extracted by adversaries. However, most of these systems do not provide passive access control. Thinking of system security, not only confidentiality but also access control is considered very important: security is potentially degraded if users have more rights or capabilities than they should actually have.

Most of the existing secure filesystems realize access control using kernel reference monitor. That is, an operating system kernel checks whether the user's access to the target file is valid or not, and performs the desired operation accordingly. This mechanism is reasonable for usual filesystems, but not desirable for secure filesystems. This is because secure fillesystems are designed for use cases where data need to be protected even when disks containing sensitive data are illegally extracted by adversaries. In such cases, kernel reference monitors may not work, as attackers can read or write data from a different operating system without such functionalities. Furthermore, this approach makes secure filesystems insufficient for emerging applications that deal with multiple users and organizations. A good example of such systems is prepaid card system. When prepaid card data are stored in secure filesystem, customers should not be able to alter the usage history (e.g., balance information, item name, price), while reading must be made possible. However, for shop owners, writing should be made possible to update the usage data, but they should be prohibited from reading card usage history, so that customer's privacy is protected. This example shows that access control protection is crucial for emerging applications, especially when it deals with price or monetary value.

Thus, an effective access control mechanism for secure filesystem is needed. Currently, two methods for access control protection are currently proposed: cryptographic access control (Harrington and Jensen 2003) and Vaults security model (Payne 2007).

Cryptographic access control utilizes public key cryptography to ensure access control. As public key can encrypt but cannot decrypt data, users having the public key have the read-only privilege to the file. However, for practical filesystems, this method is considered to be inflexible. For example, deprivation of access rights from a single user is very difficult, as it requires the data to be re-encrypted with a new key pair, and the new private and public key must be delivered securely to the users who still have the access privileges.

On the other hand, Vaults security model assumes a special storage called GPRIV (global private vault), which allows access only to the secure operating system kernel.

Under this assumption, Payne (2007) has proved that secure filesystem with access control protection can be achieved without any lack of flexibility in conventional filesystems. However, Payne does not provide any real implementation, nor mentions whether GPRIV can actually be realized.

5.2   Overview of T-Kernel/SS

Using T-Kernel/SE (T-Kernel Standard Extension 2016) as the underlying real-time operating system, T-Kernel/SS (Secure Storage) presents a suite of four filesystems, which enables users to choose the right filesystem depending on the performance-security tradeoff of use cases at hand. In order to ensure user-friendliness, T-Kernel/SS is so designed as to allow transparent access to any of the constituent filesystems. This means any file on any of the four filesystems can be accessed via the same API functions. This allows users to access secure filesystem in a transparent manner without requiting detailed knowledge on each mechanism. The four filesysyems are described below.

Standard Filesystem (STDFS). Conventional filesystem without any protection.

Tamper-Resistant Secure Storage. Tamper-resistant secure storage (TRSS) is a simple method that stores all data in tamper-resistant storage (eTRON chip) equipped with built-in access control functionality. This approach mainly aims at protecting access control without losing flexibility, which is not easy in pure cryptographic access control.

Figure 9 illustrates how access control can be protected, showing the write operation as an example. Accessing TRSS requires two steps of operations: mutual authentication, and file access request. The first part, the mutual authentication, is needed for users to authenticate themselves against the chip, and vice versa. When the authentication is successful, a temporary session key is shared between the filesystem service and the chip (Sect. 2.1), so that further communications between these two components are protected. Then, using this session key, the filesystem requests the chip to write the specific data on a specified file stored in chip. As this request is encrypted and signed using the session key, adversaries cannot impersonate the authenticated

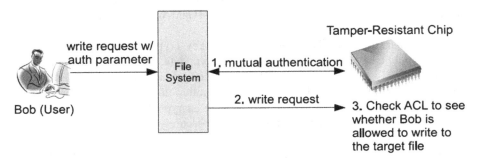

Fig. 9. TRSS mechanism overview.

user. Upon receiving the request, the chip checks the Access control list (ACL) stored in the chip to see whether the authenticated user is allowed to perform the desired operation on the file. If this validation succeeds, file operation is performed.

This mechanism enables access control protection, as policy enforcement is done not by the kernel reference monitor, but by the ACL stored inside the tamper-resistant hardware. Furthermore, the granularity of access control is high as apart from read and write, as discussed in Sect. 2.1, other privileges can also be defined, for example, delete, ACL modification, rename, move, etc. On the other hand, TRSS is not suitable for applications that require a great amount of data to be stored. This is because tamper-resistant storage can only store small amount of data and is much expensive compared to disks. Therefore, TRSS is opted for use cases where small-sized but important values are to be stored. For instance, digital receipt (as discussed in Sect. 4.1), monetary data, electronic tickets, credit cards, and right certificates, etc. To sum up, TRSS is considered suitable for applications that need strong protection and fine-grained access control.

Standard Cryptographic Filesystem (CFS-STD). Usual cryptographic filesystem, except that the encryption keys are stored on chip. Although the encryption keys are stored in chip, file data are encrypted or decrypted by software after reading the key from chip. Thus, no means of access control protection on files is provided, except for file encryption keys.

Cryptographic Filesystem with Access Control (CFS-AC). CFS-AC resembles TRSS in that the core operations needed for accessing files are controlled by ACLs in the tamper-resistant chip. However, instead of storing file data in the chip, CFS-AC stores the encryption key and ACLs on chip, and encrypted data are written on disk. Note that ACLs here do not define access rights for files; instead, they define access privileges for encryption keys (Table 2). Because write operation requires encryption and read operation requires decryption in cryptographic filesystems, read and write privilege enforcement is protected by the key ACL on chip.

Table 2. Key access control list in eTRON.

	Owner	Issuer	Others
Update key	ACL0	Always authorized	ACL1
Read key	ACL2		ACL3
Change ACL	ACL4		ACL5
Delete key	ACL8		ACL9
Encrypt file	ACLc		ACLd
Decrypt file	ACLe		ACLf

Figure 10 illustrates how CFS-AC works, taking write operation as an example. Mutual authentication and session key establishment is done the same way as in TRSS, but the successive steps are different. After the correct authentication, the filesystem requests the chip to encrypt the file data with a specified key, so that the data can be

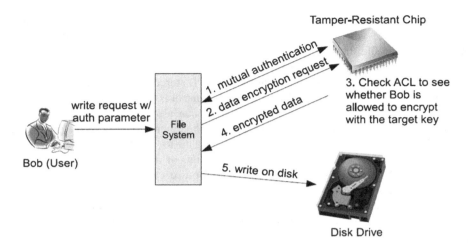

Fig. 10. CFS-AC mechanism overview.

written on disk. Upon receiving the request, the chip checks the key ACL to determine whether the authenticated user is allowed to encrypt with the specified key. If it is allowed, the chip returns the encrypted data to the filesystem, and finally the filesystem writes down the encrypted data on disk.

Alike TRSS, this mechanism also enables access control protection for reads and writes, as policy is enforced by the ACL stored inside the tamper-resistant hardware. Furthermore, because the data themselves are stored on disk and only the encryption keys and ACLs are stored on chip, the storage cost is inexpensive. It should also be noted that, unlike cryptographic access control (Harrington and Jensen 2003), deprivation of user privileges can be easily done in CFS-AC by simply changing the ACL in chip after a proper authentication.

6 Discussion

Apart from the three applications described in the last two sections, the tamper-resistant eTRON architecture has been used to develop secure applications in other domains as well. Examples include privacy-preserving convergence of real and virtual shopping using activity-based authentication (Yap et al. 2012) and a secure framework for delegation of access-control rights in healthcare informatics (Khan and Sakamura 2012).

The major security advantage of the eTRON architecture is its use of public key cryptography. The two-phase session establishment protocol is robust against attacks. Man-in-the-middle (MITM) attack is not possible in the key generation phase due to checking of certificates. However, an attacker E may send her own commit value, r_E to both A and B. Obviously doing so will not enable E to establish a pair of keys with A and B as in classical MITM scenario, as she cannot forge A or B's private key; nevertheless it would impede A and B to enter into a secured communication session.

Had there been no key confirmation phase, this anomaly would have been undetected. The eTNet architecture for inter-smartcard communication in a peer-to-peer manner has also been proven to be robust against MITM attack (Yashiro et al. 2011).

On functionality basis, the provision for transfer of electronic entity is a unique feature. For many applications, this transfer feature can provide added value of service, for example, allowing a user to seamlessly transfer a concert ticket to her friend. There are systems which support transfer of digital tokens in a centralized manner, but eTRON/eTNet adopts a completely peer-to-peer approach. Needless to say, peer-to-peer approaches are intuitively securer as they do not require assuming trust on central servers. Moreover, eTRON supports application development on multiple platforms, including T-Kernel, Unix OS, MacOSX, and Windows. The client and utility libraries provide rich set of APIs for application development.

eTRON comes across with a solid security architecture for smartcard-based enterprise applications. Hardware security and tamper resistance is of utmost importance as there is a limit to what software protection can do as with information becoming truly ubiquitous, fundamental concepts like ownership and trust have to be rethought (Anderson 1994; Sakamura 2003). Tamper-resistant chips like eTRON which carry our valuable pieces of information can be very effective for thwarting various attacks (Stankovic 2014; Anderson and Kuhn 1996). eTRON incorporates a robust access control mechanism which is very suitable for applications like electronic tickets, location-based services and so on. eTRON also has provision for seamless and peer-to-peer transfer of electronic entities between user eTRON devices. At present, only 'transfer' of entities is supported; it would be interesting if 'exchange' of entities can be supported in a secure way. Also, the issuer of entity possesses all rights by default. Although this works fine for e-tickets and other similar e-commerce applications, this may not be suitable for some business models. We leave these two issues as our future work. To sum up, eTRON is an efficient and highly secure architecture for enterprise IT applications.

7 Conclusion

In this chapter, with a view to presenting eTRON as a generic architecture for secure and efficient enterprise-level e-service development, we have introduced some of its security features, and three representative applications – which are fully implemented and tested – in three application domains of e-commerce, security in location-based services, and filesystem security. As eTRON's underlying architecture uses public key cryptography, eTRON applications are securer compared to e-services that rely on shared key cryptography. The eTRON architecture also includes a secure peer-to-peer mechanism for inter-eTRON-node communication – provision for which is either absent in other e-services or achieved through some kind of intermediate central servers, introducing an additional layer in the trust chain. Besides strong security features, it provides a rich set of API commands to enable programmers to develop e-services easily and transparently.

Acknowledgments. We cordially thank the YRP Ubiquitous Computing Laboratory for providing the eTRON hardware. The research reported in Sects. 3, 4 and 5 were carried out under the "Secure Ubiquitous Computing Platform" project supported by the Ministry of Education, Culture, Sports, Science and Technology (MEXT), Japan.

Appendix

1. The following shows API specification from eTRON Client Library for creating a file.

   unl_etron_ent_ecre_fil – Create File

   ▷ Function
   UNL_etron_ERR unl_etron_ent_ecre_fil(UNL_etron_ENTITY *ent, UNL_etron_SID sid, UNL_etron_FID fid, UNL_etron_uint8 type, UNL_etron_uint16 blk, UNL_etron_uint16 cnt, UNL_etron_FACL facl, unsigned int reptm, int tmout);

   ▷ Argument
   ent : Entity
   sid : Session ID
   fid : File ID
   type : File type (static/dynamic) Only static for eTRON/8 and 16
   blk : File start address (Not available for eTRON/16)
   cnt : File size (Octet number)
   facl : File access control list initial value
   reptm : Maximum number of trials
   tmout : Timeout time specification [ms]

   ▷ Return Value

   0 : Successful

   <0 : Error

   ▷ Description
   This issues a command to the ent eTRON entity to create the file specified by fid. This specifies tmout as the timeout time and executes according to the time specified by reptm. If the trial result is all timeout, a timeout error will be returned. If another error occurs, the trial is aborted and an error will be returned.

2. The following shows API specification from eTRON Client Library for reading a file.

unl_etron_ent_eref_fil – Acquire File Status

▷ Function

UNL_etron_ERR unl_etron_ent_eref_fil(UNL_etron_ENTITY *ent, UNL_etron_SID sid, UNL_etron_FID fid, void *filsts, unsigned int reptm, int tmout);

▷ Argument

ent : Entity

sid : Session ID

fid : File ID

filsts : Storage location for acquired file status (Depends on eTRON/8 or eTRON/16)

reptm : Maximum number of trials

tmout : Timeout time specification [ms]

▷ Return Value

0 : Successful

<0 : Error

▷ Description

This issues a command to the ent eTRON entity to acquire the file status specified by fid. The acquired data is stored in filsts. This data depends on the protocol. This specifies tmout as the timeout time and executes according to the time specified by reptm. If the trial result is all timeout, a timeout error will be returned. If another error occurs, the trial is aborted and an error will be returned.

References

Anderson, R.: Why cryptosystems fail. Commun. ACM **37**, 32–40 (1994)

Anderson, R., Kuhn, M.: Tamper resistance - a cautionary note. In: The Second USENIX Workshop on Electronic Commerce Proceedings, pp. 1–11 (1996)

Bilabo-Osorio, B., Dutta, S., Lanvin, B.: Global information technology report 2013: growth and jobs in a hyperconnected world. In: World Economic Forum (2013)

Harrington, A., Jensen, C.: Cryptographic access control in a distributed file system. In: Proceedings of the Eighth ACM Symposium on Access Control Models and Technologies, pp. 158–165 (2003)

Khan, M.F.F., et al.: A secure and flexible electronic-ticket system. In: Proceedings of 33rd Annual IEEE International Computer Software and Applications Conference, pp. 421–426 (2009)

Khan, M.F.F., Sakamura, K.: Context-awareness: exploring the imperative shared context of security and ubiquitous computing. In: Proceedings of 14th International Conference on Information Integration and Web-Based Applications and Services, pp. 101–110 (2012)

Koshizuka, N., Sakamura, K.: Ubiquitous ID: standards for ubiquitous computing and the internet of things. IEEE Pervasive Comput. **9**(4), 98–101 (2010)

Krikke, J.: T-Engine: Japan's ubiquitous computing architecture is ready for prime Time. IEEE Pervasive Comput. **4**(2), 4–9 (2005)

Matsuyama, K., Fujimura, K.: Distributed digital-ticket management for rights trading system. In: Proceedings of ACM Conference on Electronic Commerce, pp. 110–118 (1999)

Mayes, K.E.: An introduction to smart cards. In: Mayes, K.E., Markantonakis, K. (eds.) Smart Cards, Tokens Security and Applications. Springer Science+Business Media, LLC, New York (2008)

Payne, C.: A cryptographic access control architecture secure against privileged attackers. In: Proceedings of the 2007 ACM Workshop on Computer Security Architecture, pp. 70–76 (2007)

Rankl, W.: Smart Card Applications: Design Models for Using and Programming Smart Cards, 3rd edn. Wiley, West Sussex (2007)

Sakamura, K.: Ubiquitous computing: making it a reality. ITU Telecom World **2003**, 1–9 (2003)

Sakamura, K., Koshizuka, N.: The eTRON wide-area distributed-system architecture for e-commerce. IEEE Micro **21**(6), 7–12 (2001)

Sony Global Felica Website (2016). http://www.sony.net/Products/felica/index.html. Accessed 27 May 2016

Stankovic, J.A.: Research directions for the internet of things. IEEE Internet Things J. **1**(1), 3–9 (2014)

T-Kernel Standard Extension (2016). http://www.tron.org/download/index.php?route=product/category&path=24. Accessed 27 May 2016

TRON FORUM (2016). http://www.tron.org/. Accessed 27 May 2016

Yap, L.F., et al.: SUCAS: smart-card-based secure user-centric attestation framework for location-based services. Int. J. Inf. Priv. Secur. Integr. **1**(2), 160–183 (2012a)

Yap, L.F., et al.: Secure consumer-oriented integrated services using activity-based attestation for converging online and in-store shopping experience. Int. J. Comput. Theory Eng. **4**(2), 165–170 (2012b)

Yashiro, T., et al.: T-Kernel/SS: a secure filesystem with access control protection using tamper-resistant chip. In: Proceedings of 5th IEEE International Workshop on Security, Trust, and Privacy for Software Applications, pp. 134–139 (2010)

Yashiro, T., et al.: eTNet: a smart card network architecture for flexible electronic commerce services. In: Proceedings of 4th IFIP International Conference on New Technologies, Mobility and Security, pp. 1–5 (2011)

Obfuscation and Diversification for Securing Cloud Computing

Shohreh Hosseinzadeh[1][(✉)], Samuel Laurén[1], Sampsa Rauti[1],
Sami Hyrynsalmi[1], Mauro Conti[2], and Ville Leppänen[1]

[1] Department of Future Technologies, University of Turku, Agora 4th Floor,
Vesilinnantie 5, 20500 Turku, Finland
{shohos, smrlau, sjprau, sthyry, ville.leppanen}@utu.fi
[2] Department of Mathematics, University of Padua, Padua, Italy
conti@math.unipd.it

Abstract. The evolution of cloud computing and advancement of its services has motivated the organizations and enterprises to move towards the cloud, in order to provide their services to their customers, with greater ease and higher efficiency. Utilizing the cloud-based services, on one hand has brought along numerous compelling benefits and, on the other hand, has raised concerns regarding the security and privacy of the data on the cloud, which is still an ongoing challenge. In this regard, there has been a large body of research on improving the security and privacy in cloud computing. In this chapter, we first study the status of security and privacy in cloud computing. Then among all the existing security techniques, we narrow our focus on *obfuscation* and *diversification* techniques. We present the state-of-the-art review in this field of study, how these two techniques have been used in cloud computing to improve security. Finally, we propose an approach that uses these two techniques with the aim of improving the security in cloud computing environment and preserve the privacy of its users.

Keywords: Cloud computing · Enterprise security · Security · Privacy · Obfuscation · Diversification

1 Introduction

The recent changes in the business world have made the organizations and enterprises more interested in using cloud to share their services and resources remotely to their users. For this purpose, cloud computing offers three different models (Mell and Grance 2011): Software as a service (SaaS), Platform as a service (PaaS), and Infrastructure as a service (IaaS). In IaaS model the services that are offered by the service provider include computing resources, storage, and virtual machines. The PaaS model presents computing platforms to the business and its end users. In SaaS, the main services offered by the service providers are the applications that are hosted and executed on the cloud and are available to the customers through the network, typically over the Internet. Depending on the need of the enterprise, a suitable delivery model is deployed.

© Springer International Publishing AG 2017
V. Chang et al. (Eds.): Enterprise Security, LNCS 10131, pp. 179–202, 2017.
DOI: 10.1007/978-3-319-54380-2_8

The advancements in the cloud computing have facilitated the business, organizations, and enterprises with services providing lower cost and higher performance, scalability, and availability. Due to these advantages, cloud computing has become a highly demanded technology and organizations are relying on cloud services more and more. However, by using the cloud, more data is stored outside the organization's perimeters, which raises concerns about the security and privacy of the data. Therefore, it is significant for the cloud service providers to employ effective practices to secure the cloud computing infrastructure and preserve the privacy of its users. In the context of the cloud computing security, there exist many different measures that protect the cloud infrastructure. Some of these measures consider the cloud as an untrusted or malicious infrastructure that the user's data should be protected from (e.g., the cloud uses the data without the user's consent). While some other measures protect the infrastructure from the external intrusions.

Obfuscation and diversification are two propitious software security techniques that have been employed in various domains, mainly to impede malware (i.e., malicious software) (Skoudis 2004). These techniques have also been used to provide security in cloud computing as well. In a previous work[1], we have systematically surveyed the studies that use obfuscation and diversification techniques with the aim of improving the security in cloud computing environment (see the details of this study in Sect. 3.1). By analyzing the collected data, we managed to identify the areas that have gained more attention by the previous research, and also the areas that have remained intact and potential for further research. The results of the survey motivated us to propose a diversification approach, aiming at improving the security in cloud computing. We demonstrate this approach by applying obfuscation on client-side JavaScript components of an application. As such, we make it complicated for a piece of malware to gain knowledge about the internal structure of the application and perform its malicious attack. Moreover, we distribute unique versions of the application to the computers, which in the end mitigates the risk of massive-scale attacks (more detail in Sect. 4).

This book chapter is structured as follows: Sect. 2 discusses the security and privacy in domain of cloud computing, available security threats, and different aspects of security, concerning the cloud computing technology. In Sect. 3 we introduce the terms and techniques that are used in the proposed approach, and we present the state of this field of study, i.e., how these techniques have previously been used to boost the security of cloud computing. In Sect. 4, we present our proposed approach in detail. Conclusions come in Sect. 5.

2   Security and Privacy in Cloud Computing

Cloud computing is an evolving technology with new capabilities and services that have remarkable benefits when compared to more traditional service providing approaches. The services are delivered with lower cost (in usage as it is pay-for-use, in

---

[1] This book chapter is a re-written extended version of our previous study (Hosseinzadeh et al. 2015).

disaster recovery, in data storage solutions), greater ease, less complexity, higher availability and scalability, and also faster deployment. These compelling benefits have motivated the enterprises to adopt cloud solutions in their architectures and deliver their services over cloud. Depending on the need of the enterprise and how large the organization is, different deployment models are available, including public clouds, private clouds, community cloud, and hybrid clouds (Mell and Grance 2011; Mather et al. 2009). Again, depending on the need of the enterprise, cloud providers offer three different delivery models, i.e., SaaS, IaaS, and PaaS. In the following we discuss various deployment models, and various business models in cloud computing (CSA 2016).

In a *public cloud* (or external cloud), a third party vendor is responsible for hosting, operating, and managing the cloud. A common infrastructure is used to serve multiple customers, which means that the customers are not required to acquire for any software, hardware, and network devices. This makes the public cloud a suitable model for the enterprises that wish to invest less and manage the costs efficiently. The security in a public cloud is managed by the third party, which leaves less control for the organization and its users over the security (Rhoton et al. 2013). A kind of opposite solution to that is *private cloud* (or internal cloud), where the organization's customers are in charge of managing the cloud. The storage, computing, and network are dedicated to the organization owning the cloud, and not shared with other organizations. This enables the customers to have a higher control on security management and have more insight about logical and physical aspects of the cloud infrastructure. *Community cloud* refers to the type of clouds that are used exclusively by a community of customers from enterprises with common requirements and concerns (e.g., policies, security requirements, and compliance considerations). The last model is *hybrid cloud* that is the composition of several clouds (private, public, and community). According to the needs and budget of the enterprise and how critical its resources are, a suitable deployment model is chosen that can serve the enterprise's needs the best. For instance, an enterprise pays more for private cloud and has better security control over its shared resources, while it spends less on a public cloud for which it has less security control (CSA 2016; Mather et al. 2009).

As mentioned before, cloud service providers use three different business models to deliver their services to the end users: IaaS, PaaS, and SaaS. IaaS is the foundation of the cloud, PaaS comes on top of that, and SaaS is built upon PaaS. Each of these delivery models has different security issues, and is prone to different types of security threats, and therefore, it requires different levels of security.

The IaaS service model offers capabilities such as storage, processing, networks, and computing resources to the consumers. The end user does not manage the underlying infrastructure of the cloud, but has control over applications, operating system and storage. IaaS has made it a lot easier for the enterprises to deliver their services, in a way that they no longer worry about provisioning and managing the infrastructure and dealing with the underlying complexities. In addition to that, it has made it cheaper for businesses, in a way that instead of paying for the data centers and hosting companies, they only need to spend for the resources they consume to IaaS providers (Mell and Grance 2011; Mather et al. 2009).

The PaaS model is built upon IaaS and offers a development environment to the developers to develop their applications, without worrying about the underlying infrastructure. The offered services consist of a complete set of software development kit, ranging from design to testing and maintenance. The consumers of this model do not have control on the beneath services (e.g. the operating system, server, network, and the storage), but they can manage the application-hosting environment (Mell and Grance 2011; Mather et al. 2009). The dark side of these advantages is that the PaaS infrastructure can also be used by a hacker to malicious purposes (e.g., running the malware codes and commands).

In the SaaS model, the service providers host the applications remotely and make them available to the users, when requested, over the Internet. SaaS is an advantageous model for the IT enterprises and their customers, as it is more cost-effective and has better operational efficiency. However, there are still concerns about the security of the data store and software, which the vendors are required to address them (Mell and Grance 2011; Mather et al. 2009).

In addition to these three main service delivery models, the cloud offers other models and the infrastructure is utilized these days for many other purposes, such as Security-as-a-Service (SECaaS). Using this service model, many security vendors deliver their security solutions using cloud services. That is to say, the security management services are outsourced to an external service provider, and delivered to the users over the Internet. SECaaS applications can be in the form of anti-virus, anti-spam, and malware detection programs. The programs operate on the cloud, instead of client-side installed software, and with no need for on-premises hardware (Varadharajan and Tupakula 2014).

Employing cloud services by an enterprise is a two-edged sword, meaning that it has both positive and negative impacts. On one hand, by outsourcing and shifting some responsibilities from the enterprise to the cloud, fewer unwanted incidents are expected to occur. This is due to the fact that the cloud providers have a more advanced and experienced position in offering more secure services that are supported by their specialized staff, and also there are incident management plans for the case of break outs. However, this transferring of the responsibilities, on the other hand, decreases the control of the enterprise over the critical services. In addition to that, storing the data outside the organization's firewalls raises concerns about potential vulnerabilities and possible leaks. For instance, if the information fall into wrong hands (e.g., exposed to hackers or competitors), it results in loss of customer's confidence, damage to the organization's reputation, and even legal and financial penalties for the organization. On this basis, enterprises that are planning to adopt cloud services put together the positive and negative impacts, weigh them up, and do risk assessment (Rhoton et al. 2013).

In spite of the benefits of adopting cloud-based services in the enterprises, there exist still some barriers. Among all, security and privacy are the most significant barriers. The fundamental challenges related to the cloud security are the security of the data storage, security in data transmission, application security, and security of the third party resources (Subashini and Kavitha 2011). Among all the security risks associated with the cloud, the followings are the top severe security threats reported by the Cloud Security Alliance (CSA) (Top Threats Working Group 2013):

- Data breach: As a result of a malicious intrusion the (sensitive) data may be disclosed to unwanted parties, including the attacker and competitors.
- Data loss: The data stored on the cloud could be lost due to an attack, unintentional/accidental deletion of the data by the service provider, and physical corruption of the system infrastructure.
- Hijacking of the accounts and traffic: Attackers by getting access to the users' credentials, through phishing and exploiting the software vulnerabilities can read or alter the users' activities. This consequently puts the confidentiality, integrity, and availability of the system at risk.
- Insecure Application Program Interfaces (API): Clients use the SW interfaces to interact with the cloud. These APIs should be sufficiently secure to protect both the consumer and the service provider.
- Denial of service: An intruder by sending illegitimate requests to the service provider attempts to occupy the resources, so to disable/slow down the cloud to process the legitimate requests.
- Malicious insider: The adversary is not always an outsider, but can be a person inside the cloud system who has an authorized access to the data and intentionally misuses such authorization.
- Abuse of the cloud service: The cloud computing serves the organizations with extensive computational power; however, this power could be misused by a malicious user to perform his belligerent action.
- Insufficient due diligence: Before the organizations move their services to the cloud, it is significant to have a proper understanding of the capabilities and adaptabilities of their resources with the cloud technologies.
- Shared technology issues: Sharing platforms, infrastructures, and applications has made the delivery of the cloud services feasible; however, such sharing has the drawback that vulnerability in a single piece of shared component can be propagated potentially to the entire cloud.

In securing the cloud computing environment various aspects should be taken into account. The International Information Systems Security Certification Consortium (ISC)^2 (ISC 2016) has presented taxonomy of the security domains concerning the cloud computing, which covers the following aspects: physical security, access control, telecommunications and network security, cryptography, application security, operation security, information security and risk management practices, and business continuity and disaster recovery planning.

Many different approaches have been proposed in the literature for overcoming these security problems, for instance multi-layered security and large scale penetration testing (Chang 2015; Chang et al. 2016; Chang and Ramachandran 2016).

Security and privacy come hand in hand, in other words, a more secure system better protects the privacy of its users. Therefore, while integrating cloud in organization's architecture, it is highly significant for the enterprise to assure that a cloud service provider is considering all the security aspects, and adequately addressing the privacy regulations.

Considering the fact that the proposed approach in this study is aimed at securing the application, and protecting SaaS and PaaS models, in the following section we study the state of cloud application security.

2.1 Application Security in Cloud Computing

Talking about the IaaS model, it is more straightforward to provide protection by hardening the platform through allowing the traffic from trusted IP addresses, running anti-virus programs, applying security patches, and so on. However, when it comes to PaaS and SaaS models, this may not be the case; since in these models, ensuring the security of the platform is the service provider's responsibility (Rhoton et al. 2013). Moreover, in SaaS, there is less transparency and visibility about how the data is stored and secured. This makes it more difficult for the enterprises to trust the service provider.

Application security covers the measures and practices taken throughout the software development life-cycle to reduce the vulnerabilities and flaws. Because of the fact that the cloud-base applications are connected directly to the Internet, cloud offers less physical security compared to traditional data centers and service providers. Also because of the co-mingled data and multi-tenancy behavior of the cloud, the cloud's applications are prone to additional attack vectors.

Recent security incidents clearly show that the exploits by taking advantage of the software flaws and vulnerabilities, make the web applications the leading targets for attacks. Web applications are the simplest and the most profitable targets, from the attackers' perspective. Especially, in the case of cloud computing that the applications are accessed through the user's browser, website security is the sole means to impede the attacks. Moreover, the security breaches through exploiting the applications and web services have shown to be pretty severe and have led to big losses. Stuxnet (Chen and Abu-Nimeh 2011) is one example of infecting the software with the aim of affecting critical physical infrastructures and industrial control systems. The other example is using SQL injection to steal the debit/credit card numbers, which in the end resulted in 1 million withdrawals from the ATM machines worldwide (CSA 2016).

In spite of the significance of the application security, it has been considered as an afterthought in many enterprises. In other words, application security has seldom been the top priority and the main focus for neither the security practitioners and nor the enterprises and less security budget has been allocated on it (CSA 2016).

On this basis, more consideration is required both from the business side by shifting more budget to application security and also from the security team to concentrate more on securing the web applications, the most exposed component of the business.

As in other domains, application security in cloud computing is a crucial component in operational IT strategy. Regardless of where an application is residing, the enterprise is responsible for ensuring the effectiveness of the security practices to protect the application. Also, as we discussed earlier, the nature of cloud computing environment introduces additional risks compared to on-premise applications and web services.

3 Obfuscation and Diversification for Securing Cloud Computing

Code obfuscation refers to the deliberate act of scrambling the program's code and transforming it in a way that it becomes harder to read (Collberg et al. 1997). This new version of the code is functionally similar to the original code, while syntactically different. This means that even though the obfuscated code has different implementation, given the same input, it produces the same output. The main purpose of code obfuscation is to make the understanding of code and its functionality more complicated and to prevent the act of malicious reverse engineering.

Figure 1 is an example of obfuscated code that clearly shows how much harder it can become to read and comprehend the code after it is obfuscated. With no doubt, within a given time an attacker may succeed in reverse engineering the obfuscated code and breaking it: however, it is harder and costlier now, compared to the original code.

```
a)
function setText(data) {
   document.getElementById("myDiv").innerHTML = data;
}
```

```
b)
function ghds3x(n) {
   h = "\x69\u006En\u0065r\x48T\u004DL";
   a="s c v o v d h e , n i";x=a.split(" ");b="gztxleWentBsyf";
   r=b.replace("z",x[7]).replace("x","E").replace("s","").replace("f","I")
   ["repl" + "ace"]("W","m")+"d"; c="my"+String.fromCharCode(68)+x[10]+"v";
   s=x[5]+x[3]+x[1]+"um"+x[7]+x[9]+"t";d=this[s][r](c);if(+!![])
   { d[h]=n; } else { d[h]=c; }
}
```

Fig. 1. a) a piece of JavaScript code, and b) an obfuscated version of the same code

In the literature, many different obfuscation mechanisms have been proposed (Popov et al. 2007; Linn and Debray 2003). Each of these mechanisms targets various parts of the code to apply the obfuscation transformation. Among all, the techniques that attempt to obfuscate the control of the program are the most commonly used (Nagra and Collberg 2009). These techniques alter the control flow of the program, or generate a fake one, so it would be more challenging for a malicious analyzer to understand the code. To this end, bogus insertion (Drape and Majumdar 2007), and opaque predicates (Collberg et al. 1998) are effective control flow obfuscation techniques.

Software diversification aims at generating unique instances of software in a way that they appear with different syntax but equivalent functionality (Cohen 1993). Diversification breaks the idea of developing and distributing the software in a monoculture manner, and introduces multiculturalism to software design. In the other words, the identical designs of the software instances make them have similar vulnerabilities and are prone to similar types of security threats. This offers the opportunity to an attacker to design an attack model to exploit those vulnerabilities and easily compromise a wide number of execution platforms (e.g., computers). The risk of this kind of massive-scale attacks can be mitigated through diversifying the software versions, so that the same attack model will not be effectual on all instances. The way a program is diversified is kept secret and pieces of malware that do not know the secret cannot interact with the environment and eventually become ineffective. However, the created secret has to be propagated to the trusted applications, so it will still be feasible for them to access the resources. In the worst case scenario, even if the attacker gains the secret of diversification of one instance, that secret is specified to that computer and a costly analysis is required to find out other secrets to attack other computers. There have been survey studies surveying software diversity (Larsen et al. 2014; Baudry and Monperrus 2015).

A particular version of diversification is *interface diversification* which is applied to internal interfaces of software (APIs or instruction sets of languages). For example, the system call interface (for accessing all kinds of resources of a system) is one typical *internal* interface which can be changed without sharing the details of new internal interface to external parties (e.g. malware) (Rauti et al. 2014). Of course, the details on diversified internal interface need to be propagated to all legal applications so that those programs can still use the system's resources (Lauren et al. 2014).

Figure 2 illustrates distribution of diversified versions of program P among the users. Each of the programs P1, P2, and P3 are unique in structure and diversified differently. Thus, one single attack model does not work for multiple systems, and

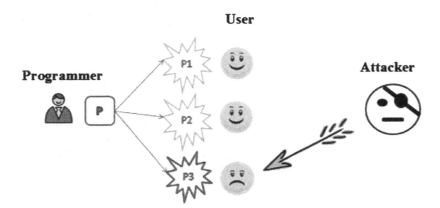

Fig. 2. Diversification generates unique versions of software. Therefore, even if one copy of software is breached, other copies are safe.

attack models need to be designed to be system-specific. When program P3 is attacked, other versions are still safe.

Program bugs left at the development time are inevitable and cause software vulnerabilities. Some of these vulnerabilities are not known, while releasing the software. Later on, a malicious person can gain knowledge about the system and its vulnerabilities, and write a piece of malware to exploit those vulnerabilities performing a successful attack. Especially, the interface diversification techniques can be helpful in preventing such zero day type of attacks, since the malicious person no longer automatically know the necessary (for malware) internal interfaces for accessing resources.

In general, diversification and obfuscation techniques do not attempt to remove these vulnerabilities, but attempt to prevent (or make it hard, at least) the attacker/malware to taking advantage of them to run its malicious code. Obfuscating and diversifying the internal interfaces of the system makes it challenging for malware to attain the required knowledge about the system, how to call the systems interfaces, in order to execute its malicious code.

3.1   Related Work on Security of Cloud Through Obfuscation and Diversification

As mentioned before, diversification and obfuscation techniques have been used in different domains to provide security, including cloud computing. In a previous study (Hosseinzadeh et al. 2015), we systematically studies in what ways these two techniques have been used in cloud computing environment with the aim of improving the security. As the result of the search, we collected 43 studies that were discussing diversification and obfuscation as the techniques for improving the security in the cloud and protect the privacy of its users, and we classified them based on how the techniques are used to this aim. After extracting data from those studies, we identified that the obfuscation and diversification techniques are used in nine different ways to boost the security and privacy of the cloud, including: (1) generating noise obfuscation, (2) client-side data obfuscation as a middleware, (3) general data obfuscation, (4) source code obfuscation, (5) location obfuscation, (6) file splitting and storing on separate clouds, (7) encryption as obfuscation, (8) diversification, and (9) cloud security by virtue of securing the browser. Figure 3 illustrates these categories with the number of studies in each group.

Many of the cloud service providers are complying with the policies and regulations in order to protect the privacy of their customers. However, there exist a wide number of service providers that may record the collected data from the customers, deduce and misuse the private information without user's consent. Hence, there is a need for practices to be taken at client side (without service provider's interference) to protect the privacy. Obfuscation and diversification techniques were employed to protect the data "from the cloud". In majority of studied works, the cloud service provider was considered as untrusted/malicious.

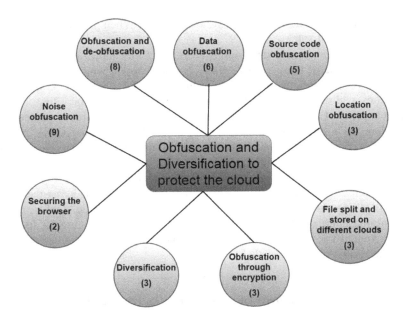

Fig. 3. The related studies on security and privacy in cloud computing through obfuscation and diversification techniques.

In the following, we explain the nine different ways that obfuscation/diversification have been used in the literature for protecting the cloud from security threats, and also protecting the user's privacy from the malicious cloud.

- Generating noise obfuscation: This approach resides on the client side and tries confuses the malicious cloud by injecting irrelevant requests that are similar to legitimate requests of the user (called noise) into the user's service requests, i.e., the requests sent from the customer to the cloud. In this way, the occurrence probability of the legitimate requests and the noise requests become the same, so it becomes difficult for the cloud to distinguish the real request. Noise generation strategy, conceals real requests coming from the users, and therefore, lessens the probability of request being revealed. As the result, the privacy of the customer is protected.

- Client-side data obfuscation as a middleware: This method protects the data from the untrusted service provider while the data is stored or processed on the cloud. A privacy managing middleware on the client side obfuscates the (sensitive) data using a secret key which is chosen and kept by the user. The obfuscated data is sent to the cloud and is processed on the cloud without being de-obfuscated. This is because the key is kept secret to the user and the cloud does not have the key to de-obfuscate the data. The result of the process is sent to the user and is de-obfuscated on the client side, so the user sees the plain data.

- General data obfuscation: In this class obfuscation, some transformations that are made into the user's data, which make them harder to read/understood. This method can be used to protect the user's identity information, the data stored on the database of the cloud, and the user's behavioral pattern. Data obfuscation makes the user's confidential harder to be exposed, and therefore, protects the user's data privacy.

- Source code obfuscation: As explained before, source code obfuscation is a technique for protecting the software from reverse engineering. This method can also be used for securing the cloud's software from attacks and risk of malware.

- Location obfuscation: As we know, there exist services that rely on the physical information of the user to provide the services. This includes privacy concerns on revealing the precise location of the user (e.g., concerns about locating and tracking down the user). To this end, obfuscating the location information is a technique to make the exact location imprecise through generalizing, or slightly altering the precise location to avoid the actual position being exposed and consequently, preserve the location privacy.

- File splitting and storing on separate clouds: The idea in this obfuscation strategy is to divide the data/files into different sectors and store them on different clouds. This approach ensures not only the security, but also the availability of the data. If one cloud is attacked, only one part will be leaked, and the other parts are safe.

- Encryption as obfuscation: Obfuscation could be attained through cryptographic techniques. For instance, homomorphic encryption and one-way hash function are examples of this obfuscation strategy. Obfuscating the data reduces the risk of data leakage and even if the data is leaked, it is quite useless, as it is scrambled. Therefore, it is a beneficial technique in preserving the confidentiality of the data on the cloud.

- Diversification: As discussed before, different components could be the target for diversification depending on the security need of the system. In cloud computing paradigm, it is proposed to continuously diversify the execution environment, so to shorten the time for the attacker to learn the execution environment and the vulnerabilities of it. The execution environment changes to a new environment, before the attacker gets the chance to obtain sufficient knowledge about it.

- Cloud security through securing the browser: In this idea a plug-in is embedded in the user's web browser, which has the capability of data obfuscation and hybrid authentication. Therein, the security and the privacy of the data are addressed in the web browser.

Table 1 lists all the papers that are discussing diversification and obfuscation as the promising security techniques in cloud computing environment. Based on how the studies use diversification/obfuscation is in cloud computing, they fall into nine different categories.

Table 1. List of the studies

No.	Description of method
Category 1: Generating noise obfuscation	
1	(Zhang et al. 2013): Injecting noise requests in user's request makes it difficult for the cloud to distinguish the legitimate request. The paper considers noise obfuscation as a way for privacy-leakage-tolerance
2	(Yang et al. 2013): This paper proposes noise generation approach as a way to obfuscate the data while the characteristic of the data is not changed. The main goal is to protect the privacy in the domain of data statics and data mining
3	(Zhang et al. 2012b): In this paper, Time-series Pattern Strategy Noise Generation (TPNGS) is used to create a pattern based on the previous requests that the user has made, and with the help of this pattern predict the occurrence probability of the future requests. This approach makes the real requests of the user vague, and protects the privacy of the client from a malicious cloud
4	(Zhang et al. 2015): In this work, noise obfuscation approach considers occurrence probability fluctuation as a way to disguise the customer's data
5	(Zhang et al. 2012c): Noise injection is discussed in this paper as a method to confuse the malicious cloud provider, with the aim of privacy protection
6	(Zhang et al. 2012a): Injecting noise (= irrelevant requests) into the user's request makes the occurrence possibility of the real and the noise requests the same, and thus make them indistinguishable
7	(Lamanna et al. 2012): This paper considers homomorphic encryption, oblivious transfer, and query obfuscation in the proxy as the techniques to protect the information from an untrusted cloud. Query obfuscation aims at generating random noisy/fake queries and confusing for the cloud
8	(Zhang et al. 2012d): Noise obfuscation disguises the occurrence probability of the user's requests. In this way, the user's personal information is kept safe, and therefore, the privacy is conserved
9	(Liu et al. 2012): In this paper, generating noise in user's requests is discussed as a way to protect the privacy
Category 2: Client-side data obfuscation as a middleware	
10	(Arockiam and Monikandan 2014): Before sending the data to the cloud, encryption and obfuscation techniques are used to ensure the confidentiality of the data. Obfuscation is used for the numerical data types, while encryption is applied on alphabetical type of data
11	(Tian et al. 2011): This paper suggests that the user's information be encrypted before being sent to the cloud. This encrypted data is decrypted only on the client side
12	(Yau and An 2010): The proposed approach protects the customer's data from malicious cloud through data obfuscation, information hiding, and separating the software and the infrastructure of the service provider
13	(Mowbray et al. 2012): This paper introduces a privacy manager that protects the user's private information by obfuscating them before delivering to the cloud. The key used for this purpose is selected by the privacy manager. The same key is used to de-obfuscate the processed data received from the cloud. They use the term obfuscation rather than encryption, since the data is partially obfuscated and some parts remain intact
14	(Pearson et al. 2009): This work presents a mathematical formulation for obfuscation, and also a privacy manager founded on obfuscation and de-obfuscation approaches

(continued)

Table 1. (*continued*)

No.	Description of method
15	(Mowbray and Pearson 2009): This paper proposes a privacy managing technique based on obfuscation and de-obfuscation approaches, to control the data transferred to the cloud. User's information is obfuscated using the key selected by user, and then sent to the cloud. This key is kept secret by the user, so the cloud is never able to de-obfuscate the data
16	(Govinda and Sathiyamoorthy 2012): In this approach customer's confidential data is obfuscated before being sent to the cloud service provider. The result of the processed data is sent back to the customer. There, the data is de-obfuscated on the client side using the user's secret key
17	(Patibandla et al. 2012): In this work, a privacy manager software is presented that obfuscates the user's sensitive data, prior to send to the cloud, based on the user's preferences
Category 3: General data obfuscation	
18	(Reiss et al. 2012): This paper proposes a systematic obfuscation approach that aims at protecting personal data. The obfuscation techniques used are: (a) transforming: changing the information into another format, (b) sub-setting: selecting a particular fraction of data, (c) culling: deleting a particular fraction of data, and (d) aggregation
19	(Kuzu et al. 2014): Data obfuscation is an advantageous solution to protect the data that is stored in the cloud's database. Besides, the access patterns could be obfuscated and protected as well
20	(Vleju 2012): The confidential information of the user can be protected through obfuscation. For instance, obfuscating the identification information conceals the user's real identity. After obfuscation is applied, the data can be deciphered only by the user
21	(Li et al. 2011): To protect the data privacy in SaaS, data obfuscation is proposed as a beneficial technique
22	(Qin et al. 2014): This paper proposes an algorithm based on obfuscation techniques to protect the confidential information that exist in CNF (Conjunctive Normal Form) format
23	(Tapiador et al. 2012): Typically, a user's decisions and behavior follow a similar pattern. Analyzing this pattern helps in foreseeing the future behavior which raises privacy concerns. Obfuscating the user's behavioral pattern, make this information inaccessible, or at least makes it harder to access
24	(Kansal et al. 2015): This paper proposes image obfuscation as a technique to hide and obfuscate an image (for instance by hiding the position of the pixels or the colors). For this purpose, the paper integrates the compression and secret sharing to produce multiple numbers of shadow images
Category 4: Source code obfuscation	
25	(Bertholon et al. 2013a): JavaScript is the language that is widely used in today's web services. To protect the JavaScript code, obfuscation is proposed to make it harder to reverse engineer
26	(Bertholon et al. 2013b): The paper presents a framework that transforms/obfuscates the source code of the C program into a jumbled form
27	(Hataba and El-Mahdy 2012): This paper is a survey of existing obfuscation techniques that aim at making the reverse engineering harder

(*continued*)

Table 1. (*continued*)

No.	Description of method
28	(Bertholon et al. 2014): JSHADOF framework is designed to obfuscate the JavaScript code. The target of the transformation is the source code in cloud computing web services
29	(Omar et al. 2014): This paper uses control-flow obfuscation and junk code insertion to present a threat-based obfuscation technique
Category 5: Location obfuscation	
30	(Karuppanan et al. 2012): This paper states that the user's private information needs to be protected from being disclosed. Location obfuscation is proposed to conceal the user's location
31	(Skvortsov et al. 2012): The paper states that the Location Services (LS) present services based on the location information of the user, which brings along privacy concerns. Location obfuscation solves this problem by making this information appear imprecise
32	(Agir et al. 2014): This paper considers location obfuscation as a way to confuse the server about the location of the user
Category 6: File splitting and storing on separate clouds	
33	(Celesti et al. 2014): In this work, data obfuscation is done through dividing the files and storing them on multiple clouds. In this way, each cloud has partial view to the file
34	(Ryan and Falvey 2012): In order to obfuscate the data, this work proposes splitting the data and storing them on geographically separated data stores
35	(Villari et al. 2013): To keep the data confidential, it is proposed to spread the data over various clouds
Category 7: Encryption as obfuscation	
36	(Padilha and Pedone 2015): The most common way to achieve obfuscation is to employ cryptographic approaches. Secret sharing is one practical example, in this regard
37	(Gao-xiang et al. 2013): This paper proposes achieving the obfuscation through homomorphic encryption
38	(Furukawa et al. 2013): This paper studies point function obfuscation which relies on one way hash functions
Category 8: Diversification	
39	(Tunc et al. 2014): Moving target defenses aim at continuously altering the execution environment of the system and its configurations, in order to make it challenging and costly for the intruder to learn about the environment and discover its vulnerabilities. This paper proposes diversification of the cloud's execution environment
40	(Yang et al. 2014): This paper proposes to continuously change the execution environment and also the platforms used to execute them. Hence, till the time that the attacker learns the execution environment, it has changed. Moreover, hardware redundancy is introduced as a way to increase the tolerance to the attacks
41	(Guo and Bhattacharya 2014): Design diversity is proposed in this paper for the cloud infrastructure. The target of the diversification is the configuration of virtual replicas. This increases the resiliency of the service, in case of possible attacks
Category 9: Cloud security through securing the browser	
42	(Prasadreddy et al. 2011): This paper proposes a plug-in for the user's web browser that offers double authentication and hybrid obfuscation for the data, and protects the security and privacy of the cloud in this way
43	(Palanques et al. 2012): In this work, obfuscation is used to extend the session's lifetime

4 Enhancing the Security of Cloud Computing Using Obfuscation and Diversification

4.1 Motivation Behind Our Idea

As discussed in Sect. 2.1 about the importance of application security in cloud computing environment and the big losses that might happen as the consequence of insecure applications, we were motivated to propose an approach to improve the cloud's security through securing the applications. Considering the fact that obfuscation and diversification techniques have shown success in impeding the malware in various domains to lessen the risk of harmful damage, we were motivated to use this techniques in our approach. To this aim, first we investigated "how these two techniques are used in cloud computing with the goal of boosting security" (Hosseinzadeh et al. 2015). We systematically reviewed all the studies that were trying to answer this research question. By answering this question, we were aiming at identifying the research gaps which lead us in our future research. After collecting and analyzing the data, we concluded that: there is a growing interest in this field of study, as the number of publications was increasing year by year. Obfuscation and diversification techniques have been used in the literature in different ways, that we presented a classification of this studies based on the way they use these techniques. The classification is presented in Sect. 3.1. Furthermore, as the result of this survey, we realized that the majority of the studied works have proposed approaches using obfuscation techniques, and few were focusing on diversification techniques. This implies that there is a room for more research on the use of diversification as a beneficial technique to bring security to cloud computing.

The previous survey shed more light on the areas that are still potential targets for further research, which motivated us to propose an efficient approach with the help of diversification and obfuscation techniques to secure the cloud's applications. We discuss the details of the proposed approach in Sects. 4.3.

4.2 Threat Model

To make using and deploying SaaS applications easy, these applications are usually available in web environment. A significant proportion of the code of these applications is usually run on the client side, which makes them vulnerable to client-side attacks. Also, the client-side interfaces are often a natural weak point that an adversary can utilize to launch an attack. In what follows, we will concentrate on this threat.

In a man-in-the-browser attack (MitB), the adversary has successfully compromised the client's endpoint application, usually the browser, by getting malware into user's system. The malware can then modify how the browser represents certain web sites and how the user can interact with them. Because the malware is operating inside user's browser, it is able to perform actions using user's authentication credentials by exploiting active log-in sessions (Gühring 2006; Laperdrix et al. 2015).

To be more specific, the malicious program infects the computer's software. The malware – often implemented as a browser extension – then waits for the user to submit some interesting data. As the data is input in the application, the malware intercepts this delivery and extracts all the data using the interfaces provided by the browser (usually by accessing the DOM interface using JavaScript) and stores the values. The malware then modifies the values using browser's interface. The malware then tells the browser to continue submitting the data to the server (or just store it locally in the web application) and the browser goes on without knowing the data has been tampered with. The modified values are now stored by the server (or locally), but neither the user nor the server knows that they are not the original values.

In the case the server generates a receipt of the performed transaction or otherwise shows the previously sent values to the user, the malware again transforms them to the original ones. The user thinks everything is fine, because it appears that the original transaction was received and stored intact. In reality, however, the stored values have been fabricated by the malicious adversary.

It is important to note that attacks of this kind have been seen in the wild (Binsalleeh et al. 2010) and there is no completely satisfactory solution to prevent them. Therefore, mitigating these attacks has become an important goal in the field of information security.

4.3   Our Proposed Approach

For this work, we decided to evaluate integrating source code level obfuscation into an existing web application written in JavaScript. Our solution is a proactive and transparent method that protects applications from data manipulation. Although it does not guarantee to completely prevent all tampering, it significantly mitigates the attack scenario we described.

An important key observation in our solution is the fact that a malicious program in the user's browser needs knowledge about the web application's internal structure in order to modify the data provided by the user. We therefore, change the application that is being executed on the user's web browser in a way that will make it very difficult for a harmful program to compromise it.

After we have applied unique obfuscation to the program, the code is unique on each user's computer. Generic and automatic large-scale malware attacks become infeasible, since the adversary needs to know what to change in the target application's code.

Given enough time, however, the attacker may be able to break the obfuscation. Taking this possibility into account, we could make attacking the web application even harder by continuously re-obfuscating it during its execution. As the internal structure of the web application is dynamically changed like this, a malicious program has only a short time to analyze it in order to modify the data.

In web environment, certain obfuscation methods can also be used to obfuscate the HTML code on the web page that is the target of protection. This makes it even harder for a piece of malware to attach itself to the web application (for example, by using known attribute names of HTML elements). In is also worth noting that in our scheme, we scramble HTML and JavaScript code but not to the actual data that is transmitted over the network. The usual cryptographic protocols like Transport Layer Security (TLS) (Dierks 2008), are still applied to this data on most web pages handling private data.

It is worth noting that when the obfuscation has been performed, the user of a web application will not notice any changes in the functionality of the application. Obfuscation is transparent to the user. We also want our solution to be transparent for the web application developer. The obfuscation is performed automatically after the code is written so the developer does not have to worry about it.

Data modification attacks are often highly dependent on the known structure of a web application. For example, the adversary might try to edit some function in the JavaScript code based on its known name. Our approach should therefore effectively mitigate these kinds of attacks by obscuring the structure of executable code.

4.4 Choice of Application

For the choice of application, we had the following criteria that the selected application had to fulfill:

1. Availability of production-ready obfuscation tooling and libraries. It can be argued, that source code level obfuscation tooling is still in its infancy and, at least in our experience gathered from this exercise, such tools are simply non-existent for many languages and environments. However, for some languages and environments – like JavaScript run in the user's browser – several obfuscation tools and libraries exist today.
2. The application had to be implemented using technologies that are common in today's web development environment. Using commonplace technologies was especially important because we wanted the experiences to be applicable to real-world web application deployment scenarios. In short, we wanted our choice of application be representative of a generic web application.

In the end, we decided to obfuscate Laverna (lav 2016), a simple note taking application that relies entirely for client side scripting for its functionality. Since Laverna contains essentially no server-side components, the main security risk it faces comes from man-in-the-browser attacks.

4.5 Implementation

Ideally, we would like the obfuscation to be seamlessly integrated into project's development work-flow. It is common for modern web-applications already contain a complex build process: resource compression, source code transpiling and request count optimization are just few of the steps that a typical application might employ. Orchestrating all these interdependent operations is a challenging task that has given a rise for a cornucopia of different build automation tools targeting the web platforms.

Laverna is not an exception on this front. The project makes heavy use of (gul 2016a), Browserify (bro 2016), and npm (npm 2016) to automate its build process and manage the complex web of dependencies required for building the application. As a part of the standard build process, Gulp transpiles stylesheets written in Less (les 2016) into css, compresses the html, produces caching manifest and runs various code quality checkers on the project.

We wanted the obfuscation to be as transparent to the software developer as possible. To this end, we decided to integrate the source code obfuscation as an additional step in Gulp's project build specification. Using common tools for the deployment process served our overall goal: evaluating the real-world challenges related to deploying obfuscation.

The concrete obfuscation implementation is composed of three third-party components: gulp-js-obfuscator (gul 2016b), js-obfuscator (jso 2016), and the service provided by javascriptobfuscator.com (jav 2016). The last of which, provides the actual source code transformations in a *software-as-a-service* like manner. js-obfuscate implements a programmatic api around the the service and gulp-js-obfuscate provides integration with Gulp's build pipeline architecture.

The results of the diversification experiment we performed on Laverna applications with our tool indicate that the program would indeed be much more difficult to understand and tamper with after diversification has been applied. For example, even with the relatively simple obfuscation transformations our tool used, the median of Halstead difficulty (the difficulty of understanding a given program) was 54.1% larger for the functions of the diversified version of the program than for the original code. Naturally, even better results would be achieved with a framework that would use a larger set of even more resilient obfuscation transformations.

4.6   Limitations of the Approach

Tooling for analyzing errors in program code is obviously important from a software development standpoint and when it comes to web development, most popular browsers come with built-in debugging capabilities. Setting break-points, single-stepping through the program code, and inspecting objects are common requirements. Unfortunately, application of source code level obfuscation makes utilizing available tooling challenging, to say the least. The problem arises because the developer interacts with the original, unobfuscated source code, but the browser only has access to the obfuscated version of the code. This is not a problem that only affects obfuscation related tooling, source-to-source transpilers have long faced similar problems. However, it could be argued that the problem is magnified for by the very nature of obfuscation, desire to make programs harder to understand.

Source maps is a technique created to solve the aforementioned problem of debugging (sou 2016). Source maps provide the browser with auxiliary debugging information about the obfuscated scripts, allowing it to map the executed statements to statements in the original source. Unfortunately, our current setup did not provide support for source maps. This problem can be somewhat remedied by applying obfuscation only to release builds of the software. While this approach works, with the added benefit of making the build process faster, it does not allow analyzing problems that might arise due to the application of obfuscation. It also limits software developer's ability to analyze possible error reports from end users.

When obfuscating any application, preserving good performance is also an important goal and a challenge. Because of the requirement for transparency, large performance losses clearly noticed by the user are not acceptable. As a response to increasing use of JavaScript frameworks and ongoing competition between web browser manufacturers, performances of the JavaScript engines have gone up in recent years. Acceptable performance and good transparency to the user are usually feasible goals even when using several obfuscation techniques in combination and the obfuscation is dynamically changed.

Employing obfuscation also often increases bandwidth consumption as the executable code grows longer. Dynamically updating the code during execution – a feature not implemented in our current proof-of-concept implementation – would also significantly increase the network traffic. All obfuscation techniques do not increase the size of code that much, though. For example, simply renaming functions does not really affect the bandwidth consumption.

The SaaS-based obfuscation backend provided by javascriptobfuscator.com supports a number of obfuscating transformations. The basic settings employ standard techniques such as variable renaming and string encoding, but more complicated transformation options are also available. Still, we felt that the service-oriented solution limited the amount of control over how the code was to be modified. Figure 4 gives an idea of what the end result of the obfuscation looks like.

```
744974656D"];define([_0xa6ab[0],_0xa6ab[1],_0xa6ab[2]],function(_0x27cax1,_0x27cax2,_0x
27cax3)_0xa6ab[3];var _0x27cax4=dbs:,getDb:function(_0x27cax5)var
_0x27cax6=_0x27cax5[_0xa6ab[4]]+_0xa6ab[5]+_0x27cax5[_0xa6ab[6]];this[_0xa6ab[7]][_0x
27cax6]=this[_0xa6ab[7]][_0x27cax6]||_0x27cax3[_0xa6ab[9]](name:_0x27cax5[_0xa6ab[4]]||
_0xa6ab[8],storeName:_0x27cax5[_0xa6ab[6]]);return
this[_0xa6ab[7]][_0x27cax6],find:function(_0x27cax7)var
_0x27cax8=_0x27cax2[_0xa6ab[10]]();this[_0xa6ab[17]](_0x27cax7[_0xa6ab[16]])[_0xa6ab[1
5]](_0x27cax7[_0xa6ab[11]],function(_0x27cax9,_0x27cax7)if(_0x27cax9)return
_0x27cax8[_0xa6ab[12]](_0x27cax9);if(!_0x27cax7)_0x27cax8[_0xa6ab[12]](_0xa6ab[13]);ret
urn _0x27cax8[_0xa6ab[14]](_0x27cax7));return
_0x27cax8[_0xa6ab[18]],findAll:function(_0x27cax7)var
_0x27cax8=_0x27cax2[_0xa6ab[10]](),_0x27caxa=this;this[_0xa6ab[17]](_0x27cax7[_0xa6ab[
16]])[_0xa6ab[23]](function(_0x27cax9,_0x27caxb)if(!_0x27caxb||!_0x27caxb[_0xa6ab[19]])re
turn _0x27cax8[_0xa6ab[14]]([]);
```

Fig. 4. Excerpt from obfuscated piece of JavaScript code.

5   Conclusion

Cloud computing is becoming an essential part of today's Information Technology. Almost all enterprises and businesses, in all sizes, have deployed (or are planning to deploy) cloud solutions for delivering their services to customers. Cloud adoption is accelerating because of the advantages that cloud computing has brought along, such as higher flexibility and capability of the infrastructures, lower costs of operation and maintenance, wider accessibility, and improved mobility and collaboration (Mather et al. 2009).

Despite of all these benefits, there are still barriers in turning into cloud. Among all, security of the data is the primary concern that holds back the projects from moving to the cloud. The cloud's security threats can be classified in different ways. Cloud Security Alliance (CSA) presented a list of top threats targeting the cloud computing environment (CSA 2016; Top Threats Working Group 2013).

In Sect. 2, we went through the security concerns of the cloud and also security aspects that need to be taken into account in cloud computing environment. We discussed that there are three main delivery models for delivering the cloud services (IaaS, PaaS, and SaaS) that each require different levels of security (Rhoton et al. 2013).

In Sect. 3, first we presented the terms and techniques used in our proposed security approach. Obfuscation and diversification are techniques that have been used to secure the software, mainly with the aim of impeding malware. These techniques have been utilized in various domains as well as in cloud computing. In a previous study we conducted a thorough survey to investigate in what way these two techniques have been previously used to enhance the security of cloud computing and protect the privacy of its users (Hosseinzadeh et al. 2015). As the result of this study, we managed to identify research gaps that motivated us to demonstrate an approach, which fills the gaps to some extent and improves the security in cloud efficiently.

In Sect. 4 we demonstrated an obfuscation (partly including diversification) approach for mainly securing the SaaS model in cloud computing. In this approach we obfuscated the client-side JavaScript components of an application, we did this to demonstrate the feasibility of applying obfuscation in the real-world. We built our solution using existing tools and services to evaluate the experience of integrating obfuscation into an existing application. Implementing the obfuscation only required a relatively small amount of work, mostly because of the use of ready-made libraries. However, the amount of work required is likely to be highly dependant on the complexity of one's target application and the thoroughness of applied obfuscation.

References

Browserify (2016). http://browserify.org. Accessed 08 Apr 2016
Cloud Security Alliance (CSA) (2016). https://cloudsecurityalliance.org/. Accessed 08 Apr 2016
Free JavaScript obfuscator Protect JavaScript code from stealing and shrink size (2016). https://javascriptobfuscator.com. Accessed 08 Apr 2016
Getting started–Less.js (2016). http://lesscss.org. Accessed 08 Apr 2016
Gulp-js-obfuscator (2016a). https://www.npmjs.com/package/gulp-js-obfuscator. Accessed 08 Apr 2016
Gulp.js The streaming build system (2016b). http://gulpjs.com. Accessed 08 Apr 2016
js-obfuscator (2016). https://www.npmjs.com/package/js-obfuscator. Accessed 08 Apr 2016
Laverna Keep your notes private (2016). https://laverna.cc. Accessed 08 Apr 2016
NMP (2016). https://www.npmjs.com. Accessed 08 Apr 2016
Source Map Revision 3 Proposal (2016). https://docs.google.com/document/d/1U1RGAehQw RypUTovF1KRlpiOFze0b-2gc6fAH0KY0k. Accessed 08 Apr 2016

The International Information Systems Security Certification Consortium (ISC)² (2016). https:// www.isc2.org/. Accessed 08 Apr 2016

Agir, B., Papaioannou, T., Narendula, R., Aberer, K., Hubaux, J.-P.: User-side adaptive protection of location privacy in participatory sensing. GeoInformatica **18**(1), 165–191 (2014)

Arockiam, L., Monikandan, S.: Efficient cloud storage confidentiality to ensure data security. In: 2014 International Conference on Computer Communication and Informatics (ICCCI), pp. 1–5 (2014)

Baudry, B., Monperrus, M.: The multiple facets of software diversity: recent developments in year 2000 and beyond. ACM Comput. Surv, **48**(1), 16:1–16:26 (2015)

Bertholon, B., Varrette, S., Bouvry, P.: JShadObf: a JavaScript obfuscator based on multi-objective optimization algorithms. In: Lopez, J., Huang, X., Sandhu, R. (eds.) NSS 2013. LNCS, vol. 7873, pp. 336–349. Springer, Heidelberg (2013). doi:10.1007/978-3-642-38631-2_25

Bertholon, B., Varrette, S., Bouvry, P.: Comparison of multi-objective optimization algorithms for the Jshadobf JavaScript obfuscator. In: 2014 IEEE International, Parallel Distributed Processing Symposium Workshops (IPDPSW), pp. 489–496 (2014)

Bertholon, B., Varrette, S., Martinez, S.: Shadobf: A c-source obfuscator based on multi-objective optimization algorithms. In: 2013 IEEE 27th International Parallel and Distributed Processing Symposium Workshops PhD Forum (IPDPSW), pp. 435–444 (2013b)

Binsalleeh, H., Ormerod, T., Boukhtouta, A., Sinha, P., Youssef, A., Debbabi, M., Wang, L.: On the analysis of the zeus botnet crimeware toolkit. In: Proceedings of the 8th Annual International Conference on Privacy, Security and Trust (PST), pp. 31–38. IEEE (2010)

Celesti, A., Fazio, M., Villari, M., Puliafito, A.: Adding long-term availability, obfuscation, and encryption to multi-cloud storage systems. J. Netw. Comput. Appl. (2014)

Chang, V.: Towards a big data system disaster recovery in a private cloud. Ad Hoc Netw. **35**, 65–82 (2015). Special Issue on Big Data Inspired Data Sensing, Processing and Networking Technologies

Chang, V., Kuo, Y.-H., Ramachandran, M.: Cloud computing adoption framework: a security framework for business clouds. Future Gener. Comput. Syst. **57**, 24–41 (2016)

Chang, V., Ramachandran, M.: Towards achieving data securCloud computing adoption framework: a security framework for business cloudsity with the cloud computing adoption framework. IEEE Trans. Serv. Comput. **9**(1), 138–151 (2016)

Chen, T.M., Abu-Nimeh, S.: Lessons from stuxnet. Computer **44**(4), 91–93 (2011)

Cohen, F.B.: Operating system protection through program evolution. Comput. Secur. **12**(6), 565–584 (1993)

Collberg, C., Thomborson, C., Low, D.: A taxonomy of obfuscating transformations. Technical report, Department of Computer Science, The University of Auckland, New Zealand (1997)

Collberg, C., Thomborson, C., Low, D.: Manufacturing cheap, resilient, and stealthy opaque constructs. In: Proceedings of the 25th ACM SIGPLAN-SIGACT Symposium on Principles of Programming Languages, POPL 1998, pp. 184–196. ACM, New York (1998)

Dierks, T.: The Transport Layer Security (TLS) protocol version 1.2 (2008)

Drape, S., Majumdar, A.: Design and evaluation of slicing obfuscation. Technical report, Department of Computer Science, The University of Auckland, New Zealand (2007)

Furukawa, R., Takenouchi, T., Mori, T.: Behavioral tendency obfuscation framework for personalization services. In: Decker, H., Lhotská, L., Link, S., Basl, J., Tjoa, A.M. (eds.) DEXA 2013. LNCS, vol. 8056, pp. 289–303. Springer, Heidelberg (2013). doi:10.1007/978-3-642-40173-2_24

Gao-xiang, G., Zheng, Y., Xiao, F.: The homomorphic encryption scheme of security obfuscation. In: Tan, T., Ruan, Q., Chen, X., Ma, H., Wang, L. (eds.) IGTA 2013. CCIS, vol. 363, pp. 127–135. Springer, Heidelberg (2013). doi:10.1007/978-3-642-37149-3_16

Govinda, K., Sathiyamoorthy, E.: Agent based security for cloud computing using obfuscation. Procedia Eng. **38**, 125–129 (2012)

Gühring, P.: Concepts against Man-in-the-Browser Attacks (2006). www.cacert.at/svn/sourcerer/CAcert/SecureClient.pdf

Guo, M., Bhattacharya, P.: Diverse virtual replicas for improving intrusion tolerance in cloud. In: Proceedings of the 9th Annual Cyber and Information Security Research Conference, CISR 2014, pp. 41–44. ACM, New York (2014)

Hataba, M., El-Mahdy, A.: Cloud protection by obfuscation: techniques and metrics. In: 2012 Seventh International Conference on P2P, Parallel, Grid, Cloud and Internet Computing (3PGCIC), pp. 369–372 (2012)

Hosseinzadeh, S., Hyrynsalmi, S., Conti, M., Leppänen, V.: Security and privacy in cloud computing via obfuscation and diversification: a survey. In: 2015 IEEE 7th International Conference on Cloud Computing Technology and Science (CloudCom), pp. 529–535 (2015)

Kansal, K., Mohanty, M., Atrey, Pradeep, K.: Scaling and cropping of wavelet-based compressed images in hidden domain. In: He, X., Luo, S., Tao, D., Xu, C., Yang, J., Hasan, M.A. (eds.) MMM 2015. LNCS, vol. 8935, pp. 430–441. Springer, Heidelberg (2015). doi:10.1007/978-3-319-14445-0_37

Karuppanan, K., AparnaMeenaa, K., Radhika, K., Suchitra, R.: Privacy adaptation for secured associations in a social cloud. In: 2012 International Conference on Advances in Computing and Communications (ICACC), pp. 194–198 (2012)

Kuzu, M., Islam, M. S., Kantarcioglu, M.: Efficient privacy-aware search over encrypted databases. In: Proceedings of the 4th ACM Conference on Data and Application Security and Privacy, CODASPY 2014, pp. 249–256. ACM, New York (2014)

Lamanna, D.D., Lodi, G., Baldoni, R.: How not to be seen in the cloud: a progressive privacy solution for desktop-as-a-service. In: Meersman, R., Panetto, H., Dillon, T., Rinderle-Ma, S., Dadam, P., Zhou, X., Pearson, S., Ferscha, A., Bergamaschi, S., Cruz, I.F. (eds.) OTM 2012. LNCS, vol. 7566, pp. 492–510. Springer, Heidelberg (2012). doi:10.1007/978-3-642-33615-7_4

Laperdrix, P., Rudametkin, W., Baudry, B.: Mitigating browser fingerprint tracking: multi-level reconfiguration and diversification. In: 2015 IEEE/ACM 10th International Symposium on Software Engineering for Adaptive and Self-Managing Systems (SEAMS), pp. 98–108 (2015)

Larsen, P., Homescu, A., Brunthaler, S., Franz, M.: SoK: automated software diversity. In: 2014 IEEE Symposium on Security and Privacy (SP), pp. 276–291 (2014)

Laurén, S., Mäki, P., Rauti, S., Hosseinzadeh, S., Hyrynsalmi, S., Leppänen, V.: Symbol diversification of Linux binaries. In: Proceedings of World Congress on Internet Security (WorldCIS-2014) (2014)

Li, L., Li, Q., Shi, Y., Zhang, K.: A new privacy-preserving scheme DOSPA for SaaS. In: Gong, Z., Luo, X., Chen, J., Lei, J., Wang, F. (eds.) Web Information Systems and Mining. LNCS, vol. 6987, pp. 328–335. Springer, Berlin Heidelberg (2011)

Linn, C., Debray, S.: Obfuscation of executable code to improve resistance to static disassembly. In: Proceedings of the 10th ACM Conference on Computer and Communications Security, CCS 2003, pp. 290–299. ACM, New York (2003)

Liu, X., Yuan, D., Zhang, G., Li, W., Cao, D., He, Q., Chen, J., Yang, Y.: Cloud workow system quality of service. In: The Design of Cloud Workow Systems, Springer Briefs in Computer Science, pp. 27–50. Springer, New York (2012)

Mather, T., Kumaraswamy, S., Latif, S.: Cloud Security and Privacy: An Enterprise Perspective on Risks and Compliance Theory in Practice. O'Reilly Media Inc., Sebastopol (2009)

Mell, P., Grance, T.: The NIST definition of cloud computing. Computer Security Division, Information Technology Laboratory, National Institute of Standards and Technology (2011)

Mowbray, M., Pearson, S.: A client-based privacy manager for cloud computing. In: Proceedings of the Fourth International ICST Conference on Communication System software and middleware, COMSWARE 2009, pp. 5:1–5:8. ACM, New York (2009)

Mowbray, M., Pearson, S., Shen, Y.: Enhancing privacy in cloud computing via policy-based obfuscation. J. Supercomput. 61(2), 267–291 (2012)

Nagra, J., Collberg, C.: Surreptitious Software: Obfuscation, Watermarking, and Tamperproofing for Software Protection. Pearson Education, Upper Saddle River (2009)

Omar, R., El-Mahdy, A., Rohou, E.: Arbitrary control-ow embedding into multiple threads for obfuscation: a preliminary complexity and performance analysis. In: Proceedings of the 2nd International Workshop on Security in Cloud Computing, SCC 2014, pp. 51–58. ACM, New York (2014)

Padilha, R., Pedone, F.: Confidentiality in the cloud. Secur. Privacy IEEE 13(1), 57–60 (2015)

Palanques, M., DiPietro, R., del Ojo, C., Malet, M., Marino, M., Felguera, T.: Secure cloud browser: model and architecture to support secure web navigation. In: 2012 IEEE 31st Symposium on Reliable Distributed Systems (SRDS), pp. 402–403 (2012)

Patibandla, R.,S.,M.,Lakshmi, Kurra, S.S., Mundukur, N.B.: A study on scalability of services and privacy issues in cloud computing. In: Ramanujam, R., Ramaswamy, S. (eds.) ICDCIT 2012. LNCS, vol. 7154, pp. 212–230. Springer, Heidelberg (2012). doi:10.1007/978-3-642-28073-3_19

Pearson, S., Shen, Y., Mowbray, M.: A privacy manager for cloud computing. In: Jaatun, M.G., Zhao, G., Rong, C. (eds.) CloudCom 2009. LNCS, vol. 5931, pp. 90–106. Springer, Heidelberg (2009). doi:10.1007/978-3-642-10665-1_9

Popov, I.V., Debray, S.K., Andrews, G.R.: Binary obfuscation using signals. In: USENIX Security (2007)

Prasadreddy, P., Rao, T., Venkat, S.: A threat free architecture for privacy assurance in cloud computing. In: 2011 IEEE World Congress on Services (SERVICES), pp. 564–568 (2011)

Qin, Y., Shen, S., Kong, J., Dai, H.: Cloud-oriented SAT solver based on obfuscating CNF formula. In: Han, W., Huang, Z., Hu, C., Zhang, H., Guo, L. (eds.) APWeb 2014. LNCS, vol. 8710, pp. 188–199. Springer, Heidelberg (2014). doi:10.1007/978-3-319-11119-3_18

Rauti, S., Laurén, S., Hosseinzadeh, S., Mäkelä, J.-M., Hyrynsalmi, S., Leppänen, V.: Diversification of system calls in Linux binaries. In: Proceedings of the 6th International Conference on Trustworthy Systems (In Trust 2014) (2014)

Reiss, C., Wilkes, J., Hellerstein, J.: Obfuscatory obscanturism: making workload traces of commercially-sensitive systems safe to release. In: 2012 IEEE Network Operations and Management Symposium (NOMS), pp. 1279–1286 (2012)

Rhoton, J., de Clercq, J., Graves, D.: Cloud Computing Protected: Security Assessment Handbook. Recursive Limited, London (2013)

Ryan, P., Falvey, S.: Trust in the clouds. Comput. Law Secur. Rev. 28(5), 513–521 (2012)

Skoudis, E.: Malware: Fighting Malicious Code. Prentice Hall Professional, Upper Saddle River (2004)

Skvortsov, P., Dürr, F., Rothermel, K.: Map-aware position sharing for location privacy in non-trusted systems. In: Kay, J., Lukowicz, P., Tokuda, H., Olivier, P., Krüger, A. (eds.) Pervasive 2012. LNCS, vol. 7319, pp. 388–405. Springer, Heidelberg (2012). doi:10.1007/978-3-642-31205-2_24

Subashini, S., Kavitha, V.: A survey on security issues in service delivery models of cloud computing. J. Netw. Comput. Appl. 34(1), 1–11 (2011)

Tapiador, J., Hernandez-Castro, J., Peris-Lopez, P.: Online randomization strategies to obfuscate user behavioral patterns. J. Netw. Syst. Manag. 20(4), 561–578 (2012)

Tian, Y., Song, B., Huh, E.-N.: Towards the development of personal cloud computing for mobile thin-clients. In: International Conference Information Science and Applications (ICISA), pp. 1–5 (2011)

Top Threats Working Group: The notorious nine: cloud computing top threats in 2013. Cloud Security Alliance (2013)

Tunc, C., Fargo, F., Al-Nashif, Y., Hariri, S., Hughes, J.: Autonomic resilient cloud management (ARCM) design and evaluation. In: 2014 International Conference on Cloud and Autonomic Computing (ICCAC), pp. 44–49 (2014)

Varadharajan, V., Tupakula, U.: Security as a service model for cloud environment. IEEE Trans. Netw. Serv. Manag. **11**(1), 60–75 (2014)

Villari, M., Celesti, A., Tusa, F., Puliafito, A.: Data reliability in multi-provider cloud storage service with RRNS. In: Canal, C., Villari, M. (eds.) Advances in Service-Oriented and Cloud Computing. Communications in Computer and Information Science, vol. 393, pp. 83–93. Springer, Heidelberg (2013)

Vleju, M.B.: A client-centric ASM-based approach to identity management in cloud computing. In: Castano, S., Vassiliadis, P., Lakshmanan, Laks, V., Lee, M.L. (eds.) ER 2012. LNCS, vol. 7518, pp. 34–43. Springer, Heidelberg (2012). doi:10.1007/978-3-642-33999-8_5

Yang, P., Gui, X., Tian, F., Yao, J., Lin, J.: A privacy-preserving data obfuscation scheme used in data statistics and data mining. In: High Performance Computing and Communications 2013 IEEE International Conference on Embedded and Ubiquitous Computing (HPCC-EUC), pp. 881–887 (2013)

Yang, Q., Cheng, C., Che, X.: A cost-aware method of privacy protection for multiple cloud service requests. In: 2014 IEEE 17th International Conference on Computational Science and Engineering (CSE), pp. 583–590 (2014)

Yau, S.S., An, H.G.: Protection of users' data confidentiality in cloud computing. In: Proceedings of the Second Asia-Pacific Symposium on Internetware, Internetware 2010, pp. 11:1–11:6. ACM, New York (2010)

Zhang, G., Liu, X., Yang, Y.: Time-series pattern based effective noise generation for privacy protection on cloud. IEEE Trans. Comput. **64**(5), 1456–1469 (2015)

Zhang, G., Yang, Y., Chen, J.: A historical probability based noise generation strategy for privacy protection in cloud computing. J. Comput. Syst. Sci. **78**(5), 1374–1381 (2012a). {JCSS} Special Issue: Cloud Computing 2011

Zhang, G., Yang, Y., Chen, J.: A privacy-leakage-tolerance based noise enhancing strategy for privacy protection in cloud computing. In: 12th IEEE International Conference on Trust, Security and Privacy in Computing and Communications (TrustCom), pp. 1–8 (2013)

Zhang, G., Yang, Y., Liu, X., Chen, J.: A time-series pattern based noise generation strategy for privacy protection in cloud computing. In: 2012 12th IEEE/ACM International Symposium on Cluster, Cloud and Grid Computing (CCGrid), pp. 458–465 (2012b)

Zhang, G., Yang, Y., Yuan, D., Chen, J.: A trust-based noise injection strategy for privacy protection in cloud. Softw.: Pract. Exp., **42**(4), 431–445 (2012c)

Zhang, G., Zhang, X., Yang, Y., Liu, C., Chen, J.: An association probability based noise generation strategy for privacy protection in cloud computing. In: Liu, C., Ludwig, H., Toumani, F., Yu, Q. (eds.) ICSOC 2012. LNCS, vol. 7636, pp. 639–647. Springer, Heidelberg (2012b). doi:10.1007/978-3-642-34321-6_50

An Approach to Organizational Cybersecurity

Jose Romero-Mariona$^{(\boxtimes)}$, Roger Hallman$^{(\boxtimes)}$, Megan Kline,
Geancarlo Palavicini, Josiah Bryan, John San Miguel, Lawrence Kerr,
Maxine Major, and Jorge Alvarez

SPAWAR Systems Center Pacific, San Diego, CA, USA
{jose.romeromariona, roger.hallman, megan.kline,
geancarlo.palavicini, josiah.bryan, john.m.sanmiguel,
lawrence.b.kerr, maxine.m.major, jorge.alvarez}@navy.mil

Abstract. Large organizations must plan for Cybersecurity throughout their entire network, taking into account network granularity and outside subcontractors. The United States Department of Defense (DoD) has large networked systems that span the globe, crossing multiple intra-organizational systems. This larger network includes Information Systems typical of enterprise networks, SCADA Systems monitoring critical infrastructure, newer Cyber-physical systems, and mobile networks. With increased connectivity within the DoD and to external organizations, Cybersecurity is seen as a critical organizational need. There is not currently a standard evaluation process to gauge whether various Cybersecurity technologies adequately meet the needs of either the DoD at large or the context of lower-tier organizations. We introduce the DoD-Centric and Independent Technology Evaluation Capability (DITEC), an enterprise-ready evaluation tool that offers a repeatable evaluation process, the ability to take prior product evaluations into account during the acquisition process, and tools to assist security non-experts in understanding which technologies meet their specific needs. This work describes DITEC and the Cyber-SCADA Evaluation Capability (C-SEC), an implementation of DITEC in a Cyber-Physical context.

1 Introduction

Large organizations are becoming more interconnected and must plan for Cybersecurity in a diverse array of systems. These systems may include information systems (e.g. a database containing employee information or sales records), legacy systems that monitor automated processes, or Cyber-physical "smart" devices. Many of the legacy systems within an organization may even predate standardized communication protocols and were never intended to be connected to broader networks of systems (Romero-Mariona et al. 2016). Governments may oversee systems of systems that co-mingle information systems with both legacy and modern Cyber-physical smart systems, connecting over both hard-wired and wireless networks. In addition to an organization-wide Cybersecurity stance, different entities within the organization will have their own context-specific requirements.

© Springer International Publishing AG 2017 (outside the USA)
V. Chang et al. (Eds.): Enterprise Security, LNCS 10131, pp. 203–222, 2017.
DOI: 10.1007/978-3-319-54380-2_9

How large organizations develop their Cybersecurity planning and implement Cybersecurity technologies varies, with acquisition decisions often being made by management personnel whose expertise is not in security. If personnel rotate through an organization on a regular basis, the security products used within a network may be changed with each new supervisor. This introduces risk into the networked system in several ways:

- Network administrators must learn how to use the new product or technology that has been forced upon them.
- The new product or technology may not be the optimal choice for the security needs of the system in the local context.
- Cybersecurity technologies are quickly evolving, and the decision to acquire the new product or technology may have involved obsolete or incomplete knowledge.

Moreover, there is no standardized method for evaluating Cybersecurity technologies (Romero-Mariona 2014), resulting in many disparate and non-repeatable evaluation processes.

In this work we introduce the DoD-Centric and Independent Technology Evaluation Capability (DITEC), a research project funded by the US Navy to assist Cybersecurity acquisition professionals in purchasing the proper technologies to secure their systems. An enterprise-level technology evaluation capability, DITEC+, is described along with a specialized implementation of DITEC's in a cyber-physical environment. The rest of this chapter is organized as follows: Sect. 2 discusses Cybersecurity for both Enterprise Information Systems and Cyber-Physical Systems along with several case studies; Sect. 3 introduces DITEC and its enterprise-level version, DITEC+; Sect. 4 describes the Cyber-SCADA Evaluation Capability (CSEC); Related works are covered in Sect. 5; Finally, concluding remarks are presented in Sect. 6.

2   Cybersecurity for Enterprise and Cyber-Physical Systems

Operational Technology (OT) components have traditionally been non-networked and isolated from the malware and exploit-filled enterprise Information Technology (IT) network. This is the case because because these components typically demand uninterrupted operations. Disruption of OT components can lead to serious economic and physical damages while risking the lives of those in close proximity to those components. Furthermore, separation of Industrial Control Systems (ICS) networks and IT networks is critical to prevent data leakage in and out of operational networks. In situations where it is infeasible to completely separate these networks, firewalls and Demilitarized Zones (DMZ) must be implemented to ensure unnecessary content does not leave or enter the ICS network, such as internal device information, malware, ransomware, or web content. However, as more OT devices are connected to the enterprise network, the more dangerous this lack of logical separation will become.

Recent Ponemon reports on Privacy and Data Security published in 2014 and 2016 (Ponemon 2014; Ponemon 2016), also found that over 90% of companies surveyed reported having a Cyberattack in the last two years. Even in the face of such dire reports, due diligence must be exercised in the investigation of potential breaches. In late 2011, a report of hackers having breached Curran-Gardner Public Water District was released by Illinois Statewide Terrorism & Intelligence Center. The report accused Russian hackers with causing a water pump to burn out and the subsequent disruption of service. ICS-CERT performed an investigation and found no evidence of a Cyberattack on the utility company causing equipment failure (ICS-CERT 2011). In the meantime, several news organizations released articles alarming the public of the incident (Krebs 2011). After thorough investigation it was found that the suspicious access to the OT network from Russian IP addresses were due to a consultant accessing the network while on vacation (Zetter 2011). The consultant had been involved in the setup of the utility's Supervisory Control and Data Acquisition (SCADA) environment, and provided support from time to time. While on vacation in Russia, he received a request from Curran-Gardner for support, and accessed the SCADA network from his hotel.

2.1 Case Studies in Organizational Cybersecurity

We briefly cover several case studies in Cybersecurity covering positive, mixed, and negative results. News of Cyberattacks that cause quantifiable damage—either in lost data, pilfered funds, or physical damage—are regular news stories, but this does not tell the whole story. There are Cybersecurity "successes" that are much less publicized, and such successes are instructive. One recurring aspect of successful Cybersecurity is regular communication with government Cybercrime experts and law enforcement. Inter-organizational threat information sharing may assist multiple organizations with improving their Cybersecurity posture. Information sharing, while a crucial aspect of an organization's Cybersecurity strategy, must be done in a way that protects proprietary information; secure and private information exchange is an active area of research.

2.1.1 Cybersecurity with Positive Results

An important Cyber-defense strategy consists of understanding the vulnerabilities that threaten each type of network while communicating with others in the field about potential threats and mitigation strategies. This requires effective network architectures that enable both uninterrupted service and secure data transfer. A successful example of this is Duke Energy (Dalesio 2015; Dalesio 2016), the Charlotte-based power company that manages nuclear plants, smart grids, dams, and other energy infrastructure. Duke Energy receives a large number of Cyberattacks every day, most of which are attributed to foreign nation states attempting to infiltrate its operational network. To mitigate these attacks and maintain sustained operations, Duke Energy routinely interfaces with the FBI and other security agencies to identify current threats to the power grid and other Internet of Things (IoT) devices such as smart meters and refrigerators, which are now connected to a larger network.

2.1.2 Cybersecurity with Mixed Results

As the number of networked devices transporting data has significantly increased in the past 5 years, many agricultural companies (e.g., Monsanto, Deer and Co.) have implemented security policies to prevent breaches (Bunge 2015). Crucial data collection, which has enabled the agriculture industry to become more efficient with greater oversight of their assets, has introduced new vulnerabilities in both physical equipment and virtual services. As a result, the industry must now think of ways to secure the flow of information. Like Duke Energy, they have begun consulting government agencies and Cybersecurity firms to secure increasingly vast networks, physical equipment, and other resources. Cyberattacks in this field can be devastating, as farmers depend on accurate information and uninterrupted operations to manage a large amount of their resources and cultivate their product.

In 2014 a server at The Climate Corporation, a company that examines weather data to offer insurance to farmers, was breached (Wyant 2014). This breach compromised credit card data and employee information. However, as a result of the IT and OT network separation, the breach did not effect any data collected by the Precision Planning equipment. If the two networks had not been either logically or physically separated, the breach would have caused a significant loss in time, money, and other resources.

2.1.3   Cybersecurity with Poor Results

On December 23, 2015 three Ukrainian power distribution companies suffered a Cyberattack that left 227,000 customers without power in the midst of the bitter, cold winter season (ICS-CERT 2016). The attack was a coordinated effort employing remote access tools to disrupt breakers, destroy systems by erasing key data from the systems (use of KillDisk malware), corrupt device firmware, and perform a denial-of-service against the companies' telephone centers to disrupt customer reporting (ICS-CERT 2011; Zetter 2011). Some reports attributed the attack to Russian hackers, due to the discovery of Black Energy 3 malware strain and the KillDisk malware found in the power distribution companies' environments (Hultquist 2016). These same tools had been used against the Ukraine in prior attacks. Given the difficult nature of attribution, there's a lack of consensus as to the group responsible for the attacks (ICS-CERT 2016; ESET 2016).

The use of Black Energy 3 for the attack has not been verified, and the mere presence of the malware does not indicate any responsible party. As alarming as the Ukraine power outage appears, developing and executing this type of attack requires considerable knowledge about the target. Unfortunately, this level of knowledge may well be in the hands of potential attackers, given the wide reach of reconnaissance operations on critical infrastructure, as in the "Energetic Bear" (aka Dragonfly) campaign (TrendMicro 2015; Symantec 2014).

In June of 2014, ICS-CERT issued alert ICS-ALERT-14-176-02A notifying the critical infrastructure community of a wave of focused attacks aimed at industrial control systems using a malware variant of the Havex remote access trojan (RAT) (ICS-CERT 2016). The Havex malware contains modules to gather information from critical infrastructure devices and ex-filtrate the data to Command & Control (C&C) servers. This provides attackers with reconnaissance information useful for future attacks. The RAT relies on the standard OLE for Process Control (OPC[1]) or

---

[1] https://opcfoundation.org/.

OPC Classic to communicate with industrial control systems (Hentunen 2014). OPC is a standard set of specification that defines an interface for machine-to-machine communication, including real-time data. It was originally developed to provide translation between dissimilar protocols used in programmable logic controllers (PLC) for interoperability. Evidence of earlier variants of the Havex RAT's being used against critical infrastructure has been reported world-wide since 2011 (Hentunen 2014). In its 2014 variant format, the RAT was embedded into critical infrastructure manufacturer's software updates in a form of watering-hole attack. The true number of world-wide infections is unknown, as any customer visiting the control systems manufacturer's websites could have downloaded their updates, and consequently installed the malware as part of the update process.

3 DITEC

Each year government and industry invest millions of dollars in Cybersecurity technologies. This money is spent on the procurement, maintenance, retirement, and replacement of security technologies. There is currently no standardized process or method enabling IT professionals to make well-informed decisions about which technologies best meet their security needs. The processes by which Cybersecurity technologies are evaluated are diverse, often performed by network engineers and IT professionals who have biased opinions of how their networks should be protected; these decision making processes are costly and non-repeatable (Romero-Mariona 2014). These disparate evaluations have hindered the development of appropriate metrics which measure the effectiveness of Cybersecurity technologies based on specific requirements and the absence of legitimate metrics inhibits the ability of evaluations to properly test manufacturer claims about Cybersecurity technologies. Evaluations that do not provide useful results based on legitimate metrics, and are not repeatable, will inevitably result in similar evaluations of technologies being performed and yielding an entirely different set of results. The Navy/DoD has concerns about this, and as such, have invested in developing the DoD-centric and Independent Technology Evaluation Capability (DITEC).

DITEC was an effort to standardize the evaluation process for Cybersecurity technologies, but was not scalable. There are numerous guidelines and frameworks that apply to the implementation of securing IT networks (e.g., National Institute of Standards and Technology (NIST) Cybersecurity Framework (NIST 2015), the DoD 8500 Series Information Assurance (IA) Controls (DoD 2014), etc.) that served as the basis for research on DITEC. These guidelines helped to establish the types of procedures, controls, threats, and features that provide the test cases for which Cybersecurity technologies are evaluated. Research was done to determine the types of technologies that were available on the market. These technology types were then classified into a three-tiered categorization based on their capabilities. A taxonomy which married the test cases and technologies was created, then matched technologies to test cases, which allowed for the creation of the evaluation metrics. Scoring algorithms were devised based on the raw scores attributed to technology evaluation, demonstrating a technology's capabilities. This scoring allows users to evaluate one technology and compare it (at a high level) against other technology types. DITEC was a prototype developed to provide a framework for standardizing evaluations. DITEC+ is the next iteration of DITEC, adding new features and capabilities to evaluations such as customizing evaluations based on a user's needs.

DITEC+ provides the Navy/DoD with an enterprise-level capability for evaluating Cybersecurity technologies. It expands upon the previously funded applied research project, DITEC, and gives the ability to streamline the process for evaluating Cybersecurity technologies by having a predetermined test plan that is scalable.

DITEC+ provides significant improvements in the user experience and capabilities. Users are able to generate baseline evaluations, as well as have the ability to add test cases based upon their needs. DITEC+ also provides users an archived database of completed evaluations to which they can apply their own set of metrics (Hallman et al. 2014). By applying their own metrics they will be able to generate a personalized evaluation without having to recreate previous efforts. In addition, DITEC+:

- supports multiple and concurrent users and technology evaluations
- provides the ability to compare various Cybersecurity technology evaluations
- developed new metrics for measuring differences across evaluations and technologies while estimating the level of Cybersecurity provided
- developed a new ranking/prioritization mechanism of evaluated technologies based on user preferences
- provides decision-making superiority from the evaluations (Hallman et al. 2014; Kerr et al. 2016).

DITEC+ leverages DITEC's three main components:

- Process—Evaluates a specific Cybersecurity technology to determine how well it meets DoD/Navy needs. DITEC+ prescribes additional/customizable steps for focused evaluations pertaining to specific stakeholders and offers those steps as a library of evaluation guidelines.
- Metrics—Measures how well each technology meets the specified needs across 125 different test cases. DITEC+ revised and improves on the DITEC Metrics module in order to enable technologies to receive a "score" based on their evaluation performance against the metrics, provides the ability to apply "weights" to each evaluation per specific items of interest identified during the process (Hallman et al. 2014). DITEC+ Metrics provide support for prioritizing results based on a variety of different aspects.
- Framework—Provides the format necessary to compare and contrast multiple technologies of a specific Cybersecurity area (Kerr et al. 2016). DITEC+ leverages the existing DITEC Framework but ensures that it is ready for enterprise- wide use, supporting multiple users and evaluations by adding robustness to the database and evaluation algorithms.

DITEC+ represents a new approach to Cybersecurity acquisition for the US Government. It enables a DoD/Navy-centric, cost-effective, streamlined evaluation of various Cybersecurity technologies, defined by a process that is standardized, flexible, repeatable, scalable, and granular metrics (developed in-house with subject matter expert support). Software applications have been implemented which leverage newly-developed visualization and scoring algorithms to support non-Cybersecurity experts in evaluating Cybersecurity technologies (Kerr et al. 2016). Finally, it integrates existing manual/paper-based efforts into a digital, automated, and completed evaluation capability.

DITEC+ is under final development (version 1 completed in 2015, with version 2 in progress) following these phases:

- Phase 1—concentrated on the initial research and requirements gathering in order to ensure that DITEC transitioned properly into DITEC+, identifying, documenting the necessary characteristics of DITEC+ and its deployment environment. Milestones achieved included completion of DITEC+ requirements, DITEC+ software design, and DITEC+ software architecture.
- Phase 2—focused on developing DITEC+ as a software tool and online collaborative environment (to enable evaluation reuse and user interaction). Tasks included (*i*) DITEC code reuse to serve as basis for DITEC+, (*ii*) implementation of new features for supporting multiple users and multiple evaluations, (*iii*) implementation of new Metrics algorithms to visualize and prioritize scores (Hallman et al. 2014), (*iv*) implement features for "suggesting" users products and evaluations based on their task at hand (Kerr et al. 2016), and (*v*) implementation of evaluation "design space" which will allow users to dynamically and visually compose evaluations on-the-fly. Milestones achieved included DITEC+ prototype and DITEC+ documentation.
- Phase 3—concentrated on the validation of DITEC+ by means of applying DITEC+ to a relevant case study, SCADA security evaluation, and demonstrating the benefits of such integration. Milestones achieved included DITEC+ SCADA customization and demonstration.

3.1 DITEC+ Phase 3

As part of DITEC+'s Phase 3, the case study of SCADA networks was developed in order to demonstrate the flexibility of the process, metrics, and framework. The results showed that while it worked, more customization was needed to be relevant in the critical infrastructures realm. As a result, the Cyber-SCADA Evaluation Capability (C-SEC) project was established in order to maximize the benefits of DITEC+'s enterprise-ready support, while focusing on the specific needs of critical infrastructures (Romero-Mariona et al. 2015).

4   C-SEC: An Implementation of DITEC

C-SEC supports Cybersecurity decision-making across new technologies by enabling a streamlined, flexible, and repeatable evaluation process against DoD-specific needs and requirements. Traditional security evaluation techniques are expensive, as they often require time and resources beyond what projects of smaller scales can afford. In addition, these evaluations tend to be non-repeatable and ultimately lack usability and applicability beyond just that one instance, thus jeopardizing their long-term return on investment (ROI) (Romero-Mariona 2014).

C-SEC has three main components:

- a software evaluation tool,
- a laboratory environment,
- an online collaborative environment.

The software evaluation tool walks non-SCADA security experts through a quick, high-level evaluation process for determining the highlights of specific technologies of interest. The laboratory environment integrates the technology of interest into a pre-scribed configuration, which then provides a more detailed evaluation. Lastly, the online collaborative environment serves as a repository of past evaluations in order to facilitate reuse of results. The following sections describe each of these components in detail.

4.1 C-SEC Evaluation Tool

The C-SEC Evaluation Tool is composed of three main parts: a process, metrics, and a framework (Romero-Mariona 2014). The approach provides not only the process necessary to determine if a certain technology meets DoD/Navy needs, but also pro-vides the metrics to measure how well those needs are met, and a framework to enable the comparison of multiple technologies of interest. Figure 1 shows all three of com-ponent parts.

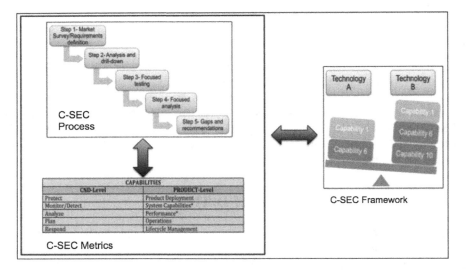

Fig. 1. C-SEC evaluation tool parts

4.1.1 C-SEC Evaluation Process

The C-SEC Evaluation Process is the first major component of the C-SEC approach. It evaluates a specific Cybersecurity technology to determine if it meets (or not) DoD/Navy needs. The following are the major steps of this aspect:

1. Market survey—High-level view of current offerings for the particular Cybersecurity technology area of interest as well as a defined set of tests to determine the compatibility of those offerings with identified needs.
2. Analysis and drill-down—Results from the market survey are analyzed and the top percentage (varies based on each study, interest, and needs) of technologies will move down to the next step.
3. Focused testing—This step takes the technologies identified during the analysis, and the drill-down, testing them more rigorously by means of test cases that go beyond the high-level used during Step 1. Often times a simulated test environment is built to test the functionality of the test subjects. In addition, documentation reviews are also used to determine if needs are met.
4. Focused analysis—This step evaluates the results for each technology tested in Focused Testing and applies metrics to determine how well each need was met.
5. Gaps and recommendations—The focused analysis results highlight current technology gaps and suggest recommendations for future research.

4.1.2 C-SEC Metrics

Metrics (especially those which relate to non-functional aspects) are a difficult problem. Traditional approaches to measuring are not well suited for aspects like security and usability (Romero-Mariona 2014). As a result, researchers, industry practitioners, and the government, lack the necessary tools to baseline and track specific characteristics of today's technologies. C-SEC provides metrics support applicable to security and usability characteristics, with relevance to academia, industry, and government sectors.

C-SEC provides metrics support across three different areas:

1. Metrics Discovery and Application—Develops DoD-specific security metrics and applies them to C-SEC Process results.
2. Metrics Manipulation—Enables manipulation and results integrity.
3. Metrics Visualization—Enables metrics traceability and decision making support.

These three areas make the C-SEC Process results usable. Figure 2 shows one of C-SEC's visualizations for metrics.

CAPABILITIES	
CND-Level	**PRODUCT-Level**
Protect	Product Deployment
Monitor/Detect	System Capabilities*
Analyze	Performance*
Plan	Operations
Respond	Lifecycle Management

Fig. 2. C-SEC metric types

4.1.2.1 Metrics Discovery and Application. The foundational step is to develop metrics and determine the best way to apply them to the C-SEC Process results. In order to provide relevant metrics to a variety of Cybersecurity technologies, we have selected ten different metrics areas, referred to as Capabilities. These Capabilities represent the highest level of granularity and cover aspects across two main areas, Computer Network Defense (CND) concepts as well as product-level. As shown in Fig. 2 below, C-SEC prescribes five types of metrics (or Capabilities) under the CND area, and five types of metrics under the product-level category. The CND-level metrics refer to the basic aspects related to security (i.e. how well does a technology support the protection, monitoring and detection, analysis, planning, and response to threats and/or attacks).

The Product-level area metrics refer to aspects more commonly associated with the daily operations of a technology. Product-level metrics look at aspects that range from the cost and difficulty of deploying a specific technology, to the complexity of maintaining that technology once it is deployed. Each type of metric applied to the results obtained from the application of the C-SEC Process is assigned a numerical value that reflects how well the specific technology under evaluation meets (or not) the objectives defined for that metric.

4.1.2.2 Metrics Manipulation. Once the C-SEC Metrics have been established and applied, C-SEC supports the manipulation of these metrics in order to better understand the technology under various "shades of light". C-SEC employs a granular approach to metrics manipulation; this enables flexibility as well as reusability of results. For example, suppose that Agency 1 just completed an evaluation of Technology X, with an emphasis on the cost, but now Agency 2 also wants to evaluate the same Technology X, but with a different emphasis on protection capabilities. Agency 2 could reuse the same C-SEC results that Agency 1 produced, and manipulate the C-SEC Metrics to put more weight into the protection aspects of the results (and less on the cost aspects) in order to obtain a different measurement of Technology X's ability to meet those needs.

C-SEC Metrics prescribe two new levels in addition to the Capability-level described in Sect. 4.1.2.1, which further break down each Capability into Sub-Capabilities, and those into Sub-Capability Elements. As an example, Fig. 3 below shows how a Capability, like Protection, is composed of two Sub-Capabilities: Vulnerability Protection and Listing (which refer to two possible ways to achieve protection). These are further broken into SubCapability Elements, such as Vulnerability Scanning and Vulnerability Reporting (which refer to two possible ways to achieve Vulnerability Protection).

This granular approach prescribes a few rules:

- Every Capability is composed of one or more Sub-Capabilities.
- Every Sub-Capability is composed of one or more Sub-Capability Elements.
- Sub-Capability Elements can be duplicated across other Sub-Capabilities.

C-SEC computes an aggregated "score" from various levels of granularity (Capability $\rightarrow$ Sub-Capability $\rightarrow$ Sub-Capability Element) as well as provides "weights" at each element to facilitate the flexibility and reuse of the C-SEC Metrics.

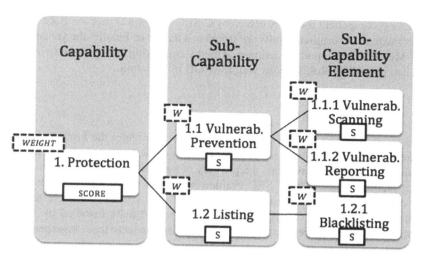

Fig. 3. C-SEC metrics granularity

This granular system is what would enable Agency 2, in our earlier example, to take the C-SEC Process results from Agency 1 and apply different weights to their scores in order to emphasize different aspects of interest.

4.1.2.3 Metrics Visualization. The last aspect supported by C-SEC Metrics is visualization, shown in Fig. 4. C- SEC Metrics provide a visualization for the manipulation of the various scores and weights applied to the C-SEC Process results, so that users can see in "real-time" the effect that changes have on the original results. The Metrics

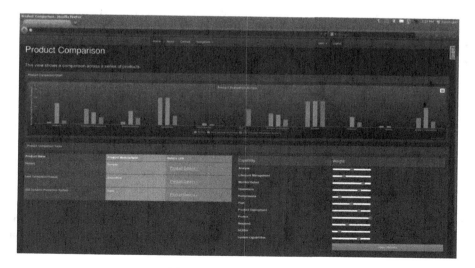

Fig. 4. C-SEC metric types

visualization component is mainly driven by C-SEC's graphical user interface (GUI) and changes made to the original results are stored in a database. Finally, the visualization of C-SEC Metrics also supports decision-making by employing Bayesian-Network models in order to provide probabilities as well as (ROI) information.

4.1.3   C-SEC Framework

The last piece of C-SEC is the Framework. This piece provides the format necessary to compare and contrast multiple technologies of a specific Cybersecurity area. Furthermore, the framework also supports a repository of past and present evaluation results in order to facilitate reuse. The C-SEC Framework serves as the key component of the online collaborative environment, through which various users can share results and reuse information. While C-SEC applications are individually installed by users (clients), the Framework serves as the hub (server) that connects them together.

4.2   C-SEC Laboratory Environment

In order to further evaluate the various security technologies of interest in more detail, we have established a SCADA laboratory environment. The C-SEC Laboratory Environment consists of several SCADA demonstration kits from various vendors, which are easily reconfigurable to simulate different environments. Using this setup, the Technology Under Evaluation (TUE) is integrated for a much more detailed evaluation beyond just the C-SEC software tool. Laboratory assets include:

- SCADA and ICS components (including, but not limited to): programmable logic control units (PLCs) (Zhu and Sastry 2010), networking equipment, valves, actuators, motors, and various other components, which create a realistic industrial environment. These components are representative of real-world equipment offered by the major SCADA and ICS suppliers.
- A DoD-mandated vulnerability scanner.
- Vulnerability visualization tool, Combinatorial Analysis Utilizing Logical Dependencies Residing on Networks (CAULDRON).
- A suite of internally developed, custom security test scripts to exercise the equipment within and beyond normal operation parameters.

CAULDRON, developed by George Mason University, is a network vulnerability visualization tool that takes vulnerability scan results in Extensible Markup Language (XML) format, parses them, and outputs a weighted network diagram (Jajodia et al. 2011). The nodes represent the IP addresses within the network and the edges show potential for information exchange. Each edge has an associated weight that represents the number of vulnerabilities between connected nodes and shows how these vulnerabilities propagate throughout the network. This tool was designed to enable network modeling; a user could create a visualization their existing network, then model how a security product would change the state of the network based on placement.

A set of scripts was developed to automate a number of well-known approaches to network penetration. These scripts are deployed on the SCADA network to test the effectiveness of security products.

The C-SEC process for testing the effectiveness of security technologies is as follows:

1. Perform a vulnerability scan to baseline SCADA equipment.
2. Install and configure security TUE.
3. Allow equipment to run for several weeks to generate data.
4. Re-scan SCADA equipment.
5. Visualize scan results on Cauldron.
6. Compare new and baseline results to determine effectiveness of security TUE.
7. Initiate scripted tests on network to validate scan results.

This process can be seen in Fig. 5.

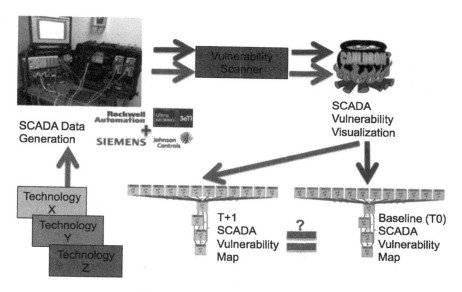

Fig. 5. C-SEC laboratory environment

4.3   C-SEC Online Collaborative Environment

The C-SEC Online Collaborative environment consists of a web application providing users with an interface to create, search, and reuse standardized evaluations of security technologies that are specifically marketed for SCADA networks. This online collaborative environment was created to standardize what is currently a disparate process for evaluating security technologies and apply a set of weights that is representative of user needs. Users have the option to perform new evaluations or choose previously completed evaluations. Allowing users to choose existing evaluations enables them to make informed decisions about which technology (or suite of technologies) to implement on their networks without necessarily performing independent evaluations. The online environment is designed for easy deployment to both enterprise and operational networks. To achieve this, C-SEC deploys as virtual machines (VMs) which are lightweight and have the ability to be hosted on almost any network. The C-SEC web server sits on top of a 64-bit Linux-based platform[2]. Using a lightweight Linux distribution enables C-SEC to have a smaller footprint. NGiNX[3] is the preferred web server to host C-SEC as it is a lightweight solution and memory-efficient, which is key when being hosted on a network with limited resources (e.g. tactical networks). NGiNX is able to handle modern concurrency issues on websites with numerous connections. uWSGI complements NGiNX by handling dynamic content.

The C-SEC website uses the Django framework because it provides required functionalities of a web framework, such as ease of use, scalability, and speed. Websites developed on Django[4] use Python as the primary programming language, as well as HTML. Django also allows for the incorporation of additional APIs, such as Highcharts[5].

Separating the database server from the webserver is an operational decision because running both services on a single machine is resource intensive. Turnkey Linux[6] is a community that takes many of the top open-source applications and creates an easily deployable server with a minimum amount of components to fully operate securely. The C-SEC database server is a Turnkey distribution built specifically host a PostgreSQL database[7]. The database for C-SEC's online collaborative environment has transitioned through a couple of different database iterations, finally settling upon PostgreSQL. PostgreSQL is one of the most feature-rich open source relational databases available.

An overarching goal for C-SEC is the development of a repository of evaluations for reuse as a cost-saving feature. When a user wants to reuse an existing evaluation, they have two options. First, they can take another user's evaluation at face value; they are satisfied with the answers provided by the other user and accept the score as is. Alternatively, they can reuse existing evaluations while overlaying a set of weights based on individual needs using the built in wizard to establish their preferences. Weights based on individual prioritizations are overlayed onto the existing evaluation data. The user also sees a visualization consisting of a bar graph of existing scores over each of the Capabilities and an overlay "wave" of their weighted preferences. This allows users to directly compare their priorities to what the technology provides according to the existing evaluation, shown in Fig. 6 (Hallman et al. 2014).

---

[2] http://linuxmint.com.

[3] https://www.nginx.com.

[4] https://www.djangoproject.com.

[5] http://www.highcharts.com.

[6] https://www.turnkeylinux.org.

[7] http://www.postgresql.org.

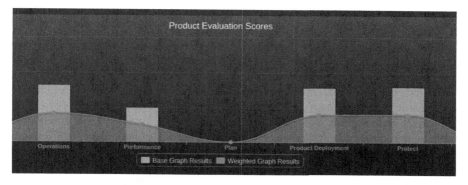

Fig. 6. C-SEC "wave" overlay comparing user priorities with existing evaluations

5   Related Work

Much research has been performed which aims to model and demonstrate methods to provide information about the operational state and security posture of IT/enterprise systems and IoT infrastructure. This research often attempts to simplify understanding of these systems to facilitate decision making for improving the operational and security posture of the system. Research into integrating both enterprise applications and networks of IoT devices must first address the similarities and differences of how both approach communications and security. Once these differences have been addressed, research can be generalized into either:

1. the development of models to understand the scope of actionable information that can be collected from a system, and
2. data collection from operational systems hosted within diverse experimental test bed configurations.

These approaches are discussed in the following sections.

5.1   IoT and Control Systems Security Issues

Enterprise systems, commonplace for many years, are well-known and very complex. Optimization strategies are continually researched to propose methods of con-figuring and securing a standard set of operating systems, hardware, and networking protocols. As the Internet of Things (IoT) provides more transparency and processflow improvement (Hsu et al. 2015), the multitude of connected devices exponentially introduces complexity and the risk of cyber threats into enterprise systems. The research field for understanding IoT-introduced complexity and cyber vulnerabilities is new, but already innovative strategies abound. Developing models to understand and optimize configurations and technology placement is the first step toward mitigating these risks.

Numerous studies cite the need to secure the IoT and the entities that need to be secured, though little speaks to how to secure the IoT (Axelrod 2015). Much of the research into securing networks of IoT devices, particularly in the domain of ICS and

SCADA, focuses on how to apply what we know about more common enterprise level devices and protocols to the IoT domain (Jing et al. 2014).

There are some important differences between ICS and traditional IT system security, particularly in the areas of risks and priorities (Drias et al. 2015). For example, many ICS require time-critical operations, where the focus is not on throughput (as in IT), but rather assurance of timely relaying of messages within the system. Availability is a critical ICS property, particularly while the potential for physical damage or injury from service failure exists. As a result some common IT strategies, such as rebooting systems when errors occur, cannot be applied to the ICS environment. ICS environments frequently prioritize availability over confidentiality and integrity, which increases the likelihood of security flaws (Cruz et al. 2015).

Other differences between traditional IT systems and ICS include support and lifecycle issues (Drias et al. 2015). While IT systems offer a wide variety of support approaches, ICS may be limited to single-vendor solutions due to the specialized nature of the system. ICS products can remain in the field for decades. This is significantly longer than typical IT systems which turn over typically every three to five years. During the functional life of an IT system, patching is generally managed in a timely fashion through various automated techniques, while ICS may not receive patches as rapidly due to the need for testing and the scope of planning for outages as devices are patched.

Historically, SCADA and ICS networks operated in isolated environments and so were not developed to support secure external communications with features such as key management and secure routing protocols (Jing et al. 2014). This is problematic, as a majority of the overhead in protecting IoT systems involves key management for encryption solutions (Fink et al. 2015). Resource usage is critical in IoT, where devices tend to be resource limited. In a traditional network composed of a number of PCs or servers, each with considerable computing resources, the impact on processing power or memory usage in performing security tasks such as monitoring or threat detection is of much less concern. While enterprise systems can glean security information based on feedback from IDS/IPS and other intelligent solutions, IoT devices lack the intelligence and resources to host applications that can report comprehensive metrics, much less security data (Jing et al. 2014).

Yu et al. (2015) discusses vulnerabilities introduced by collaborative implementations of IoT devices. Due to the vast diversity and computational simplicity of IoT devices and prolific unpatched vulnerabilities, a network-based solution, rather than a host-based solution, is the key to IoT security. The proposition is that of a software-based solution which dynamically adapts network security to a changing operational environment (Yu et al. 2015). Security in IoT does not rely on adding point solutions, but end-to-end solutions (Fink et al. 2015).

A simple IF-This-Then-That (IFTTT) style of instructions commonly implemented in IoT tends to ignore the complexity of device interactions, and thus the security interpretation of a combination of known states. Because threat signatures need to be collected in order to make intelligent security decisions, policy extraction must be implemented as a separate utility from firewalls and other IoT management protocols. Researchers Yu et al. propose a brute force method of identifying all devices and possible device states, then deriving the environmental context and security posture from combinations of these states (Yu et al. 2015).

Software Defined Networking (SDN) is used to control a network of IoT devices through a hierarchical control structure with logical partitioning of devices based on only essential device interactions (Yu et al. 2015). In order to implement Network Functionality Virtualization (NFV) of essential devices, micro-middleboxes (μmboxes) can be implemented as lightweight, rapidly configurable VMs running the lightweight Click OS. These μmboxes could be deployed and reconfigured to adapt to the changing security needs of their respective domains within the system.

5.2 Security Models

Because of the vast diversity of IoT appliances, protocols, and configurations, the development of conceptual models to understand and extract meaningful security data from IoT networks is a rapidly growing field of research. These models generally do not evaluate individual device interactions, but rather understand the types of interaction or behaviors as a whole. Information gained from this research aids decision-makers in understanding the scope and behaviors of their interconnected devices.

Risk in ICS can be categorized as residing at either the network level or the system level (Meltzer 2015). The network level allows for security measures such as examining vulnerabilities in ICS protocols, for example, DNP3. New security devices specific to IoT and ICS domains, such as one-way data communication diodes, remote access devices, and industrial protocol translating gateways target security concerns at the network level. A robust architecture featuring network segmentation and appropriate network gateways facilitates ICS process monitoring while minimizing the potential for service disruptions (Meltzer 2015). At the system level, application of appropriate system controls and automation provide a platform from which to implement capabilities such as threat detection. Standards help guide the decision-making process.

The use of a model is beneficial to understanding a system, but even better if it provides insight on the efficiency of operations and potential optimization strategies for that system. Ramachandran et al. (2015) propose a Fine Grain Security Model (FGSM) which offers a multi-layered Cybersecurity strategy that takes advantage of multiple technologies. Specifically, the FGSM layers consist of access management, intrusion detection and prevention technologies, and encryption technologies. The FGSM has bee integrated into the Cloud Computing Adoption Framework (CCAF) by Chang and Kuo (2016). The Enterprise Security Pattern (ESA) model (Moral-García et al. 2014) aims to provide transparency to security infrastructure and policies of an enterprise system. This model integrates assets, environment (context), stakeholders, threats, and technologies for an enterprise system. Given the definitions for each of those values, a method of modeling the interactions, dependencies, and cascading effects resulting from a failure in any of those areas.

ESA proposes meta-models for each category to better understand the system from each of the focus areas. For example, information assets models aim to help establish cost-effective policies to preserve and maintain confidentiality, integrity, and availability of those assets. A security realm model considers the security classification of each system and sub-system in a way that standardizes enterprise security and reduces financial and administrative overhead. A separate security technology model optimizes the software development lifecycle and the purchase and placement of architectural components.

Considering how IoT integration could be addressed in context of enterprise system models, the ESA model proposes a pattern that addresses secure external access to a production environment. This model considers information flow and controls between the enterprise system, which wants to see what the IoT system is doing, and the IoT system which needs to have its own, undisrupted computational processes.

These models can then be chained together to produce a comprehensive solution. The ESA model proposes a solution of four abstract chaining models: Computation Independent Model, Platform Independent Model, Platform Specific Model, and the Product Dependent Model. Each model feeds relevant information into subsequent models to facilitate understanding of the context of the model and reinforce intelligent decision making.

6 Conclusion

In this chapter, we covered a number of Cybersecurity problems that large organizations must navigate. Among these problems are issues of decision making in the acquisition process, communication, human resource management, etc. Case studies showed that communication—with law enforcement and between organizations—was a key aspect of a successful Cybersecurity strategy, although there are many research efforts on safer inter-organization information sharing. The US Navy has funded DITEC to address the lack of a standardized, reusable process for evaluating Cybersecurity products. DITEC+ is an enterprise-level evaluation capability and C-SEC is an instance of DITEC+ focused on SCADA security technologies, a matter of interest as legacy OT systems are connected with standardized, open Internet protocols.

The DITEC+ project offers decision makers a tool that helps them understand the capabilities of Cybersecurity technologies, and assists them in gauging which products are best suited to their specific system. C-SEC demonstrates that this approach to Cybersecurity acquisition is extendable diverse networked environments. SCADA is one of many networked systems used by the DoD and it would be beneficial to have instances of DITEC+ in those contexts as well. Moreover, as new Cybersecurity technologies come onto the market, DITEC+ and its extensions offer the prospect of evaluation capabilities with only minimal adjustment. While not the only factor in a successful strategy, understanding context-specific security needs and which technologies best suit them is an important part of any organization's Cybersecurity effort. DITEC+ and its extensions address this challenge.

References

Axelrod, C.W.: Enforcing security, safety and privacy for the internet of things. In: 2015 IEEE Long Island Systems, Applications and Technology Conference (LISAT), pp. 1–6. IEEE (2015)

Bunge, J.: Agriculture giants boost cybersecurity to shield farm data (2015)

Chang, V., Kuo, Y.-H., Ramachmandaran, M.: Cloud computing adoption framework: a security framework for business clouds. Future Gener. Comput. Syst. **57**, 24–41 (2016)

Cruz, T., Barrigas, J., Proena, J., Graziano, A., Panzieri, S., Lev, L., Simões, P.: Improving network security monitoring for industrial control systems. In: 2015 IFIP/IEEE International Symposium on Integrated Network Management (I), pp. 878–881. IEEE (2015)

Dalesio, E.P.: Duke energy executive says utility battles off steady cyberattacks. Charlotte Obs. (2015)

Dalesio, E.P.: Duke Energy Corp. CEO Lynn Good says the volume of cyberattacks on the country's largest electric company is astonishing. Charlotte Obs. (2016)

DoD: Cybersecurity/Information Assurance (IA). United States Department of Defense, Defense Contract Management Agency (2014)

Drias, Z., Serhrouchni, A., Vogel, O.: Taxonomy of attacks on industrial control protocols. In: 2015 International Conference on Protocol Engineering (ICPE) and International Conference on New Technologies of Distributed Systems (NTDS), pp. 1–6. IEEE (2015)

ESET: ESET finds connection between cyber espionage and electricity outage in Ukraine. Technical report (2016)

Fink, G.A., Zarzhitsky, D.V., Carroll, T.E., Farquhar, E.D.: Security and privacy grand challenges for the internet of things. In: 2015 International Conference on Collaboration Technologies and Systems (CTS), pp. 27–34 (2015)

Hallman, R., Romero-Mariona, J., Kline, M., San Miguel, J.: DITEC user priority designation (UPD) algorithm: an approach to prioritizing technology evaluations. Technical report, DTIC Document (2014)

Hentunen, D.: Havex hunts for ICS/SCADA systems (2014)

Hsu, A.P.T., Lee, W.T., Trappey, A.J.C., Trappey, C.V., Chang, A.C.: Using system dynamics analysis for performance evaluation of IoT enabled one-stop logistic services. In: IEEE International Conference on Systems, Man, and Cybernetics (SMC), pp. 1291–1296 (2015)

Hultquist, J.: Sandworm team and the Ukrainian power authority attacks (2016)

ICS-CERT: ICSB-11-327-01-Illinois Water Pump Failure Report, United States Department Of Homeland Security (DHS) Industrial Control Systems Cyber-Emergency Response Team (ICS-CERT). Technical report (2011)

ICS-CERT: ICS-CERT alerts, United States Department of Homeland Security (DHS) Industrial Control Systems Cyber-Emergency Response Team (ICS-CERT) (2016)

Jajodia, S., Noel, S., Kalapa, P., Albanese, M., Williams, J.: Cauldron mission-centric cyber situational awareness with defense in depth. In: Military Communications Conference 2011, MILCOM 2011, pp. 1339–1344 (2011)

Jing, Q., Vasilakos, A.V., Wan, J., Lu, J., Qiu, D.: Security of the internet of things: perspectives and challenges. Wirel. Netw. **20**(8), 2481–2501 (2014)

Kerr, L., Hallman, R., Major, M., Romero-Mariona, J., Bryan, J., Kline, M., San Miguel, J., Coronado, B.: TMT: technology matching tool for SCADA network security. In: 2016 Cybersecurity Symposium. University of Idaho, Springer, Heidelberg (2016, in press)

Krebs, B.: DHS blasts reports of Illinois water station hack (2011)

Meltzer, D.: Securing the industrial internet of things. ISSA J., 24–30 (2015)

Moral-García, S., Moral-Rubio, S., Rosado, D.G., Fernández, E.B., Fernández-Medina, E.: Enterprise security pattern: a new type of security pattern. Secur. Commun. Netw. **7**(11), 1670–1690 (2014)

NIST: Cybersecurity Framework. National Institute for Standards and Technology, 100 Bureau Drive Gaithersburg, MD 20899 (2015)

Ponemon, I.: Fourth annual benchmark study on patient privacy and data security. Technical report (2014)

Ponemon, I.: Sixth annual benchmark study on privacy & security of healthcare data. Technical report (2016)

Ramachandran, M., Chang, V., Li, C.-S.: The improved cloud computing adoption framework to deliver secure services. In: Proceedings of ESaaSA 2015-2nd International Workshop on Emerging Software as a Service and Analytics, in conjunction with the 5th International Conference on Cloud Computing and Services Science-CLOSER 2015, pp. 73–79. Scitepress (2015)

Romero-Mariona, J.: DITEC (DoD-centric and independent technology evaluation capability): a process for testing security. In: 2014 IEEE Seventh International Conference on Software Testing, Verification and Validation Workshops (ICSTW), pp. 24–25 (2014)

Romero-Mariona, J., Hallman, R., Kline, M., San Miguel, J., Major, M., Kerr, L.: Security in the industrial internet of things - the C-SEC approach. In: Proceedings of the International Conference on Internet of Things and Big Data, pp. 421–428. INSTICC, SCITEPRESS Science and Technology Publications (2016)

Romero-Mariona, J., Kline, M., Miguel, J.S.: C-SEC (cyber SCADA evaluation capability): securing critical infrastructures. In: 2015 IEEE International Symposium on Software Reliability Engineering Workshops (ISSREW), pp. 38–38. IEEE (2015)

Symantec: Dragonfly: western energy companies under sabotage threat. Technical report (2014)

TrendMicro: Report on cyber-security and critical infrastructure in the americas. Technical report, Organization of American States (2015)

Wyant, S.: Monsanto confirms security breach at precision planting unit (2014)

Yu, T., Sekar, V., Seshan, S., Agarwal, Y., Xu, C.: Handling a trillion (unfixable) flaws on a billion devices: rethinking network security for the internet-of-things. In: Proceedings of the 14th ACM Workshop on Hot Topics in Networks, HotNets-XIV, pp. 5:1– 5:7. ACM (2015)

Zetter, K.: Exclusive: comedy of errors led to false water-pump hack report (2011)

Zhu, B., Sastry, S.: SCADA-specific intrusion detection/prevention systems: a survey and taxonomy. In: Proceedings of the 1st Workshop on Secure Control Systems (SCS) (2010)

Using Goal-Question-Metric (GQM) Approach to Assess Security in Cloud Storage

Fara Yahya[✉], Robert J. Walters, and Gary B. Wills

University of Southampton, Southampton, UK
fara.yahya@soton.ac.uk

Abstract. Assessing the security of data stored in cloud storage can be carried out by developing goal-based measurement items. The measurement items can be utilized to construct a security assessment model based on practical needs. The measurement items can assist in acquiring support decision making on the implementation of a security frameworks. This paper discusses the Goal-Question-Metrics (GQM) approach and its application towards constructing measurement items for a security metric. It also attempts to provide practical guidance and example of measurements using GQM. An application of the GQM paradigm towards the development of a security metric is presented. The metrics obtained will assist organizations to meet their requirements for a cloud storage security framework.

Keywords: Cloud storage · Goal-Question-Metric · Security measurement · Security metric

1 Introduction

As data stored in the cloud become more complex, connected, and dynamic in nature, the related security management becomes more challenging. There is a need for systematic techniques with which to obtain quantitative evidence of the systems' security performance. Measurement is widely practiced in engineering and management as means of increasing the understanding of complex real world phenomena and enabling informed and adaptive decision-making. At the moment, domain-specific expertise is the standard knowledge used to manage security. There is a need for more general methods to provide measures for security management. Research on measuring security as a systematic discipline is still in its infancy, although there are examples of industrial security measurement practices. Security Metrics (SM) can be applied to provide security evidence for security engineering, risk and security management, and internal and external evaluation.

The main contributions of this paper is to develop a security assessment model that provides quantitative high level security assessments of cloud storage for IT security practitioners. The SM are expected to assess the relative level of security offered by organizations, cloud storage providers (CSPs) or cloud architectures.

The purpose of our paper is to present a Goal-Question-Metric approach that will support the definition of tailored SM to assess the security of data held in cloud storage. We will start by presenting how security is measured in computer science and cloud

© Springer International Publishing AG 2017
V. Chang et al. (Eds.): Enterprise Security, LNCS 10131, pp. 223–240, 2017.
DOI: 10.1007/978-3-319-54380-2_10

storage. Then, we will discuss cloud storage security challenges and security goals. Later, we will introduce GQM approach to derive SM related to the cloud storage context.

2 Background

Security is a key concern in society. The term is usually defined as a set of different concepts related to "protection" (Colobran 2016). Computer security means to protect information. It manages prevention and detection of unauthorized actions by users of a computer. Security overall covers mainly three aspects: confidentiality, integrity and availability (CIA). These aspects are the topmost considerations in designing a security measure. Currently, computer security has been extended to include security attributes such as authenticity, authorization, identification, and non-repudiation (Microsoft 2015). Each of these aspects refers to security objectives while security threats are specific to the systems (Gonzales et al. 2015). Despite the fact that security is key in society, several questions are still debatable (Baldwin 1997). How much security is needed? How could security be measured? Which security degree could be achieved? The term SM has a range of meanings, with no widely accepted definition. Measuring security is an interesting issue because the concept is challenging. SM reflect some security attributes quantitatively (Pendleton et al. 2016).

3 Measuring Security in Cloud Storage

Measuring security is important in order to predict future situations and take appropriate countermeasures in advance (Colobran 2016). A measurement is defined as "*a quantitatively expressed reduction of uncertainty based on one or more observations*" (Hubbard 2014). Traditionally, security in computer science is based on objective indicators that supply a level of security. Subjective measures are used in fields of computer visualizations (Torkhani et al. 2015). They make sense when data is difficult to obtain; when the associated concepts are difficult to measure, e.g. "measuring user satisfaction etc." (Jahedi and Méndez 2014). Subjective measures can be collected from survey questions or by some sort of assessment made by experts. In the IT field there are also several subjective measures like the "usability" concept for example. Indeed measurements such as the "degree of understanding of security issues among computer users, remain somewhat subjective" (Payne 2006).

According to Cisco Global Cloud Index, cloud storage users will store 1.6 Gigabytes data per month by 2019, compared to 992 megabytes data per month in 2014 (Cisco 2014). The projection of cloud storage growth per user is presented in Fig. 1. With this trend, it has been shown that more and more data will reside in cloud storage and it is expected to grow further. As the cloud becomes the tool of choice for data storage services, the number of cloud storage providers (CSPs) is also increasing. From these providers, users have a wide selection of services available to move their data into the cloud. However, the responsibility for maintaining the security of sensitive data stored therein remains paramount (Zissis and Lekkas 2012).

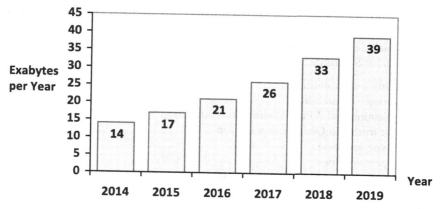

Fig. 1. The cloud storage growth per user (Cisco 2014)

Cloud storage provides a facility for those users who mainly require highly scalable storage on demand that is accessible globally. Despite the benefits cloud storage may bring to users through convenience and lower cost, it also may bring security concerns. These worries have been identified by various researchers (CSA 2010, 2013a; GTISC and GTRI 2013; Sabahi 2011; Shaikh and Haider 2011) who conclude that security concerns are increasing significantly every year.

Recent reports by Cloud Security Alliance (CSA 2013a) and Georgia Technology Information Security Center (GTISC and GTRI 2013) reveal a trend of insecure APIs, data loss and leakage concerns, as outsiders gain access to unencrypted data. Several simple methods are employed: a user password may be discovered by brute force, and unencrypted local files or folders located in the cloud can easily be accessed. The cloud service itself can also be compromised. In these cases, users and CSPs should implement security measures before the data is stored online.

CSPs have been implementing controls to secure access to sensitive data in the cloud, such as two-factor authentication, encryption, etc., making access to the data more difficult for attackers (Mather et al. 2009). Then again, an increase in security controls affects the usability of the data and therefore may cause the system to be avoided by users (Honan 2012; Zarandioon et al. 2012; Zhang and Chen 2012, Zhao and Yue 2014; Zissis and Lekkas 2012). Most CSPs are unwilling to reduce the efficiency of access to cloud storage because users expect equally efficient access into secured data as into plain text data. Security protection based on security components and mitigating its concerns is foreseen as one of the efforts to overcome this issue.

4 Security Challenges in Cloud Storage

According to an IDC IT Cloud survey, 74% of IT executives and CIOs mentioned security as the top concern in cloud services. The cloud providers should be able to provide suitable security controls (Subashini and Kavitha 2011). Data security is an important factor for cloud adoption. An approach that provides real time data protection and blocks threats and isolate affected data in a Data Center is one of the ways to overcome data security issues (Chang and Ramachandran 2016).

In the cloud, application software and databases are operated in large data centres. This poses several new security challenges (Singh et al. 2012; Wang et al. 2012). These challenges include but are not limited to the following (Ryan 2013; Srinivasan and Rodrigues 2012; Subashini and Kavitha 2011; Wang et al. 2012):

- accessibility vulnerabilities
- virtualization vulnerabilities
- web application and APIs vulnerabilities such as:
  - SQL (Structured Query Language) injection
  - cross-site scripting
- physical access issues
- privacy and control concerns as third parties have physical control of data
- identity and credential management issues
- issues associated with integrity and confidentiality such as data verification, tampering, data loss and theft
- issues related to authentication of devices and IP spoofing

Computer storage is where data is held. Storage has been divided into primary storage, which holds data in memory (RAM) and other "built in" devices such as the processor's L1 cache, and secondary storage, which holds data on hard disks, tapes, and other devices requiring input/output operations (Rouse 2005). Primary storage is much faster to access than secondary storage because of its proximity of the storage to the processor or because of the nature of the storage devices. On the other hand, secondary storage can hold much more data than primary storage, and this includes external hard disks and USB flash drives (Rouse 2005).

Cloud storage is known as utility storage if delivered through public cloud service providers (Wu et al. 2010). On the other hand, private service providers offer the same scalability, flexibility, and storage mechanism with restrictions or non-public access. Cloud storage runs on a virtualization platform providing end users and applications with a scalable and provisioned virtual storage architecture. Generally, cloud storage is accessed through an API (Ju et al. 2011; Wu et al. 2010).

5 Definition

Cloud storage is defined as a cloud computing model that stores data on distributed servers and is accessible anywhere through the Internet. A cloud service provider maintains, operates, and manages storage servers that are built using virtualization techniques (Wu et al. 2010).

6 Architecture

Cloud storage architectures contain a front end that exports an API to communicate with the backend storage (Ju et al. 2011), as shown in Fig. 2. At this layer, there are Web service, file-based Internet SCSI or iSCSI front ends (Jones 2010). This layer is the first communication point between the user and the service provider. Users access

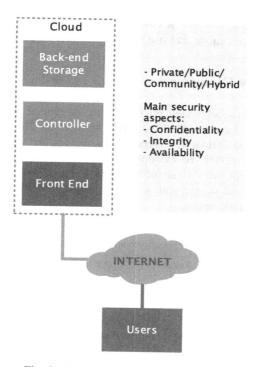

Fig. 2. Generic cloud storage architecture

the services using their credentials. The midpoint component is a layer called *controller* that interconnects the front end API to the backend storage. This layer has a variety of features such as virtualization, replication and data-placement algorithms with geographical location. Finally, the back-end consists of physical storage for data. This may be a central protocol that runs dedicated programs or a traditional back-end to the physical disks.

7 Frameworks for Security

A framework is a basic structure underlying a system or concept. It is a broad overview, outline, or skeleton of interlinked items which supports a particular approach to a specific objective and serves as a guide that can be modified as required by adding or deleting items (Firesmith 2004). IT security frameworks and standards can be helpful in addressing many areas such as encryption, application security, and disaster recovery. An information security framework is a series of documented processes that are used to define policies and procedures around the implementation and ongoing management of information security controls in an enterprise environment (Granneman 2013).

These frameworks are basically a blueprint for building an information security programme to manage risk and reduce vulnerabilities. Information security can utilise these frameworks to define and prioritise the tasks required to build security into an organization. Frameworks can also be customised to solve specific security problems to meet the required specifications and use (Firesmith 2004; Granneman 2013).

8   Cloud Security Frameworks

Several frameworks have addressed cloud security in general (Brock and Goscinski 2010; Firesmith 2004; Takabi et al. 2010; Zissis and Lekkas 2012), and cloud storage in particular (Mapp et al. 2014). Researchers have also applied security components as specific objectives. A review of existing frameworks for cloud security to obtain common security components is summarized in Table 1. We have also addressed issues and threats in cloud storage with security components (Yahya et al. 2014, 2015). Descriptions are presented below.

Table 1. Summary of security components from existing studies

Author	Firesmith (2004)	Takabi et al. (2010)	Brock and Goscinski (2010)	Zissis and Lekkas (2012)	Mapp et al. (2014)
Confidentiality	√	√	√	√	√
Integrity	√	√	√	√	√
Availability	√	√	√	√	√
Non-repudiation	√				
Authenticity			√	√	√
Reliability			√	√	√

8.1   Confidentiality

One of the common security components is the protection of data by allowing only the intended recipient to read the information. This refers to confidentiality. Data should be handled correctly to prevent unauthorised exposure (Firesmith 2004). Brock and Goscinski (2010) has characterize security concerns of clouds by proposing a Cloud Security Framework (CSF) that takes into consideration cloud infrastructure protection to ensure confidentiality. Data can be protected by applying access controls, authentication and authorization while handling data effectively.

8.2   Integrity

The ability of a system or mechanism to detect changes or modifications to an original data ensures integrity. Some techniques implement integrity across a packet header and/or data field by creating a hash across the contents of the packet (Firesmith 2004). A systems integrity approach will review the architecture of a system and its implementation. A system designed and maintained with important aspects, which include contingency planning for power failures and disaster recovery, is also part of a system integrity (Firesmith 2004; Mapp et al. 2014).

8.3   Availability

Availability is the idea that the data is accessible to all authorised users at all times. Its unavailability may occur in a physical way, as the failure of critical network components, power disruptions, and physical plant disruptions, either malicious or natural (Firesmith 2004; Takabi et al. 2010). Availability can also be impacted in a logical way, in the form of improper addressing or routing, and through the use of Denial-Of-Service attacks, which are the deliberate insertion of unwanted data into the network (Brock and Goscinski 2010). This is often associated with address spoofing, which associates the introduction of unwanted data with a trusted end node. Zissis and Lekkas (2012) recommended user-specific security components for users.

8.4   Non-repudiation

The purpose of non-repudiation is to assign attribution, i.e. provenance, to a message that a third party could verify and be confident that it cannot be disputed. It can also prevent a recipient of a message from denying a message was received. Firesmith (2004) developed a detailed specification which attempts to provide a comprehensive security framework. It consists of nine layers: access control, attack harm detection, non-repudiation, integrity, security auditing, physical protection, privacy and confidentiality, recovery, and prosecution. This framework provides a detailed analysis of the required functionality and therefore is able to serve as a reference model. This framework is widely adopted but has not been addressed within the cloud context. It was created at a general level to provide an overview of security components in information systems.

8.5   Authenticity

The authenticity of data refers to its original conception by its owner or author. Maintaining this relationship of data and network communications is performed with the use of public key encryption and a process called digital signing (Brock and Goscinski 2010; Zissis and Lekkas 2012). To create a digital signature, a hash is created across the data. A hash is sometimes referred to as a message that ensures the data is coming from an authentic source (Mapp et al. 2014). When ownership of a digital signature secret key is bound to a specific user, it demonstrates that the data was sent by a valid user. Thus, authenticating the source of data.

8.6   Reliability

Reliability refers to the ability of a system to provide consistent intended service (Brock and Goscinski 2010; Zissis and Lekkas 2012). Mapp et al. (2014) suggested a security framework using capabilities that are required to provide the operational reliability and flexibility needed in cloud environments. The proposed functions are developed into mechanisms using a capability-based approach. The development is implemented for an e-Health system that monitors patients. However, it is described as a process and does not have specific security components for cloud storage.

9 International and Industry Standards, Best Practice, and Guidelines

The interest in cloud computing has led an explicit and constant effort to assess the latest trends in security (Honer 2013). The interest in cloud computing has led an explicit and constant effort to assess the latest trends in security (Honer 2013). Effective governance in cloud computing environments follows from well-developed information security processes as part of the organization's obligations (CSA 2013a; Srinivasan and Rodrigues 2012). In this section, IT industry standards in relation to promoting security are reviewed.

When the cloud was first introduced, the Cloud Security Alliance (CSA), a non-profit organization developed and published cloud security best practice (CSA 2009). Almost all major cloud providers (such as Amazon, Oracle, RedHat, and Salesforce) are members of the CSA. Their efforts include identifying the top concerns. A survey of industry experts was conducted by CSA to collect professional opinion of the vulnerabilities within cloud computing. In the latest edition, experts have identified data loss and breaches, and insecure APIs as the critical concerns to cloud security (CSA 2013a, 2013c). A compliance standard, called Cloud Control Matrix (CCM), was developed to provide standard security controls that can guide providers and help users in the assessment of the risks associated with a provider (CSA 2013b). The CCM is specifically designed as a control framework with security concepts aligned to CSA guidance in 13 domains. It also describes the relationship with industry-accepted security standards, regulations, and control frameworks (such as COBIT, ISO 27001/ 27002, PCI, NIST etc.) (CSA 2013b).

The National Institute of Standards and Technology, Security and Privacy Controls for Federal Information Systems and Organizations (NIST SP 800-53 Revision 4) was created to assist organizations in making the appropriate selection of security controls for information systems by introducing security control baselines (NIST 2013). Security control baselines are used as a starting point for the security control selection process and are based on the security category and associated impact level of information systems determined in accordance with FIPS Publication 199 and FIPS Publication 200 (NIST 2004). The baselines address the security needs of a comprehensive and varied set of constituencies, and are developed from several assumptions, including common environmental, operational, and functional considerations. However, the baselines also assume typical concerns facing common information systems (NIST 2013) but not specifically in the context of a cloud or cloud storage. Moreover, the suggestion of security protections based on categories of impact (low, moderate and high) has also not been included in the latest revision.

The European Network and Information Security Agency (ENISA) developed an authoritative security reference that listed risks, vulnerabilities, and a survey of related research recommendations. It consists of a report and practical guides designed for managing security in the cloud. In the asset management section, security measures highlight the point that service providers should review user data sensitivity. Another recommendation is that providers request information from users whether deploying their data in the cloud is deemed as sensitive enough to require additional security protection. Service providers are also encouraged to apply appropriate segregation between systems with different classifications (Catteddu and Hogben, 2009). The recommendation was only made in general and then only if there are sensitive data.

The United Kingdom Centre for the Protection of National Infrastructure (CPNI) has also provided critical security controls for cyber defence as baselines for high-priority information security measures and controls (CPNI 2014b). They can be applied across an organization to improve its cyber defence. The Council on Cyber-security is coordinating the development of these controls. In their guidelines, the 20 controls (and sub-controls) concentrate on technical measures and activities. The main goal is assisting organizations in prioritising efforts to secure against the current and most common attacks. Besides that, comprehensive security should take into account other areas of security such as policy, organizational structure, and physical security. CPNI has added these in their latest guideline publication (CPNI 2014a). However, this guideline has not discussed cloud security in depth but some recommendations can also be applied to the cloud context.

In 2011, the Australian Signals Directorate (ASD) published 35 best practice strategies to mitigate targeted cyber intrusions (ASD 2014b) but it was simplified into four top mitigation strategies in 2012 (ASD 2012) focusing on application whitelisting, patching applications and operating systems, using the latest version, and minimising administrative privileges. The strategies are ranked in order of overall effectiveness and are based on ASD's analysis of reported security incidents and vulnerabilities. These are derived from ASD security testing and audits on Australian government networks. At the same time, the top four mitigation strategies are expected to effectively help in achieving a defence-in-depth ICT system. The combination of all four strategies, if correctly implemented, will protect an organization from low to moderately sophisticated intrusion attempts.

The Australian Government Information Security Manual (ISM) was published in 2014 and is the standard which governs the security of government ICT systems (ASD 2014a). It has 15 security aspects including: physical security, personnel security, communications security, information technology security, product security, media security, software security, email security, access control, secure administration, network security, cryptography, cross-domain security, data transfers and content filtering, and working off–site. There is an interesting section on protecting classified information and suggestions on encryption methods to protect confidential, secret and top secret information as shown in Table 1. The ISM comprises three documents targeting different levels within the organization, making the ISM accessible to more users and promoting information security awareness in Australian government agencies.

These industry-accepted standards, guidelines and best practice are reviewed and mapped against the security requirements discussed in the previous section (Brock and Goscinski 2010; Firesmith 2004; Mapp et al. 2014; Takabi et al. 2010; Zissis and Lekkas 2012). The Cloud Control Matrix (CCM) has been used as a reference document to crosscheck with other standards. NIST and ENISA are already included in CCM but are separated in this research in the context of cloud storage as it discusses information security in general. CPNI and ASD are not included in CCM as they provide the latest security guidelines and therefore have been thoroughly analysed. The summary is shown in Table 2.

Table 2. Mapping of components to existing security controls in international and industry standards, guidelines, best practice

Organization	CSA (2013b)	NIST (2013)	ENISA (2009)	CPNI (2014b)	ASD (2014a)
Confidentiality	√	√	√	√	√
Integrity	√	√	√	√	√
Availability	√	√	√	√	√
Non-repudiation	√				
Authenticity	√		√	√	√
Reliability			√	√	√

10 Protecting Sensitive Enterprise Data in Cloud Storage

The Institute for Security and Open Methodologies (ISECOM) states that security provides protection where a separation is created between the assets and the threat (ISECOM 2001). These separations are generically called "controls" and sometimes include changes to the asset or the threat. The degree of resistance to or protection from harm may apply to any vulnerable and valuable asset, such as a person, community, nation, or enterprise organizations.

The cloud has enhanced security in many ways. For instance, the cloud provider is trusted to implement better and more recent security technologies and practices than the data owner (Ryan 2013). Conversely, data is stored outside the control of the data owner, which inevitably introduces security issues (Srinivasan and Rodrigues 2012; Subashini and Kavitha 2011; Suntharam et al. 2013). Many controls in the cloud, for example in securing access, are tackled by controls implemented by organizations and CSPs to secure access to sensitive data (Al-sabri and Al-saleem 2013; Calero et al. 2010; Kamara et al. 2011; Zhao and Yue 2014). Most CSPs are reluctant to decrease the efficiency of accessing the cloud storage as users expect similarly efficient access to secured data as with plain data. Some of the drawbacks of having excessive security controls in the cloud are (Honan 2012; Zarandioon et al. 2012; Zhang and Chen 2012; Zhao and Yue 2014; Zissis and Lekkas 2012):

- Decreased availability – the user may need to use a private cloud or an intranet to be able to access data in a controlled network. Some organizations require a security measure to be installed such as a Virtual Private Network.
- Needs robust infrastructure – a suitable infrastructure is needed to run encryption that is able to decrypt and encrypt data stored in the cloud. Misconfiguration may result in needing more computing resources.
- Costly data protection – some organizations require extra measures for identification, such as fingerprint readers and iris scanners. These are expensive and prone to error. The fingerprints are also a single piece of data that resembles a unique identity and can be stolen.
- Inconvenience – the most secure system has reduced use if it is hard to access. Requiring users to remember complicated passwords might keep data safer, but

users may easily forget their passwords. This may require users to reset passwords and remember new combinations.

- Some data needs less protection – during the formative years of the web, as everything went online, passwords worked well. This was mainly due to the small amount of data to protect. Currently, having a single level of protection i.e. password may be insufficient as the threat landscape has evolved.

Security issues in the cloud have surrounded enterprise organizations with the growth of data held in cloud storage. As mentioned in the previous section, cloud storage has been widely utilized by users. Table 3 provides a brief representation of regional information on Internet users (adoption percentage) and the number of cloud storage users (based on the percentage of Internet users) for year 2019. The projection depicts the rise of cloud storage adoption rate by global users and enterprise organizations.

Table 3. Regional cloud storage users by 2019 (Cisco 2014)

Region	Internet users in millions (% of population)	Cloud storage users in millions (% of internet users)
Asia Pacific	2,022 (49%)	1,176 (58%)
Central and Eastern Europe	321 (66%)	134 (42%)
Latin America	355 (54%)	141 (40%)
Middle East and Africa	401 (25%)	65 (16%)
North America	311 (83%)	257 (83%)
Western Europe	341 (80%)	272 (80%)

The concerns towards the security of data in the cloud have encouraged studies undertaken in the area of cloud storage security; this involved developing frameworks to guide enterprise users and CSPs. This has encouraged governing bodies and agencies to publish standards, best practice and guidelines that can be used as references by enterprise organizations adopting cloud storage into their global cloud solutions. Cloud Security Alliance (CSA) in particular has been actively developing guidelines and the Cloud Control Matrix (CCM) is among the important ones that map the controls to other standards protection domains. The National Institute of Standards and Technology (NIST) published NIST 800-53 R4 that presented a risk-based approach in establishing responsibilities for implementing important controls in the cloud. Existing standards, best practices, and guidelines has provide recommendations for the cloud in general but has not put specific emphasis on cloud storage.

Previous research has shown that organizations and CSPs have implemented many controls to ensure security and data protection. However, some measures involve many controls that most enterprise are reluctant to impose, as it is likely to decrease the efficiency of accessing cloud storage. Applying controls based on goal-driven security components and concerns is proposed to protect data efficiently in cloud storage. The proposed solution can be used to better assess an enterprise security goal and policy implementation whether existing policies and controls are in place, measures have been taken or vice versa. The next section discusses methods for deriving security metrics from security goals.

11 Methods for Deriving Security Metrics from Security Goals

According to (Kassou and Kjiri 2012), there are three approaches that support metrics derivation from goals: GQM (Goal-Question-Metric) approach (Basili et al. 1994), GAM (Goal-Argument-Metric) (Cyra and Górski 2008) and BSC (Balanced Scorecard Framework) (Buglione and Abran 2000). GQM Approach provides an outline of process that defines goals, refining them into questions and then specifying measurements and finally data to be collected. GAM is a goal-oriented methodology for defining measurement plans. BSC is a framework that look into several dimensions for describing, implementing and managing strategy at different levels of an organization by linking objectives, initiatives and measures to an organization's strategy.

Considering the purpose and the general approach (top down derivation and bottom-up interpretation) GQM and GAM look the same. The differences relate to the way of defining and maintaining the relationship between the measurement goals and the metrics. In GAM, the goals and sub-goals are denoted as claims and then the analysis focuses on classifying which data and which properties of the data (further sub-goals) are needed to fulfill these claims whereas in GQM referring to a goal, several questions are defined in such a way that obtaining the answers to the questions leads to the achievement of the measurement goal then based on the questions, metrics are defined, which provide quantitative information then treated as answers to the questions (Basili et al. 1994).

GQM Goals are referred to as a mission, while BSC goals are referred to a certain perspective and a certain particular tier in the organizational pyramid (hierarchy). Besides, GQM can be defined as a technique for deriving quantitative measures from a list of goals while BSC can be viewed as performance management framework that uses a GQM-like technique to derive the indicators (Buglione and Abran 2000).

Table 4 shows GQM, GAM and BSC comparison and similarities.

Table 4. GQM, GAM and BSC approach (adapted from (Buglione and Abran 2000; Kassou and Kjiri 2012))

Approach level	Measurement approach		
	GQM	GAM	BSC
Conceptual - Objects	Goal	Claim	Goal
Operational - Assessment	Question	Assertion	Driver
Quantitative - Objective/Subjective	Metric	Metric	Indicator

12 Goal-Question-Metric (GQM) Approach

This section will present the Goal-Question-Metrics and provide example of its application in security research. The Goal-Question-Metric (GQM) approach is based upon the assumption that for an organization to measure in a purposeful way it must first specify goals for itself and its projects, then it must match those goals to the data that are intended to define those goals operationally, and finally provide a framework for interpreting the data with respect to the stated goals. The GQM paradigm (Basili et al. 1994; Basili 1992, 1993) is based on the theory that all measurement should be goal-oriented i.e., there has to be some rationale and need for collecting measurements & each measurement collected is stated in terms of the major goals. Questions are then derived from the goals and help to refine, articulate, and determine if the goals can be achieved. The metrics or measurements that are collected are then used to answer the questions in a quantifiable manner.

A GQM Model is a hierarchical structure as presented in Fig. 3 starting from a goal (specifying purpose of measurement, object/issue to measured, and viewpoint from which measure is taken). GQM defines a measurement model on three levels:

1. Conceptual level (Goal)

   A goal is defined for an object, for a range of reasons, with respect to different models of value, from different perspectives and relative to a specific domain.
2. Operational level (Question)

   A set of questions is utilized to define models of the object of study and after that emphases on that object to describe the evaluation or accomplishment of a particular goal.
3. Quantitative level (Metric)

   A set of measurements, taking into account the models, associated with every question in order to answer it quantifiably.

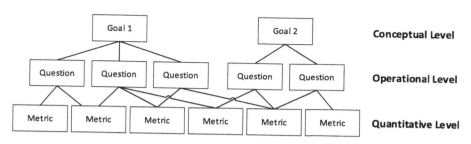

Fig. 3. GQM hierarchical approach

13 Application of GQM

Security requirements are actually a set of conditions that describe properties such as confidentiality, integrity, availability, authenticity, and non-repudiation etc. of the systems security goal (Islam and Falcarin 2011). It is a set of requirements which consider organization policies, security goals and security policies. The security requirements identified here are based on the security goal identified in cloud storage security challenges and threats in previous research (Yahya et al. 2014, 2015). According to (Kassou and Kjiri 2012), there are four steps to build SM using GQM as follows.

14   Building Security Viewpoint

For each security goal, we need to define the viewpoint of the security context related to control that is provided by other viewpoints: Infrastructure, Governance etc.

1. Developing Goals
   Based on Cloud Security Alliance Control Matrix (CCM) and other controls from the literature, we have identified security goals; confidentiality, integrity, availability, non-repudiation, authenticity, and reliability (Yahya et al. 2014, 2015). Each security goals are have been related to the security of data in cloud storage.
2. Refining Security Goals into questions and deriving metrics
   We present in Table 5, an example of security goal; showing the confidentiality of data stored in cloud storage can be achieved by having controls such as identity management, access management and controls.

Table 5. Example of GQM application (In assessing the confidentiality of data accessed in cloud storage)

Goal		Question	Metric
Purpose	Assessing	Co1. Identity Management Sub-questions:	
Issue/Component	the Confidentiality	Co1.1. Implementation of identity management policy?	Rating score*
Object/Process	of Data accessed in cloud storage	Co1.2. Has user-based authentication process/solutions?	Yes/No
Where	in organization	Co1.3. Uses standards to delegate authentication?	Rating score*
Viewpoint	from the stakeholder's viewpoint	Co2. Access management	
		Co2.1. Implementation of access management policy?	Rating score*
		Co2.2. How many access points to the cloud storage?	Number of access points
		Co2.3. Percentage of enforcement points?	Percentage
		.	
		..	
		...	

* Rating Score 1 - No Plan to Implement, 2 - Planning to Implement, 3 - Do not know/Not sure, 4 - Partially Implement, 5 - Fully Implement

3. Detailing metrics

A set of questions and sub questions follows the key indicator. An example includes, identity management, authentication, access management, access points etc.

The four steps is explained in the context of the stakeholders. In this scenario, the stakeholders are IT managers in data centers that manages cloud storage. IT managers are responsible to maintain an organization's effectiveness and efficiency by defining, delivering, and supporting strategic plans for implementing secure information technologies i.e. ensuring that security policy and controls are in place and implemented in an organization. Therefore, security goals in an organization can be assessed and achieved.

15 Conclusion

We have presented a Goal-Question-Metric (GQM) approach to define Security Metrics (SM) to assess the security control features of cloud storage systems. Once defined, these SM can be applied to evaluate the level of security through the following assessment process.

1. Characterize environment assessment – evaluate cloud storage (infrastructure, storage, etc.)
2. Identify Measurement Goals – select security goals and their associated metrics
3. Develop Measurement Plan – assess security controls based on existing studies (frameworks and standards, etc.)
4. Use Measurement Results – use assessment results for showing compliance to cloud storage security framework

Evaluating cloud storage security can be useful for organizations that use cloud storage to: (i) Use the assessment result to ensure the safety of their cloud storage; (ii) Enhance their security implementations to be aligned with their current or target security policy (iii) Improve the quality of their security processes according to the security capability level they are targeting.

In this paper we have presented several approaches for deriving security metrics from security goals; GQM, GAM & BSC. We have also made a comparison of the approach in the context of security. GQM was introduced as a solution to present our work. A brief explanation on how we develop the security metrics are described with details on the process. Our solution proposes a GQM approach to derive security metrics from cloud storage security key indicators (focusing on control characteristics) and their related security goals. Metrics that we have defined and their implementation evidence can used to support organizations in assessing security in cloud storage especially for control features, to enhance the protections in cloud storage.

References

Al-sabri, H.M., Al-saleem, S.M.: Building a cloud storage encryption (CSE) architecture for enhancing cloud security. IJCSI Int. J. Comput. Sci. **10**(2), 259–266 (2013)

ASD: Top four mitigation strategies to protect your ICT system. Australian Signals Directorate (ASD) (2012). http://www.asd.gov.au/publications/protect/Top_4_Mitigations.pdf. Accessed 22 Aug 2014

ASD: Australian Government Information Security Manual Controls. Australian Signals Directorate (ASD), Australian Signals Directorate (2014a). http://www.asd.gov.au/publications/Information_Security_Manual_2014_Principles.pdf. Accessed 12 Oct 2014

ASD: Strategies to mitigate targeted cyber intrusions - mitigation details. Australian Signals Directorate (ASD). Australian Signals Directorate (2014b). www.asd.gov.au/publications/Mitigation_Strategies_2011.pdf. Accessed 16 Aug 2014

Baldwin, D.: The concept of security. Rev. Int. Stud. **23**(01), 5–26 (1997)

Basili, V.R.: Software Modeling And Measurement: The Goal/Question/Metric Paradigm. Quality (1992)

Basili, V.R.: Applying the Goal/Question/Metric Paradigm in the Experience Factory. Software Quality Assurance and Measurement A Worldwide Perspective (1993)

Basili, V.R., Caldiera, G., Rombach, H.D.: Goal Question Metric Paradigm. Encyclopedia of Software Engineering. Wiley, New York (1994). doi:10.1002/0471028959.sof142

Brock, M., Goscinski, A.: Toward a framework for cloud security. In: Hsu, C.H., Yang, L.T., Park, J.H., Yeo, S.S. (eds.) Algorithms and Architectures for Parallel Processing. ICA3PP 2010. LNCS, vol. 6082, pp. 254–263. Springer, Heidelberg (2010)

Buglione, L., Abran, A.: Balanced scorecards and GQM: what are the differences? In: 3rd European Software Measurement Conference, FESMA-AEMES 2000, pp. 18–20 (2000)

Calero, J.M.A., Edwards, N., Kirschnik, J., Wilcock, L., Wray, M.: Toward a multi-tenancy authorization system for cloud services. Secur. Priv. IEEE **8**(6), 48–55 (2010)

Catteddu, D., Hogben, G.: Cloud computing: benefits, risks and recommendations for information security. White Paper. European Network and Information Security Agency (ENISA) (2009)

Chang, V., Ramachandran, M.: Towards achieving data security with the cloud computing adoption framework. IEEE Trans. Serv. Comput. **9**(1), 138–151 (2016). doi:10.1109/TSC.2015.2491281

Cisco: Cisco Global Cloud Index : Forecast and Methodology, 2011–2016. White Paper, 1–41 (2014). http://www.cisco.com/en/US/solutions/collateral/ns341/ns525/ns537/ns705/ns1175/Cloud_Index_White_Paper.html#wp9000816

Colobran, M.: Modeling human perceived security: a conceptual framework and its application to health. Comput. Hum. Behav. **62**, 1–8 (2016). doi:10.1016/j.chb.2016.03.050

CPNI: Reducing the cyber risk in 10 critical areas. White Paper, Centre for the Protection of National Infrastructure (CPNI) (2014a). https://www.gov.uk/government/uploads/system/uploads/attachment_data/file/395716/10_steps_ten_critical_areas.pdf. Accessed 22 Aug 2014

CPNI: The critical security controls for effective cyber defense V5.0 report. Centre for the Protection of National Infrastructure (CPNI) (2014b). http://www.cpni.gov.uk/documents/publications/2014/2014-04-11-critical-security-controls.pdf?epslanguage=en-gb. Accessed 22 Aug 2014

CSA: Security Guidance for Critical Areas of Focus in Cloud Computing V2.1, White Paper. Cloud Security Alliance (CSA) (2009). doi:10.1016/S1353-4858(99)90042-9

CSA: Top Threats to Cloud Computing V1.0 Report. Cloud Security Alliance (CSA) (2010). https://cloudsecurityalliance.org/topthreats/csathreats.v1.0.pdf. Accessed 22 Aug 2014

CSA: Cloud computing vulnerability incidents : a statistical overview report. Cloud Security Alliance (CSA) (2013a). https://cloudsecurityalliance.org/download/cloud-computing-vulnerability-incidents-a-statistical-overview/. Accessed 22 Aug 2014

CSA: The Cloud Control Matrix V3.0.1. White Paper, Cloud Security Alliance (CSA) (2013b). https://cloudsecurityalliance.org/download/cloud-controls-matrix-v3-0-1. Accessed 22 Aug 2014

CSA: The Notorious Nine: Cloud Computing Top Threats in 2013 Report. Cloud Security Alliance (CSA) (2013c). https://downloads.cloudsecurityalliance.org/initiatives/top_threats/The_Notorious_Nine_Cloud_Computing_Top_Threats_in_2013.pdf. Accessed 22 Aug 2014

Cyra, L., Górski, J.: Extending GQM by arguement structures. In: CEE-SET 2007, vol. 44(5), pp. 26–39 (2008). doi:10.1016/j.ipm.2008.03.002

Firesmith, D.: Specifying reusable security requirements. J. Object Technol. 3(1), 61–75 (2004). doi:10.5381/jot.2004.3.1.c6

Gonzales, D., Kaplan, J., Saltzman, E., Winkelman, Z., Woods, D.: Cloud-trust - a security assessment model for infrastructure as a service (IaaS) clouds. IEEE Trans. Cloud Comput. 14 (2015). doi:10.1109/TCC.2015.2415794

Granneman, J.: IT security frameworks and standards: Choosing the right one (2013). http://searchsecurity.techtarget.com/tip/IT-security-frameworks-and-standards-Choosing-the-right-one. Accessed 12 Aug 2015

GTISC and GTRI (2013): Emerging cyber threats report 2014. Georgia Tech Information Security Center (GTISC) and Georgia Tech Research Institute (GTRI), Georgia Tech Cyber Security Summit (2013). https://www.gtisc.gatech.edu/pdf/Threats_Report_2014.pdf. Accessed 22 Aug 2014

Honan, M.: Kill the password: why a string of characters can't protect us anymore. WIRED, pp. 9–16 (2012)

Honer, P.: Cloud computing security requirements and solutions: a systematic literature review. In: 19th Twente Student Conference on IT, Enshede, The Netherlands (2013). doi:10.1007/978-3-642-40861-8_42

Hubbard, D.W.: How to Measure Anything: Finding the Value of Intangibles in Business. Wiley, New York (2014)

ISECOM: ISECOM - Open Source Security Testing Methodology Manual (OSSTMM). Institute for Security and Open Methodologies (ISECOM) (2001). http://www.isecom.org/mirror/OSSTMM.3.pdf. Accessed 22 Aug 2014

Islam, S., Falcarin, P.: Measuring security requirements for software security. In: IEEE 10th International Conference in Cybernetic Intelligent System (CIS), pp. 70–75 (2011). doi:10.1109/CIS.2011.6169137

Jahedi, S., Méndez, F.: On the advantages and disadvantages of subjective measures. J. Econ. Behav. Organ. 98, 97–114 (2014). doi:10.1016/j.jebo.2013.12.016

Jones, M.T.: Anatomy of a cloud storage infrastructure: models, features, and internals. White Paper. Developer Works, IBM Corporation 2010. http://www.ibm.com/developerworks/cloud/library/cl-cloudstorage/cl-cloudstorage-pdf.pdf. Accessed 8 Sept 2014

Ju, J., Wu, J., Fu, J., Lin, Z.: A survey on cloud storage. J. Comput. 6(8), 1764–1771 (2011). doi:10.4304/jcp.6.8.1764-1771

Kamara, S., Papamanthou, C., Roeder, T.: CS2 : a searchable cryptographic cloud storage system. Microsoft Research, pp. 1–25 (2011)

Kassou, M., Kjiri, L.: A goal question metric approach for evaluating security in a service oriented architecture context. Int. J. Comput. Sci. Issues 9, 1–12 (2012)

Mapp, G., Aiash, M., Ondiege, B., Clarke, M.: Exploring a new security framework for cloud storage using capabilities. In: Proceedings of IEEE 8th International Symposium on Service Oriented System Engineering (SOSE), pp. 484–489 (2014). doi:10.1109/SOSE.2014.69

Mather, T., Kumaraswamy, S., Latif, S.: Cloud Security and Privacy: An Enterprise Perspective on Risks and Compliance. International Journal of Policy and Administration. O'Reilly Media Inc., Sebastopol (2009)

Microsoft: Security Threats. Microsoft Developer Network (MSDN) (2015). https://msdn.microsoft.com/en-us/library/cc723507.aspx. Accessed 22 Apr 2015

NIST: Standards for Security Categorization of Federal Information and Information Systems. National Institute of Standards and Technology (NIST), Special Publication FIPS 199 (2004)

NIST: Security and Privacy Controls for Federal Information Systems and Organizations. National Institute of Standards and Technology (NIST), Special Publication 800-53 Revision 4 (2013)

Payne, S.C.: A Guide to Security Metrics. SANS Institute (2006)

Pendleton, M., Garcia-Lebron, R., Xu, S.: A Survey on Security Metrics (2016). arXiv Preprint arXiv:1601.05792

Rouse, M.: What is storage? TechTarget (2005). http://searchstorage.techtarget.com/definition/storage. Accessed 12 Mar 2015

Ryan, M.D.: Cloud computing security: the scientific challenge, and a survey of solutions. J. Syst. Softw. **86**(9), 2263–2268 (2013). doi:10.1016/j.jss.2012.12.025

Sabahi, F.: Cloud computing security threats and responses. In: 2011 IEEE 3rd International Conference on Communication Software and Networks, pp. 245–249 (2011). doi:10.1109/ICCSN.2011.6014715

Shaikh, F.B., Haider, S.: Security threats in cloud computing. In: 6th International Conference on Internet Technology and Secured Transactions, Abu Dhabi, UAE, 11–14 December 2011

Singh, R., Kumar, S., Agrahari, S.K.: Ensuring data storage security in cloud computing. IOSR J. Eng. **2**(12), 17–21 (2012)

Srinivasan, M.K., Rodrigues, P.: State-of-the-art cloud computing security taxonomies - a classification of security challenges in the present cloud. In: ICACCI 2012, pp. 470–476 (2012)

Subashini, S., Kavitha, V.: A survey on security issues in service delivery models of cloud computing. J. Netw. Comput. Appl. **34**(1), 1–11 (2011). doi:10.1016/j.jnca.2010.07.006

Suntharam, V.S., Reddy, K.V., Puspalatha, N.: Data storage security in cloud computing and verification of metadata by encryption. Int. J. Comput. Sci. Electron. Eng. **2**(3), 1–9 (2013)

Takabi, H., Joshi, J.B.D., Ahn, G.J.: SecureCloud: towards a comprehensive security framework for cloud computing environments. In: Proceedings of International Computer Software and Applications Conference, pp. 393–398 (2010). doi:10.1109/COMPSACW.2010.74

Torkhani, F., Wang, K., Chassery, J.M.: Perceptual quality assessment of 3D dynamic meshes: subjective and objective studies. Signal Process. Image Commun. **31**, 185–204 (2015). doi:10.1016/j.image.2014.12.008

Wang, C., Wang, Q., Ren, K., Cao, N., Lou, W.: Toward secure and dependable storage services in cloud computing. IEEE Trans. Serv. Comput. **5**, 220–232 (2012). doi:10.1109/TSC.2011.24

Wu, J., Ping, L., Ge, X., Ya, W., Fu, J.: Cloud storage as the infrastructure of cloud computing. In: Proceedings of 2010 International Conference on Intelligent Computing and Cognitive Informatics, ICICCI 2010, pp. 380–383 (2010). doi:10.1109/ICICCI.2010.119

Yahya, F., Chang, V., Walters, R.J., Wills, G.B.: Security challenges in cloud storage. In: 6th IEEE International Conference on Cloud Computing Technology and Science. Enterprise Security 2014, pp. 1051–1056 (2014). doi:10.1109/CloudCom.2014.171

Yahya, F., Walters, R.J., Wills, G.B.: Modelling threats with security requirements in cloud storage. Int. J. Inf. Secur. Res. (IJISR) **5**(2), 551–558 (2015)

Zarandioon, S., Yao, D(., Ganapathy, V.: K2C: cryptographic cloud storage with lazy revocation and anonymous access. In: Rajarajan, M., Piper, F., Wang, H., Kesidis, G. (eds.) SecureComm 2011. LNICSSITE, vol. 96, pp. 59–76. Springer, Heidelberg (2012). doi:10.1007/978-3-642-31909-9_4

Zhang, R., Chen, P.: A dynamic cryptographic access control scheme in cloud storage services. In: Proceedings of 2012 8th International Conference on Computing and Networking Technology (INC, ICCIS and ICMIC), ICCNT 2012, pp. 50–55 (2012). doi:10.4156/ijipm.vol4.issue1.13

Zhao, R., Yue, C.: Toward a secure and usable cloud-based password manager for web browsers. Comput. Secur. **46**, 32–47 (2014). doi:10.1016/j.cose.2014.07.003

Zissis, D., Lekkas, D.: Addressing cloud computing security issues. Future Gener. Comput. Syst. **28**(3), 583–592 (2012). doi:10.1016/j.future.2010.12.006

Security in Organisations: Governance, Risks and Vulnerabilities in Moving to the Cloud

Madini O. Alassafi[✉], Raid K. Hussain, Ghada Ghashgari,
R.J. Walters, and G.B. Wills

University of Southampton, Southampton, UK
moa2g15@soton.ac.uk

Abstract. Any organisation using the internet to conduct business is vulnerable to violation of security. Currently security in most organizations relates to protection of data and the management of their business information systems. Hence, security is often defined as the protection of information, the system, and hardware; that use, store and relocates that information. Governing information and the secure use of Information Technology (IT) is essential in order to reduce the possible risks and improve an Organisation's reputation, confidence and trust with its customers. One of the importance success factors for an organization to adopt and use the cloud effectively is information security governance (ISG). As a consequence, this chapter clarifies the concept of governance and the necessity of its two factors IT governance (ITG) and ISG.

Enterprise governance is directing and controlling the organization by the board of directors and executive management in order to ensure the success of the organization. ITG and ISG are integral part of corporate governance. ITG is about the structure that links IT processes, resources and information to support organisation's objectives. IT brings several risks and threats that need to be considered. Therefore, Information security should not be considered as just a technical issue but governance challenge that needs proactive approach. ISG consists of leadership, organisational structure, processes, compliance and technology. In order to promote the adoption of cloud computing, it is important to recognize that an important and specific issue related to cloud computing is the potential and perceived security risks posed by implementing such technology. Adopting the cloud has several risks such as malicious insider threats and data breaches. An example of cloud risk is virtualization that is one of the concepts used for constructing cloud computing, which has its own security risks, but they are not specific to the cloud. Virtualization is related to open-source shared application server, database, and middleware components. The multi-tenancy model has introduced security problems as it is based on virtualization and sharing resources (hard disk, application software, and virtual machine) on the same physical machine. This chapter will present an overview of information security governance, the risks and vulnerabilities when moving to the cloud.

1 Introduction

Cloud computing is a delivery model for information and services using existing technology like virtualization, distributed computing, utility computing and web services. Security is the key issues for cloud computing success as cloud users feel a lack

© Springer International Publishing AG 2017
V. Chang et al. (Eds.): Enterprise Security, LNCS 10131, pp. 241–258, 2017.
DOI: 10.1007/978-3-319-54380-2_11

of control over their data stored in cloud computing. One of the most problematic elements of cyber security is the quickly and constantly evolving nature of security attacks, risks and threats. The security issues need to be governed to ensure that the organisation can survive and thrive. Ongoing attention and countermeasures are required to protect organisational data and information assets. Governing cyber security is required for the sustainability of an organisation through effective direction and control of all the possible security risks, threats, and vulnerabilities. Since one of the key aspects of governance is mitigating security risks in the enterprise environment in general and in cloud computing in particular, cloud adoption security risks as well as security issues in virtualization layer in cloud computing have to be addressed.

Information security governance (ISG) is a sub set discipline of corporate governance. Businesses that rely on information technology (IT) to hold and process their data and information have many advantages over non-IT approaches, but it also brings cyber security threats (IT Governance Institute 2003). Consequently, for the sustainability of the organisations they should use ISG at all levels of the organisation with consideration of all the significant security risks that may influence the organisation negatively in achieving its mission, goals and objectives. As well as aligning their strategies with the organisational objectives. Several Information security governance best practice standard-based frameworks are available, but there is no fixed framework for an organisation as it depends on several factors (Calder and Moir 2009). Because Information security governance is one of the important success factors for an organisation adopting and successfully using cloud, this article clarifies the concept of governance and the necessity of its factors. The security of the cloud, associated privacy concerns, causes many organisations to "*apply the brakes*" as they think through their particular cloud computing concerns. Security concerns include physical security and simple access to facilities and equipment, as well as logical security, industry compliance requirements, auditability, and more (Pearson 2013). Furthermore, the security risks have potential influence on the acceptance of cloud computing in most of the world. One of the main problems notable by big organisations is the amount of cost on the IT infrastructure. When an organisation is considering using cloud computing, there is a need for professional's cyber security skills for designing and building a cloud (Chang 2015). In addition, before using cloud computing, every organisation should consider the multiple dimensionality posed by security risks (Weng and Hung 2014).

Security risks affect different infrastructure layers, which are the application layer, network layer, data storage layer, virtualization layer, trust layer and authentication and access control layer. Virtualization is one of the main concepts used for constructing cloud computing. It is the foundation for sharing resources for multiple cloud users but it has related security risks for instance, virtual machine (VM) isolation, VM migration, VM drawback, VM escape, VM sprawl, and VM image sharing. Multi-tenancy is one of the characteristics of cloud computing which is used to shared Infrastructure, application and platform resources among multiple users (Abd et al. 2015). Security experts consider multi tenancy as vulnerable.

This chapter consists of three sections, security governance, cloud security risks and cloud virtualization issues. The first section provides an overview of the governance concept in an organisation and its necessity. This section begins with corporate governance followed by its two components IT and security governance including an explanation of each concept and the necessity to be implemented in an organisation. Furthermore, some of the best practises principles and standards as well as effective factors are highlighted. The second section provides an overview of the security and security risks in cloud computing and a clear definition of both considering features that related to the cloud computing adoption and cloud security risks that affect the cloud computing adoption. The third section provides an overview of virtualization and multi- tenancy starting with an explanation of each component. Then the main security risks related to virtualization security layer are illustrated.

2 Information Security Governance

In order to examine Security Governance and its place in an organisation, we first examine the role of Corporate Governance and Information Technology Governance.

2.1 Corporate Governance (CG)

Corporate governance (CG) is *"the system by which companies are directed and controlled"* (Cadbury 1992) and it has been defined as:

> *"The set of relationships between a company's board, its shareholders and other stakeholders. It also provides the structure through which the objectives of the company are set, and the means of attaining those objectives, and monitoring performance are determined"* (OECD 1999).

The main objective of good CG is the enhancement of the organisational value and success in the long-term view for its all stakeholders and shareholders (Müller 2003). A vital factor in economic growth, financial stability, social development, good decision-making, and successful operation in an organisation is good CG. Moreover, CG ensures security confidence by monitoring and controlling the operation of the organisation (OECD 2004).

Governance is the responsibility of the board of directors. Therefore, setting organisation's strategic and goals, supervising the management, providing leadership and reporting to shareholders that all subject to laws and regulations are their responsibility (Cadbury 1992). Governance is unlike management because boards do not manage day-to-day activity but direct and control the organisation, ensure that shareholders and stakeholders desires are met (Love et al. 2010), and create an appropriate organisational culture to achieve organisation's goals (de Oliveira Alves et al. 2006). Therefore, the organization is directed by producing the policies, standards and procedures and controlled by measuring, monitoring and reporting compliance (Von Solms 2006 and von Solms 2001).

Corporate governance became a world-wide topic in 1980s after many corporate crises and the financial collapses in several developed economies that raised questions regarding the ethics of their CG (Lessambo 2013). There were several investigations in UK notably after the collapse of Maxwell Communication Corporation plc in 1991, in order to improve CG the Cadbury report was published in 1992, and the Greenbury report in 1995 (Jones and Pollitt 2004). Due to the powerful interest and the high quality process of Cadbury's committee investigation, Cadbury report on the Financial Aspects of Corporate Governance has been distinguished from all other reports and has been implemented internationally (Lessambo 2013).

The cadbury code of best practice was developed to strengthen the effectiveness of the board system in order to achieve high standards of corporate governance, financial reporting and auditing confidence based on compliance with disclosure, and clear understanding of responsibilities and expectations of each person involved. The code is based on three main principles, openness and information disclosure, integrity of financial reports and honesty, and accountability of the board and shareholders.

The Organisation for Economic Cooperation and Development (OECD) is an international corporate governance system. OECD framework is based on Cadbury code (Bouchnez 2007; Mallin 2002). The principles of the framework aim to raise the consideration of managing conflicts of interest by enhancing transparency and information disclosure. The principles encompass five main areas; shareholders rights, equitable treatment, transparency and board responsibilities (Bouchnez 2007; Mallin 2002).

There is no single universal framework of CG that fits all organisations because the actions of the boards and the frameworks are subject to their country's law and regulations (Cadbury 1992; OECD 2004).

By adopting CG framework, an organisation will have the opportunity to use their resources efficiently with accountability for its stewardship, and align the interests of individual, organisation, and society (Weill and Ross 2004). CG is not just about complying with rules and regulations; CG is about principles (OECD 2004).

2.2 IT Governance (ITG)

Information technology (IT) is critical to enterprise success. It assists the enterprise to accomplish a competitive advantage since it increases the enterprise efficiency and productivity and reduces cost. However, IT creates different types of risks and threats such as hardware and software failure, human error, computer viruses and social engineering. Therefore, understanding of IT issues and strategy is required for secure and successful operational sustainability and extensibility of an organisation, if it is to be controlled and governed efficiently (IT Governance Institute 2003). Long-term success of an organisation requires that IT and business be strongly tied together in order to maximize the benefits of IT and reduce its uncertainty (Posthumusa and Von Solms 2005). IT governance (ITG) is the means for deciding who makes what decisions about the use of IT and the accountability framework creation that drives the desired behavior in the use of IT (Weill and Ross 2004). ITG has been defined as

"The structure of relationships which links IT processes, IT resources and information to organisation strategies and objectives to direct and control the organisation in order to achieve the organisation's strategies and objective" (Abu-Musa 2007).

ITG is the responsibility of the board of directors and executive management in particular because IT expectation and reality often do not match. ITG is a subset discipline of corporate governance, and should not be considered in isolation (IT Governance Institute 2003). Thus, to accomplish the objective of corporate performance, ITG should be developed based on the principles of corporate governance (Weill 2004). Ko and Fink (2010) illustrated the concept of ITG by framing its scope of functions since the concept is not yet consistent and mature because of the disconnection and the concentration between the industries, developers of the ITG best practice frameworks. Ko and Fink (2010) grouped the view of ITG into three collaborative and complimentary dimensions: structure, process and people. The structure dimension consists of the structure of the IT functions, IT decision-making authority, and the mechanism for the organisation to manage its IT. The process component includes IT activities that have to be aligned with strategic business objectives, and performance tracking for organisational improvement achievement and positive outcomes sustainability. People is the third collaborative dimension that has received less attention in literature. Leadership is one of the ITG key success factors that distinguishes the organisations with top performance from the others ones. Leadership is required to ensure that IT activities achieve the goal of the organisation. Furthermore, clear understanding of roles and responsibilities, commitment and participation with transparency, and awareness and understanding are the sub components of the dimension. As it can be seen, all of these ITG components and sub components work and cooperate with each other (Ko and Fink 2010).

ITG best practices, standard-based frameworks, have been developed by internationally recognized organisations. These frameworks are control objectives for Information and related technology (COBIT), and ISO/IEO 38500. COBIT has been developed by IT Governance Institute (ITGI) which is part of Information systems audit and control (ISACA). Its objectives are the alignment of IT and business, maximize the benefits of the use of IT, the use of IT resource responsibly, and manage and mitigate IT risks (Ko and Fink 2010). ISO/IEO 38500 has been published by ISO organisation, and its aim is the effective, efficient, and acceptable use of IT in all organisations (Sylvester 2011). Both COBIT and ISO/IEO 38500 are principle-base and provide a high-level governance framework that focuses on what to be done rather than how, and these are the most comprehensive ITG frameworks (Sylvester 2011). The main principles of COBIT 5 are meeting stakeholder needs, covering the enterprise end-to-end, applying a single integrated framework, enabling a holistic approach, and separating governance from management (Vander Wal et al. 2012). While ISO 38500 is based on six principles responsibility, strategy, acquisition, performance, conformance, human behavior (ISO 38500:2008).

There is no universal ITG framework or standard that has the best ITG structure and effective processes and implementation because ITG on an organisation depends on several factors (Calder and Moir 2009). Successful implementation of an ITG framework requires stakeholders' involvement from all business levels (Rau 2004). In addition to the management support and leadership from all management levels (Calder and Moir 2009).

2.3   Information Security Governance (ISG)

Data and information held on IT systems are valuable and critical to the business of the organisation because the value of a business is concentrated in the value of its information. Most organisations rely on IT to store and process information; therefore, it is essential to maintain Information Security. In the ever-changing technological environment, the threats to Information Security from viruses, hackers, criminals, and terrorists are increasing as well as the threats to information from errors, loss, misuse, or disclosure. Consequently, organisations need to incorporate effective information security program into the everyday practice performed that must be proactive, and cope with the technological changes and the growing cybersecurity risks effectively (IT Governance Institute 2006). Information security includes the protection of information assets in all of its forms; digital physical and people as well as information systems in all of its situations in transit, processing or storage from attack, damage or misuse (Love et al. 2010). The main objectives of Information Security are protecting information confidentiality by ensuring that it is accessible only by authorized people and only disclosed to authorized people; preserving information integrity by safeguarding its accuracy and completeness and preventing unauthorized modification; promoting information availability by ensuring its availability when it is required by authorized people; and exchanging information with trust, authenticity and non-repudiation (IFAC 1998; IT Governance Institute 2006; ISO 17799).

For effective and successful information security, active involvement of executive and senior management is required in order to evaluate emerging security threats and the organisation's response to them, and to provide strong cyber security leadership. This involvement is the integration of Information Security with CG, the overall governance. Information Security needs to be addressed at the strategic level of the organisation, top-down process, in order to support organisational strategy and objectives. As a consequence, Information Security should not be considered as a solely a technical issue, but a governance challenge that involves, reporting, accountability and risk management (National Cybersecurity Summit Task Force 2004; IT Governance Institute 2006). The implementation of governance concepts and principles on the issues of Information Security is Information Security governance (ISG). Johnston and Hale (2009) confirmed empirically that the effectiveness of an information security program relies on the strategy the organisation uses for its information security planning. They confirmed that an organisations that address their information security from the bottom up, use reactive IS plans and segregate information security from their strategic directive; in other words, isolate the governance from the management of information security, have ineffective information security programs and can fall victim to internal and external cybersecurity attacks.

The ITGI (2006) has defined ISG as,

"The set of responsibilities and practices exercised by the board and executive management with the goal of providing strategic direction, ensuring that objectives are achieved, ascertaining that risks are managed appropriately and verifying that the organisation's resources are used responsibly."

Moulton and Coles (2003) defined ISG as,

"The establishment and maintenance of a control environment to manage the risks relating to the confidentiality, integrity and availability of information and its supporting processes and systems"

ISG assures that Information Security strategies are aligned with organisational strategy; support organisational objectives, and are consistent with the laws and regulations via policies and internal controls compliance. Compliance places responsibility and accountability for IS at all levels of the organisation to manage and reduce security risks (Bowen et al. 2006).

When organisations update or apply new legal requirements, the responsibilities of management's governance can change significantly which can cause changes to the way information security is approached. The framework of ISG supports organisations to undertake requirements and manage new risks within the organisation (Moulton and Coles 2003).

ISG consists of leadership, organisational structure, processes, compliance and technology. It also requires executive management leadership to be proactive and strategic in order to ensure that the activities of information security are supported and understood at all organisational levels and aligned with organisational objectives (Love et al. 2010). Organisational structure is a rational set of arrangements and mechanisms (Weill and Ross 2004, p. 183) about how ISG functions are carried out, controlled and coordinated, and is dependent on the overall organisation structure (Bowen et al. 2006). ISG processes are the Information Security activities that support organisational objectives. These main components of ISG ensure that the confidentiality, integrity and availability of organisation's electronic assets are maintained all the time and information is never compromised (von Solms 2001). Employing ISG properly allows organisations to align Information Security with their strategy in order to support their objectives (strategic alignment), deliver business value to all stakeholders, ensure management of risk and resource, measure organisational performance to ensure that organisational objectives are achieved (IT Governance Institute 2006), and comply with regulation standards and agreement (ISO 27014).

Because their strategy is becoming a major issue of concern for all types of organisations around the world, an effective ISG framework is required. Task Force and Entrust (2004) confirmed that adopting a framework is an important action in assisting organisations with integrating ISG into their CG practices, securing information, improving the efficiency of organisational processes, complying with regulations, and cultivating an acceptable IS culture. In addition, ITGI (2006) clarifies that ISG is essential because it improves organisation's reputation, confidence and trust with customer relationship and with whom business is conducted, reducing operational costs by providing predictable outcomes and mitigating risks that may interrupt operations.

ISO/IEC 27014 (2013) and COBIT 5 for their strategy are two ISG best practice standard-based frameworks that have been developed by internationally recognized organisations.

Similar to ITG, there is no single best ISG framework or standard because organisations are different according to their requirements and risk tolerance (Love et al. 2010).

3   Security Risks in Cloud Computing

Implementing ISG is based on understanding the security risk, within an organisation. Security is the most important challenge and it is still the biggest concern in cloud computing, this is because of the uncertainty about privacy and security of information in cloud, at every level (Avram 2014). Before using cloud computing, every organisation should consider the multiple dimensionality of security risk (Weng and Hung 2014). Organisations around the world are facing the problem of protecting individual's private information and by adopting cloud computing, it is not clear whether it will provide security for such information (Alharthi et al. 2015).

ISO27001 defined the security as, *"Preservation of confidentiality, integrity and availability of information; in addition, other properties such as authenticity, accountability, non-repudiation, and reliability can also be involved"*

Moreover, there is a list of cloud computing concerns; security is often at the top of the list (Sen 2013). Cloud computing might introduce different risks to many organisations from traditional IT and the security risks be influenced significantly by the type of cloud service and cloud deployment model.

According to Cloud Security Alliance Definition the Cloud Computing Security is

"The set of control-based technologies and policies designed to follow to regulatory compliance rules and protect information, data applications and infrastructure associated with cloud computing use" (Rashdi et al. 2013).

When an analogy is drawn between criminals and hackers, experts of cloud computing agree that cloud security is a step behind the development of technology in implementing it. There are various security issues for cloud computing as it includes several technologies including operating system, networking, virtualization, concurrency control, database and load balancing. Therefore, security issues in most of these technologies are applicable to cloud computing. For example, the network that communicates the systems in the cloud must be secure. Moreover, the virtualization model in cloud computing leads to more security concerns. Data security includes encrypting the data with securing that a suitable policy are applying for data sharing. Besides, resource allocation and memory management systems must be also secure (Sen 2013).

The full utilization of cloud based services by any organisation or by any individual depends on the security of their personal information, which is the biggest concern (von Solms and van Niekerk 2013). Irrespective of whether it is a service provider an organisation or an individual, there are security issues that concern every stakeholder in adoption of cloud. The security can be summarized into these principles: confidentiality, availability, and integrity (CIA) (Cherdantseva and Hilton 2013). Therefore, If any one of the three Confidentiality, Integrity, or Availability, can be threaten, it can have a serious significance for the organisations (Cherdantseva and Hilton 2013). CIA are important to understand the security principles and they can be defined as following:

Confidentiality: a system should ensure that only authorised user's access information.

Integrity: a system should ensure completeness, accuracy, and absence of unauthorised modifications in all its components.

Availability: a system should ensure that all system's components are available and operational when authorised users require them.

The principles of CIA are important to known set of threats, and occasionally law requires some of these principles. Despite the security benefits of cloud computing the cloud services which are applications successively anywhere in the cloud computing infrastructures by inside network or the internet and the most benefit of security in positions to cloud computing is the data securely and safely. Hence, cloud computing has important prospective to develop security and flexibility. According to European Network and Information Security Agency (ENISA), the following are the security benefits of cloud computing:

- Security and the benefits of scale
- Security as a market differentiator
- More timely and effective and efficient updates and defaults
- Rapid, smart scaling of resources
- Standardised interfaces for managed security services
- Audit and evidence-gathering
- Audit and Service Level Agreements (SLAs) force better risk management
- Benefits of resource concentration

When it comes to define the risk, it is the possible impact or result of happening on assets of an organisation. In economic positions, the risks have recognised like a value at risks that is arithmetical measure, which describes the significance of a loss via the confidence level or the chance of happening (Chang et al. 2015).

Despite all benefits of cloud computing, there are some risks that hinder government organisations or even public sectors to adopt cloud computing (Chang 2013). Most of the risks on cloud computing addressed as:

- Time Risk: considered one of the most risk affecting the decision of the cloud computing. Time risks include (time to recognise and situations environment of using cloud computing, compliance with protect the data, time to explore and implementing a new solution and time to know and work in with the service level agreement (SLAs) terms) (Elena and Johnson 2015).
- Performance Risk: consumers always want confidence and transparency about the performance of the cloud system and how it succeeded as well, since the cloud dynamically offering a service, which meets performance needs and holds operating costs low (Nist 2012).
- Social or Reputational Risk: considered of the technical risks due to meet customer demand. Social risk for using cloud services is very high because of the possibility

damage and loss of standing in matter of leakage of particular data and unavailability of the cloud services (Chang 2013).

- Financial Risk: including prospective costs from reputational damage from the cloud provider in security data breaches. Financial risk is importance perceived security risks of cloud service because the cloud services need to show qualifications and performances before spending money on new IT systems (Gentzoglanis 2011; Chang 2014).
- Security Risk: most of studied shows that the security risk is the most importance should considered when adopting cloud computing services in government organisations or even private sector and it typically ranked the top cloud computing adoption concerns (Elena and Johnson 2015). Security risks are the major impediment and information always comes with security and risk problems. According to the Cloud Security Alliance, the security of cloud computing is the biggest concern for the organisations. The security risks linked with each cloud delivery model are different and reliant on a varied collection of factors including the sensitivity of information possessions, cloud architectures and security control complicated in a specific cloud environment. However, the characteristics of cloud computing increased number of users of cloud poses concerns regarding security risks in cloud computing because of shared resources in the cloud (Sen 2013).

Implementing cloud computing in any organisation means that all the data is shifted to external cloud which increases the exposure of threats from hackers (Sen 2013). Therefore, before implementing cloud computing, be aware of potential security risks in the organisation is very important. Since, there are many different ways of classifying security risks. Furthermore, these classifying appropriate in a wider model of cloud associated to risks. For example Centre for Protection of National of in Infrastructure organisation (CPNI) covered the most of security risks in the practical cloud service transaction depending on their accompanied a survey of industry experts to collect specialised judgement on the highest weaknesses within cloud computing *as Insider user, External attacker, Data Leakage, Data segregation, User access, Data quality, Change management, Denial of Service, Physical disruption and Exploiting weak recovery procedures.* Generally, the cloud computing are similar those used in further IT environments in term of security control. But, the clients give up the control to the provider of the cloud and there is connected of the risks that the CSP do not satisfactorily address the security that have to be control or even that service level agreement (SLAs) don't consist of any providing of the important security services (Pearson 2013).

These risks are reliant on the service cloud model that are used. The cloud providers have to be controlled because the further security the customers is responsible for. Consequently, the customers of infrastructure as a service wants to construct in security as they are mainly responsible to that, while in the software as a service environments security controls and its possibility as the privacy and the compliance are converted in the agreements for service. It is important that for the customers or users to understand what the cloud provider holder the issues such as configuration management and cover management when they build new operating system or upgrade it to new one likely the IT security hardware and software which the provider is consuming and how to be protected. In other case of IaaS and PaaS, the cloud providers have to be simplify the type of IT security. So, the users are expected to put into place. Moreover, by SaaS, the users is still wishes to offer access security over its own their systems, that could also being to know how management system or a local access control their applications (Pearson 2013).

The risks to information assets established in the cloud can vary according to the cloud delivery service models used by cloud user organisations. Table 1 provides some of risks for cloud according to CIA security model and their linked to each of the cloud delivery models. Some of the security risks in cloud computing can affect the services in the cloud (IaaS, PaaS and SaaS) posing threats on the CIA of the systems in these services. However, some risks only affect two or one of the service models.

Table 1. Cloud services security risks on CIA

Security principles	Risks	Cloud service models (SaaS, PaaS and IaaS)		
Confidentiality	Insider user	SaaS	PaaS	IaaS
	External attacker	SaaS	PaaS	
	Data Leakage	SaaS	PaaS	
Integrity	Data segregation	SaaS	PaaS	
	User access	SaaS	PaaS	IaaS
	Data quality	SaaS	PaaS	
Availability	Change management	SaaS	PaaS	IaaS
	Denial of Service	SaaS	PaaS	IaaS
	Physical disruption			IaaS
	Exploiting weak recovery procedures	SaaS	PaaS	IaaS

4   Virtualization Security Risks in Cloud Computing

The National Institute of Standards and Technology stated that security risks are the main obstacle that delays the adoption of cloud computing (Kshetri 2013). Cloud computing has some vulnerabilities that might affect the core principles of information security. Vulnerability in cloud computing refers to weaknesses in the system that might be exploited by an attacker to obtain unauthorized access to the resources. Whereas, threats refer to vulnerability being abused by an attacker to obtain unauthorised access to the resources (Hashizume et al. 2013). In the survey of the literature by Modi et al. (2013) show security issues at different layer in cloud computing and they are:

- The application level issues.
- The network level issues.
- The data storage level issues.
- Virtualization level issues.
- Authentication and access control level.
- Trust layer level issues.

Virtualization is an important component in cloud computing and it helps cloud computing to deliver its services. In the next section, virtualization is explained along with some of the security concerns in more detail.

4.1 Virtualization

Virtualization has a crucial role in cloud computing as it is helping the IT industries to lower the cost and improve the performance of their applications (Sabahi 2011). Virtualization means

> *"A way of making a physical computer function as if it were two or more computers where each non-physical or virtualized computer is provided with the same basic architecture as that of a generic physical computer. Virtualization technology therefore allows the installation of an operating system on hardware that does not really exist"* (Carlin 2011).

In virtualization, the resources can be joint or spilt through multiple environments. These environments are called virtual machines (VMs). The virtual machine host the guest operating system (Buyya et al. 2009). A hypervisor is one of visualization components which permit the guest OS to be hosted on host computer (Sabahi 2011).

One of the characteristics of cloud computing is multi-tenancy. Shared infrastructure and partitioning virtualization are provided by multi-tenancy to facilitate better utilize computing resources (Abd et al. 2015). Multi-tenancy is defined as

> *"Multi-tenancy is a property of a system where multiple customers, so-called tenants, transparently share the system's resources, such as services, applications, databases, or hardware, with the aim of lowering costs, while still being able to exclusively configure the system to the needs of the tenant"* (Kabbedijk et al. 2015).

There are two kinds of multi-tenancy: the multiple instance and native multi-tenancy. In multiple instance, each tenant served by devoted application instance from a shared OS, hardware and middleware server in a hosted environment. However, the native multi-tenancy one instance of a program can serve several tenants over many hosting resources. In a SaaS model, multi-tenancy can be applied to four different software layer: application layer, middleware layer, the virtual layer and the OS layer (Espadas et al. 2013).

While Multi-tenancy has brought significant benefit to cloud computing as it reduces cost and save energy, it has however from the perspective of security expert brought vulnerabilities as it may affect the confidentiality of the data held on the server (Aljahdali et al. 2013). Wu et al. (2010) admitted that eliminating the virtualization layer will avoid the security hazards caused by multi-tenancy but this will exclude a vital advantage for cloud service providers like VM mobility. VM mobility is very helpful in saving energy. However, normal security techniques used in Multi-tenancy cannot mitigated some threats when both attacker and victim are on the same physical machine (the server). To secure this vulnerability, it is important to understand how the attack is performed. Firstly, a target VM is identified by a network probing mechanism. The network probing mechanism is used to find the physical topology of a network that contains the servers connected to the network and the internet protocols (IP), which are used to recognise the victim. Secondly, by taking advantage of multi tenancy the attacker's VM is allocated close to victim's VM using a brute force attack. A brute force attack is a mechanism that is used by an attacker to run an attack operation multiple times until a breach is achieved. Brute force is one of the most common data breaches attack methods used by attackers. Finally, a side channel attack is generated based on the information gathered from the network probing to extract data from the victim's VM (Aljahdali et al. 2013).

In the virtualized (multi-tenancy) environment, each user is allocated a virtual machine that host a guest operating system. The virtual machines (VMs) that belong to different users can share the same physical resources that allows resource pooling. A virtual machine monitor is used to control the VMs and allow the many OS to run on the same physical hardware (Ali et al. 2015). The virtualized (multi-tenancy) environment has introduced security issues for instance VM isolation. VM isolation is the VMs that are running on the same physical hardware need to be isolated from each other. In spite of the VMs being logically isolated, they will still need to be isolated physically as they share the same physical storage and memory. Sharing the same hardware might lead to data breaches and cross VM attacks (Gonzalez et al. 2011).

Moreover, VM migration happens due to load balancing, maintenance and fault tolerance, a VM can be moved from one physical hardware to another without shutting down the VM. This process might expose the data to the network that lead to privacy and integrity concern. The migrated VM can be compromised by an attacker to relocate the VM to an infected monitor or compromised server (Zhang and Chen 2012).

Furthermore, VM rollback occurs when VM can be rollback to pervious state when it is necessarily. This facility provides flexibility to the user but it raise a security problems. Moreover, it might render VM to a vulnerability that was solved previously (Hashizume et al. 2013). In addition, VM escape: the VVM or the monitor is a software that manage the VMs and the access to hardware. The VM escape happen when the malicious user trying to escape from the control of the monitor. The VM escape can provide the attacker the ability to access other VMs in the same hardware or might bring the monitor down (Jansen 2011). Subsequently, VM sprawl: it is happen when a number of VMs are increasing on the host system and most of them are in the idle state. This situation lead to wasting the resources of the host machine in a large scale (Sunil Rao and Santhi Thilagam 2015).

Finally, VM image sharing: A user can use the VM image from the repository or can create his/her own VM image. A malicious user can upload an infected image that contains malware to be used by other users. An infected VM image can be used to monitor the users' data and activities (Ali et al. 2015).

5 Recommendation

In this section, security governance, virtualisation and security risks subjects that affect the organisation when moving to the cloud are described and a set of recommendations related to these domains are further illustrated in Table 2.

Table 2. Security in organisation with recommendations

Domains	Subjects	Description and recommendation	References
Information security governance	Strategic alignment	Information security should not consider just technical issues but of strategic level governance concerns in order to align the security processes and practices with organisational strategy and support organizational goals and objectives	National Cybersecurity Summit Task Force (2004) and IT Governance Institute (2006)
	Active involvement	Active involvement of senior management is required in order to evaluate emerging security risks and threats, and the organisation's response to them	National Cyber Security Summit Task Force (2004); IT Governance Institute (2006) and Abu-Musa (2007)
	Management leadership	It is important to have proactive and strategic leadership in order to ensure that the activities of information security are supported and understood at all organisational levels, and aligned with organisational objectives. In addition to that, when staff members see the management concern and attention to security, they understand the necessity and importance of security, therefore, its benefit the creation of security culture	Love et al. (2010)
	Effective IS program	Organisations need to integrate an effective information security program into the everyday practice performed that must be proactive, and cope with technological changes and growing cybersecurity risks effectively	IT Governance Institute (2006)
	Adopting ISG best practice framework	Adopting ISG framework is an important action in assisting organisations with integrating ISG into their CG practices, securing information, improving the efficiency of organisational processes, complying with regulations, and cultivating an acceptable IS culture	National Cyber Security Summit Task Force (2004) and Entrust (2004)
Cloud security risks	Security principles (CIA)	If any one of the three Confidentiality, Integrity, or Availability, is threatened, it can have serious consequences for the organisations	Cherdantseva and Hilton (2013)

(continued)

Table 2. (*continued*)

Domains	Subjects	Description and recommendation	References
	Risks in cloud computing	In economic case, the risks have to known as a value at risks which is numerical measure, that defines the significance of a loss by the confidence level or the chance of happening	Chang et al. (2015)
	Risks with cloud service models	The risks are dependent on the cloud service models that are used. The cloud providers must be controlled because of the additional security the require. However, it is important that for the users to be familiar with what the cloud provider does to control issues such as configuration and cover management when they build new operating systems or upgrade them	Pearson (2013)
	Security risks	Before using cloud computing, every organisation needs to consider the multiple dimensionality of security risks. For example, the network that communicates the systems in the cloud must be secure. Moreover, the security risks linked with each cloud delivery model are different and reliant on a varied collection of factors including the sensitivity of information and cloud architectures	Weng and Hung (2014); Sen (2013)
Security issues in virtualization layer	Security issues	Services in cloud computing are delivered through virtualization as they share the hardware among many users	Sabahi (2011)
	Multi-tenancy	Confidentiality of the data held on the server might be vulnerable as it is sharing the same hardware	Aljahdali et al. (2013)

6 Conclusion of This Chapter

In conclusion, the life blood of an organisation is its data and information, therefore, compromising them could harm the organisation. Governing the information security and aligning these strategies with organisational objectives is essential to the sustainability and the success of an organisation. Information security governance is a subset of corporate governance, and a task within the organisational structure of a company is to ensure that the organisation will survive and thrive. There is no universal governance model and there are no right or wrong governance frameworks, or standards because each organisation has its own culture, law and regulations, requirements, and risks. Security risks and virtualization in cloud computing have obtained attention from organisations.

Directing and controlling the use of IT in all the organizational levels is important in order to reduce all the possible risks. There are several risk triggers when adopting the cloud that need to be governed such as malicious insiders and account hijacking. Moreover, virtualization issues in cloud computing such as virtual machine image sharing is one of the most threaten issues that need to be directed and controlled. By governing the possible risks including such risks the organisation will survive and thrive.

References

Abd, S.K., Salih, R.T., Hashim, F.: Cloud computing security risks with authorization access for secure multi-tenancy based on AAAS protocol. In: IEEE Region 10 Conference TENCON, pp. 1–5 (2015)

Abu-Musa, A.: Exploring information technology governance (ITG) in developing countries: an empirical study. Int. J. Digit. Account. Res. 7(13), 71–120 (2007)

Alharthi, A., et al.: An overview of cloud services adoption challenges in higher education institutions (2015)

Ali, M., Khan, S.U., Vasilakos, A.V.: Security in cloud computing: opportunities and challenges. Inf. Sci. 305, 357–383 (2015). http://linkinghub.elsevier.com/retrieve/pii/S0020025515000638

Aljahdali, H., Townend, P., Xu, J.: Enhancing multi-tenancy security in the cloud IaaS model over public deployment. In: Proceedings of the 2013 IEEE 7th International Symposium on Service-Oriented System Engineering, SOSE 2013, pp. 385–390 (2013)

Avram, M.G.: Advantages and challenges of adopting cloud computing from an enterprise perspective. Procedia Technol. 12, 529–534 (2014). http://www.sciencedirect.com/science/article/pii/S221201731300710X

Bowen, P., Hash, J., Wilson, M.: Information Security Handbook: A Guide for Managers. NIST Special Publication 800-100, National Institute of Standards and Technology, Gaithersburg (2006)

Bouchnez, L.: Principles of corporate governance: the OECD perspective. Eur. Co. Law 4(3), 109–115 (2007)

Buyya, R., et al.: Cloud computing and emerging IT platforms: vision, hype, and reality for delivering computing as the 5th utility. Future Gener. Comput. Syst. 25, 17 (2009). http://portal.acm.org/citation.cfm?id=1528937.1529211

Cadbury, A.: The Financial Aspects of Corporate Governance, p. 90 (1992)

Calder, A., Moir, S.: IT Governance, Implementing Frameworks and Standards for the Corporate Governance of IT (2009)

Carlin, S.: Cloud computing security. Artif. Intell. 3, 14–16 (2011)

Chang, V.: The business intelligence as a service in the cloud. Future Gener. Comput. Syst. 37, 512–534 (2014). http://dx.doi.org/10.1016/j.future.2013.12.028

Chang, V.: A proposed model to analyse risk and return for a large computing system adoption. Doctoral dissertation, University of Southampton (2013)

Chang, V., Kuo, Y.-H., Ramachandran, M.: Cloud computing adoption framework–a security framework for business clouds. Future Gener. Comput. Syst. 57, 24–41 (2015). https://doi.org/10.1016/j.future.2015.09.031

Chang, V., Walters, R.J., Wills, G.B.: Organisational sustainability modelling—an emerging service and analytics model for evaluating cloud computing adoption with two case studies. Int. J. Inf. Manag., 1–13 (2015). http://linkinghub.elsevier.com/retrieve/pii/S0268401215000882

Cherdantseva, Y., Hilton, J.: A reference model of information assurance and security. In: 2013 International Conference on Availability, Reliability and Security, pp. 546–555 (2013)

de Oliveira Alves, G., de Costa Carmo, L., de Almeida, A.: Enterprise security governance a practical guide to implement and control information security governance (ISG). In: Business-Driven IT Management, 2006, pp. 71–80 (2006)

Entrust: Information Security Governance (ISG): an essential element of corporate governance (2004). http://itresearch.forbes.com/detail/RES/1082396487_702.html

Elena, G., Johnson, C.W.: Factors influencing risk acceptance of c loud computing services in the UK. 5(2) (2015)

Espadas, J., et al.: A tenant-based resource allocation model for scaling Software-as-a-Service applications over cloud computing infrastructures. Future Gener. Comput. Syst. 29(1), 273–286 (2013)

Weng, F., Hung, M.-C.: Competition and challenge on adopting cloud ERP. Int. J. Innov. Manag. Technol. 5(4), 309–313 (2014). http://www.ijimt.org/index.php?m=content&c=index&a=show&catid=56&id=832

Gentzoglanis, A.: Risk, financial modeling and cloud computing: a new approach. Computer 9, 147–151 (2011)

Gonzalez, N., et al.: A quantitative analysis of current security concerns and solutions for cloud computing. In: 2011 IEEE Third International Conference on Cloud Computing Technology and Science, pp. 231–238 (2011)

Hashizume, K., et al.: An analysis of security issues for cloud computing. J. Internet Serv. Appl. 4(5), 1–13 (2013)

IFAC: International Information Technology Guidelines: Managing Security of Information, New York (1998)

IT Governance Institute: Board Briefing on IT Governance, 2nd edn. (2003)

IT Governance Institute: Information Security Governance: Guidance for Boards of Directors and Executive Management, 2nd edn. IT Governance Institute (2006)

ISO/IEC 17799: ISO/IEC 17799:2005 code of practice for information security management. In: International Organization for Standardization and the International Electrotechnical Commission, Geneva (2005). http://www.iso.org/iso/catalogue_detail?csnumber=39612

ISO/IEC 27014: ISO/IEC 27014 governance of information security. In: International Organization for Standardization and the International Electrotechnical Commission, Geneva (2013). http://www.iso.org/iso/iso_catalogue/catalogue_tc/catalogue_detail.htm?csnumber=43754

Johnston, A.C., Hale, R.: Improved security through information security governance. Commun. ACM 52(1), 126 (2009)

Jones, I., Pollitt, M.: Understanding how issues in corporate governance develop: Cadbury report to Higgs review. Corp. Gov.: Int. Rev. 12(2), 162–171 (2004)

Jansen, W.A.: Cloud hooks: security and privacy issues in cloud computing. In: Proceedings of the Annual Hawaii International Conference on System Sciences, (iv), p. 42 (2011)

Kabbedijk, J., et al.: Defining multi-tenancy: a systematic mapping study on the academic and the industrial perspective. J. Syst. Softw. 100, 139–148 (2015)

Ko, D., Fink, D.: Information technology governance: an evaluation of the theory-practice gap. Corp. Gov. 10(5), 662–674 (2010)

Kshetri, N.: Privacy and security issues in cloud computing: the role of institutions and institutional evolution. Telecommun. Policy 37(4–5), 372–386 (2013)

Lessambo, F.I.: The International Corporate Governance System, p. 488 (2013)

Love, P., et al.: GTAG Information Security Governance, p. 134 (2010)

Mallin, C.: The relationship between corporate governance, transparency and financial disclosure. Corp. Gov.: Int. Rev. 10(4), 253–255 (2002)

Müller, K.: Corporate governance and globalization: the role and responsibilities of investors. In: Selected Issues in Corporate Governance: Regional and Country Experiences, New York, Geneva, United Nations. Publication No. UNCTAD/ITE/TEB/2003/3 (2003)

Modi, C., et al.: A survey on security issues and solutions at different layers of cloud computing. J. Supercomput. **63**(2), 561–592 (2013)

Moulton, R., Coles, R.S.: Applying information security governance. Comput. Secur. **22**(7), 580–584 (2003). http://www.sciencedirect.com/science/article/pii/S0167404803007053

Nist: Cloud computing: a review of features, benefits, and risks, and recommendations for secure, efficient implementations. ITL (2012)

National Cyber Security Summit Task Force: Information security governance: a call to action. Corporate Governance Task Force Report CS1/05-0037 (2004). www.technet.org/resources/InfoSecGov4_04.pdf0

OECD: Principles of Corporate Governance. Organization for Economic Co-operation and Development (1999). http://www.oecd.org/officialdocuments/publicdisplaydocumentpdf/?cote=C/MIN(99)6&docLanguage=En

OECD: Principles of Corporate Governance. Organization for Economic Co-operation and Development (2004). http://www.oecd.org/corporate/ca/corporategovernanceprinciples/31557724.pdf

Pearson, S.: Privacy and Security for Cloud Computing, pp. 3–42. Springer, London (2013)

Posthumusa, S., Von Solms, R.: IT oversight: an important function of corporate governance. Comput. Fraud Secur. **2005**(6), 11–17 (2005)

Rashdi, A., et al.: Cloud Security Standards (2013)

Rau, K.G.: Effective governance of IT: design objectives, roles, and relationships. Inf. Syst. Manag. **21**(4), 35–42 (2004)

Sabahi, F.: Virtualization-level security in cloud computing. In: 2011 IEEE 3rd International Conference on Communication Software and Networks, pp. 250–254 (2011)

Sen, J.: Security and privacy issues in cloud computing. In: Architectures and Protocols for Secure Information Technology, (iv), p. 42 (2013)

Sylvester, D.: ISO 38500—Why Another Standard? Cobit Focus, 2 (2011). https://www.isaca.org/Knowledge-Center/Documents/COBIT-Focus-ISO-38500-Why-Another-Standard.pdf

Sunil Rao, K., Santhi Thilagam, P.: Heuristics based server consolidation with residual resource defragmentation in cloud data centers. Future Gener. Comput. Syst. **50**, 87–98 (2015)

Vander Wal, K., Lainhard, J., Tessin, P.: A COBIT 5 overview. ISACA (2012). www.isaca.org

Von Solms, R., van Niekerk, J.: From information security to cyber security. Comput. Secur. **38**, 97–102 (2013). http://www.sciencedirect.com/science/article/pii/S0167404813000801

von Solms, B.: Corporate governance and information security. Comput. Secur. 20, 215–218 (2001)

Von Solms, R., von Solms, S.B.: Information security governance: a model based on the direct-control cycle. Comput. Secur. **25**(6), 408–412 (2006)

Weill, P., Ross, J.W.: IT governance on one page. Cisr Wp No 349, p. 18, March 2004

Wu, R., et al.: Information flow control in cloud computing. In: 2010 6th International Conference on Collaborative Computing: Networking, Applications and Worksharing (CollaborateCom), pp. 1–7 (2010)

Weill, P.: Don't just lead, govern: how top-performing firms govern IT. MIS Q. Exec. **3**(1), 1–17 (2004b)

Zhang, F., Chen, H.: Security-preserving live migration of virtual machines in the cloud. J. Netw. Syst. Manag. **21**, 562–587 (2012)

Protecting Document Outside Enterprise Network: A Confirmed Framework

Zeyad S. Aaber, Gary B. Wills[✉], and Richard M. Crowder

University of Southampton, Southampton, England
{zsalgl3, gbw, rmc}@soton.ac.uk

Abstract. Sharing e-documents are important components of any enterprise workflow. Keeping these e-documents secure is fundamental to enterprise security, especially in multi-site enterprises or when sharing e-documents with third party. For that purpose, enterprises use document management software. However, document leakage is the most challenging security issue. These leaks are mainly caused by internal attack wither intentional or due to accident and employee ignorance. After exploring the landscape of the current e-document sharing security issues, this chapter proposes a framework to address these issues. The proposed framework is adapting current technologies in new novel approach to deliver a secure environment to share e-documents and track them. The confirmed framework secures documents not only inside the enterprise, but also when they leave the enterprise boundaries via networks or portable devices. As the author's knowledge extends, there is no other work similar to what this paper provide regarding proposing such a framework. The framework provides a persistent and secure environment through the e-document life cycle and ability to track the document. The framework components design is based on analysing the literature of the current issues and available solutions. These components were confirmed after surveying security professionals and interviewing fourteen security experts. The framework includes components utilising active document concept, digital right management concept, context awareness, and a central certification authority service.

Keywords: Active document · Secure document sharing · DRM · Enterprise document security · Self-protecting documents

1 Introduction

Currently, e-documents can contain a variety of information produced by an enterprise such as reports, product documentations, financial information, help and user manual documents. To manage these documents the enterprise uses software systems to digitise (if not already produced by software) and store these documents. The main systems currently in use are Electronic Document Management System (DMS), Electronic Records Management (ERM), Enterprise Content Management (ECM), and Data Loss (leakage) Prevention (DLP) (Smallwood 2012). These systems allow the enterprise to control the usage and document access according to security policies. In real life, these systems leak documents especially in enterprises that have multiple sites, employees working at home or elsewhere, or sharing documents with other parties.

© Springer International Publishing AG 2017
V. Chang et al. (Eds.): Enterprise Security, LNCS 10131, pp. 259–275, 2017.
DOI: 10.1007/978-3-319-54380-2_12

Document leakage can cause serious damage to any organisation in any domain. For example, the health care domain is not an exception, National Health Service (NHS) suspended one of its staff when he sent an email to his home email address containing pay slip details for entire staff of his hospital (Greatrex 2010). An engineering employee at General Motor stole hybrid car trade secrets and sold them to a Chinese rival manufacturer (Smallwood 2012). Software Engineering Institute at Carnegie Mellon University conducted a survey in 2013. The survey identified that 53% of the organisation participating in the survey agreed that "damage caused by insider attacks is more damaging than outsider attacks" (Software Engineering Institute 2013b). Another fact concluded from the same survey is that 68% of the insider attacks are either unintentional exposure of enterprise private data or Intellectual Property (IP) theft. Recent investigation by Computer Emergency Response Team (CERT) shows that document leakage and insider user threats are increasing in the enterprise environment (Software Engineering Institute 2013a). Moreover, the documents leaked by an insider are usually carefully chosen and therefore they have critical information.

Currently software systems are mainly used to secure documents on the enterprise's computers inside network boundaries. Virtual Private Network (VPN) is used to extend the enterprise network and connect remote employees to enable and control document usage when using these systems. Software systems like ERM and ECM are not commonly used in enterprises when high level of document protection is essential. There are many reasons why such a software is not satisfying enterprise security requirements. One reason is that employees can keep a copies of documents on their computer and the system (ERM or ECM) cannot track the usage of this copy (Smallwood 2012). Another reason is compatibility issues, and providing the same level of protection to all kind of documents (Manasdeep 2012). Generally, ERM and ECM are having simple structure from security point of view and this make them less likely to be used by enterprises.

DMS is the most commonly used software to secure enterprise documents (Randazzo et al. 2005). Currently, DMS become complicated software system that provide secure document sharing inside the enterprise network. Early versions of DMS goes back to 1989 and at that time it facilitates only PKI and SMTP technologies (Wilbur et al. 1989). With time, more technologies has been integrated inside the DMS structure to provide robustness to the system. This make the DMS very resource hungry and expensive. Therefore, Small and Medium size Enterprises (SME) usually cannot effort the cost (The Department for Business Innovation and Skills 2014). When such SME subcontract with bigger enterprise, the latter usually has to choose between two approaches; either force the SME (the subcontractor) to use the same DMS, or trust the SME security precautions and share documents in less secure format. Either approaches do not prevent insider attacker from leaking sensitive document. Equally important, DMS uses the same technology combination to protect the documents regardless their security classification.

Another software system used to prevent document leakage is Data Leakage Prevention (DLP) (Lee et al. 2015). These systems work like a reverse firewall by monitoring the enterprise network traffic for any data that improperly transmitted. This does prevent document leakage when the document is transmitted in plain format but not efficient when it encrypted or encapsulated in another compressed format.

None of the systems discussed earlier prevents insider document leakage caused by using portable storage devices (USB storage, mobile phones and smart portable devices). This chapter proposes a novel framework to share documents securely over a network or over portable devices. The structure of the remaining sections in this chapter are as follows. Previous work includes literature review of the active document concept and then security related research about active document. Latter paragraph will be the structure of the confirmed framework. Then explaining the research methodology that been used to confirm the framework components and finishing with the conclusions and expected future work.

2 Previous Work

This section will trace the development of the active document concept and discuss the most recent and similar work that combines these concepts.

Active Document as a concept first introduced by Quint and Vatton (1994). They suggested that a document could be active when the document has a set of features in addition to its basic logical structure and the *"document manipulation system"* has the ability to read these features by using some mechanisms. They emphasised the benefit of the active document concept on cooperative editing and authoring document such as user interface and on document indexing. Most of the research since had been focused on the same aspect (collaborative document authoring and editing) without mentioning any security enhancements as the next paragraphs discusses.

Most of the research done on the active document concept were to facilitate collaboration and not focusing on security usage until recently. Document-centred collaboration is one of the early research products published by LaMarca et al. (1999). They detailed the earlier related work that done before them. These previous studies failed to primarily depend on extended document properties like (Giampaolo 1999) and (Richter and Cabrera 1998). Their approach based on separating the coordination information stored in the document from the actual document data that presented by the associated program. As a result, the document carries its sematic within, which can be read by a middle-ware they designed for that purpose. This middle ware will read this semantic information and convert them to actions on the fly. In 2000 they introduce their prototype project *"Placeless Document System"* to explore the new features they propose (Dourish et al. 2000a, 2000b). At that point, they use the phrase *"Active Properties"* to represent the sematic information stored inside the document by their middle ware. These active properties extend the default document properties and metadata to represent document structure as well as behaviour. They published their analysis of the placeless document system as case study of using active document in collaborative environment (Dourish 2003).

In the same direction of using active document concept in collaboration, Nam and Bae (2002) introduced a framework for processing active documents in business domain (Nam and Bae 2002). The active document in their terminology is a document that contains both business rules and data. Their framework focused on combining business rules and data for a web form at the client side and then validates the business rules before triggering any event on the database server side. However, their proposed framework works on web forms with Database management system back end in particular oracle. Moreover, they did not mention any things regarding any security aspect that may face their framework. Furthermore, they focused on the cooperative work on online documents more than securing the document produced from that work (Nam et al. 2004).

Another work by Abiteboul et al. (2009), they used the words "active document" again but this time to capture user interaction with Web 2.0 applications (Abiteboul et al. 2009). This time they used the active document to add some semantic to the documents available in the web.

Latest work related to using active document for collaboration was done by Neumann and Lenz (2010). They introduced a content-oriented workflow system for the medical care domain. They used the term "active document" to describe a software agent that reflects to the user role to display information that proper to his access level (Neumann and Lenz 2010). They adopt the same principle that was introduced by LaMarca et al. (1999) which mainly focused on the differentiation between the content and coordination information to facilitate easy use of their proposed workflow system "The alpha-Flow". One year later Todorova and Neumann (2011) introduce a project to make use of the active properties in the previous "alpha-Flow" system to build an auxiliary small system that adds more features to the main system in distributed environment (Todorova and Neumann 2011). And that was the last contribution of them regarding active document and active properties. Although they introduce new point of view for the patient record in health or medical domain, they failed to address the benefits of their system from a security point of view. Aspects like confidentiality, privacy, access control and integrity are not covered in their system. Moreover, they tailor-built their system to match the health domain requirements and there is no guarantee to work on other domains.

The most recent and security related concept of active document introduced by Munier et al. (2012). They proposed a new Enterprise Digital Right Management (E-DRM) architecture for secure file sharing over the cloud among various parties (main organisation and subcontractors or outsourcing entity). Data encapsulation is used to store security related information (access control, audit, and metadata) as well as "Security Kernel", which is basically a piece of code to perform the security checks and decisions (Munier et al. 2012). To read the document the user needs to have a "licence" explicitly describing his/her right to access the document and a "Trusted Viewer". The trusted viewer could be a lightweight viewer embedded inside the document itself or by using heavy trusted viewer by using Application-programming interface (API). Another way to view the document content is to export the data to eXtensible Mark-up Language (XML) to be displayed in any regular XML viewer or any conventional viewer. At either way, the security kernel will accept or reject the user access, collecting and attaching metadata of the action and finally calculation new data as the action going along. After that the document stores the new data and waits to connect to a server, specialised for synchronisation propose, to synchronise the new data (Munier et al. 2012).

The architecture proposed by Munier et al. (2012) tries to bind the management and security in one solution, this binding works in the provided scenario but may not work as a general solution. The collaboration part of the binding needs a server for synchronising the data between different versions of the document. This adds more vulnerability to the proposed system by bringing the cloud computing issues and communication threats like man in the middle or spoofing attacks.

Munier et al. (2014) published another work about the same previous idea to emphasise the role of metadata in their system. Where each document contains metadata about the author, date, reviews, notes, and other editorial information. They make use of these metadata to automate the security and collaborative editing in their model. Nevertheless, compromising the information they extract from the metadata (for example geo-tagging information) could result in some privacy issues since they expose privet enterprise information.

Another approach to secure document outside enterprise network adapting active document concept is introduced by Chen et al. (2015). They proposed a system that encapsulate both the data and the access control policy in "SelfProtect Opject SPF". Their system compiles the actual data need to protect with the access policy into new Dynamic Linked library DLL file. This file then can be shared cross the enterprise or with other parties. The DLL file will be opened in normal presentation software depending on the original data type compiled in it. When the user opens the DLL file in secure environment that matches the compiled policy requirements, he/she will be asked to provide a name or other security tokens in order to view the document contents. Before the file discloses its contents, the "Policy Decision Point PDP" will check the attached policy requirements with online service to validate it. This approach provides another way to hide the data and controls its usages. However, the SPF has all the actual data inside, and compiling data and policy files into DLL is not secure enough. Using reverse engineering and other decompiling techniques will give the attacker the ability to retrieve the original data (Metula 2009).

3 The Confirmed Framework Concepts

The framework is utilising three main concepts "Active Document", Information/digital Right Management and Certificate authority. "Active Document" a concept is mentioned for the first time by Quint and Vatton (1994). They defined "Active document" as a "result from a combination of some specific features in documents and some mechanisms in a document manipulation system". This concept, by opening new possibilities, makes the meta-data of the document more interesting hence; it can change the behaviour of the presentation software. These new possibilities actually used in collaborative document editing management in "Placeless Document" project (Dourish et al. 2000a, 2000b). The proposed framework insert piece of information and codes inside the document. The injected document will have the ability to provide more security information without access to the actual document data as well the capacity to perform simple tasks.

Another concept is adopted by the framework is the Digital/Information right Management. It provides continuous protection for the document inside its wrapper (Tassel 2006). The wrapper is usually used to replace the actual document presentation software in order to control the operations performed on the document (copy, past, cut, delete and print). Moreover, it is used to provide a secure channel to authenticate the users and enforce the organisation security policy. The framework aims to transforms each machine in which it installed whether it inside or outside the organisation as a wrapper for the document. This facilitates identification of each machine and user inside the organisation, furthermore, setting the privilege of that user or machine. Instead of using new software wrapper, the framework aims to integrate seamlessly with the existing presentation software. This integration with the presentation software, which the user is familiar with their interface, facilitates monitoring user operations performed on that document. This approach enables the framework to enforce the security policy of the organisation with more granularity.

Since the proposed framework utilise DRM concept it needs to adapt the certification authority concept. DRM concept adapting public key infrastructure (PKI) to deliver documents when requested by the user. PKI uses certificate to bind user to a public key and other information (Loren 1978). This binding may become invalid with time when some of the user information changes or when private key of the user compromised. The certification authority concept make sure that the binding always valid (Zhou et al. 2002). This concept will be utilised in the proposed framework to insure the integrity of document shared using a network or the internet (Kumar and Tech 2012; Chang and Ramachandran 2016).

4 The Framework Structure

The novelty in the proposed framework comes from the way it combines existing concepts and the documents are secure regardless of the delivery approach. The confirmed framework had some modification since it first introduced (Aaber et al. 2014). The proposed framework depends on the following concepts Active document, DRM, and certification authority service. The framework ensures that the document is secure in all the stages of the document life cycle regardless the document distribution channel (though network or portable storage devices). Document life cycle have four main stages which are; creation, distribution, usage and storage (Fig. 1). The confirmed

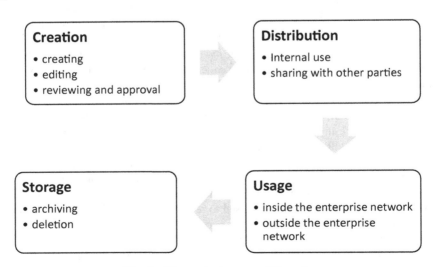

Fig. 1. Electronic document life cycle

framework ensure that documents are useless before and after the usage stage of their life cycle. Documents created in a machine using the proposed framework contains only part of the encrypted document data when it transferred inside or outside the network boundaries. Each time the user request an operation (read or edit) on a document the framework will check the security policy requirements, and then contact the certification authority for other security requirements, to download the remaining document data.

The main goals of the proposed framework are:

First, it provides means to extend organisation A document security policy to be applicable on the entire organisation A sites and when the document transferred to organisation B. this will reduce the threat of insider attack due to employee ignorance or accident document lose.

Second, documents produced in this framework are useless outside the framework environment. Since, their contents are incomplete and they need to communicate with a certification authority via the proposed framework to download the remaining data. This will secure the document when it transferred over network or portable devices.

The framework is composed from three main components Active Document, System Functions and certification authority. Active document is the actual document created by the user on a machine using the framework. System Functions are set of modules that perform security services. Certification authority provides updated binding between user and document and download services. Following sections explain each component in more detail. The proposed framework structure is shown in Fig. 2.

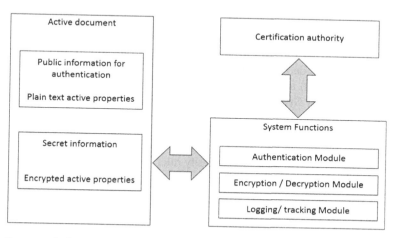

Fig. 2. Framework Structure showing the main three components of the framework. Active document, certification authority and the system functions.

Active Document: An active document is a document that has active security properties created in a machine uses the proposed framework. These active properties are divided into two main parts, first is the public information and second is the secret information. Public information (Pre-Processing information) is plain text Default Security Policy and Active Properties that help the System Functions to detect, authenticate, and check the integrity of the document. The default security policy used by the System Functions to check for the initial security requirements. Secret Information (Post-Processing information) is encrypted data that contains security parameters. These parameters are:

- Access control policy: the required user authentication information and mechanisms.
- Context parameter: when, where, what for each user authorised to open this document.
- Verification code for the active information in the Public Information. It is a hash value for the Public Information in the document.
- Security Mechanism Parameter: contains technical information about encryption technique, content verification, and retention policy. This technical information is for the System Functions in order to decrypt Actual Encrypted Data.
- Actual Encrypted Data: part of the actual data of the document. This data is encrypted for the second time and can be only accessed if all the validations from public information and verification code are passed.

4.1 System Functions

The Framework Files are the actual files that contain programming code to perform the System Functions. The authors assume that each enterprise will customise the Framework Files to fit its security policy. The customisation includes access control policy, context parameters and default document retention settings. Framework Files are customised executable files distributed by the enterprise to work as a background service in computer machine. They integrate with the operating system and the presentation software (the default program that is used to view the documents like Office suites, and PDF readers) to monitor and control their activities. In addition, they have special function called System Functions that perform security operations (encrypt, decrypt, and hashing).

System Functions are automated background service in the operating system responsible for the encryption/decryption, monitor presentation software operations and translate the active properties into security rules. The system functions divided into three main modules:

- Authentication Module: this module reads the public active properties of the active document.
- Encryption/Decryption Module: this module decrypts the actual data inside the active document.
- Logging/Tracking Module: this module logs all the operation done on the document and send it back to the certification authority.

Certification Authority: It provide continuously updated secure binding between the encryption keys and their authors (Zhou et al. 2002). The certification authority

(CA) provide secure download services in addition to its default functions. This secure download service will be the channel which used by enterprise to share its security policy requirements. The CA could belong the enterprise itself or it could be provided by a third party. The trust issues of CA are out of the scope of this research. The workflow of CA is as follow:

1. Enterprise A security officer submits their Framework Files to the CA. And chose what this Framework Files aimed for, are they for every one to download or for specific enterprise to share documents with.
2. The CA assigns pair of keys (public and private) to encrypt the enterprise Framework Files.
3. Exchanging the keys with enterprise A. Then CA sends the owner a sharable download link for the encrypted Framework Files.
4. Enterprise A send that link with enterprise B, which aim to securely share documents with.
5. Enterprise B download and install the Framework Files on their computers, and they ready to work on documents from enterprise A.
6. Once an Active Document sent to enterprise B from enterprise A, the Framework Files will interpret its active properties and check for the integrity of the document with the CA.
7. Then the document will be opened or discarded depends on the integrity feedback from the CA. The integrity checking required to access to the Public Information part of the Active Document.
8. if the document integrity check was clear, the Framework Files will decrypt the Secret Information part of the Active Document. And then download the remaining document part on the computer.
9. When the Active Document in use the Framework Files will monitor and control its usage (saving in other name, printing, or screen printing). When the user finish using the document the Framework Files will send session information to the CA to track this document usage.

This workflow ensures secure delivery of the Framework Files and remaining data for the document. And provide the ability to track users activity on the document.

4.2 Document Access Scenarios

When a document created by an author inside environment has the framework installed in it, the framework will implant active properties inside that document. These active properties depends on security requirements determined by the author. The framework will ask the author for these security requirements once the document closed. The author will set only active properties that allowed by the enterprise security officer. The security officer sets active properties that related to the enterprise security policy and the security functions implant them by default. The proposed framework will divide the document contents into two or more parts and encrypt then using PKI with different keys. Then the framework will transfer one of those parts to the certification authority and delete it from the author's machine. This deleted part will be downloaded from the

CA each time the document opened. So that when the document shared with any one, it required authoring enterprise framework files installed to translate the active properties into security rules. After that, the framework will contact the CA to download the remaining of the document contents. See Fig. 3.

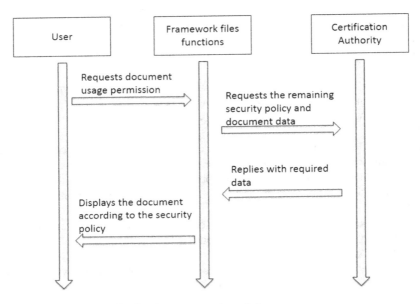

Fig. 3. Access scenario activity sequence

The expected scenario is that organisation A provides its customised version of framework Files to reflect its security policy. A trusted third party could provide the CA service or it can be provided by organisation A itself. Then, organisation A shares the download link for the customised Framework Files with organisation B. When both organisations install the Framework Files, they are ready to share documents and extend security policies.

The Active Document will have two main components Pre-Processing information and Post-Processing information. Pre-Processing information public information that can be read by any operating system. Yet, it is interpreted differently on machine that has Framework Files installed. This information is used to authenticate and track document usage and to set the minimum-security policy parameters at the destination machine. While Post-Processing information are encrypted information using asymmetric key encryption that will be used to. The content of this information are the following:

- Security parameter (access control, environment-monitoring level and context).
- Active properties to verify document content integrity.
- Part of or all the actual document content.

After the document is verified and user is authenticated the framework functions will start decrypt the Post-Processing information to retrieve the remaining security policy parameters. The System Function will translate these parameters into security policy roles, which they are authoring organisation security policy. Finally, the remaining document content downloaded from the certification authority. These steps are shown in more details in Fig. 4. The document retention policy is also part of the Post-Processing information.

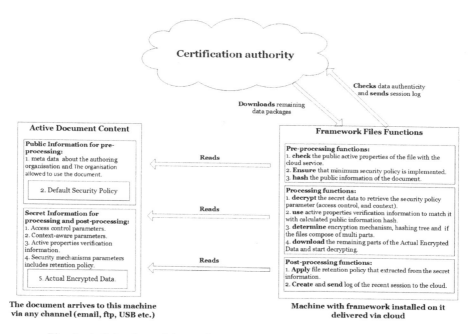

Fig. 4. Activity flow of the confirmed framework document-access scenario

5 Framework Components Confirmation

In order to refine and confirm the framework components methodological triangulation was performed (Recker 2013). It involved combining and comparing data discovered from a detailed literature review, an expert review and a questionnaire survey. The triangulation is performed in three stages since each method should be applied independently (Jupp 2006). This approach utilized a methodological triangulation of literature review, expert reviews and a questionnaire survey. The expert review was based on conducting semi-structured interviews with sixteen cyber security experts from the four investigated domains (government, healthcare, education, and business). The findings from these reviews were used to confirm the initial framework (Aaber et al. 2015). An online survey conducted, 113 cyber security professionals responded to the online survey. The results were used to confirm the reviewed framework.

5.1   Expert Review

Expert review conducted with sixteen expert in total. These experts had at least five years' experience in working in cyber security within one or more of the suggested domains. They were approached with an email contains overview about the framework, aim of the interviews and a consent form. The purpose of this expert review was to review the factors and components identified from literature and to identify further factors if there is any. For that matter, a saturation was reached from the tenth interview. After the tenth interview no new information were added. The reviews were constructed in the form of semi-structured interviews that the researcher obtained permission to record. There were twenty questions classified in four main categories (general questions, factors effect document security, and framework components).

All the interviews were positively constructive and with detailed discussion. That aside, all the experts confirmed that the proposed framework has the right components. Yet, there are some characteristics and technologies that were at the centre of the debate. The detail of the technology to used to implement the framework is out of the interview scope. The most frequently debated questions and the researcher's answer are listed below:

1. **Question:** What type of encryption will be used?
   Answer: this is not determined yet. It will be determined first step in the future proof of concept.
2. **Question:** The ability of the file to detect the environment once it copied or downloaded (auto run) at the receiver machine.
   Answer: the file will check the environment once the user tries to open it not the moment it lands at the receiver computer.
3. **Question:** What if the body of the document that contains the actual information is copied using bit-by-bit operations from Dos or Linux and the attacker has many tries to crack it?
   Answer: the document body is useless by its own. Since it part of the original body and the remaining is provided by the framework.
4. **Question:** What is the security measure for communication channel when sharing a document via email or network.
   Answer: channel security is out of my research. However, the document itself is not useful without the framework.

The experts suggested using some technologies but did not proposed replacements for the proposed components. They were really interested by the concept of keeping the same software and there is no need for training of the end users. Ten of the experts, including seven from the UK, where focusing on training cost and time They suggest to use cloud and Security Assertion Mark-up Language (SAML) as delivery mechanisms to share and force security policies. SAML is an Extensible Mark-up Language (XML) based data format used to exchange authorisation and authentication. Moreover, the XML signature may be used to verify the SAML source and the data integrity. Some of them suggest using Attribute Based Access Control System (XACML) to provide more granularity to user access right.

The result of the feedback from the expert interviews notes were reflected on the initial framework design described in (Aaber et al. 2015). Most of the discussion with the expert was about technologies and mechanisms that may be used in the framework and which is better. They were good remarks and points made in the discussion but they are more useful in the implementation level not for the conceptual level for this research is at.

5.2   Survey Results

The triangulation method is used to explore and confirm the literature finding. The method was successful in exploring the aspect of the proposed framework. The expert in general, were interested in a secure solution that is low cost, customisable and scalable. Furthermore, they provided constrictive comment regarding framework components. These comments were used to modify the initial framework components (Aaber et al. 2015). The modified framework component that reflect the expert feedback now ready to be confirmed by the selected samples from a professional IT community.

This survey was performed by administering an online questionnaire to confirm the factors in the updated framework resulting from the expert review. Ninety participant did complete the survey. These participants were reached via security groups in academia, business and healthcare. It was decided to administer the questionnaire online as this method is convenient for respondents. Respondents were approached by email or via social media (LinkedIn) and asked to complete the online questionnaire.

The questionnaire is divided into two main parts. The first part, asks couple of nominal questions about the respondents' organization type, demographic data, and experience to confirm their eligibility for this study. The second part was constructed using a five point Likert-type scale (Bhattacherjee 2012) with the following ratings: strongly agree = 1; agree = 2; neutral = 3; disagree = 4 and strongly disagree = 5. The purpose of the questions in the second part is to confirm the proposed framework components. The survey data was processed using SPSS software.

Following Tables 1 and 2 related to the first part of the survey, show general information about the participants and their opinion about the literature findings. The participant opinions is very clear that human negligence and different domains security policy are their most concern.

The survey is used to confirm the components of the modified framework as well as the issues that challenge securing document in enterprise environment. For the latter, the

Table 1. Domain frequency for survey participants total number n = 90

Domain	Frequency	Percentage
Healthcare	15	16.7%
Education	34	37.8%
Business	14	15.6%
Government	18	20%
Other	9	10%

Table 2. Survey response for the identified issues for securing document in enterprise environment

Issue	Response	No. of cases	Percentage
Human negligence	Strongly agree	25	27.8%
	Agree	38	42.2%
	Neutral	22	24.4%
	Disagree	3	3.3%
	Strongly disagree	2	2.2%
Different domains different security policy	Strongly agree	37	41.1%
	Agree	20	22.2%
	Neutral	16	17.8%
	Disagree	17	18.9%
	Strongly disagree	0	0%
Legislations	Strongly agree	18	20%
	Agree	5	5.6%
	Neutral	25	27.8%
	Disagree	20	22.2%
	Strongly disagree	22	24.4%

results were confirming the importance and frequency of the first two issues identified by the research. On the other hand, the survey results show common disagreement about lacking legal framework as an issue for protecting enterprise documents. This finding states that security policy rules and legal implication related to document security are well known. Moreover, this supports indirectly the first and second issues.

The other part of the survey is to confirm the proposed framework components. The participants asked eight questions about the three main components of the framework. Hence, the answers were weighted from 1–5, then the mean value was three. Table 3 shows the basic statistical analysis of the answers. Two types of errors are considered when calculating the minimum acceptable sample size (Bhattacherjee 2012). Type1 or α errors which occur when rejecting a true null hypothesis and type2 or β errors occur when a false null hypothesis is not rejected. The likelihood of these error occurring can be reduced by increasing the sample size, therefore, the sample size was 90 instead of 15 (Bhattacherjee 2012). By convention, α is set to 0.05 for a 95% confidence and $(1-\beta)$ is set to 0.9 for 10% of missing an association (Bhattacherjee 2012). Another parameter considered is effect size, which refers to the magnitude of the association between the predictor and outcome variables. Cohen (1988) defines three different effect sizes: small $(d = 0.2)$, medium (d-0.5) and large $(d = 0.8)$. In this study G* Power software was used to calculate the minimum sample size (Faul et al. 2009). The calculation was performed for a t-test to find the difference in mean from constant. From this calculation it was determined that the minimum sample size is 15. The detailed statistical analysis is beyond of this chapter scope.

In summary, the three components of the framework were confirmed with significant low value of hypothesis rejection. The confirmed framework aims to secure electronic documents when they leave the boundaries (firewalls) of the authoring enterprise. Based on the issues identified in the literature and confirmed through the survey, the framework proposing a new combination of technologies to solve these issues. The initial proposed framework structure modified to reflect the discussion with the security experts interviewed. The concepts behind the framework components are still the same and can be summarised in the following points:

- Active document (AD): a document that has a set of properties more than the ordinary metadata. These properties called "Active Properties" and can be read by other particular software (Quint and Vatton 1994).
- Certification authority (CA): It used in this context as delivery and distribution channel. The term in this context, refer to a web site that trusted by both parties to share the "System Functions files".
- Persistent security: it means that the system is secure through all its states if certain characteristics are met (Bossi et al. 2004). There are different methods to control and monitor a system characteristics. common method is to install a software that replaces all default programs that open certain files type, this concept is used in Digital Right Management (DRM) solutions to secure digital media and documents. On the other hand, this research uses customised Framework Files to perform security tasks (document usage monitor and control), in this context it called "System Functions".

These three concepts combined form the core of the confirmed framework components. The framework may use certain technology to facilitate its implementation. Technologies like XACML to provide standardised security policy communication (Lorch et al. 2003). Another technology is the Erasure Code for reliable content delivery (Rizzo 1997). All these technologies and specification is out of this research for the time being, it will be relevant in the prof of concept of the framework.

6 Conclusion

Securing documents have always been a continuous and expensive task for enterprises. However, some may fail to keep their document safe outside their network boundaries. The research identified the main two issues related to document leakage from enterprises. These issues are human negligence and the absence of unified affordable security tracking platform for document sharing cross different domain. These issues are confirmed statistically and via discussion with experts in the security field. The authors proposed a framework to address these two issues and this book chapter shows the confirmed framework. The framework combines three main concepts to provide a platform in which enterprise can securely share their document and track it usage. This framework enable enterprises to share document outside enterprise boundaries securely by utilising a novel combination of concepts. It utilises the Active document, DRM, and certification authority concepts to provide secure document sharing regardless the delivery channels. The framework is confirmed by using triangulation methodology (literature review, expert review and professionals' survey). This confirmed framework works with any document delivery mechanism (network sharing, email or portable devices).

Recently, self-protecting documents, active documents, smart content documents and context aware document are get more attention from security researchers. These concepts are not new, but they are using deferent approaches and technology combinations to secure the document content.

References

Aaber, Z.S., et al.: Preventing document leakage through active document. In: 2014 World Congress on Internet Security, WorldCIS 2014, pp. 53–58 (2014)

Aaber, Z.S., et al.: Towards a framework for securing a document outside an organisational firewall. In: Proceedings of the International Conference on Cloud Computing Technology and Science, CloudCom, pp. 1057–1062 (2015)

Abiteboul, S., Bourhis, P., Marinoiu, B.: Efficient maintenance techniques for views over active documents. In: Proceedings of the 12th International Conference on Extending Database Technology Advances in Database Technology – EDBT 2009, p. 1076. ACM Press, New York (2009)

Bhattacherjee, A.: Social Science Research: Principles, Methods, and Practices (2012)

Bossi, A., et al.: Verifying persistent security properties. Comput. Lang. Syst. Struct. Spec. Issue 30(3–4), 231–258 (2004)

Chang, V., Ramachandran, M.: Towards achieving data security with the cloud computing adoption framework. IEEE Trans. Serv. Comput. 9(1), 138–151 (2016)

Nam, C.-K., Bae, J.-H.J.: A framework for processing active documents. In: Proceedings of 6th Russian-Korean International Symposium on Science and Technology KORUS-2002 (Cat. No.,02EX565), pp. 122–125. IEEE (2002)

Dourish, P., Edwards, W.K., et al.: A programming model for active documents. In: Proceedings of the 13th Annual ACM Symposium on User Interface Software and Technology - UIST 2000, pp. 41–50. ACM Press, New York (2000a)

Dourish, P., Edwards, W.K., et al.: Extending document management systems with user-specific active properties. ACM Trans. Inf. Syst. 18(2), 140–170 (2000b)

Dourish, P.: The appropriation of interactive technologies: some lessons from placeless documents. Comput. Support. Coop. Work (CSCW) 12(4), 465–490 (2003)

Faul, F., et al.: Statistical power analyses using G*Power 3.1: tests for correlation and regression analyses. Behav. Res. Methods 41(4), 1149–1160 (2009)

Giampaolo, D.: Practical File System Design with the Be File System, 1st edn. Morgan Kaufmann, San Mateo (1999)

Greatrex, J.: Bungling West Midlands medics lose 12,000 private patient records-Birmingham mail. Sunday Mercury (2010)

Jupp, V.: The SAGE Dictionary of Social Research Methods. SAGE Publications Ltd., London (2006)

Kumar, C.D. Tech, M.: Use of Secure Distributed Online Certification Authority, 2(1) (2012)

LaMarca, A., Edwards, W., Dourish, P.: Taking the work out of workflow: mechanisms for document-centered collaboration. ECSCW 1999, September, pp. 12–16 (1999)

Lee, H., et al.: New approach for detecting leakage of internal information; using emotional recognition technology. TIIS 9(11), 4662–4680 (2015)

Lorch, M., et al.: First experiences using XACML for access control in distributed systems. In: Proceedings of the 2003 ACM Workshop on XML Security XMLSEC 2003, 47(C), p. 25 (2003)

Loren, M.K.: Toward a practical public-key cryptosystem. Unpublished doctoral dissertation, Department of Electrical Engineering, Massachusetts Institute of Technology, Cambridge (1978)

Manasdeep: Information rights management implementation and challenges, Mumbai (2012)

Metula, E.: NET Framework Rootkits: Backdoors Inside Your Framework. BlackHat, Amsterdam (2009)

Munier, M., Lalanne, V., Ardoy, P.-Y., Ricarde, M.: Legal issues about metadata data privacy vs information security. In: Garcia-Alfaro, J., Lioudakis, G., Cuppens-Boulahia, N., Foley, S., Fitzgerald, W.M. (eds.) DPM/SETOP-2013. LNCS, vol. 8247, pp. 162–177. Springer, Heidelberg (2014). doi:10.1007/978-3-642-54568-9_11

Munier, M., Lalanne, V., Ricarde, M.: Self-protecting documents for cloud storage security. In: 2012 IEEE 11th International Conference on Trust, Security and Privacy in Computing and Communications, pp. 1231–1238. IEEE (2012)

Nam, C., Lim, J., Kang, I.: Declarative development of web applications with active documents. In: 2004 Proceedings of the 8th Russian-Korean International Symposium on Science and Technology, KORUS 2004, pp. 68–72. IEEE (2004)

Neumann, C.P., Lenz, R.: The alpha-flow use-case of breast cancer treatment - modeling inter-institutional healthcare workflows by active documents. In: 2010 19th IEEE International Workshops on Enabling Technologies: Infrastructures for Collaborative Enterprises, pp. 17–22. IEEE (2010)

Quint, V., Vatton, I.: Making structured documents active. Electron. Publ. 7(November 1993), 55–74 (1994)

Randazzo, M.R., et al.: Insider threat study: Illicit cyber activity in the banking and finance sector (2005). http://www.dtic.mil/cgi-bin/GetTRDoc?Location=U2&doc=GetTRDoc.pdf&AD=ADA441249

Recker, J.: Scientific Research in Information Systems: A Beginner's Guide. Springer, Heidelberg (2013)

Richter, J., Cabrera, L.F.: A File System for the 21st Century: Previewing the Windows NT 5.0 File System-Many programming tasks will be simplified by innovations in NTFS, the Windows NT 5.0 file system. Microsoft Systems Journal-US Edn., pp. 19–36 (1998)

Rizzo, L.: Effective erasure codes for reliable computer communication protocols. SIGCOMM Comput. Commun. Rev. 27(2), 24–36 (1997)

Smallwood, R.: Safeguarding Critical E-Documents: Implementing a Program for Securing Confidential Information Assets. Wiley, Hoboken (2012)

Software Engineering Institute: 2012 CyberSecurity Watch Survey (2013a). http://resources.sei.cmu.edu/asset_files/Presentation/2013_017_101_57766.pdf

Software Engineering Institute: 2013 US State of Cybercrime Survey (2013b). http://resources.sei.cmu.edu/asset_files/Presentation/2013_017_101_58739.pdf

Van Tassel, J.: Digital Rights Management. Elsevier Inc., Oxford (2006)

The Department for Business Innovation and Skills: Information Security Breaches Survey 2014: Technical report (2014). https://www.gov.uk/government/publications/information-security-breaches-survey-2014

Todorova, A., Neumann, C.: alpha-Props: a rule-based approach to "active properties" for document-oriented process support in inter-institutional environments. In: Lecture Notes in Informatics (LNI) (2011)

Wilbur, S., et al.: Secure automated document delivery. In: 1989 Fifth Annual Proceedings of Computer Security Applications Conference, pp. 348–356 (1989)

Zhou, L., Schneider, F.B., Van Renesse, R.: COCA: a secure distributed online certification authority. ACM Trans. Comput. Syst. 20(4), 329–368 (2002)

Author Index

Printed in the United States
By Bookmasters